Selfie Democracy

Selfie Democracy

The New Digital Politics of Disruption and Insurrection

Elizabeth Losh

The MIT Press
Cambridge, Massachusetts
London, England

The MIT Press would like to thank the anonymous peer reviewers who provided comments on drafts of this book. The generous work of academic experts is essential for establishing the authority and quality of our publications. We acknowledge with gratitude the contributions of these otherwise uncredited readers.

This book was set in ITC Stone Serif Std and ITC Stone Sans Std by New Best-set Typesetters Ltd. Printed and bound in the United States of America.

Library of Congress Cataloging-in-Publication Data is available.

ISBN: 978-0-262-04705-0

10 9 8 7 6 5 4 3 2 1

For Mel Horan

Contents

Introduction: Unwiring Democracy

In a candid photograph taken at the G8 Summit in 2010, several of the world's most powerful leaders peered at a device in President Barack Obama's hand (figure 0.1). Although his BlackBerry, which allowed remote access to email and the internet, was hardly a novelty by then, there was great global interest in emulating his new digital politics.[1]

Others were watching Obama's BlackBerry closely, too. A journalist described the president's phone as a symbol of "hard-working, tech-obsessed professionals" that connected Obama with his political base, just as Reagan's cowboy hat represented ties to rural voters.[2] Some thought that Obama's obvious digital proficiency might challenge stereotypes about race and technical knowledge that presented Black Americans as always being on the wrong side of the digital divide.[3] Efficiency consultants worried that the device might introduce distraction by dividing the president's attention between his screen and affairs of state.[4] Security experts were concerned with a different threat—that a smartphone might reveal the president's location to terrorists or allow hackers to access classified documents.[5]

Years later, Obama would laugh about the BlackBerry's eventual obsolescence and the limitations of using mobile tools designed to conduct secure communication. "'Good news Mr. President, we're going to give you a smartphone instead of a BlackBerry,'" Obama said during an appearance on *The Tonight Show*. "I'm excited, I get the thing, and they're like, 'Well, Mr. President, for security reasons—this is a great phone, state-of-the-art—but it doesn't take pictures, you can't text, the phone doesn't work, you know, you can't play your music on it.'" Comparing his spy-proof gadget to a toy phone that a three-year-old might use, Obama expressed envy for the much greater functionality that his teenage daughters enjoyed with their everyday smartphones.[6]

Figure 0.1
Barack Obama at the G8 Summit in Muskoka, Canada on June 25, 2010, surrounded by French President Nicolas Sarkozy, German Chancellor Angela Merkel, Russian President Dmitry Medvedev, and Italian Prime Minister Silvio Berlusconi. Official White House Photo by Pete Souza.

Of course, taking pictures, texting, and playing music on a smartphone were already political acts. The smartphone continues to serve as a major vehicle for civic expression and partisan influence. For many citizens, it has also become their main interface with the state. Because of this transformation, digital literacy and ideological persuasion are inextricably linked.

The president of the United States gives speeches, answers questions at news conferences, and signs legislation with the smartphone secured out of sight, but the device has become a political actor in its own right, thanks to social media. As a consumer of these technologies, the president reinforces certain cultural assumptions about the power of smartphone use. These assumptions perpetuate myths about connection, transparency, participation, and access. These myths are further amplified in rhetoric borrowed from Silicon Valley about how these technologies supposedly strengthen social bonds, enable exploration, encourage engagement, and overcome barriers.

Barack Obama and Donald Trump are usually cast as ideological opposites, but, during their presidencies, they were both seen as strongly attached to their non-human companions. Obama might have been the anti-Trump and Trump the anti-Obama, but they both used mobile computing in ways that redefined the office of president. Now such devices have become difficult for any world leader to renounce.

Mobile media-making and constant internet access have changed political engagement at all scales—from local regulations to international law—and transformed all branches of government. Not all of these changes have been for the better. Masked by the appeal of greater direct democracy, both tech companies and authoritarian figures have amassed power largely through image management and opinion framing rather than through a true broadening of civic life. The "disruption" promoted by tech companies to existing economic and social institutions inevitably destabilizes our political frameworks as well.

This book exposes the unintended consequences of wireless technologies on political leadership and shows how seemingly benign mobile devices that hold out the promise of direct democracy undermine representative forms of government. Trump's time in office is often viewed as a reaction to the Obama presidency, but Trump took up Obama's call to abolish intermediaries, and he followed it to its most extreme conclusions. For both men, the intermediaries that stood between the president and his people included elected representatives, professional diplomats, and high-profile journalists, along with the "bureaucrats" and "middlemen" long vilified in conventional political discourse. Trump's ideas about using technologies for connection, access, transparency, and participation might appear perverse in rewarding sycophancy, influence peddling, paranoia, and insurrection, but there is a logic that connects the two administrations that this book will trace.

This account of recent history offers a way for citizens to understand a common repertoire of digital practices acted out by users from both the right and the left and thus to rethink our contemporary state of political polarization and alienation. This is not to say that the right and the left do not offer different moral visions when it comes to ever-present digital communication. Democrats have insisted that Republicans are too nostalgic for the past and too slow to adapt, while Republicans have accused Democrats of loving new technologies too uncritically and promoting "left-coast" values in the process. Furthermore, these contrasting ideologies present very different imagined users who reflect cultural stereotypes that are rooted in identity politics. As this book will show, attitudes about technology tend to reflect a political group's particular anxieties about class, gender, and race.

Interestingly, when it comes to race, both political parties tend to share what André Brock has called a "deficit perspective on minority technology," in which people of color are assumed to be lacking in skills and resources.[7] Liberals argue for retraining and redistribution, and conservatives complain about overreach and handouts, but both center the assumption of Silicon Valley engineers—most of whom are white, male, and affluent—that the underprivileged are incompetent.

Despite differences between types of technology users, certain universals about technology use persist. User experiences like taking pictures, texting, and playing music are designed to be the same.[8] The interchangeable interfaces of social media platforms encourage similar attitudes across the political spectrum regarding online citizenship.

These platforms remind all users, regardless of party affiliation, to give constant attention to their feeds. As users become familiar with what content generates likes, comments, and shares from the people that they care about, they make common risk/reward calculations about what to post to maximize engagement within their social circles. Thus, mobile devices and social media incentivize citizens to perform attention-getting acts of political self-expression and encourage feelings of direct contact with powerful leaders, who might appear as notable characters in their digital lives. These political leaders often seem to share their constituents' disapproval of intervening gatekeepers, who seemingly want to reinforce traditional barriers between the electorate and the elected. By contrast, journalists and elected officials who amplify the leader's messages uncritically are rewarded with celebrity status and larger audiences.

Both Obama and Trump offered a mode of political engagement that was neither the representative democracy they shunned nor the direct democracy they promised. Instead, this mode encouraged a dialectical process of identity performance that oscillated rapidly between digital empowerment and disempowerment. This is selfie democracy.

The Myth of the Obamaphone

On October 17, 2012—long before he became a presidential candidate—Donald J. Trump posted a message on Twitter with a now familiar tone:

"Great—now Supreme Court Justices are talking about a constitutional right to a cell phone bit.ly/Wn22Kq Obama, just stop already."[9] Unlike Trump's far more prolific tweets from this period calling for the release of Obama's birth certificate, this tweet about whether US citizens were legally entitled to wireless digital communication was relatively obscure, even to his followers. Only a few hundred people engaged with his post.

Several political liberals pointed to the inaccuracy of Trump's message. The concept of a constitutional "right" to a cell phone came from retired Supreme Court justice John Paul Stevens, not from the White House or from current members of the court. At an event hosted by a nonprofit organization lobbying for tougher gun control, the former justice had been asked about the doctrine of self-defense as justification for the right to bear arms. In response, Stevens suggested that "maybe you have some kind of constitutional right to have a cell phone with a predialed 911 number at your bedside, and that might provide you with a little better protection than a gun."[10]

Since then, the idea that a cell phone could be viewed as a weapon of self-defense has gained traction. In addition to summoning help, a smartphone can be used to document abuses of power and to upload the evidence to social media. Thus, a cell phone can deter unjustified police actions, the mistreatment of people in prisons, government corruption, or civil rights violations.[11] Of course, the phone has also been used as a weapon to discredit voter registration efforts, policies to protect vulnerable populations on college campuses, legalized abortion, and other progressive causes.

The link Trump included in his tweet belonged to the right-wing website CNSNews, run by the conservative Media Research Center. With its generic name, CNSNews could easily be confused with more established journalistic outlets such as CBS or CNN, but it was a decidedly more partisan site. Before Trump's tweet, CNSNews had already run several stories challenging the necessity of cell phones in contemporary life, including as tools for public safety. For example, on the same day the site ran a story about charitable donations of cell phones to battered women, it posted another story about how cell phones might tie domestic violence victims to their abusers with "electronic leashes."

Just a few months before Trump retweeted the story questioning the "right" to a cell phone, CNSNews had mocked an even more radical proposition: what if owning a cell phone could be considered a civic duty? In a March 2012 story, the site reported that sitting Supreme Court justice Stephen Breyer had suggested that owning a cell phone might one day be legally required in case citizens needed to contact emergency services while away from home. Just as Congress had mandated in 2010 that all US residents purchase health insurance coverage, so too might the government demand its citizens have cell phone plans.[12]

Trump's tweet seemed to be a complaint about government overreach. But if liberals saw Trump's reference to Obama as a non sequitur, conservatives immediately understood the unspoken premise that tied the cell phone story to the 44th president. During the 2012 presidential campaign, which was in its final days when Trump tweeted his message, the myth that the government was handing out free smartphones with cellular service had become a powerful narrative for focusing right-wing outrage. Supposedly, this cell phone distribution program was intended to secure the loyalties of minority, inner-city voters. These so-called Obamaphones became the perfect myth to tie the country's first Black president and his Silicon Valley rhetoric to an unequal plan for doling out the nation's technological resources.

One racially charged story on the Drudge Report had gone viral just a few weeks before Trump's tweet. It featured a Black woman praising the Obamaphone program.

Woman: Obama!

Interviewer: You got Obamaphone?

Woman: Yes! Everybody in Cleveland low minority get Obamaphone! Keep Obama in president, you know. He gave us a phone.

Interviewer: He gave you a phone?

Woman: He'll do more.

Interviewer: How'd he give you a phone?

Woman: You sign up. If you're on food stamps, you're on social security, you got low income, you disability . . .[13]

Conservative pundits seized on "the Obamaphone lady" immediately. Right-wing radio personality Rush Limbaugh reduced her to an object of scorn: "She may not know who George Washington is or Abraham Lincoln, but she knows how to get an Obama phone."[14] Conspiracy theorist Alex Jones invited her on to his online TV show *InfoWars*, where the two agreed about the dangers of government surveillance. Soon she became a kind of internet celebrity, like other kooky viral stars enjoying a dubious moment of fame.[15] There were video remixes and ring tones. The original video racked up over nine million views.

It was a meme that many Obama-haters would have known without any direct reference. The week of Trump's tweet, the clip of the woman praising Obamaphones appeared in an anti-Obama attack ad for Republican challenger Mitt Romney. Taglines in the spot included "HAVE BARACK OBAMA'S POLICIES EMPOWERED OR ENSLAVED AMERICANS?" and "THE OBAMA RECORD: 1 IN 7 AMERICANS ON FOOD STAMPS." Although the advertisement was ostensibly produced by a political action committee, or PAC, called the Tea Party Victory Fund, the spot appears to have had financial and strategic ties to the party establishment.[16]

Hidden beneath the avalanche of Obamaphone memes was a fragment of truth. A federal program called Lifeline, established in 1985, had been providing universal access to telephone service, subsidized by a small monthly fee paid by all users. The modest program didn't cover expensive calling services or long-distance charges, but it offered a basic utility at a low cost. The Lifeline program was updated in 1996 when the Telecommunications Act created the Universal Service Fund, which pooled contributions from mobile phone carriers to offer expanded services to low-income customers. The funds were also used to build cell towers in rural areas, connect schools and libraries to the internet, and provide communications services to rural health-care centers. Significantly, the federal code was changed to explicitly include non-discriminatory language, making access available "to all the people of the United States, without discrimination on the basis of race, color, religion, national origin, or sex."

Some Lifeline providers embraced the Obamaphone brand and incorporated the term into their sidewalk pitches, paid search results, and appeals on their websites. For example, the landing page of Obamaphone.com features a photo of President Obama speaking on a landline in the Oval Office, thereby enhancing the authority of the company.

As a low-income graduate student with a meager teaching assistant's salary, I used the Lifeline service in the eighties and don't recall much stigma being attached to beneficiaries at the time. But by the mid-'90s, much as other forms of social welfare came to be suspect, universal telephone service was now disparaged, particularly when it expanded to include wireless coverage.

The simple proposition that people with low incomes should have access to basic services and information was reframed as a giveaway to people of color who didn't deserve such a sophisticated device. In fact, the smartphone could connect the disadvantaged to the internet in a more cost-effective way that was much more practical than relying on home computer ownership or broadband service. Given that people living in precarious situations might change addresses frequently, a cell phone provided consistent access to connectivity. In the original policy documents, the phone's utility for job hunting, even if the person was unhoused, was stated as a benefit. People with mobile access could also begin to use financial services online.

Yet like the food stamps program that provided grocery assistance to the poor, conservatives viewed this universal service as wasteful spending that was ripe for fraud and abuse. Many local news programs aired stories showing undercover reporters acquiring free cell phones without providing any proof of financial hardship, some collecting multiple devices. A Denver broadcast described phones being handed out "like Halloween candy." A Tulsa program showed a man with "two duffle-bags full" of mobile devices. In Baltimore, newscasters claimed drug dealers were benefiting from the plethora of cell phones flooding the streets. The subtext for these depictions of scams and double-dealing was reflexive moral outrage about government handouts. Critics referred to the program as "phone stamps."

These reports from local news channels often advanced a racial narrative about cell phone ownership. In most cases, white reporters spoke with authority about stories in which Black people appeared to benefit from illegitimate cell phone acquisitions, either as dealers collecting unjustified commissions or as unscrupulous customers lying about their accounts. Nonbroadcast sources were even more explicit with their racism. They uploaded user-generated Obamaphone videos to YouTube in which Black cell phone users were shown as unkempt or inarticulate, much like the Obamaphone lady video picked up by the Drudge Report.

Black scholars of digital media have shown how the Obamaphone and the Obamaphone lady came to symbolize racialized high-tech welfare.[17] Changing the phrase "Lifeline" to "Obamaphone" also undercut the essential nature of cell phone service for the otherwise disconnected and recast it as a partisan issue. This strategy diverted attention from access to an invisible (i.e., scarce) public infrastructure to possession of a visible personal electronic device. It made a gadget the focus of debate rather than a persistent lack of services.

The idea of the Obamaphone as a technology designed for the urban poor persisted in conservative policy making for years. As recently as 2018, a congressional report issued this critical assessment: "Lifeline—sometimes called 'Obamaphones'—provides subsidies to about 12.3 million low-income Americans for telephone, wireless, and broadband service, at a cost of about $1.5 billion per year. . . . Yet due to a loosely monitored oversight arrangement, Lifeline is highly susceptible to fraud, waste, and abuse."[18]

Trump's 2012 tweet mocking a "right" to own a cell phone focused on a specific kind of right, one assumed to be founded in natural law, self-preservation, and a might-makes-right understanding of the world consistent with Trump's general moral philosophy. Extending an ethical claim for a right to ownership to members of an underclass offended his sensibilities, particularly when the tool was judged a luxury rather than a necessity and was associated with other rights to economic participation.

In the spirit of Justice Stevens's thought experiment, it might be useful to consider all the rights that a system of mobile computational telecommunications subsidies might affirm, particularly when the nondiscriminatory language of the 1996 legislation is applied. For example, if one acquires a device at freegovernmentcellphones.net, is a political right or a civil right being exercised? Activists who denounce the confiscation of cell phones or suspension of wireless service by authoritarian regimes might even claim that there are human rights issues involved.

Rather than seeing the smartphone simply as an aid for protecting bodily integrity, experts in human–computer interaction tend to view it as an extension of mental agency and consciousness. The cell phone is usually held close to the body—along with the keys and the wallet that it may soon replace. It has become entrusted with activities once traditionally handled by older technologies for personal authentication and financial exchange.

The smartphone—like the mind—also facilitates cognition by offloading memories, navigation functions, and other conscious and unconscious aspects of mental life. It allows for both an extension of and a separation from the traditional boundaries of the self. Our bodies are now enhanced by an apparatus that records, stores, and displays information and connects us to distributed networks. How might political sovereignty be reshaped by our new cyborg identities, particularly when the most intimate spheres of personal decision-making are influenced by the algorithms ready-to-hand? As the smartphone and other mobile applications are reshaping civic participation, attitudes about freedom, civil rights, and national security are also changing.

One particularly useful way to examine these profound transformations in conceptions of political sovereignty is to examine the digital practices of our political leaders. Based on interviews with White House insiders, archival research, and a trove of public data, this book tells the story of how our leaders are developing personalized communication styles in a rapidly changing media landscape of ever-present connection technologies and cascading disasters. It reveals important insights about the digital practices of the most significant actors in recent American politics—Barack Obama and Donald Trump as presidents and Hillary Clinton and Joe Biden as presidential candidates—and how their approaches to domestic governance and crisis management relate to their technological choices. This book also views the smartphone as a political actor in the lives of cabinet members, legislative leaders, and prominent activists in ways that clarify its transformative role in the democratic aspirations of average citizens.

The Smartphone in the Oval Office

Former president Barack Obama was associated with a broad range of digital practices during his time in the White House, from shooting selfies to directing drones. In contrast, the presidency of Donald Trump was largely affiliated with behavior normalized by a single technology company: Twitter. But the digital literacy of both presidents involved a complex repertoire of technologies, platforms, devices, and advisors. Trump's content surfing and status checking might be cast as a pathological digital obsession, but he also evolved a relatively nuanced online rhetorical strategy over time and in response to feedback from a range of communities. Many leading social media companies played a significant part in shaping his rise to power and his governing style.

Both Trump and Obama also appropriated the language of Silicon Valley in similar ways and echoed the same themes of transparency, personalization, participation, and direct access. Political scientists and pollsters may continue to debate the characteristics of the so-called Obama–Trump voter, who voted for both the 44th and 45th presidents, and they might question what would inspire the same citizen to vote for such diametrically opposed candidates.[19] But it is obvious that both campaigns deployed a language of direct digital democracy and operationalized similar themes of radical change. Both Obama and Trump uttered populist appeals as candidates that were reflected in their digital practices as leaders.

Access to compact and unobtrusive mobile computing is certainly transforming politics and civic discourse at all levels. The constant presence of these always-on devices realizes the dream of Xerox PARC head Mark Weiser, who coined the term "ubiquitous computing" long before these technologies were practical or widely available. At a time when a president's mobile phone would have been the size of a brick and carried by the muscle men of the Secret Service, Weiser imagined a future in which computers would be available "throughout the physical environment" and become "invisible to the user."[20] Such tiny electronic servants are now close to the bodies of most political leaders in the developed world, just as they are nestled in the pockets and purses of their constituents. Because they "push" notifications and "pull" data from queries, these servants may also prove to be masters. Therefore, it matters that presidents serve as models for what to do and what *not* to do with mobile communication technology, and it also matters that they learn from the digital behaviors of their followers.

This book examines the unintended consequences of this transition to a new way of doing democracy, a change that has taken place with remarkably little public comment or critical reflection. Part of this absence of informed commentary has to do with with the fact that technologists and humanists are often siloed, although there is an energetic cohort of researchers studying the legal, ethical, cultural, and political consequences of pervasive computing technologies. Many of these people analyze important policy topics like network neutrality, digital surveillance, the governance of global platforms like Facebook or Google, and the prevalence of false or misleading data online. Many studying digital culture have examined the topic of ubiquitous computing with a focus on protecting individual privacy and other civil liberties. However, relatively few of these interdisciplinary thinkers have written about the smartphone's prevalence as an everyday instrument of communication, its political impacts on deliberative processes for resolving conflicts, and the consequences of its false promises of direct democracy.

To appeal to citizens' desires for digital direct democracy, both administrations emphasized what I call "the rhetoric of connection," "the rhetoric of transparency," "the rhetoric of participation," and "the rhetoric of access."[21] Both Obama and Trump consistently emphasized the associations of the term "rhetoric" with distraction and deception, but I use the term frequently in this book to refer to the verbal and visual crafting of public image, a practice both presidents clearly cared about. In addition to more traditional channels of communication, rhetoric also operates through algorithms, database structures, and interface design. We live in a culture inundated with obvious messages, but the operations that order, filter, and curate these messages for us are often invisible. Understanding these less explicit techniques of influence and expression is an important part of analyzing contemporary political rhetoric.

In another White House photo, the 44th president and the future 46th president are looking at the screen of a mobile device together while, in the background, a female staffer uses a desktop workstation to perform the office labor required by the bureaucratic state (figure 0.2). Obama's broad smile as he gazes at the screen communicates the pleasure of consuming

Figure 0.2
Vice President Joe Biden and President Barack Obama look at an app on an iPhone in the Outer Oval Office, Saturday, July 16, 2011. Official White House Photo by Pete Souza.

digital media. The photograph shows a moment of intimacy, both between two political leaders sharing a bond and between humans and a digital device.

Much as presidents now demonstrate how to use mobile devices to express political and social solidarity, the digital designers, strategists, and content creators in the White House during this transformative period have attempted to influence our behavior as networked citizens and to shape the structures of our democratic expression. Similarly, their counterparts in Silicon Valley have spawned a new set of practices very different from those associated with watching television or speaking on the telephone. As citizens doing democracy in everyday life, we would do well to imagine what features on our devices might better enable us to be heard, to combat wrongdoing by the state, and to mobilize political agency.

1 Obama's Rhetoric of Connection

Although Obama left office years ago, the website of the Obama White House has been preserved intact. The banner image shows the president striding across the White House lawn. The navigation works. The search window still operates. Visitors can find executive orders, official speeches, and press briefings, as if Obama's presidency had never ended.

At least one of the website's creators looks back fondly on this digital record. In a lengthy interview held a few blocks away from the White House, Macon Phillips, the former director of digital strategy for the president of the United States, reminisced about being part of Obama's youthful, tech-savvy team. He described a group that "sincerely believed in the opportunity of social media," not only to spread messages to audiences more effectively but also to learn from these audiences, "to tap into networks of expertise and to tap into new ways of solving problems and ultimately to empower people to help shape those policies."[1]

Phillips explained how the initial digital team took shape long before the Obama WhiteHouse.gov site went live. It began with the launch of the digital strategy and technology firm Blue State Digital in 2004. The firm's previous experience running a national race had been with Vermont governor and progressive politician Howard Dean, when they pioneered new methods for using websites and targeted emails. The Dean campaign's strategy to reach younger voters included an online game, *Howard Dean for Iowa*, that simulated the kinds of grassroots activities performed by real Dean volunteers.[2]

Looking back to the early '00s, it could be argued that the Democratic Party was surprisingly slow to understand the power of online communities as a means for political organization. I vividly remember meeting Terry

McAuliffe, who was chair of the Democratic National Committee (DNC) from 2001 to 2005, at an intimate Hollywood fundraiser where he made his pitch for data-driven get-out-the-vote efforts. McAuliffe boasted that the DNC could now access extremely granular information about magazine subscriptions and grocery store purchases that might illuminate patterns in voter loyalty. In other words, an independent voter who subscribed to *Guns & Ammo* might be less persuadable than a subscriber to *Food & Wine*. With more data, resources could be more appropriately invested in mailers, phone calls, and door-to-door campaigning to target different demographics.

Yet the digital dossiers that McAuliffe was compiling presupposed that the voter was only a consumer, rather than a creator, of content. His data provided little information about how a citizen navigated choices or contributed to an information environment. For example, purchasing a backyard bird bath might indicate an enthusiasm for protecting animal species, but a purchase record couldn't tell campaign strategists much about how a potential voter might communicate a passion for birding to others or the political valences of this hobby. In contrast, a Facebook post about birdwatching might offer a wealth of information about a voter's personal political opinions. Social media posts provide data in the form of images that is enhanced with metadata in the form of descriptive labels, and the activities of production and consumption are intertwined, particularly as users comment on other people's posts.

From his L Street office, Phillips recalled joining Blue State Digital in 2005. "There wasn't really a developed marketplace for this stuff. This is prior to social media, even YouTube. So it was really about how you used email, websites, and other kinds of tools to organize people and raise money."[3] He described how he "just basically marveled at the idea that you could send emails to a lot of people, and they pulled out their credit cards."[4] Another early Blue State employee, Tom Cochran, who would follow Phillips to the White House and later to the State Department, recalled feeling like he was risking "career suicide" to work in a "frat-like start-up," even though the mission of offering "cool tools and technologies" to progressive candidates was extremely appealing.[5]

The firm aspired to capitalize on big data and to explore paradigms of persuasion that party establishment figures like McAuliffe could never have imagined. As political communication scholar David Karpf notes, digital technology allowed new constituencies to "more easily *speak*" and enabled organizations to "more effectively *listen*."[6] Blue State was interested in listening in on the digital behavior of potential voters using the insights derived from online engagement. Furthermore, thanks to digital delivery methods, understanding people's preferences about messaging was now much cheaper and more precise than conventional polling and market research. Blue State Digital was already ahead of new trends in measuring political sentiment and persuasive appeals.[7]

By the time Obama decided to run for the White House using the new strategies being refined by Blue State Digital, social network sites like You-Tube and Facebook had made the concept of "online community" more familiar to Americans outside of the tech industry. Chris Hughes, one of the cofounders of Facebook, helped design the campaign's online organizing efforts. Although the campaign used multipurpose platforms like Facebook and YouTube, they also created a dedicated platform: My.BarackObama. com. The URL was often abbreviated to MyBO, which was pronounced like "my bow" rather than the acronym for "my body odor." The site made a few conventionally "back end" features for insiders visible to regular "front end" users. For example, it allowed its empowered cadre of users access to databases of potential voters. MyBO also reinforced an ethos of group effort with its frequent psychological appeals to encourage investment in its project of collective storytelling.[8] Although Obama was initially considered a political underdog in the 2008 Democratic primary because he was running against Hillary Clinton, a more established candidate, his campaign quickly narrowed the gap with a more intuitive and multifunctional web presence. Significantly, the digital campaign aligned itself with a particular design aesthetic that emphasized personal and mobile computing rather than computing on a desktop.[9]

The digital campaign was eager to appeal to constituents who were new to social media platforms, so the tech team devised video tutorials to explain MyBO's features to the uninitiated. The available suite of MyBO tools allowed more than a million members to create individualized profiles, contact likely voters in shared zip codes, launch personalized crowdfunding pages, post blog entries, and join affinity groups. Among the plethora of choices for affinity groups were those for tango dancers, air traffic controllers, and single mothers.[10] In addition to harvesting personal information—including one's birthdate—the site's functionality incorporated new digital mapping technologies that merged online and face-to-face campaigning.

The older technology of SMS (Short Message Service) text messaging was also important for instilling a sense of connection. Potential Obama voters regularly received text messages on their mobile phones that were designed to make them feel personally addressed, included, and invested in the campaign. Even if the same message went to a hundred thousand other people, individual texts sent to a single user could enhance feelings of intimacy and immediacy.

Once the race narrowed to Obama and McCain, Republican strategists bemoaned being bested by the superior approach of Blue State Digital, particularly for targeting younger voters: "I get Obama's text messages, and every one is exactly what it should be. It is never pointless, it is always worth reading, and it has an action for you to take."[11] Although "pull" technologies like mining social network data would prove to be important in later campaigns, it is important not to ignore how "push" technologies like text messaging really revolutionized campaigning in 2008.

The Remix Candidate

During Obama's first presidential candidacy, his campaign employed unconventional tactics to try to gain voter support via YouTube, most notably by parlaying the popularity of online mash-up videos in which content from one video was combined or "remixed" with another. For example, the "Vote Different" video fused footage from a speech by Hillary Clinton, Obama's Democratic primary opponent, with an Apple Superbowl ad that had an Orwellian *1984* theme.[12] The "Yes We Can" video blended footage from an Obama stump speech with clips of pop singers and celebrities singing an inspirational anthem about the possibilities of winning the election.[13] Both YouTube videos were clearly referencing ideas about how political speech was constituted dialogically, and they represented that back-and-forth dynamic visually, either as a contrast between Clinton's passive supporters and Obama's active ones in "Vote Different" or as a call and response between Obama and his followers in "Yes We Can." Although the videos were not affiliated with the campaign, they were met with tacit approval from official Obama operatives.

The aesthetics of the Obama remix videos also signaled defiance of conventional rules about intellectual property. Since most remix videos never seek formal permission from copyright holders to use spliced-in audio and images, they tend to blur boundaries between production and consumption. The unsanctioned borrowing in "Vote Different" concerned the video's substance—the copyrighted material came from a commercial entity—and in "Yes We Can" it concerned merely style.

These election videos seemed to appeal to an audience shaped by what digital rights advocate and law professor Lawrence Lessig has deemed "remix culture." According to Lessig, remix is "a critical expression of creative freedom" that "no free society should restrict," because it combines liberatory political possibilities with technological affordances now that a "read-write" culture was possible.[14] These remix practices promote active individual expression in which every citizen can participate creatively.

Staffers for the Republican McCain campaign tried to gain traction with YouTube videos of their own. Their most popular attempt was "Celeb," a video that compared Obama to Paris Hilton and Britney Spears, two paparazzi starlets known for overexposing their personal lives.[15] The "Celeb" video was intended to further boost McCain's already superior standing in the polls for "trustworthy" characteristics that usually correlated strongly with votes on election day.[16] Unfortunately for McCain, YouTube's search features optimized the visibility of response videos that skewered the original premise with parody. A few days later, "Paris Hilton Responds to McCain Ad" appeared with Hilton herself announcing her run for the White House. Although both Obama and McCain were lampooned in the video, the opening montage juxtaposed footage of the elderly McCain with images of real and fictional oldsters, such as Yoda, the Crypt Keeper, Colonel Sanders, Larry King, and the Golden Girls.[17]

To make matters worse, McCain's campaign was mocked for trying to use digital technologies at all. Because McCain's image was so dependent on projecting the twentieth-century authenticity of their candidate, any kind of twenty-first-century technological showmanship could be easily lambasted. When green-screen footage of McCain giving a speech was leaked by a studio technician, do-it-yourselfers created a variety of remixes, which included casting the Senate veteran and former war hero in the Julie Andrews role in *The Sound of Music*.

With its frequent use of YouTube, the Obama campaign was implicitly endorsing Google, which had become the corporate parent of YouTube in 2006. YouTube soon became the second most popular search engine after Google. There were also specific design features that shaped the character of Obama's campaign on YouTube.[18] The platform's efficient and standard-ized compression and streaming technologies made more bandwidth avail-able for interaction and traffic management, which in turn revolutionized how people experienced online video.[19] Before YouTube, most people who wanted to watch an online video had to wait for a file to download from a static web page and then hope that the format would run on their per-sonal machine. Uploading was even more time-consuming and knowledge-intensive than downloading. With YouTube, people could easily watch and upload videos from their mobile phones, search for relevant content, and like, share, and comment. Metrics from those activities were also visible on the site.

What did it mean in 2008 to have a YouTube candidate running for president? How was this experience different from engaging with a can-didate who communicated primarily through television, radio, or news-papers? The media theorist Geert Lovink has argued that audiences "no longer watch films or TV" as communal events because they only "watch databases" in the form of personalized flows of information targeted at individual consumers.[20]

As YouTube began to colonize the landscape of media consumption in the mid-'00s, popularity as a metric offered some sense-making capacity within the kaleidoscopic slot machine of YouTube searches. Now "views," "likes," and "shares" could be used to calibrate the popularity of content on social media platforms. As Alexandra Juhasz has observed, YouTube was fundamentally about "popularity," and this this new kind of "postmodern television" rewarded affinities with familiar "faces, formats, and feelings."[21]

Other media scholars have asserted that because "YouTube launched without knowing exactly what it was going to be for," its "relative under-determination" facilitated "openness, scale, and diversity."[22] This initially unformed character of the YouTube platform also allowed Obama as a rela-tive neophyte in party politics to use the platform as a site of experimen-tation to see what kinds of content would encourage users to claim the material as their own. After all, YouTube videos were often reposted on secondary social media sites so that the embedded material could be per-sonalized with additional framing and curation. In this way, average people could claim a kind of ownership of footage generated by the Obama cam-paign, and the Obama campaign could appropriate footage uploaded by average people.

The Obama Media Ecology

YouTube allowed MyBO to post videos easily, quickly, and cheaply and to analyze data about the kind of content that was most likely to be watched, reposted, and discussed. It is also worth remembering that the main MyBO site wasn't the only web address the campaign employed. For example, in October of 2008, Obama and McCain sparred over which candidate's tax plan would most benefit the middle class. To attempt to settle the question, a YouTube video directed potential voters to Taxcut.BarackObama.com, an interactive subdomain with a "tax calculator" that generated individualized savings predictions. The user filled in information about income, marital status, number of dependents, mortgage debt, and college expenses. The same information could have been communicated via a static table, but the ability to see one's data as personalized and to magically transform input into output was much more persuasive and appealing. Competing tax calculators were available elsewhere on the web,[23] but Obama's Blue State Digital tax calculator was much more polished. It displayed virtuoso web design for the time, and—like the rest of My.BarackObama.com—it invited engagement. According to one scholar of rhetoric, Obama campaign algorithms invited visitors to "fill in the gaps" and supply missing information, just as an audience might supply unspoken assumptions when listening to a conventional speech.[24]

Macon Phillips pointed out that depictions of volunteers on the website were often as important as those of the candidate himself. The design of MyBO's architecture advanced a humanized political narrative by showcasing the experiences of dozens of individual supporters. "We would feature a lot of volunteers out there organizing. We would create content of regular people doing things to help the campaign that we would then share with other regular people to encourage them to do things. . . . We really tried to elevate what we called 'champions of change,' just regular people from around the country that were doing things consistent with what the president thought was important, . . . letting them be the face of that policy issue rather than Obama." This user-generated content populated the site with the good deeds of the volunteers, and it made the MyBO social network seem energetic and active. Many people updated their statuses frequently and engaged with the content of others, hoping to merit attention from the candidate or senior staffers.

In *Yes We Did: An Inside Look at How Social Media Built the Obama Brand*, media strategist and Obama campaign staffer Rahaf Harfoush describes some of the strategies used to promote interaction. For example, the campaign's designers sought to gamify participation among supporters by encouraging competitive goal setting. "Members were ranked against each other and could lose their standing if another member accumulated more points."[25] Successive versions of these self-monitoring features were refined as more user data made it possible to understand how the level of difficulty in achieving particular goals might incentivize (or disincentivize) MyBO members with different degrees of political commitment or free time. The formula for calculating the activity index was tweaked to reward only the most recent activities and to assign more weight to off-line actions like hosting events than to online actions like joining a MyBO group.

Using MyBO's rich suite of authoring tools, users could display the content they desired, even content that challenged the positions of the candidate himself. For example, an insurgent group of MyBO users began organizing against Obama's planned vote as senator to expand the Foreign Intelligence Surveillance Act, a move opposed by many internet privacy advocates. The pro-privacy contingent had been initially very attracted to Obama's stances on digital rights issues, which had aligned with civil libertarians who were determined to preserve the presumption of innocence, but they grew wary that he might be becoming part of the political establishment that supported warrantless surveillance programs. Although MyBO users' resistance to his FISA position did not impact Obama's ultimate policy choice to side with the Senate majority, members of his digital team agreed that they had to acknowledge the conflict to maintain his credibility and his followers' support. In this way the mainstream culture MyBO espoused could accommodate the resistant subculture it had enabled.

While the Obama campaign's digital strategy was fairly traditional in its dissemination of controlled content by disciplined operatives, it utilized channels optimized specifically for smartphones. Within weeks of announcing his run for the presidency, Obama opened an account (@BarackObama) on Twitter in March 2007. Yet Obama's tweets from 2007 and 2008 look oddly cryptic compared to today's more declarative political soundbites that are often crafted for recirculation via other media. Many of Obama's older tweets merely linked to longform announcements of important updates without summarizing the information in the announcements.

Even the announcement of Obama's final FISA decision on Twitter was tantalizingly inaccessible: "Made an important decision today and wanted to share it with you. Visit http://my.barackobama.com/mydecision."

Organizing for America and Organizing for the Self

During the Obama years, technologies of connection enabled new forms of monitoring driven by data analytics that sliced and diced complex information to disambiguate and classify. For MyBO users, these new forms included mechanisms for self-surveillance and personal datafication. Obama fans could create blog posts or fundraising pages. They could also post photos on their profiles, frequently ones in which pictures of themselves had been run through an "Obama-izer" to emulate the iconic "Hope" image created by street artist Shepard Fairey. Finally, they could numerically track their progress in completing assigned campaign tasks or achieving statistical goals as volunteers.

Media scholar Jill Walker Rettberg has argued that such digitally mediated practices of self-representation facilitate "seeing ourselves through technology." Algorithmically enabled self-presentation makes some aspects of ourselves more legible while making others less legible to our own self-consciousness. Rettberg points out that written, visual, and quantitative types of self-representation all have long histories—diaries, self-portraits, and ledgers have recorded this kind of information for centuries.

The MyBO interface served as a mirror reflecting an image of what digital citizenship should look like, based on the verbal, visual, or statistical characteristics of ideal users. The MyBO interface defined its ideal user as an optimized "quantified self." The right kind of "stats" marked the user as exceptional, and those numbers contributed to the user's self-understanding of his or her own moral worth. Although all MyBO users were distinct individuals with unique expressive capacities, all users were measured by the same seemingly neutral, objective, and egalitarian standards for achievement.

Statistical practices from life writing, goal setting, accounting, and even athletics and gaming may have informed how MyBO users interpreted the site's numerical representations of their own political participation. As any dieter or step counter knows, quantifying the self can offer both consolations and frustrations.[26] Self-tracking can challenge stereotypes about health, wellness, and success, but it can also subject individuals to enhanced scrutiny and surveillance.[27] The careful recording of an individual's traits is a practice rooted in histories of colonialism, slavery, and eugenics,[28] but today such quantitative measures reflect the ruthless logic of the neoliberal marketplace. Like people monitoring the rise and fall of their credit scores, MyBO users had to constantly attend to their perpetually fluctuating numbers. Furthermore, MyBO users weren't always in complete control when it came to maximizing their individual scores, because many of the assigned tasks for fundraising or voter outreach favored those with existing class privilege, social status, and economic capital.

Looking back to Obama's 2008 campaign, we can see how the personalization of political action through user-focused digital technologies would eventually transform patterns of connection in social movements of all kinds.[29] Even those designated as social media "followers" now expected to be addressed as individuals and to be recognized as distinct political entities within larger groups mobilized for change. Shared experiences of inequality or precarity that might drive massive collective protests, both in the streets and online, would transform into a rhetoric of diverse personal experience manifesting in an array of distinct forms.[30]

Personalization might have appeared to enhance direct democracy by allowing people to speak as individuals rather than as interchangeable constituents of political parties or congressional districts, but it has also detracted from the unified messaging, organizational coherence, and communal ethos necessary for true solidarity.[31] With its highly personalized design strategy and an interface optimized for novelty, the MyBO site depended on constant updating by temporarily invested users who were relatively new to the platform. Although MyBO logged an impressive number of total subscribers, many of those users only created skeletal profiles and spent little time with the site's activities of self-monitoring, personal measurement, status checking, and social connection. Most users committed only to completing short-term, relatively simple tasks rather than engaging in sustained discussions or complex deliberations. Few users integrated the site into their permanent routines, and connections between users largely remained superficial.

After Obama's inauguration in 2009, MyBO became Organizing for America, which would serve as the DNC's grassroots digital organization. As former *Nation* editor Micah Sifry recounted in his article "Obama's Lost Army," MyBO's transition into the Democratic Party establishment was not uncontested.[32] Many wanted to see a more independent successor organization with a distributed network of users who would continue to welcome new political participants. According to a concept document written by boosters of this idea, an organization called Movement 2.0, or M2.0, could "serve both to educate supporters" and to "gather the input to help shape" the president's legislative agenda while serving as an autonomous nonprofit organization focused on governance rather than elections.[33] Instead, Sifry told the unhappy story of a core group of idealistic campaign advisors, tech executives, and academics obstructed by traditional party insiders defending the status quo. Sifry asserted that the decision to tie the site to the party establishment might have doomed its promise as a left-wing counter to the right-wing online populism that blossomed with the Tea Party.

However, some insiders blamed members of Obama's own tech team for abandoning grassroots organizing in favor of more lucrative opportunities. Kate Albright-Hanna wrote that "New Media was dead, but a corpse called 'Digital' rose to take its place."[34] According to Albright-Hanna, this new entity was "bloodless, technocratic, and made of big data" and "rolled its eyes at narrative, on the ground feedback, and human political instinct." As the focus changed to surveillance, number crunching, and algorithmic manipulation of the Democratic political base, digital strategy became a "sure-fire, can't-lose, totally smart approach to crushing the competition."

While visiting the old pages of My.BarackObama.com, I discovered that many links led to Domain Name System errors with apologetic messages like "Something went wrong (but it's not your fault)." Although I was encouraged to "try again in a few minutes," the online community once comprising over a million users failed to manifest itself again. But MyBO became obsolete long before it degenerated into broken links and apologies. Sifry described a conspiracy to undermine democratic digital participation orchestrated from above, but MyBO lost much of its reason for existence from below. After users helped get Obama elected, interest in the more modest grassroots goals of increasing voter turnout and political participation waned. Obama's White House became the new focus. His was expected to be the most transparent administration in history.

2 Obama's Rhetoric of Transparency

Even before Obama's 2008 triumph at the polls, his digital team was preparing for the launch of Change.gov. Change.gov took a novel approach to digital transitions by elevating the role of the president-elect. This new federal government website was supposed to be a staging area for policy announcements and plans to achieve lofty goals. Before the president-elect and his future vice president Joe Biden moved into the more established online spaces of WhiteHouse.gov, their operation took advantage of an official interim digital platform.

The Clinton to Bush transition in the physical White House had been a messy one—literally. Republican staffers arrived to find Vaseline-smeared desks, glued drawers, unplugged refrigerators, whited-out computer keyboards, scattered bumper stickers, and obscene voice mail greetings.[1] Government-issued cell phones were also missing.[2] By contrast, Jane Cook, a Bush-era webmaster, remembered no animosity in the digital transition of power at WhiteHouse.gov. However, the Clinton presidency—which created WhiteHouse.gov in 1994—seemed to have put little thought into managing the handoff.[3] On George W. Bush's inauguration day, federal contractors hastily erected a skeleton page to replace the website celebrating "President William J. Clinton: Eight Years of Peace, Progress and Prosperity."[4] The razor-thin margins of the Bush/Gore election led to contestation that lasted many weeks after election day. With Bush winning Florida by only 537 votes, recounts were demanded, and legal challenges had to work their way through the court system. According to Cook, this uncertainty made it difficult to have a polished web presence in place to celebrate the new administration.[5]

Due to their negative experiences with the transfer of power, the Bush web team worked assiduously on a peaceful digital transition with the

Obama team. The last update to the Bush White House page showed the first family welcoming the Obamas.[6] Yet not everything went perfectly when the Obama IT team took over. Tom Cochran, a Blue State Digital veteran and the first director of new media technologies for Obama, recounted with regret how "servers were unplugged" and "accounts wiped out," sometimes for civil servants who had been with the government for over a quarter of a century. People discovered that files that they had scrupulously maintained over decades had been erased overnight.

Change.gov promised a radical transformation. The site allowed average people to apply directly for presidential appointments in the Obama administration by filling out an online form. This was done to show that the new White House was rejecting the cronyism of the political spoils system, which rewarded loyalty by giving jobs to known supporters. I filled out an application myself to explore the desired qualifications. I noticed that the skills, experience, and education requirements were remarkably generic. Seemingly anyone was welcome to apply and could thus feel encouraged and included.

I never heard back from the White House about any potential job prospects. What I did receive were regular emails from Democratic Party power broker John Podesta with subject lines such as "Give Your Ideas Directly to the President," "Video: The President-elect's plan," and "It's time." Just as the campaign had grown a huge bank of contacts through the MyBO platform, the administration seemed to be creating a similar database of Change.gov users.

Change.gov also sought to archive evidence of citizen participation as the inauguration approached. "An American Moment: Your Story" explicitly encouraged users to share their own content: "We're counting on citizens from every walk of life to get involved. Share your experiences and your ideas—tell us what you'd like the Obama–Biden administration to do and where you'd like the country to go."[7] As with the job application portal, users of the American Moment site had to provide their email addresses. They were also encouraged to upload a photo to illustrate their story. Other parts of the site included areas for information, discussion, and inquiry, such as "Citizen's Briefing Book," "Join the Discussion," "Your Seat at the Table," and "Open for Questions."[8]

On digital rights issues, Change.gov sent decidedly mixed messages about its use of intellectual property. On the page titled "Copyright Notice" was a proud announcement that the site used a Creative Commons Attribution 3.0 License. Such "copyleft" (as opposed to "copyright") licenses had been created by forward-thinking legal experts who thought that traditional copyright was often inappropriate in the digital age because it stifled the creativity of online remixes, mash-ups, and amateur imitation and consequently silenced many forms of online political speech. Change.gov informed users that they had granted "a non-exclusive, irrevocable, royalty-free license to the rest of the world for their submissions" in keeping with the sharing ethos of Creative Commons. At the same time, Change.gov sternly asserted the rights of traditional copyright holders, such as music studios and movie producers, and warned against violations of the Digital Millennium Copyright Act.

The First Social Media Inauguration

1.8 million people gathered in Washington, DC to watch Obama's inauguration in 2008. At the time, I had a sick sinking feeling about the event's impermanence. I looked at what my friends were posting on social media, whether they were out shivering on the Washington Mall or partying in the warmth of elite galas. I was dismayed to watch this massive archive of digital images being entrusted to social media companies rather than cultural preservationists.

The historical record had never been more rich, inclusive, and varied, thanks to mobile digital technology. But it had also never been more at risk due to the frequent obsolescence of proprietary platforms and media storage systems. When users signed away their rights to Silicon Valley companies in exchange for using these services, the situation only got worse.

In the days leading up to the event, I talked to Dan Cohen, who was director of the Center for History and New Media at George Mason University. He agreed there were many problems with "online memory-making with decentralized user contributions" that were dependent on organizations "not in the forever business."[9] He thought that all those pictures and messages should be part of a digital public archive that could be explored by researchers and average citizens centuries into the future. The social media companies absorbing the collective memories of the Obama inauguration weren't incentivized to serve as stewards and custodians, and they weren't charged with the responsibility of making data accessible and legible for posterity. Such companies might be interested in harvesting as much data as possible in order to mine it for potential monetization, but it was in their proprietary interest to keep much of this information obscured.

I also talked to Kris Carpenter from the Internet Archive, a nonprofit digital library, who reassured me that volunteers would be dispersed among the crowd on inauguration Tuesday, armed with laptops and "every adapter they can think of." The volunteers would collect data from cell phones and digital cameras and provide the metadata for cataloging information to identify sources on the spot. When I checked in with her a few weeks after the inauguration, she admitted that the effort had been a bust. They didn't have enough personnel or equipment to begin with, and the cold weather had further discouraged volunteer turnout.

The problem with relying on sites like Facebook to store our collective memories is that social media platforms were never designed to be national archives; they were designed to generate advertising revenue and marketing data by capitalizing on the digital collections of others. In other words, these companies were interested in mining archives, not maintaining them.

The widespread social media coverage of Obama's 2009 inauguration allowed millions of people who were thousands of miles away from Washington, DC to experience a feeling of copresence during the ceremony, celebrations, and counter-protests. Newspapers, such as the venerable *Telegraph*, were also learning to follow hashtags for the first time during their inauguration reporting.[10] People observing the event were encouraged to follow #inauguration, #obamainaug, and #inaug09.

Facebook partnered with CNN to allow live commentary on the broadcaster's video stream of the event. On the history-making morning of January 20, about 600,000 people—a "mind-blowing" number for the time[11]—posted on Facebook during CNN's mixed-media spectacle. Over a billion people were estimated to have watched the inauguration "on their TVs and computers," according to *Wired*, which noted that the BBC had a thirty-minute interruption of their digital stream.[12] Google's traffic showed heavy use of their search engine by an international audience tuning in. Metrics peaked as people like Aretha Franklin appeared on the stage.[13] On Facebook, the visitors to Washington continued to share. Many users were seeing a faster and more varied stream of content from "friends" than they had ever seen before.

The New Digital Technocrats

A new generation of technocrats came into the White House with Obama that day in January. They differed radically from information technology professionals from earlier eras. Previous generations had come from the worlds of the military, academia, or traditional business management. These earlier technocrats understood their prime directive to be the maintenance of files.

Filing was a pre-digital technology made more efficient by computerization. A century ago, German philosopher Max Weber described how "the management of the modern office" was "based upon written documents," which were "preserved" by "a staff of subaltern officials and scribes of all sorts."[14] When computer operating systems like Unix came into use by the federal government, files remained at the core of the state's identity.

As the Spanish sociologist Manuel Castells has observed, during the late twentieth century a newer culture of software development emerged with fractious networked subcultures such as "the techno-meritocratic culture," "the hacker culture," "the virtual communitarian culture," and "the entrepreneurial culture"[15] in a sometimes volatile "intersection of big science, military research, and libertarian culture."[16] As the new Obama White House staffers interacted with old-guard IT managers, they encountered resistance from the entrenched techno-meritocratic culture that wanted to preserve the bureaucratic hierarchies of civil service employment and file management procedures.

Tom Cochran described how the fraught relationship "between Silicon Valley and Washington, DC" could make negotiation between the two office cultures impossible. "Both sides think that they are the smartest in the room," he lamented.[17] However, some of the Blue State tech workers eventually became habituated to the way that Washington worked, as they began to see the value of maintaining tradition. Cochran laughed about how even he came to react negatively to the next wave of tech employees, "twenty-four-year-old start-up founders in t-shirts saying, 'Washington is broken,'" even though he himself had agreed with many of their arguments just a few months earlier and had come from the same start-up culture himself.

While the older generation of technocrats focused on preservation, the new generation focused on access. The previous maze of Byzantine rules was to be replaced with wide-open windows that would allow anyone to shine a light inside the government. To popularize these new policies, the metaphors of "sunlight" or "sunshine" became common figures of speech in the administration's rhetoric about transparency. The White House borrowed language from political transparency organizations like the Sunlight Foundation (founded in 2006) and the American Society of Newspaper Editors, which sponsored Sunshine Week (founded in 2005). The adage from Supreme Court Justice Louis Brandeis that "sunlight is said to be the best of disinfectants" was quoted on the White House website over a dozen times during the Obama years.

Transparency was also a popular theme in Silicon Valley, one that was supposed to improve efficiency by getting the most out of a corporation's "human capital."[18] CEOs like Facebook's Mark Zuckerberg worked in open offices without walls or cubicles, so everyone's workplace activity was visible.[19] The "transparency report," issued by companies like Google and Twitter, eventually became a recognized public relations genre.[20]

The Open Source Revolution

One explanation for the optimism among new technocrats had to do with the rise of the API (Application Programming Interface), a software intermediary that allowed two applications to communicate with each other. Specifically, APIs provided structured mechanisms for new applications to pull data from existing applications. Although the proliferation of different social media platforms and types of mobile devices could have caused total chaos, the forces for integration were powerful, too.

Open file formats like JSON (JavaScript Object Notation) were rapidly adopted by companies like Twitter, Facebook, and Flickr during this period.[21] JSON was designed to be light, promote legibility with human-readable text, and make outputting data easy. JSON was also designed in ways that helped the ecologies of social media grow sustainably, particularly as use exploded with the proliferation of applications for mobile devices. Developers reaped the benefits of these standardized open formats.

Commercial interest was not the only driver of API growth. Fan communities and non-governmental organizations used APIs as a way to gather, manage, and circulate statistical knowledge collectively. Public web-based APIs could allow interested people to download large spreadsheets from an organization's website with the push of a virtual button. This data could also be visualized to make significant patterns of information more apparent and meaningful.[22]

Another factor encouraging the new generation of digital technocrats was the so-called smart cities movement that was embedding technology into every aspect of urban infrastructure.[23] APIs were being used in tech-enriched cities to make public transportation more user-friendly and efficient, to encourage more sustainable energy consumption, and to manage services like waste removal and policing. Other technologies were important to the smart cities movement as well. Radio-frequency identification could make transactions simpler with smart cards, license plate tracking could improve flow on toll roads and parking structures, and city-specific applications for mobile phones could dispense location-aware information in real time. If new digital technologies could improve life at the local level, perhaps these same technologies could transform the delivery of services and management of infrastructure for the entire country.

The central concern for many tech employees coming into the Obama administration was scalability. Those with previous experience with smart cities or digital town halls (covered in the next chapter) worried that what worked well in a metropolis with fewer than a million people, such as San Francisco or Seattle, might become totally dysfunctional at the federal scale. In contrast, those with tech company experience might have managed user bases with hundreds of millions of members, but they were often unfamiliar with the legal, ethical, and bureaucratic obligations of government work and its historical precedents and civil service rules.

The Presidential Records Act was a particularly prickly thorn in the side of Obama's digital crew. It had been passed in 1978 while the impact of the Nixon Watergate scandal was still strong. The act's mandate that all presidential records be preserved starting in 1981 did not translate easily to the digital age. For example, if an electronic file had thousands of nearly identical versions, did each one need to be saved and labeled? The process of collecting data for posterity could often be cumbersome. Cochran recalled many struggles around figuring out how to archive social media, and he chuckled about the "craziness" of "rooms of government bureaucrats taking screenshots of Facebook and emailing them" to comply with their interpretation of the act.[24]

Obama's campaign promises also posed challenges for his digital staff. Obama had vowed that bills passed by Congress would be posted online for the public to see for at least five days before receiving the president's signature.[25] After the inauguration, very few pieces of actual legislation received this "sunlight before signing" treatment, even in Obama's critical first few months in office.[26] As then-director of digital strategy Macon Phillips explained on the White House blog, "implementation procedures and some initial issues with the congressional calendar" hampered delivering on the promise.[27]

Despite these reality checks, celebrations of high-tech transparency began on Obama's first full day in office, when the president issued a memorandum to heads of departments and agencies on "Transparency and Open Government." Transparency was key to what Phillips described as the three cornerstones of the new government: "transparency," "participation," and "communication."[28] According to Obama's directive, transparency "promotes accountability and provides information for citizens about what their Government is doing." The new transparency policy designated federal information as a "national asset" that had to be disclosed "rapidly in forms that the public can readily find and use." Furthermore, executive departments and agencies were expected to "harness new technologies to put information about their operations and decisions online and readily available to the public." Finally, executive departments and agencies were urged to "solicit public feedback to identify information of greatest use to the public."[29]

Each one of these elements represented challenges for the new technocrats. Protecting public information "assets" from Silicon Valley monetization was difficult to do while maintaining open architectures. It was also hard to make information understandable to a general audience equipped with much less data literacy than the administration's number crunchers and tech whizzes. In addition, there were trade-offs between releasing data in truly open formats, which required more arcane technical knowledge, and releasing data in commercial formats that had closed algorithms but were more commonly in use. Nonetheless, by 2012, Transparency.gov was dispensing all sorts of information with maps, graphs, charts, and visualizations to show how federal spending was being allocated. The numbers on everything from oil spill contracts to grants in higher education were available to be mined.

Searching for Transparency

During Obama's eight years in office, the design of the White House website remained relatively consistent, conveying institutional permanence. For instance, the homepage navigation menu changed only slightly between 2009 and early 2017. Reading from left to right, "*the* BRIEFING ROOM," "*the* AGENDA," "*the* ADMINISTRATION," "ABOUT *the* WHITE HOUSE," "*our* GOVERNMENT," and "CONTACT *us*" gradually became "BRIEFING ROOM," "ISSUES," "THE ADMINIS-TRATION," and "1600 PENN."[30] Other small changes included the replacement of serif with sans serif fonts and the addition of a more prominent search box. As a kind of interactive interface for input, the search box encouraged users to engage.

Search boxes are also associated with transparency; facilitating unobstructed inquiry by making large quantities of information accessible suggests there is nothing to hide. The Obama White House website was designed as a portal to other public open data websites that allowed citizens to see the inner workings of government for themselves. It was conceived as a launchpad for perusing budgets, poring over regulatory language, or monitoring the activities of government officials. Despite its prominent position on the site, however, the search box was rarely used. Most users accessed WhiteHouse.gov materials through Google searches rather than via the site's own search interface.

Like most public-facing institutional websites, the back end of Obama's WhiteHouse.gov was constructed using resources from multiple technology providers. According to Cochran, the "most targeted website in the world" utilized software from Drupal, Akamai, Acquia, and Apache Solr to handle needs like content management, networked content delivery, cloud services, and indexing. Eager to avoid "reinventing the wheel," Cochran eventually switched the WhiteHouse.gov search engine to one developed by the government's General Services Administration that was powered by Microsoft's search engine Bing. But he remained aware that "all the studies that user experience experts do" show that "user search is rarely search" because "people just go back to Google" when they want to find information.

Certainly, search algorithms conceal as well as reveal. Search engines filter and rank results. Google distinguished itself from early competitors like AltaVista and Ask Jeeves by understanding the enormous value of human behavior in improving the indexing done by machines. Google, like most search engines from the 1990s, initially relied on programs called "web crawlers," also known as a "spiders" or "spiderbots," that moved through links on the World Wide Web, accessed their HTML pages, and copied their content so that other programs could classify this material and make it easily findable. Google's page rank algorithm was effective at monitoring how successful users perceived its searches to be, combining the labor of human users with the labor of nonhuman crawlers. As media theorist Benjamin Bratton observes, a search engine "does not produce new content for its *Users*, but rather structures the value of content that other *Users* provide."[31]

This recursive loop loads search algorithms up with users' cultural biases, atop the original biases structured into the initial search algorithms by Silicon Valley programmers. The digital media scholar Safiya Umoja Noble questions Google's pose of neutrality in her work on the company's tendency to serve up racist and sexist search results. Noble criticizes "algorithms of oppression" that create new systems of digital redlining in the backgrounds of our computationally mediated daily lives.[32] Substantive moral and ethical questions need to be asked about purportedly objective search results, particularly when people of color are tagged with hurtful racist stereotypes.

And even as tech corporations like Google promote rhetorics of openness, their business models necessarily reward proprietary secrecy and elite forms of expertise. Such companies may laud open-source software development as a training ground for their programmers or open standards as the basis of the interoperability from which they profit, but their commitments to genuine transparency are often extremely superficial.

Promoting Open Government

A 2009 video of Macon Phillips and chief information officer Vivek Kundra explaining the functionality USASpending.gov exhibits the administration's optimism about its early open data initiatives. In the video, Kundra boasts about providing "tools around analysis that allow you to do comparative analysis" that will enable users to serve as "watchdog," "auditor," and "innovator."[33] Kundra enthuses about how users will "be able to take that data and slice and dice and cube it and mash it up in different ways." He gushes about how "you could actually get XML feeds from the platform itself, and you could design your own online community that follows how a project is performing."

XML stands for Extensible Markup Language. It is used to structure data for storage and transport. XML files include both tags and text, allowing digital composers to use existing website tagging architecture to create distinctive classification systems. In other words, XML is a metalanguage that allows users to define their own customized markup languages and to annotate existing digital content by organizing it into particular buckets of similar data. For example, using XML, I could mark up an online dining menu with tags like <item>nachos</item>, <price>4.99</price>, or <appetizer vegetarian="true">. Using these tags, a computer could easily tabulate all the orders and summarize what the restaurant received as income and what products were delivered to customers. The vast and heterogeneous corpus of information on government websites—currently written in prose as speeches, executive orders, legislation, reports, court decisions, and many other genres of political expression—could be reduced to data that could be processed for more sensible decision-making.

Certainly Kundra was right that XML made data more readable and rational by providing useful classifiers to simplify information processing across multiple sites. However, using specialized data lingo like "XML" in an online video intended for a general audience might have reinforced existing stereotypes about educated elite snobbery and the exclusion of less privileged and more precarious classes. In other words, how might a senior citizen, food service worker, or truck driver make sense of Kundra's Silicon Valley jargon?

At the same time that the Obama administration was centralizing information for one-stop perusal at sites like Transparency.gov and USASpending.gov, it was setting up innumerable single-issue websites. Each new site joined an alphabet soup of other .gov sites that were not clearly connected to specific federal agencies. For example, FoodSafetyWorkingGroup.gov was established in 2009 to bring together expertise from the Department of Health and Human Services and the Department of Agriculture in response to persistent problems with foodborne illnesses and contamination. The site appears to have been taken off-line in 2017 during the Trump administration.

Most of these specially coined Obama-era domain names employed aspirational language associated with a robust social safety net, such as

Recovery.gov, Opportunity.gov, HeathReform.gov, FinancialStability.gov, AStrongMiddleClass.gov, and MakingHomeAffordable.gov. However, some —like Distraction.gov or Flu.gov—were named after the hazards from which the welfare state could provide protection. Other choices in website naming raised questions about why some issues deserved a federal.gov website while others didn't. For instance, the administration created Fatherhood.gov in April of 2011, but it never created a Motherhood.gov.

The Costs of Transparency

Kin Lane, a self-described "API evangelist" and former presidential innovation fellow, left the administration sixty days after he joined it. Lane was a software engineer with interests in the potential synergies of technology, business, and politics. Even though he was part of a robust cohort of forty-three fellows recruited by the Obama administration, he felt that he couldn't make much impact on an entrenched and defensive federal culture, and the G-14 salary, high cost of living in the nation's capital, and periodic suspension of government payrolls during periods of legislative brinksmanship only made things worse.[34]

In an interview for this book, Lane described what unfolded after his initial placement in the Veterans Administration (VA) in the summer of 2013.[35] The VA is an agency with broad responsibilities that include providing health care, dispensing benefits, arranging for burials, and constructing memorials. Lane initially focused on the most basic task of helping the agency "understand the mandate" from the administration about transparency and defining "what is public data" and "what should be shared."[36] He discovered that agency units often wanted to shift responsibility to other entities. Even teams that appeared eager to embrace accountability might "give you smoke, stuff that is already on their website" rather than doing the hard work of harvesting new data or making existing data accessible, machine readable, and enriched with metadata that would make it more valuable to users.

Lane came to understand that the VA's resistance to digital transparency was often perfectly rational. "I learned that people are really looking to hurt federal agencies. You might publish material publicly that might seem harmless, but it can be weaponized to punish and politicize." In the era of "journalists doing gotcha stories," WikiLeaks, and an entrenched political culture of extreme polarization, Lane saw the consequences of revealing disappointing or embarrassing numbers that were more likely to demoralize federal employees than to energize them.

Although transparency was supposed to lower federal costs, putting real-time, open-access information online could also elevate federal expenditures dramatically. When "corporations scrape the data every minute looking for changes" in order to profit from free information, agencies incur "bandwidth costs," "server costs," and "commercial costs associated with transparency." As Lane asked, "if you are Google, should you be able to pound government servers for free?" There were concerns about profiteering as well. "Some of this stuff can impact markets," Lane observed. Records from sub-branches of government like the Department of Labor couldn't always be released in real time. Yet being too slow or secretive with data release risked exploitation for insider trading by those with access to such information before it was made available to the public.

As Lane's mission expanded beyond Veterans Affairs to include working with other agencies, he began to recognize that the unintended consequences of transparency could be profound. He experienced a glaring "spotlight on government" rather than the gentle warmth of "sunshine" transparency had promised.

The elimination of information gatekeeping had sounded appealing, but dumping "a million records in PDF format" was "not helping reporters make sense of this data." However, converting enormous PDF archives into usable spreadsheets and then cleaning that tabulated data is an enormous task that requires attention to detail and millions of man-hours.

The Obama administration also had serious privacy concerns about the push for transparency. Law enforcement agents who could be identified in federal data feared retaliation from organized crime enterprises. Data from the Department of Housing and Urban Development could put victims of domestic violence at risk of being tracked down by their abusers. There were also often problems implementing authentication systems for government workers accessing private or confidential information housed on federal servers, and these problems were heightened by the fact that federal agencies tended to operate in a competitive environment of mutual mistrust.

Macon Phillips agreed about the pitfalls of transparency. "It's a whole lot easier to tear something down than to build it. No one ever wrote stories about how great all of the data that we published was. We were seen as increasing the threat vector for the press to pick up negative stories."[37] Phillips gave the example of publishing all of the data from the American Recovery and Reinvestment Act of 2009. This legislation was intended to provide an economic stimulus and bailout package to address the financial crisis that had plagued the last months of the Bush administration. "Someone's going to find something in there that's bad, which one could argue is really valuable. But from a press and communications standpoint it meant we were typically only getting black marks and not gold stars."

The double bind faced by the Obama administration was thus that there could never be enough transparency and that there would always be too much. As legal scholar Mark Fenster argues, transparency always functions as both an end and a means. As Fenster explains, "the term *transparency* simultaneously describes both an aspirational goal—full openness to the public—and the core problem that must be overcome in order for that goal to be met—the separation between the state and public."[38] Transparency is supposed to unite the public and the state, but it always reveals a division that propagates suspicion rather than trust.

According to digital democracy skeptic Evgeny Morozov, some government secrecy is needed for nuanced coalition building, flexible decision-making, and maintenance of collective trust. Getting rid of "sleazy corruption, backroom deals, and inefficient horse trading" might sound like an admirable goal,[39] but the puritanical pursuit of absolute transparency can undermine the expectations for private communication that are necessary for functioning deliberation. Morozov also criticized the Obama administration's hypocrisy in preaching transparency while it "prosecuted leakers and whistle-blowers," "expanded the government's classification program," and "forbad reporters from disclosing the names of federal workers."[40]

Input and Output Transparency

Many administration officials knew from the outset that transparency wouldn't be simple to achieve. One of Obama's key appointments in advancing his transparency agenda was Harvard Law professor Cass Sunstein as administrator of the Office of Information and Regulatory Affairs. OIRA (pronounced "oh-eye-ruh") was established as part of the Office of Management and Budget.

Sunstein had argued for an approach that he characterized as "libertarian paternalism," which differed significantly from simple transparency. According to Sunstein, government officials would serve as "choice architects" for the masses by presenting information in a manner that facilitated better outcomes. In this way federal agencies could achieve the goals of a more prosperous and sustainable society using principles of behavioral economics by designing systems to "nudge" citizens toward better choices. In other words, transparency alone would fail if it were not connected to clear decision-making opportunities.

Furthermore, Sunstein recognized that legalistic approaches to transparency could result in the burying of critical information in too much data or fine print, thereby disclosing nothing by disclosing everything. For example, one of the signature transparency achievements of the Obama administration that Sunstein praised was the Credit Card Accountability, Responsibility, and Disclosure Act of 2009, which required credit card companies to redesign monthly statements to be more informative, particularly about the long-term costs of paying only the minimum due. Not only was the information on the new statements more transparent, but it was also more actionable.

Sunstein expressed jaded opinions about the benefits of transparency for its own sake, particularly as it affected the efficacy of the government. After his tenure in the White House, Sunstein remained enthusiastic about the value of what he called "output transparency," which involved transparency about what the government *produced*, such as findings about environmental pollution, but he was leerier of "input transparency," which involved transparency about what the government *consumed*, such as "who, within government, said what to whom, and when."[41]

As an example of effective output transparency, Sunstein pointed to information about workplace fatalities from the Occupational Safety and Health Administration that was posted prominently on the landing page of OSHA.gov. On a real-time news ticker, visitors could see "11/09/2015 UT: Larry Nickell killed in fall while installing solar panel" or "11/12/2015 TX: Steven Reyna asphyxiated from CO2 exposure."[42] Users were only one click away from a site for downloading fatality reports with open and interoperable CSV (comma-separated value) files. CSV files are formatted using only commas and line breaks to represent a table-structured format, allowing data to be saved in small, bare-bones files. They are popular because they can be read by commercial spreadsheet software, such as Microsoft Excel, and thus the data can be more easily processed. According to Sunstein, this output data could be applied to decision-making, whether directly—by average people looking online at the numbers for themselves—or indirectly—by average people using handy mobile phone applications that had ingested repurposed government data. In contrast, Sunstein believed that input transparency had higher costs and fewer benefits than output transparency because it was "pre-decisional" in character.

Transparency can also exacerbate existing societal inequality. In the post-Obama era, dozens of books have been published that caution against the assumption that a data-driven society will necessarily be a better one. Among these titles are Cathy O'Neil's *Weapons of Math Destruction*, Virginia Eubanks's *Automating Inequality*, and Andrew Guthrie Ferguson's *The Rise of Big Data Policing*. Each of these volumes show the unintended consequences of information harvesting on a massive scale. They also observe that the poisonous legacies of data-gathering efforts from the pre-digital era still exist, such as the neighborhood redlining that led to racial and economic segregation. Although Black voters were an important sector of Obama's political base, his administration's talking points about transparency weren't particularly popular with this core constituency. Black citizens, who appeared hypervisible in the dominant society, were already subjected to more privacy violations than their white counterparts.[43]

As media theorist Wendy Hui Kyong Chun pointed out in a 2010 interview, "transparency can't be the answer to all our political questions," because "things can be transparent and still unfair," and "things can be transparent and actually more unfair, because certain people are exposed, and exposure is not always the same."[44] Chun asserted that "exposure is the beginning of a dialogue, which is always about power relations." According to Chun, those who were exposed by the data-gathering mechanisms of the state tended to be the most vulnerable and precarious citizens—the poor, the sick, the criminalized, and children—who were also the least able to participate as equals in shared discussions about democracy.

When making a complex world legible becomes the main goal of the state, the messy lives of its citizens tend to suffer. Top-down planning efforts often begin with the violence of the ledger and the map, whether it is through uprooting people from their homes in the Tennessee Valley during the New Deal or forcing others into strategic hamlets during the

Vietnam War. As the state uses tools that categorize assets and sort people into social categories, it often ignores the informal agreements and flexible arrangements upon which human life depends.[45] In other words, these all-seeing Obama databases could be blind to people's lived experiences.

The Google President

While campaigning for president in 2007, Obama gave a talk on the Google campus in Mountain View, CA, in which he claimed that he and Google shared similar commitments to "changing the world from the bottom up, not the top down."[46] For Obama, "the Google story" was not only a narrative of "good jobs"; it was also a tale of Google's quest for seeing "things that are unseen." From this inspirational account of Google's visionary track record, Obama jumped into his own plans for open government initiatives to encourage greater transparency. As a senator, he sponsored a bill dubbed the "Google for Government" bill to create a searchable website about government spending.[47]

Obama's history with Google goes all the way back to the summer of 2004, when he joined one of Google's TGIF events. During his visit he watched master displays of search traffic and expressed admiration for the company's many banks of computer servers. In *The Audacity of Hope*, Obama fondly recounts his experience of meeting founders Sergey Brin and Larry Page, and he repeats the founders' well-known egalitarian origin story that links their wealthy company to its supposedly humble beginnings in a dorm room and a garage.[48] He repeated this founding myth in his 2007 speech at Google. In a 2013 White House speech devoted to Obama's "New Management Agenda," the president reminisced about his 2007 visit and added that he had "promised to appoint the nation's first CTO—Chief Technology Officer" when he visited Google.[49]

Certainly, Obama was not the first president to champion transparency. Coming out of early twentieth-century Progressive Era politics, the Keep Commission was founded by President Theodore Roosevelt in 1905 to promote efficiency and accountability among federal agencies.[50] And all throughout that pre-digital century, the Government Printing Office made statistical information widely available to many constituencies.

Neither was Obama the first president to advocate for digital transparency specifically. Under Obama's predecessor, George W. Bush, federal bureaucrats made information available online about meetings held between OIRA and outside groups, and they also created the portal at Regulations.gov to sunlight all federal agencies' rulemaking proceedings.[51] During the Clinton administration, the website of the National Performance Review led by Vice President Al Gore posted information from a range of government agencies.[52]

Obama wasn't even the first president to associate the powers of the federal government with a search engine. Clinton administration staffers had boasted that the government-funded search engine *FirstGov* would introduce "a single point-of-entry to one of the largest and most useful collection of web pages in the world" by allowing users "to search all 27 million federal agency web pages at one time" so quickly that it could mine "half a billion documents in less than one-quarter of a second" and "handle millions of searches a day."[53]

However, Obama was unique in closely associating his presidency with Google, a multi-billion-dollar privately owned search engine company. The administration's overly close relationship was a topic of concern for many civil libertarians from the start. The search engine giant had launched AdSense in 2003, introduced its own web-based email service in 2004, rolled out Google Maps in 2005, and acquired YouTube in 2006. By the 2009 inauguration, the company seemed poised to further expand its cross-platform data-mining efforts. Google lobbyist Johanna Shelton visited the White House 128 times during Obama's tenure, an astonishing measure of corporate influence.[54] Shelton was far from the only Google employee to be welcomed. The Google Transparency Project has created a color-coded information visualization that shows connections representing hundreds of meetings between White House officials and Google employees.[55]

Nearly 250 people transitioned from Google employment to government service or vice versa over during the Obama administration.[56] Given the strong need for technical expertise in a self-described digital administration, it was not surprising that the federal government sought to lure employees from Google, but the diffusion of personnel habituated to Google's corporate culture inevitably also influenced policy attitudes.

The Google corporation benefited from copious White House publicity that depicted the company as a philanthropic entity promoting diversity in STEM (science, technology, engineering, and mathematics) fields. For example, in 2011 three female winners of the Google Global Science Fair toured the Oval Office with the president,[57] and in 2013 the White House blog ran a long piece devoted to the four winners of the Google Science Fair.[58] Coverage of these Google fairs emphasized the racial diversity of participants and the strong showing of female competitors, thus advertising a counterfactual spectacle of inclusivity in tech culture along with the Google brand.

The story of Google's founding also became a parable about the promise of the immigrant entrepreneur. A picture of Sergey Brin appeared during the 2016 State of the Union Address, and the words to the left of his headshot read "SERGEY BRIN IS A US IMMIGRANT: HE'S ALSO A CO-FOUNDER OF GOOGLE."[59] Another image of Brin appeared on a WhiteHouse.gov page about the Administration's response to the Syrian refugee crisis that described how Brin "fled the Soviet Union with his family at the age of 6." The image was accompanied by the hashtag #RefugeesWelcome.[60]

Despite the adulation of the company coming from the White House, members of Google's corporate leadership did not necessarily reciprocate with praise for Obama. Eric Schmidt, who served as the company's CEO from 2001 to 2011, presented a harsh assessment of Obama's presidency in his 2013 coauthored book *The New Digital Age*.[61] The references to Obama were about potential interference, punishment, and surveillance directed by the White House. The former president was associated with cyberwarfare against Iran and other nations, the prosecution of WikiLeaks informants, and the expansion of secret drone programs using unmanned vehicles for lethal force. Rather than a mutually beneficial partnership between Silicon Valley and the White House, Schmidt depicted an asymmetrical power relationship between a mighty government and its vulnerable digital citizens.

In contrast, Google as a corporate entity celebrated the Obama White House. On the company's marketing resources page directed at potential corporate clients, it featured Obama's campaign as a case study demonstrating the economic value of its customer base. Notably, the company chose the 2012 campaign as the focus of analysis rather than the 2008 campaign that had used more grassroots DIY techniques. It credited Obama's digital strategists with knowing the basics of "right message, right audience" and "building an engagement hub" while pitching particular Google products used successfully by the Obama team, such as "TrueView ads" and "YouTube homepage mastheads."[62] They even included an endorsement from Nate Lubin, former director of digital marketing for Obama for America.

The Googlization of Government

The close connections between Google and the Obama White House were philosophical as well as pragmatic. When writing about the "special bond" between the two entities, conservative scholar Adam J. White draws attention to their similarities of worldview.

> Both view society's challenges today as social-engineering problems, whose resolutions depend mainly on facts and objective reasoning. Both view information as being at once ruthlessly value-free and yet, when properly grasped, a powerful force for ideological and social reform. And so both aspire to reshape Americans' informational context, ensuring that we make choices based only upon what they consider the right kinds of facts—while denying that there would be any values or politics embedded in the effort.[63]

In making the messy world of political discourse and individual aspirations machine readable and rationalizable as code, White claims that both Google and Obama promote monopolization that limits competition from alternative perspectives.

Critics on the left also insisted that the coziness between Google and the Obama administration was unhealthy for the political process. Siva Vaidhyanathan called this phenomenon the "the Googlization of government."[64] As Vaidhyanathan observed, Obama frequently compared good experiences that citizens should have with their government to positive experiences that customers already had with their software companies. For example, in his "New Management Agenda" speech, Obama likened using government services to online shopping for cars and computers. Such analogies presented premises as conclusions. By comparing government to a business, democratic citizenship became equated with consumer satisfaction.[65]

The convenient personalization of search engines, social network platforms, and locative mobile technologies promoted by Google have a dark side: compromised privacy. Search queries feel relatively anonymous because they lack face-to-face interaction, and because user input seems to disappear each time a uniform search box is refreshed.

In addition to the built-in obfuscation of the page-ranking algorithm, other technologies in the Google supply chain are designed to optimize the conditions of what Shoshana Zuboff has dubbed "surveillance capitalism." This fundamentally "parasitic" form of capitalism "claims human experience as free raw material for hidden commercial practices" while undermining "market democracy" by deploying superior predictive powers and concentrating "wealth, knowledge, and power" through algorithms.[66]

For Zuboff, this "coup from above" began with Google's decision to monetize surplus behavioral data that had previously been used only to refine its search engine. This corporate strategy required an expansion of the company's surveillance efforts to include monitoring email, transportation wayfinding, and private exchanges within smart homes. Zuboff has also argued that there were historical factors that prevented regulators in the United States from acting quickly enough to head off this new kind of monopoly, particularly as Google appealed to the federal government's ideals about free expression.

Zuboff has laid much of the blame for Google's cultural, economic, and political dominance on the Obama administration. In the Bush-era, the company certainly exploited anxieties about terrorism, but it solidified its position during the Obama White House years. According to Zuboff, the company created a "fortress" around its interests by offering the Obama campaign sophisticated analytics about the electorate, placing Google executives on key committees, infiltrating the White House staff, lobbying extensively, and colonizing academia and advocacy organizations to minimize resistance. Campaign donations and powerful tech lobbying aimed at Democrats were also important influences.

The Cookie President

Today, typing the word "cookie" into the old Obama White House site brings up a number of results, mostly recipes: sugar cookies for Halloween, gingerbread for Christmas, and "Passover Chocolate Chip Mandel Broit." There are messages about healthy eating from former First Lady Michelle Obama, since "cookies" were a food for growing bodies to avoid. On the page about the White House privacy policy there is also a less prominent entry for cookies: "Cookies: A small piece of data sent from a website and stored in a user's web browser while the user is browsing that website."

Allegedly, the name either came from the "magic cookies" that were designed for the Unix operating system or from the story of Hansel and Gretel dropping crumbs to find their way out of the forest. In its definition of "cookie," the White House uses minimizing language. Not only are cookies "pieces" of data, but they are also "small" pieces.

Although it was one of the least covered technology stories of 2009, the Obama administration's changes to the White House cookie policy were significant. Before Obama came into office, using cookies to collect user data from web browsing was explicitly prohibited. A 2000 memorandum from Jacob J. Lew, the director of the Office for Management and Budget, which regulated federal bureaucracy, was clear that the country's "unique laws and traditions about government access to citizens' personal information" should bar the use of cookies on government websites. Cookies could only be used under very specific conditions if they served a critical national interest. Anti-cookie regulations included mandating "clear and conspicuous notice," proving "a compelling need to gather the data on the site," and providing "appropriate and publicly disclosed privacy safeguards for handling of information," in addition to "personal approval by the head of the agency."[67] A few weeks later the Chief Information Officers Council issued the so-called Cookies Letter, which concurred with Lew's "presumption against the tracking of personal information provided as a result of interacting with a federal web site."[68]

The Clinton White House had implemented the initial version of this anti-cookie policy after a specific scandal had alarmed civil libertarians. Privacy advocates had been outraged by the conduct of a government contractor, DoubleClick, that had installed cookies on the Office of Drug Control Policy website. The company had supposedly wanted to gauge which anti-drug advertisements generated the most click-throughs to anti-drug information on government websites. However, the company could also merge seemingly anonymous data gathered from the cookies with personal data stored in other databases. This led to an investigation of DoubleClick's monitoring software by the Federal Trade Commission. Drug policy experts who favored treatment over prosecution warned that such cookies might dissuade users from seeking information about the dangers of illegal substances. "People shouldn't have to worry when they're getting information from the government that the government is getting information from them," an administration official observed.[69]

Although George W. Bush's White House expanded its online information-gathering efforts after the September 11 attacks,[70] the anti-cookie policy remained in place. Jane Cook, the president's "web gal," recalled intense discussions about protecting user privacy.

In 2001 cookies were still new to the scene, just a few years old. We discussed using cookies on WhiteHouse.gov in 2001 because we wanted to know more about the users of WhiteHouse.gov so we could make the site better. However some people were suspicious of sites that used cookies, particularly government websites at the time. People feared that "big brother" was spying on them. The president and his administration should not spy on US citizens.[71]

The Bush web team ultimately decided to use the Lew memorandum and the Cookie Letter as guidance. The privacy status quo was largely maintained.

The Obama administration put changes in motion very quickly. One objection to the old anti-cookie policy was practical. Obama was the first social media president. His rise to political power coincided with the founding of many social media companies: Facebook and Flickr in 2004, YouTube in 2005, and Twitter in 2006. He had clearly benefited from those new social media platforms. As a candidate Obama had an active YouTube channel and Facebook presence and was an early adopter of Twitter. Content posted on these services or embedded from these services was subject to the practices of liberal information gathering that made these internet companies so successful. Creating special government social media companies without cookies would be expensive and likely less popular than their corporate counterparts.[72]

The cookie policy was also viewed as antiquated from a personalization standpoint. Political organizations that focused on traditional media and appealed primarily to mass television or radio audiences were very different from those emphasizing digital narrowcasting. After all, the Obama campaign had built its momentum through targeted advertising and individualized digital messaging. In former campaign staffer Rahaf Harfoush's memoir, a key chapter on analytics and online advertisements explained how driving and monitoring web traffic was key to campaign strategy. Obama's analytics team "studied everything from page views to email open rates."[73]

When the Obama administration began dismantling the anti-cookie policy, some privacy experts sounded alarms. But it was difficult to criticize a president who had been so supportive of internet freedom issues such as network neutrality, increased broadband access, and digital portals for e-government. Nonetheless, tech blogger Christopher Soghoian persisted in raising objections.

As a graduate student, Soghoian had achieved national fame for his strong pro-privacy sentiments. After September 11, when providing government-issued identification became a requirement for flying on airplanes, Soghoian created an electronic boarding pass generator that hypothetically could allow one to board a plane without matching documents. Although his intentions were framed as satire, Soghoian's apartment was ransacked by federal officers, and he and his university advisor were detained for questioning. Just as Soghoian had been a critic of privacy overreach during the Bush-era, he became a vocal faultfinder of the Obama technology staff, who he believed were compromising the anonymity of online browsing.

In a 2009 interview Soghoian explained his main concerns about YouTube's "cushy deal" with the White House: "I started to highlight some of the problems associated with the president's use of YouTube, the fact that these videos were being embedded directly into the White House website, and the fact that YouTube was given just so much data on persons." He objected to the "specific cut-out from strict federal privacy rules that exempted YouTube's collection of data from the White House website." While Soghoian acknowledged that the White House responded quite rapidly with "quick changes," he was ultimately unhappy with the outcome. According to Soghoian, "the language in the White House privacy policy that specifically excluded YouTube" was only "softened" to "include other companies," named as "third-party video-sharing sites." By "expanding it to other companies," perhaps the exemption was less of a "cushy deal" for YouTube, but it also could be seen as "making it worse."[74]

Soghoian submitted an official letter to Chief Information Officer Vivek Kundra asserting that privacy guidelines "should focus on the degree of personally identifiable information contained within cookies, rather than their intended usage."[75] Fans of optimization in the White House argued that cookies were essential for high-quality customer service. Without a granular understanding of web traffic patterns, they insisted, it would be difficult to help constituents find what they needed on government domains and to judge the performance of their web design. In his letter Soghoian lambasted such approaches as giving ground to "behavioral advertising," which he saw as both intrusive and ill-conceived. The opt-out procedures for those who wished to preserve the cookie-free browsing privileges that they had previously enjoyed were also onerous. Although he later worked within the administration, Soghoian wasn't about to go down quietly when it came to the cookie policy. By pointing out the hypocrisy of claiming transparency but secretly spying on citizens, critics hoped to embarrass the Obama administration into returning to Bush-era norms.

In an interievw, Macon Phillips was philosophical about Soghoian's whistleblowing. "I really appreciated the comments that he had, and they led me to speak with people at the Center for Democracy and Technology about this issue. And then ultimately, we engaged YouTube, and YouTube ended up creating a no-cookies version of their player so that we were able to embed YouTube content without the tracking mechanisms."[76] According to Phillips, in some ways Soghoian's desire to flag a potential conflict of interest actually strengthened the public-private technology partnership. Exposure of the cookies issue enhanced "the White House's ability to help push privacy issues," and it also improved the Google-owned company's offerings of products and features, which "were developed and published on YouTube."

There were certainly cultural reasons that the White House was willing to make concessions to privacy advocates and admit that third-party services like YouTube could be problematic. As a 2009 White House blog entry explained, both "federal employees" and "the public" raised questions.[77] Many of the technology experts who were brought on to assist the White House felt that their mission was transparency rather than personalization. For example, Kin Lane described personalization as a "double-edged sword" that was also a "gateway to surveillance."[78] Those who had come from Silicon Valley often said they had chosen government service to pursue goals for digital democracy that were impossible to develop on commercial platforms. Sadly, the administration's commitments to avoiding dependence on data-harvesting companies were often short-lived.

Nonetheless, the Obama White House continued to engage in debates about personalization and privacy and to urge technology companies to include "do not track" options. For example, in 2012 the White House announced that Twitter had agreed to implement a "one-click," "do-not-track" feature on their microblogging service, which it attributed to "collaboration amongst business, privacy advocates, technical experts, academics, standards organizations and government."[79] Phillips argued that these privacy versus access debates were ultimately healthy for technology initiatives in the White House; conflicts between government and technology firms served as a driver for innovation in the public sector where dedicated social media and search tools needed to be developed for non-commercial uses.

Looking back at the controversy, Tom Cochran agreed that there were "reasonable and logical questions of privacy" where the government was involved. But he expressed puzzlement that "people didn't have the same fears of Facebook and Google" at the time. Unlike Silicon Valley companies, the government required "many more safeguards and cautions" about data gathering and "rules and limitations in how to use information." Whereas people like Soghoian expressed concerns about the rapaciousness of social media companies, Cochran described a relatively innocent time when the government could still make a principled stand for users' rights.[80]

Yet even as the Obama White House implemented open standards and offered data in accessible formats like XML, JSON, and CSV, the administration was also applying other common tech-industry practices that were clearly at odds with its stated transparency goals. White House staffers wanted to reach constituents with user-friendly appeals and to offer video content that featured their young telegenic leader, which meant using "free" platforms that facilitated playing and sharing videos on social networks. They also wanted to gather data from these users to understand how to control as many branches of government as possible in a volatile political situation in which they felt threatened by a rise of Republican activism and the success of Tea Party candidates.

This tack in strategy was not illogical. Unlike giving data *to* people, which could have unintended negative consequences, gathering data *from* people could help maintain a winning position. After all, the metrics of personalization, customized experiences, and narrowly targeted appeals had helped Obama get elected.

Less examined were the ethics of Silicon Valley that were imported into the White House during this critical period. Writer and activist Jillian York has called this ethical system "silicon values,"[81] a philosophy rooted in a mix of libertarianism, social engineering, and willful ignorance. Obama celebrated these values in White House rhetoric, reinforcing a prevailing disregard for consumer protection and privacy. That said, his tech teams' choices were not necessarily malevolent. They were driven by the understandable preferences for convenience, integration, and success, qualities that Google exemplified.

Obama's call for transparency was perhaps his clearest and most ambitious mandate. The enthusiasm of his staffers and the availability of open-access formats made it possible to bring together previously disconnected pieces of information archived by the government. Hopes were also high that new data tools and policies would serve the public interest rather than private commerce. In practice, transparency proved to be a much more challenging proposition. It turned out that open data could be weaponized against the White House and prove a threat to its most vulnerable constituencies. The president's transparency ideals were also compromised by his close relationship with Google and the many ties to the company among his technical staffers. The administration's willingness to use cookies and other tools of surveillance capitalism also eroded its moral high ground. Such coziness with Silicon Valley raised serious questions about the administration's regulatory will. Looking back, it seemed inevitable that the White House would be unable to thwart Google's progression toward market dominance. As the next chapter will show, this pattern with Google was replicated with Facebook and other social media companies. However, these alliances were justified by a different pillar in the administration's digital strategy: the pillar of participation.

3 Obama's Rhetoric of Participation

Aaron Fisher was one of the college interns who worked with Obama's Office of Digital Strategy during the summer of 2012. He described himself as part of a cohort of "really young people" who were "all young, all idealistic."[1] An enormous influx of people like Fisher was needed in the digital unit, particularly as Obama geared up for his reelection campaign and needed to prove he had delivered on past promises. White House staffers had been attempting to realize an ambitious goal: facilitating more direct input from citizens and more personal responsiveness to their individual queries.

It was hoped that political participation in the United States could be completely reimagined using new technologies. Average people could finally have a greater role in governing the country, and direct political participation would finally be achieved. "Citizen participation will be a priority for the Administration," Obama's chief digital strategist Macon Phillips announced shortly after the 2009 inauguration, "and the internet will play an important role in that."[2]

To facilitate more direct citizen participation during the Obama administration, a remarkable amount of trust was placed in the youthful White House staffers who managed online petition systems and social media accounts. Fisher was actually more experienced than most, having already interned at Twitter the previous summer. In fact, he had been at Twitter during Obama's 2011 Twitter Town Hall, in a reliability engineering division where he was responsible for testing the platform's capacity to prevent itself from going down during the event, as it occasionally and very noticeably did during its early years of service.[3]

Young newcomers like Fisher were expected to educate their political elders about the digital etiquette for interacting with constituents. Fisher recalled with amusement teaching senior officials "how to tweet." Interns were allowed to follow their instincts as they handled the huge volume of internet traffic without too much interference. Fisher described how the digital strategy team experimented with a cumbersome content management system before reverting to simpler methods. Access to Facebook and Twitter logins was granted "after you have proven that you can be trusted," and supervision often took the form of what Fisher called a "hey, can you look at this?" approach, which avoided "waiting to go through a pipeline."

However, not everyone in the Obama government had free rein to interact with the public unimpeded on social media. Comments by some government officials were moderated by other government officials. For example, when global digital rights activist Rebecca MacKinnon complained about Chinese bloggers being placed under house arrest, she received a seemingly neutral and perfunctory reply from one of the State Department's social media accounts: "we're looking into it." Because of the sensitivity of US-China relations, even that minimal gesture was controversial. The "we're looking into it" message was soon deleted.[4] The staffer had clearly tweeted out of turn.

Existing bureaucratic structures—including legal restrictions—also prohibited some direct attempts to engage with citizens online. For example, the 1995 Paperwork Reduction Act, which required that US federal agencies obtain Office of Management and Budget approval before requesting or collecting most types of information from the public, prohibited the president in 2009 from posting a prompt on Twitter when he wanted to gather stories about health-care experiences from average citizens. After extensive legal consultation, the administration wrote a memo to the Office of Management and Budget complaining that the rule interfered with the administration's commitment to "transparency, public participation, and collaboration."[5] Fifteen months later, a response memo was issued entitled "Social Media, Web-Based Interactive Technologies, and the Paperwork Reduction Act," which permitted questions on social media as "general solicitations" that were exempted from the law.[6] Thus it was finally decided that "the president could end a tweet with a question mark."[7] But many other issues about direct democracy on digital platforms remained.

In the early months of the Obama administration, I interviewed Professor Christopher Kelty about the feasibility of the new White House's approach to political participation. Kelty studied the topic of participation broadly—from citizen science to citizen journalism—and had led a National Science Foundation-funded research project focused on the subject.[8]

In Kelty's opinion, social media was an imperfect vehicle for the kind of radical transformation in political participation that might be possible to achieve with technology. Kelty clarified that participation could be both "good and bad." When participation was "bound up with the new media and communication technologies that saturate our lives," it was necessary to acknowledge that the vast assemblage of "servers, clouds, mobile phones, tablets, cameras, passwords, and satellites" provided "personal freedom, expressiveness, and mobility," but it also inserted "insidious devices of surveillance and paranoia" into citizens' daily lives.[9]

Although online interaction between citizens and their political leaders was highly mediated by software and hardware, technology companies frequently invoked the language of direct democracy to emphasize the potential of personal devices to enable access to the powerful. New social media corporations highlighted the customer's power to vote, rank, review, or recommend. They also appealed to ideals of meritocracy, community, and selflessness supposedly demonstrated by their users online.

From Town Hall Candidate to Town Hall President

As with the Obama White House's transparency initiatives, the administration's citizen participation initiatives were part of a longer history. One of the first "electronic town halls" was proposed by Amitai Etzioni in 1972. He claimed that his Minerva system would be ready by 1985 to "allow masses of citizens to have discussions with each other" and "enable them to reach group decisions without leaving their homes." With the Minerva system, he promised to restore "the kind of participatory democracy available to the members of small communities such as the Greek polis, New England towns, and Israeli Kibbutzim."[10]

In the 1992 presidential election, independent candidate Ross Perot promoted his own version of an "electronic town hall." Since 1969, Perot had been interested in the idea of one-hour public conversations followed by computerized voting. Traditional gatekeepers were less enthusiastic. *Time* magazine dismissed the concept as "an illusion" embellished with "the other trappings of direct techno-democracy" that lacked a substantive plan for implementing the results of deliberative processes. "Mass electronic communication is really one-way communication, top-down," they insisted. According to the *Time* editors, "direct democracy is such a manipulatable sham that every two-bit Mussolini adopts it as his own." Furthermore, the "American experiment" flourished because it was as an "experiment in democratic indirectness" that preserved the value of "filtering institutions."[11]

By the 1990s, however, digital town halls had become increasingly common at the city scale. Experiments in direct digital democracy were especially likely to occur in urban areas near Silicon Valley in Northern California and near "Silicon Beach" in Southern California, where the digital effects and game industries were booming on the outskirts of Los Angeles.[12] For example, the small beachfront city of Santa Monica introduced PEN—the Public Electronic Network—in 1989.[13] PEN provided an alternative public space online that operated very differently from city council meetings and empowered small clusters of citizens, particularly activists and community organizers. As a site for articulating creative responses to issues like homelessness, affordable housing, traffic congestion, or green space, PEN could point to some successes. However, online harassment and abuse raised challenges that were unusual for a municipal government to handle.[14]

Town-hall-style presidential debates, which allow questions from average citizens, have been in use since the 1992 debate between George H.W. Bush and Bill Clinton.[15] Because town hall debates allow for unscripted interchanges, there have been occasional attempts to hijack them for self-promotion or publicity stunts. For example, in 2012, Pizza Hut offered a lifetime of free pizza in exchange for a "favorite toppings" question from an audience member.[16]

While many remained leery of the town hall concept, by the Obama era, technology companies saw an opportunity for publicity by including remote participants online. And Obama was a particularly enthusiastic debater when CNN collaborated with YouTube in 2007 to produce the first Democratic Party debate using video questions from users.

The CNN/YouTube debate was an important turning point for the Obama campaign, as the media-savvy candidate showed himself to be confident in addressing online audiences. Race and gender were highlighted as major concerns for the CNN/YouTube audience. Obama was asked to field a question about reparations for slavery, and then both Obama and Hillary Clinton were challenged to respond to the issue of identity politics.

"Whenever I read an editorial about one of you," a questioner noted, "the author never fails to mention the issue of race or gender, respectively. Either one is not authentically Black enough, or the other is not satisfactorily feminine."[17]

Obama scored some laughs by talking about his experiences as a Black man hailing taxi cabs in New York City. He also answered questions about expanding military service opportunities to women and about gay marriage.

The answer from Obama that drew the most attention called upon Americans to support direct talks with foreign leaders from countries such as Iran, Syria, Venezuela, Cuba, and North Korea. Without formal diplomatic relations, these nations had become pariah states. Obama drew upon the legacies of Ronald Reagan and John F. Kennedy to argue for maintaining communication with these governments and criticized current policies of "not talking to countries" as "punishment." These remarks may have been enhanced by the inclusion of videos from international YouTubers, such as those featuring questions from an aid group in a Darfur refugee camp and a member of the military forces serving in Okinawa, Japan.

Shortly after appearing in the debate, Obama remarked that he "thought YouTube did a terrific job" and praised the "American people" for "asking questions" and "paying attention to this race."[18]

Obama also lauded the internet-based format for being "funnier than most of the other debates."[19] Videos that invited laughs from the audience included one with an animated snowman about global warming and another from a lesbian Brooklyn comic. However, many other irreverent videos were screened out. For example, people in costume were frequently excluded by moderators, and a popular video joking about former movie star and current California governor Arnold Schwarzenegger was also pulled from contention.

In contrast, it seemed acceptable that many of the candidates' videos incorporated jokes. For example, the white-haired Christopher Dodd appeared with a white rabbit during his clip, and the telegenic and expensively coiffed John Edwards submitted a music video set to the song "Hair."

By using established YouTube formulas, many candidates were clearly reaching out to the youth vote. Even the relatively staid Hillary Clinton used an established YouTube genre, the words-on-cards style, which was popular in many YouTube videos at the time.

YouTube was barely two years old by the time of the debate, and candidates were scrambling to learn how to use it. With so many presidential contenders and so many new internet platforms, candidates rushed to engage with internet celebrities. For example, Georgetown University senior James Kotecki made satiric political videos starring pencil puppets. He had built a following on his channel by doling out advice to candidates. As a result, politicians in the 2008 race were willing to be interviewed in his college dorm room. Others recorded response videos that addressed Kotecki. The cable television ratings for the YouTube debates (there was also a Republican Party debate on the platform) were not particularly impressive, but viewers in the 18–34 demographic courted by advertisers proved to be much more likely to tune in.[20]

Experts in political communication had hoped that this new format would encourage more civic engagement, particularly by younger citizens. Youth had been turning away from broadcast networks and toward social media in droves. Content analysis of the 8,000 video questions submitted indicated that politically underrepresented or disengaged populations "were present in a significant number" with content that was "politically substantive."[21] However, another research team argued that the spectacle had only reinforced the superior position of journalists in "agenda control," since reporters were clearly able to formulate better questions than average citizens and to maintain their position of prominence as gatekeepers curating submissions.[22]

In 2016 YouTube partnered with NBC News for another Democratic Party debate. This time, the broadcast network moderators and pundits were even more noticeable. The YouTubers featured were also much more likely to have had already achieved celebrity status on the platform. According to the network, these internet celebrities were included by virtue of their position as "prominent voices on YouTube."[23] For example, among Black YouTube celebrities, Marques Brownlee, a YouTuber famous for videos related to technology, asked about warrantless access to people's digital files. Comedian and video blogger Franchesca Ramsey asked about unindicted cases of police violence. Brownlee and Ramsey had millions of subscribers and were far from the average citizens highlighted on the earlier incarnation of the

YouTube Democratic Party debate. They also implicitly invoked an ethos of identity politics.

White House Town Halls

After the 2009 inauguration, there were high hopes for YouTube town halls in the White House. Now that attention could be turned from electioneering to governance, the participatory power of direct democracy seemed important to harness. For the first White House YouTube town hall, 103,512 people submitted 76,031 questions and cast 4,713,083 votes on which issues to highlight. Although Obama had publicized a ranking system that allowed users to upvote material on "Open for Questions," he seemed to avoid answering the most popular questions. Instead, he focused on responding to viewers who presented a spectacle of respectability deemed more appropriate to his political messaging.

For example, when marijuana legalization proved to be one of the most popular questions generated by online polling, Obama laughed off the public's interest in the issue. About halfway through "Open for Questions," Obama chose to "interrupt" the proceedings to acknowledge that a question "ranked fairly high" about "whether legalizing marijuana would improve the economy and job creation." To this, he got a laugh with following punchline answer: "I don't know what this says about the online audience."[24]

The event was streamed live on the web to sixty-four thousand participants, and it was also broadcast on television. Although the event opened with a traditional introduction and presidential speech, attention soon shifted to the text and webcam content appearing on two large, flat-screen computer monitors. Strangely, Obama often sought to distance himself from new communication technologies. For example, in response to a question about outsourcing jobs, Obama referred to "all the gizmos that you guys are carrying . . . all the phones, the Blackberries, the this and the that, plugging in all kinds of stuff in your house."[25] Notably, his focus was on the devices that "you" average citizens carried rather than he carried as the chief executive and on "your house" rather than the White House.

Much like the radio town halls organized by the League for Political Education or those held in cities like Detroit or New York by urban reformers during the first half of the twentieth century, these internet town halls emphasized questions from ordinary citizens and orderly assemblies of seated audience members who clearly respected their roles as passive spectators.

In *Town Hall Meetings and the Death of Deliberation*, Jonathan Beecher Field differentiates this kind of town hall spectacle, which showcases the leader's public performance of empathetic listening, from actual democratic processes that make voting and collective decision-making the main outcome from the airing of citizens' concerns. Field notes a major difference between "a legislative body open to any legal voter within the jurisdiction"[26] and "a public gathering that mimics a deliberative democratic process but does not offer any direct power to the people assembled."[27]

Field also argues that the style of the town meeting had become dominant long before the digital age. From the time of Alexis de Tocqueville's nineteenth-century writings on *Democracy in America*, New England town meetings had been romanticized as an ideal form of direct democracy. For example, sentimental depictions of the town meeting were used in Norman Rockwell's *Freedom of Speech*, which depicted a heroic everyman standing up from the assembled crowd to illustrate one of Roosevelt's "Four Freedoms." According to Field, the aesthetic of the town hall meeting in today's culture has been extended beyond politics. In the post-Obama era, the format has also been appropriated by corporations and universities who use this neoliberal strategy of simulated inclusion and affective performance as a way to quash potential dissent or solidarity building.

Obama experimented with several different town hall formats on various platforms. He later incorporated synchronous video chatting using Google Hangouts to dramatize his real-time responsiveness to his constituents. At the Hangouts event he dispensed with the live White House audience and was instead shown in isolation interacting with remote users through his computer. Town halls on other social media platforms followed, including one on Facebook in April 2011 and ones on Twitter and LinkedIn a few months later. In 2012 he hosted an AMA ("Ask Me Anything") on Reddit.

By the 2012 presidential election, social media had become an established aspect of television coverage. By this time, however, citizens who used social media were depicted as commentators rather than participators in the political sphere, and they tended to replicate the media's focus on the horserace between candidates rather than highlight key policy issues.[28]

CitizenTube

Perhaps no story better illustrated the disappointments of digital direct democracy than the tale of CitizenTube, YouTube's political video blog. Launched in 2007 with a mission to "add fuel to the revolution that is YouTube politics," CitizenTube promised to serve as a two-way communication channel capable of influencing political powerbrokers. As the channel that solicited questions for the Democratic and Republican CNN/YouTube debates, it was well positioned to be influential.[29] Its opening pitch was full of questions to promote viewer engagement: "What issue matters most to you? What do you think about the politics of your neighborhood, your district, your state, your province, your country . . . your world? And what are you going to do about it?"[30] In promising that it could offer "a place where everyone, from users to candidates, has the same chance to be seen and heard," it predicted that the "best ideas" would inevitably "win." On February 10, 2010, Obama answered questions from CitizenTube that were neither "chosen by the White House" nor "seen by the president."[31]

Although CitizenTube pledged to be an outlet for all kinds of people concerned with all kinds of issues, from "EU membership" and "Native American sovereignty" to "Your noisy neighbor" and "Pothole on your street," the channel's most popular videos were conventional interviews with politicians in representative government, such as Barack Obama, Bill Clinton, John McCain, John Edwards, and Ron Paul.

The last video on CitizenTube was posted in 2013. Before the channel was deactivated, it had become clogged with spam. It was even taken down at one point for violating YouTube's own policies.[32]

Facebook's Rhetoric of Participation

While democratic institutions were experimenting with digital technologies, digital technology companies were also imitating democratic institutions. For example, in 2009 Facebook held an "election" to vote on its terms of use. The opportunity for users to vote was announced with great fanfare.

> Today we announced new opportunities for users to play a meaningful role in determining the policies governing our site. We released the first proposals subject to these procedures—The Facebook Principles, a set of values that will guide the development of the service, and Statement of Rights and Responsibilities

that governs Facebook's operations. Users will have the opportunity to review, comment and vote on these documents over the coming weeks and, if they are approved, other future policy changes.[33]

In a sanctimonious posting called "Governing the Facebook Service in an Open and Transparent Way," the company asserted the following claim: "Our main goal at Facebook is to help make the world more open and transparent. We believe that if we want to lead the world in this direction, then we must set an example by running our service in this way."[34]

Of course, Facebook's shareholders probably believed that the main goal of the company was to make money by using a huge database of user-generated content for purposes like online advertising and data harvesting. But Facebook was positioning itself in the *Zeitgeist* of participatory culture. Using buzzwords common to the Obama administration—like "transparent" and "open"—was an effective way to burnish the Facebook brand.

The Facebook election was described by the *Los Angeles Times* as "homework," and only 0.32 percent of users even bothered to weigh in.[35] This voter apathy was understandable; there were only two choices. Neither version of internet legalese laid any groundwork for serious commitment to consumer protection. Yet some blamed the voters, arguing that the poor turnout allowed Facebook to go from a "democracy" to a "dictatorship."[36]

In a 2009 interview, media scholar Henry Jenkins argued that the Facebook election was meaningful to the platform's users as a chance to "vote for the mechanisms of control of your own community," even if it was "a poor substitute for more open democratic processes." He asserted that the mechanism for input on Facebook's governance was neither worse nor better than America's current political system. According to Jenkins, it was a "realistic representation of how Washington works today" in that users only were presented "choices between the two options," much like the ballot produced by the two-party political system, which ignored how "citizens would like to project into the future of their government."

As a regular voter in political elections, it is difficult for me to accept the cynical idea that a Facebook election isn't any worse than a real election. For starters, the company's terms of use are inherently undemocratic; users must agree to the terms to even enter the platform. It is impossible to reject a license agreement in the spirit of civil disobedience and still enter Facebook's highly constrained spaces for discussion and debate.

Notably, Facebook CEO Mark Zuckerberg invited users to online town halls about "Proposed Facebook Principles and a Proposed Statement of Rights and Responsibilities." Again, it is worth considering how the town hall now serves as a spectacle in which actual policy making rarely takes place. Such town halls are merely ceremonial airings of public views to produce a pre-ordained conclusion.

Nonetheless, some Obama officials lauded Facebook as a model for democratic participation. For example, Beth Noveck, who led Obama's Open Government Initiative as deputy chief technology officer from 2009 to 2011, claimed that "ubiquitous social networking technologies like Facebook and MySpace, in which participants 'friend' and 'poke' those in their personal networks, can teach us more about the idiom of participation than the legalistic practices in which so few of us actually participate."[37] Noveck asserted that government only gave citizens participation "in theory," whereas Facebook and other social media companies offered it "in practice."

We the People

On September 22, 2011, the White House launched We the People, a section of the WhiteHouse.gov website devoted to online petitions. All one needed to start or sign a petition was a White House account. Enrolling in the service required citizens to supply a first and last name, a zip code, and an email address to verify authenticity. Later versions included a math problem to screen out bots. Petitions that surpassed a certain threshold of signatures were to be reviewed by administration officials. Officials were then obligated to issue official responses.

From the beginning, one of the biggest challenges for We the People was its own success. As participation levels grew, managing the flood of petitions required gatekeeping. First the threshold was raised to 25,000 signatures in thirty days, and then it was raised to 100,000.[38] As with the YouTube town hall, one issue rose to popularity quickly: the legalization of marijuana almost immediately dominated the site.[39]

Composing responses to some popular petitions was difficult when they were made popular out of humor, thereby subverting the process. For example, the demand that the White House "acknowledge an extraterrestrial presence engaging the human race" required a lengthy answer that affirmed scientific findings and contradicted conspiratorial thinking, even though many had only signed as a joke. Frustrated users of the site created petitions about the misleading use of the word "petition," arguing that their direct appeals were not having much impact.[40]

We the People was one of the signature digital direct democracy projects of the Obama administration. It also drew upon a long history of political philosophy. Because petitioning predates even English common law, some legal experts have characterized the right to petition as foundational to the US political system. One scholar described petitioning as "the likely source of other expressive rights," such as "speech, press, and assembly."[41] By being able to bring a petition directly to a sovereign leader, political subjects can bypass the barriers of representative government.

For the Obama administration, We the People was intended to deliver on its direct democracy promise. However, official responses were largely symbolic. Even a leading example of the program's success—supporting the rights of citizens to unlock their cell phones for use with other carriers—may have been a policy position already in the works.

Because of their obscure location and bland appearance, digital petitions were much easier to ignore than traditional analog petitions. In televised spectacles, paper petitions could show tangible evidence of widespread public support. One of the most successful twentieth-century petition campaigns in the United States was launched by Candy Lightner, the founder of Mothers Against Drunk Driving (MADD), whose thirteen-year-old daughter was killed in a hit-and-run accident in 1980. To build its awareness campaign, MADD organized large-scale public protests and developed local chapters to agitate for more stringent regulations and for victims' rights. In addition to their petition drives, MADD orchestrated ambitious direct mail campaigns.[42] Their operatives could deluge legislators with material from paper petitions and postcard campaigns. The delivery of their documents to the steps of the seats of power created dramatic media events.

Despite the absence of such public flourishes of political theater, staffers inside the White House paid close attention to We the People petitions. Digital administrators who monitored the petitions' progress even came to see We the People as a potential platform for engaging productively with otherwise unruly online opponents. Petitions that spread misinformation or undermined trust in the government could be responded to directly, which was usually impossible when right-wing social media rumors were spread on blogs or forums that had mechanisms for filtering out pro-Obama arguments. As such, We the People was as much a site for listening as it was for speaking.

Director of digital strategy Macon Phillips reasoned that "if people care about an issue, it's incumbent on their leader to know about that and to pay attention to it."[43] He also explained that in a "world of so much noise" it could be essential "to have a direct line to your critics." As Phillips put it, "I think people tend to forget that social media may allow you to yell and tweet, blast out your stuff. It also gives you an opportunity to pay attention to other people and learn things."

As an example of this potential for unfiltered engagement, Phillips cited the fact that his team was able to use We the People email addresses to contact followers of conspiracy theorist Alex Jones who had organized a petition to deport the British talk show host Piers Morgan because Morgan had stirred their ire by advocating for gun control. After the Obama administration issued its formal statement on the Morgan petition, which defended both First and Second Amendment rights, signers were asked to complete a short survey. One of the questions asked if the petitioners had learned anything new in the process, and about a third of them said that they did, according to Phillips.

We the People offered the administration a tool to measure "the intensity and focus of different groups," Phillips said, and it gave the administration "a chance to address" online communities "with our own words." Theoretically this potential for dialogue presented alternatives to politically polarized publics and promoted respectful conversation. Phillips's colleague Tom Cochran argued that the platform "inspired a crowdsourced mentality that galvanized people around good ideas" and "streamlined the process for bringing attention to critical issues."[44]

Aaron Fisher looked back on We the People as an exercise intended to "reaffirm this mystical creature exists," a collective popular "we" capable of authoring founding legislation and articulating essential political principles. By this measure, even the young idealistic intern was disillusioned. During his short time at the White House he saw it transformed into the "work of trolls."[45]

At the end of Obama's second term, Cochran made a public plea to the incoming Trump administration for "maintaining digital momentum" to

continue to allow "people to influence legislation, collaboratively inno-
vate with government agencies and, most importantly, participate in their
government."[46] We the People was one of his central examples of a digital
direct democracy program that needed to be sustained.

One popular petition on We the People called for Trump's resignation;
others demanded the release of his tax returns or placement of his businesses' assets in a blind trust. Not a single such petition received the promised White House response from Trump officials. At the end of Trump's
first year in office, the administration announced that it would be termi-
nating We the People temporarily to achieve what they claimed would be
a million-dollar savings to taxpayers. It returned after a one-month hia-
tus,[47] but the government was still not responding to top petitions. By
the end of Trump's term in office, the top petition read almost exactly
like a Trump tweet: "★INDICT & ARREST Moon Jae-in for SMUGGLING
the ChinaVirus into the US & ENDANGERING the national security of US
& ROK!"[48]

Unlike CitizenTube, We the People offered actual lessons to be learned
about online political participation for future administrations. Although
White House staff who maintained the site day-to-day had to manage
insincere trolls and deluded conspiracy theorists, the energy and size of
the site's broader audience imbued their labor with an invigorating sense
of meaning.

Certainly, such crowdsourcing is problematic in many ways. It tends to
privilege people with digital literacy, technical resources, superior status
in the dominant culture, and access to means of amplification via social
media platforms. Nonetheless, crowdsourcing as a force for shaping economic, cultural, and political production is not going away anytime soon.[49]
The Obama administration's encounter with such a wide variety of crowdsourced efforts merits further attention, and an entire book could easily be
written about its case studies.

The Fact-Checking President

Not all of the Obama White House's attempts at direct digital democracy
were accepted as projects with good intentions. On August 4, 2009, Macon
Phillips posted "Facts Are Stubborn Things" on the White House blog to
solicit user input about fake news.

> There is a lot of disinformation about health insurance reform out there, span-
> ning from control of personal finances to end of life care. These rumors often
> travel just below the surface via chain emails or through casual conversation.
> Since we can't keep track of all of them here at the White House, we're asking for
> your help. If you get an email or see something on the web about health insur-
> ance reform that seems fishy, send it to flag@whitehouse.gov.[50]

Quickly this call to action was seen as an attempt to censor conservative
media sources. The mechanism for gathering data was perceived as an effort
to compile an "enemies list."

The very next day, Texas Republican Senator John Cornyn issued a letter
to the White House that objected to harvesting "the names, email addresses,
IP addresses, and private speech of U.S. citizens."[51] The theme of "turning
supporters into snitches" was amplified on Fox News.[52] Although the program was quickly discontinued and the email address deactivated, Cornyn
continued to call for the Obama administration to purge any data gathered
from its thirteen days of operation.[53] A federal lawsuit was filed by a conservative physicians' organization in Arizona and a Black pro-life group in
Washington, DC on the grounds that the White House had "unlawfully
collected information on political speech."[54]

Although the lawsuit was eventually dismissed, Phillips remembered the
controversy as a harrowing time. He never had to testify, but he did have to
consult with White House counsel, which reinforced the gravity of the situation. "It was also the only time my grand mom saw my name on television
because Fox News ran John Cornyn's letter to the president."[55]

The conservative media outrage ecosystem also spawned a plethora of
content on YouTube. As Phillips recalled, "videos went out with my name"
and there were "Nazi chants" that depicted him as a servant of totalitari-
anism. Phillips was surprised by these reactions because he considered the
project to be in keeping with other digital direct democracy efforts. Phillips
claimed he only had the "best intentions," and he insisted that "no lists of
critics were ever created or disseminated."

The Legacies of Online Participation

During Obama's years in office, citizens were exhorted to participate more
actively and directly in their government through a variety of digital venues, including the video town halls and online petition sites discussed

in this chapter. Yet fears that trolls and other bad actors might dominate online discussion often inhibited the possibilities for truly transformative change.

If anything, experts like Christopher Kelty thought that the Obama White House had not been nearly ambitious enough when it came to re-imagining political participation. Despite the hype and promises, it was dis-appointing that these initiatives were primarily used to legitimate existing plans for agenda setting rather than to encourage substantive deliberation and real policy making. As Kelty pointed out, it is now "more and more possible for people to conceive of voting remotely—not having to go to a polling place on a specific day and casting their vote at that moment, but rather voting more or less continually—and voting not just for a *candidate* who is a representative, but for any given *issue*."[56]

Kelty chuckled about Americans' antiquated attitudes toward political participation, despite all of the other ways that their society and culture had been radically transformed by technology during their lifetimes. Rather than explore the real possibilities for using computer networks for "direct democracy on a massive scale," Americans were resigned to the status quo. "Because the Greeks voted the same way that we did, it will always be that way."[57]

Political participation is most easily measured by counting votes or quan-tifying petition signatures. However, citizens also participate in their gov-ernments by joining campaigns and political parties, making themselves visible in protests, educating themselves about issues, consuming stories about politics, and pursuing civic mindedness as a daily practice. Baratunde Thurston has argued that citizens would likely be more engaged and ener-gized if they thought of "citizen" as a verb rather than as a noun. He has encouraged his podcast and TED Talk audiences to learn from various mod-els of "how to citizen" from a range of leaders and activists.[58] In digital cul-ture, civic participation may be signaled by making, sharing, or validating user-generated content on social media and mobile devices, which could potentially encompass a much broader range of political expression that is not defined by the two-party system.

Some media scholars have rightfully argued that it may be more impor-tant to examine the "participation gap" between the weak and the power-ful rather than the more obvious "digital divide" that was once seen as the main obstacle to a truly inclusive democratic culture.[59] Now that almost everyone in the United States owns a powerful smartphone that can be connected to a vast digital network through intuitive software, the cause of digital equality has seemingly been won.

Nonetheless, as the next chapter will argue, the questions of access that were emphasized in Bill Clinton's White House continued to be important for Obama's, especially as "access" became associated with "disintermediation." The digital team installed in the White House was strongly committed to removing middlemen wherever possible. Disintermediation seemed desirable as a way to reduce obstacles between constituents and the state and to increase efficiency among government agencies. It also required new approaches to inclusivity that welcomed citizens into their own government.

4 Obama's Rhetoric of Access

During his eight years in office, Barack Obama recorded almost four hundred weekly addresses in a standardized format in which he spoke directly to the American people. His face maintained a fixed gaze and serious expression when talking about mass shootings, natural disasters, and other tragedies. He was more animated when delivering holiday messages for Christmas, Diwali, and Nowruz. When discussing policy matters like energy or the economy, he often pointed his right index finger as he spoke.

The Obama administration was clearly drawing on nostalgic tropes of a government father figure, a role that was epitomized by Franklin Roosevelt's weekly radio addresses intended to calm national anxieties during the Great Depression and World War II. The convention of the "fireside chat" was so powerful that Obama was often seated next to a fireplace during his weekly addresses.

David Ryfe has argued that Roosevelt employed key techniques from the mass communication industries of the twentieth century: "the idiom of stardom the movies had established, the idiom of fellowship that commercial advertising had disseminated, and the idiom of domesticity the radio had naturalized."[1] According to Ryfe, Roosevelt's carefully crafted messages solidified a new relationship between the presidency and the public. Listeners were encouraged to be interested in motivation and character, open to advice about exercising their choices, and receptive to being addressed in their own households. Although Obama's videos harkened back to Roosevelt, he used the conventions of internet performance from his own time, which better suited twenty-first-century attitudes about celebrity, relatability, and accessibility.

Macon Phillips remembered the YouTube weekly address originating during a hectic time in the transition between Bush and Obama. He recalled that "the idea for putting them on YouTube may have come from a midnight email from a press person to me right after we won the election."[2] Using the YouTube platform made it "easy enough to publish," and the higher quality HD format made content available to news networks around the world.

In planning for shooting, it became apparent to Phillips that "time on the president's calendar" was "really valuable," particularly because "this was a weekly amount of time," a commitment of about thirty minutes that had to be carved out on Obama's schedule from other matters of state. Like any routine, a uniform template required less rehearsal and fewer retakes. Yet Phillips wanted to pursue any "opportunity to be more creative" with the content by "answering questions," "being more topical," or "having a live element." However, "the traditional press operation at the White House" felt strongly "as a communications operation" that it was important to stick with the typical format directed to the "sort of the people who expected the presidential address" and "were used to it being a certain way." According to Phillips, "we weren't targeting BuzzFeed readers with the weekly address. It was definitely more of like a rural radio type thing."[3]

Scrutinizing the output from about a hundred Obama White House weekly addresses that had been scraped from YouTube, I zoomed in and looked for patterns.[4] The Software Studies Lab used shot-detection software that generated a new frame every time there was an edit in a scene; more complicated production techniques showed up as longer strips with a greater variety of shots (figure 4.1). The most elaborate montages were shot in places far from Washington, DC, such as at the site of a Louisiana oil spill or on an automobile assembly line. Most weekly addresses, however, used much simpler camerawork and were generally composed of only four or five shots.

The weekly addresses followed a formula with relatively little variation. This is why the data from the weekly addresses was also attractive to computer scientists who were interested in studying body language and gestures. To the left of Obama's talking head there was usually an American flag, and to the right was often a flower arrangement. The backgrounds generally showcased the same stately rooms in the White House: the Library, the Roosevelt Room, the Map Room, the Blue Room, the Red Room, and the Diplomatic Reception Room. The most common tags labeling the speeches from Obama's first months in office were "Economy" and "Health Care." Unlike for other public appearances by the president, there

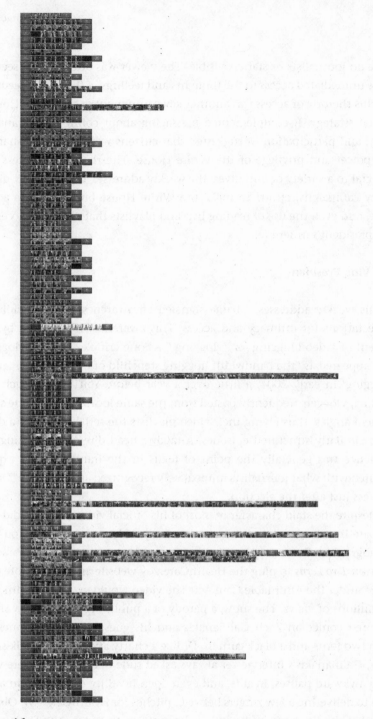

Figure 4.1
Output from weekly addresses generated by the Software Studies lab. Images courtesy of Lev Manovich.

were no journalists or staffers visible. The viewer was offered what seemed to be unmediated access to the thoughts and feelings of the chief executive.

This rhetoric of access was another key component of the White House's digital strategy. It complemented messaging about connection, transparency, and participation. It suggested that citizens were invited to share in the power and privilege of the White House. The rhetoric of access was integral to a variety of initiatives: the weekly addresses, digital public diplomacy campaigns, efforts to make the White House building more accessible, and even the use of reading lists and playlists that conveyed access to the president's inner life.

The Vlog President

In his weekly addresses, Obama signaled an awareness of new audience expectations for intimacy and access. This awareness was shaped by the advent of video blogging, or "vlogging." As one critic explained, vlogging had appeared as "the bandwidth hogging stepchild of podcasting or 'audio blogging' in early 2004, a little over a year before YouTube."[5] Much like Obama, vloggers frequently posted from the same locations using the same camera angles, thus giving their video playlists the serial format of a diary with similarly structured episodes. A talking head directly addressing the audience was generally the point of focus in the frame. Obama experimented with what journalists immediately recognized as "vlog style"[6] in an address just after the election.

Despite the staid character of most of his official videos, Obama did participate in some viral content creation to appeal to the younger YouTube demographic. For example, Obama appeared on the popular web series *Between Two Ferns* to plug the HealthCare.gov website and to promote coverage under the Affordable Care Act. The video would eventually earn tens of millions of views. The show, a parody of a public access interview show, featured comedian Zach Galifianakis and his guests on a bare-bones set with two ferns and a black curtain. Unlike a chatty and convivial talk show host, Galifianakis's interviewer always asked rude questions, so there were long awkward pauses, insults, and even open hostility on display. In addition to delivering a few zingers between pitches for HealthCare.gov, Obama revealed the final gag by dropping the curtains to expose the Diplomatic Reception Room. The conceit was that Galifianakis had been clandestinely recording *Between Two Ferns* in the White House, just as Obama had been regularly producing his weekly addresses there.

In addition to challenging White House protocol by pursuing such viral moments, the younger digital staffers also tried to introduce new elements of office culture that included remote work. However, analog-oriented rules dictated that work be performed on-site. Phillips watched the clash between "the policies and operation of the White House" and "the realities of 2009" firsthand. As Phillips observed, "when your entire technology operation is premised on the desktop model, it meant that in order to launch the weekly address, which we released at 6:30 Saturday mornings, I had to physically come into the White House on Saturday mornings to go to my desktop to press 'publish.'"

The Public Diplomacy President

It is significant that Obama delivered one of his most important speeches via YouTube. In an hour-long oration, speaking in the "timeless city of Cairo," he acknowledged hurtful legacies of colonialism and the Cold War, as well as the uncertainty brought by "modernity" and "globalism."[7] From the podium, Obama thanked the two Egyptian universities that hosted his talk, but the main audience that he was addressing was much larger—"the Muslim World"—and he was trying to reach it directly through the internet with an ambitious public diplomacy campaign. Using Web 2.0 technologies, the administration was determined to expand "people-to-people" interchanges that bypassed the formalities of professionally trained diplomats and other intermediaries.

News reports documented how Obama's remarks in Cairo were synchronized with a "flurry of messages" on the White House's Twitter feed, while the White House Facebook page "posted highlights while Obama was still speaking," and the State Department "sent free text messages about the speech."[8] Videos of the speech were made available with subtitles in Arabic, Turkish, Hebrew, and French. With YouTube, Obama had an opportunity to speak directly to citizens of countries that were potential geopolitical threats and to humanize his powerful position as a world leader.

At the time of the speech YouTube was already occupying a significant role in public discussions about civil society and human rights in Egypt. Blogger Wael Abbas achieved notoriety for publishing a 2006 video of

Cairo police officers beating, torturing, and sexually abusing a bus driver. Abbas also posted an interview with the driver that described his humiliating ordeal.[9]

Of course, providing a platform for debate about contentious issues like police brutality had not been a core concern for YouTube as a social media company. Controversial uses could complicate its business model. In 2007 YouTube removed Abbas's account on grounds of violating rules about "inappropriate material."[10] However, by the time of the Arab Spring, the bus driver video had become a cultural touchstone. Clips from the original video frequently appeared in musical remixes that spliced together footage from several sources and often combined visuals showing protests with images of abuse.[11]

As the United States began designing promotional videos for international consumption, the administration again found itself confounded by federal laws written for the analog era. International broadcasting services such as Voice of America had been authorized and funded by the 1948 Smith-Mundt Act. Because the legislation was passed at a time when concerns about state-sponsored propaganda had seemed justified, in the wake of having fought totalitarian governments, the act included a proviso that materials intended to persuade audiences abroad must not be disseminated in the United States. This was done to avoid any appearance of indoctrinating American citizens. Given that YouTube content can be accessed from any country where it is not blocked, videos intended for predominantly Muslim countries or other regions rife with anti-American sentiment were easily accessible in the United States. As a result of this anachronistic prohibition on domestic distribution, the State Department was not sure if it would be able to benefit from the "YouTube effect" that caused videos to rapidly gain attention all around the world, thus bypassing the censorship imposed by authoritarian regimes.[12] Moreover, because channels promoting American interests needed to use streaming services to reach the broadest audiences, the entire new media approach in public diplomacy was limited by the Smith-Mundt Act.[13]

Diplomats saw that YouTube videos could reshape foreign affairs and destabilize ideas about who counted as a legitimate representative. Consequently, US overtures needed to be directed toward building "sustained, meaningful connections" with "citizens, industries, and groups," according to public diplomacy expert Anne-Marie Slaughter.[14] She also cautioned that antagonists could be skillful creators of viral videos with explosive and 'violent content. In other words, online spaces that allowed citizen-to-citizen access could be sites for both negotiating peace and conducting war.[15]

Unquestionably, video platforms like YouTube that showcased popular content have played an important role in public diplomacy. To communicate directly with populations from autocratic nations or failed states, all-purpose social media channels centered on entertainment were much less likely to be blocked by repressive governments than were internet domains dedicated to investigative journalism or documenting human rights abuses. Ethan Zuckerman has called this the "cute cat" theory of digital activism,[16] because sites like YouTube can be used for non-political purposes—like sharing videos of cats—and political ones. When a "cute cat" platform is blocked in a country like Turkey, citizens who might otherwise care little about politics notice, and they are also less likely to accept the regime's justifications for censorship.

Given the Obama administration's focus on internet freedom, posting material to YouTube and other social media sites created dilemmas about content moderation. For example, journalists at *Wired* magazine noticed that officials "initially disabled the comment function on YouTube and prevented response videos from appearing alongside" Obama's weekly address videos.[17]

In the name of promoting civil liberties, the administration made a conscious effort to tolerate some dissent from international audiences for the sake of the pluralism it celebrated. For example, blogs on America.gov, which included *Obama Today*, allowed a curated selection of moderated comments in response to Obama's 2009 address to the "Muslim World," some of which were mildly critical of American policy. In contrast, the section of the Facebook page for the White House that was dedicated to the Cairo speech received a deluge of thousands of comments. When real-time reactions began streaming in quickly, it was difficult for digital staffers to respond appropriately. Yet blocking or ignoring critical comments from outsiders was counterproductive because these actions thwarted access, reinforced "fortress America" stereotypes, and scuttled hopes of projecting hospitality and generosity.

The Street View White House

The rhetoric of access also extended to the home front. In 2012 the administration released a video about how Google Street View would now include the interiors of the White House.[18] As inspiring music plays, Google employees roll a modified version of their Street View apparatus, adapted for indoor use, through the narrow hallways of the historic building. The compound eye atop the machine captures a 360-degree view of famous rooms as it is trundled from location to location. However, the trolley is too high for some doorways and has to be gently leaned back by workers to fit through.

In the video, Diana Skaar of Google Art Project promotes the access being offered to regular citizens. She enthuses about how people will be able to experience the wonders of this important place in American history and memory without the expense and hassle of traveling to Washington for a public tour. Google team member Chris Fiock praises the "incredible sites" and "incredible artwork" of the White House and shares his favorite viewpoint: a window in the Blue Room that looks out on the Washington Monument. He also explains that it is his first trip to Washington. By impli-cation, Google Street View will make it possible for others to take their own first journeys to the nation's capital.

Cultural theorist Lauren Berlant describes the pilgrimage to Washington as a critical ritual that can either solidify "infantile citizenship" or trans-form early emotional attachments to a parental state into a more mature form of political subjectivity.

> Usually made in tandem with families or classes of students, the trip to the capital makes pedagogy a patriotic performance, one in which the tourist "playing at being American" is called on to coordinate the multiple domains of time, space, sensation, exchange, knowledge, and power that represent the scene of what we might call "total" citizenship.[19]

Berlant is skeptical about how much is actually learned from these travel experiences, since the transition from innocence to experience is often structured by ideological clichés. For example, a classic film like *Mr. Smith Goes to Washington* is scripted around a conventional narrative of "an ambivalent encounter between America as a theoretical ideality and Amer-ica as a site of practical politics."

Berlant also tells the story of the Black writer Audre Lorde's childhood visit to Washington and the episodes of humiliation and trauma that she experienced there. Unlike Fiock, who is white, Lourde encountered a seg-regated city that excluded her from celebrations of citizenship. For Ber-lant these pilgrimages are important because they are highly mediated and not directly experienced. Even when citizens are physically present in the corridors of power and can witness the capital firsthand, their psyches are flooded with images and sounds from previous representations of the city.

In contrast, Google's version of Washington, DC promises unmediated access. There seem to be no secret service agents or tour guides to constrain the user's movements through the empty White House. It is possible to get close to precious artworks and furnishings that have become sacred to a common cultural heritage and to feel the opulence and intimacy of the place. There is no requirement to follow a particular trajectory through the floor plan. Unlike a real tour, there are no closing or opening hours. One can linger within the White House architecture as long as one wishes.

Unfortunately, a virtual presence in DC forecloses any possibilities for real political action. Protest is impossible, and consequently the civic imagination becomes impoverished rather than enriched by this technology. Visitors are invisible to everyone except Google. They can't disrupt a session of Congress, lie down on the steps of the Supreme Court, or unfurl a banner in front of the White House as cameras roll.[20] Because other people are erased from the building, the potential for coordinating with fellow demonstrators is also nullified.[21] A visitor to the White House via Street View can only act as the politest of guests, unseen and unheard in its sterile interiors.

Upon a closer look at the Street View experience, one can see unsmiling guards posted at the front entrance. Guards block inaccessible rooms throughout the interior as well. Even in the visible space, there are many invisible barriers. For example, by clicking the zoom feature, the user can look out the window at the Washington monument, but the chair in front of the window limits how close to the pane of glass a virtual visitor can come. Street View also offers only a kind of clunky vehicular mobility through the space. It's difficult to get very close to fireplaces or pianos, and going up the stairs step-by-step is impossible, although one can be abruptly transported to the upper floor.

Although Google Street View seems to promise a liberatory experience of exploration, it was designed—like all Google products—to promote other Google applications and services, gather user data that can be monetized, and refine the system's navigation and design features as cheaply as possible. When customers use Google's interfaces they are also being classified by its systems. For example, based on a user's prior search history, Google uses algorithmic profiling to somewhat arbitrarily assign an age and a gender to the user.[22]

In other words, as spatial domains become increasingly likely to be augmented by personalized ubiquitous computing, and our day-to-day decision-making becomes more intimately connected to our "smart" mobile devices, we should be wary of services that seem to promote ideologies of unfettered search and exploration. Corporate entities like Google are overtaking venues traditionally available for shared discussion and debate. Places like Washington, DC have at times surged with the raucous crowds of social movements. In Street View, these places are reduced to interfaces for navigating between recognizable landmarks.

The French philosopher Antoinette Rouvroy has warned that we are living in an age of "algorithmic governmentality" which facilitates "a colonization of public space by a hypertrophied private sphere."[23] According to Rouvroy, algorithmic technologies function as security apparatuses that insulate users from any human experience of "the common." For her "the common" is premised on difference rather than similarity because it is a "place of co-appearance where beings are addressed and talk about themselves to one another, with all their dissymmetries and 'disparateness'."[24] A ubiquitous computing society that records each user as an individual can extend that person's private preferences into the environment she or he experiences, providing a digital shield from potential conflict and disagreement.

The 360-Degree President

Toward the very end of Obama's presidency, media company Felix & Paul Studios created another 360-degree tour of the White House. "The People's House" was designed for a new, smoother VR (virtual reality) format optimized for YouTube, which could be viewed either through a head-mounted display (such as an Oculus RIFT or a Samsung Gear VR) or on a smartphone. The project won the 2017 Creative Arts Emmy for an Outstanding Original Interactive Program and has received over a quarter of a million YouTube views. In the video, the user follows a fixed course through the building, which is limited to twenty-two minutes of tour time.

On this virtual visit, the user has company—the president and First Lady serve as guides.[25] When the Diplomatic Reception Room is featured near the end of the tour, Barack Obama explains that George Washington believed such oval rooms could serve "as a symbol of democracy" because "the president could stand in the center to greet everyone at a similar distance, and nobody gets stuck in a corner."[26] Obama goes on to explain that Franklin Delano Roosevelt "recorded his famous fireside chats" in the room when it was adapted to serve as a production studio. A clip of Roosevelt's voice talking about how he "used the radio" then plays.

According to Obama, all modern presidents since then have used media technologies to "communicate directly with the American people" in a history of address that includes "radio, television and now the web and social media."[27] In Obama's telling, "what you are participating in right now" in the VR experience is "another step in the story of our progress" that is intended "to meet citizens where they are." This narrative of successive waves of disintermediation and personalization actually shifts much more rapidly. Because the Obama administration used YouTube as a platform, it had to constantly adjust its tactics to adapt to changing user agreements, algorithmic logics, and genres of content creation.

The Playlist President

As Obama prepared for leaving office, he geared up for a new role imbued with a different kind of celebrity. He was preparing to occupy a unique position of stewardship for his own cultural legacy. Some might say that he began his transition even earlier by capitalizing on the vogue for posting favorite books and media.

Obama released his first summer reading list in 2009. Unlike other launches, the announcement was not an artfully staged media event. Instead, the deputy press secretary read off the president's list of titles to be read on vacation during a press briefing.[28] The list could have been interpreted as another one of Obama's pedagogical projects because it promoted a distinctive type of civic education and literacy. The five initial titles were *The Way Home* by George Pelecanos, *Hot, Flat, and Crowded* by Tom Friedman, *Lush Life* by Richard Price, *Plainsong* by Kent Haruf, and *John Adams* by David McCullough.

Although his selections were highly didactic, Obama's summer reading lists resembled book recommendations shared among friends. He skipped his reading lists in the busy summers of 2012 and 2013 but offered recommendations in subsequent years. As the paradigm of his legacy moved from political leader to cultural influencer, the lists were released officially on WhiteHouse.gov. He continued the practice after leaving office using other platforms; he released his 2019 list, which led off with the collected works of the recently deceased Nobel Prize winner Toni Morrison, on Instagram.

Obama's choices sometimes seemed to express reservations about the very practices of digital culture that had likely brought him into office. For example, on the summer reading lists were Nicholas Carr's *The Shallows*, which warns about stunted brain activity supposedly caused by online surfing, and Naomi Alderman's *The Power*, which tells the story of young girls learning from internet videos how to electrocute people using the energy in their bodies.

Significantly, almost all of his lists were recommendations for "summer" reading and thus suggested the books were sideline pursuits rather than fodder for sustained intellectual activity. In this way Obama's reading lists represent what rhetorician Thomas Rickert has called "ambient rhetoric"; the books are media relegated to the background, setting the mood for summer vacation rather than articulating any particular message.[29]

In 2015, while still in office, Obama expanded his summer recommendations to music and released two playlists on the new White House Spotify account. One playlist was for day and one was for night.[30] In 2016, a political reporter for the *New York Times* noticed a pattern. Although the president's musical taste was "open-minded, even eclectic," including tunes from genres like "surf rock, soul, blues and hip-hop," his selection lacked "even a nod to country music, widely played in Southern states where Mr. Obama could benefit from more people relating to him."[31] Obama remedied this oversight in 2019 by including Lil Nas X's "Old Town Road" featuring country star Billy Ray Cyrus, although the song—created by a Black queer artist—was initially excluded from the country charts. Perhaps Obama's enthusiasm for curating ambient audible media was shaped by his prior experiences with audiobooks—he read the entire text of his bestselling memoirs *Dreams from My Father* and *The Audacity of Hope* himself.

In contrast to human-curated playlists, many social media platforms have recommendation engines that queue up media on autoplay. This design feature encourages users to engage with the platform for hours in one sitting. By the time Obama left office, more social media users were encountering algorithmically recommended content rather than content recommended by human linking, embedding, or commenting. To sustain engagement, these recommendation engines also tended to offer up content that was more emotionally and ideologically charged.[32]

We can follow the arc of the internet in the twenty-first century from optimism to pessimism—along with the up-and-down trajectory of American popular political culture in general—by examining gradual changes in social media practices and platform governance. In doing so, we can trace how platforms built to be democratizing with utopian possibilities became largely the property of a few corporate conglomerates. It is easy to assume that we can chart the transition from the communalism of Obama to the neoliberalism of Trump and find the critical moment when Silicon Valley companies finally dropped the pretenses of participatory culture and openness and the public became resigned to their opaque and extractive policies. But it is also possible that surveillance capitalism and political polarization was there all along, and that the conditions for their development were already in place, although they were disguised by rhetorics of connection, transparency, participation, and access.

5 Representing Representation

When conservative pundits saw an image of Barack Obama posing for a "selfie" with two other heads of state at the funeral of former South African president Nelson Mandela (figure 5.1), they pounced. The selfie taking seemed to provide irrefutable evidence of the telegenic president's tendencies toward disrespectful self-aggrandizement. Right-wing commentators clucked over the signs of flawed character and criticized Obama for succumbing to the narcissistic distractions of the personal screen. Not surprisingly Donald Trump retweeted a message of disapproval about his nemesis: "@Lisa_Smith70 'A real president wouldn't take a selfie during ANY memorial service. #NelsonMandelaMemorial.'"

Some of the criticism about the Obama funeral selfie echoed earlier comments about his supposed lack of decorum in promoting technology use. For example, Obama gave an iPod to Queen Elizabeth II during her state visit to the White House in 2009 to the consternation of political traditionalists.[1] The right-wing blog *Gateway Pundit* ran several stories about Obama's gadget gift. Because the iPod included audio files of Obama's inauguration and some of his speeches, the *Gateway Pundit* dubbed him a "royal narcissist."[2] After the selfie scandal, the site saw the opportunity to reapply one of its favorite denigrating nicknames for Obama: "narcissist-in-chief."[3]

Obama was often cast by conservative critics as pandering to the digital generation's exhibitionism, self-affirmation, and self-love. They accused him of attempting to seem youthful in ways that only made him appear immature. Of course, presidents have often been criticized for overvaluing self-image, but Fox News went so far as to declare Obama's selfie to be an "international incident."[4]

Researchers Nancy Baym and Kate Miltner analyzed news coverage of the "Selfiegate" incident to see how the story was framed. They looked

Figure 5.1
President Barack Obama and British Prime Minister David Cameron pose for a picture with Denmark's Prime Minister Helle Thorning-Schmidt next to US First Lady
Michelle Obama during the memorial service of South African former president Nelson Mandela at the FNB Stadium in Johannesburg on December 10, 2013. Image
credit: Roberto Schmidt/AFP/Getty Images.

at reporting in the three countries represented by the three leaders who
appeared in the image: Denmark, Great Britain, and the United States.
They claimed that the image was influential because it was "not actually
a selfie, but a depiction of the act of taking a selfie" and thus "polysemic
in ways that evoke multiple, simultaneous cultural shifts and anxieties."[5]
They argued that the picture "captures the increased popularity of selfie
taking, raising questions about who takes selfies and under what circum-
stances," as well as "the infusion of technological gadgets into events
where they were previously absent." The image also speaks to "shifts in the
social fabric that led to a man of color being president and a woman being
prime minister."

In this way the Mandela funeral selfie is an image representing representation. It operates through depictions of traditional politics (because

heads of state both signify the body politic as sovereigns and craft their own media images), identity politics (because women and people of color are often excluded as marginalized groups and yet serve as signifiers of political transformation), and technology (because a media device documents a particular scene and is also present as an actor in the frame).

Nicholas Mirzoeff, a critic of visual culture, also considered Obama's selfie to be worthy of interpretation because it encapsulated how an image could serve as "the interface between the way we think we look and the way others see us."[6] Thus the photo was both an image of seeing and an image of being seen. For him this kind of selfie conflated "machine image" and "digital performance."[7] Critics of visual culture like Mirzoeff assert that powerful images often give implicit instructions to viewers about what and how to see.[8] According to this school of thought, pictures are not passive objects to be interpreted by a neutral observer—they are the active agents of indoctrination by visual culture. Thus, an image might provide a guide for its own decoding.

For example, the famous "3D glasses" image of Obama (figure 5.2) vividly places visual culture on display. The photograph shows each person in the audience looking through their own individual lenses while sharing a moment of communal spectatorship.[9] Unlike most Obama photos, none of the gazes connect people together in the frame. And yet there is a certain egalitarianism in the assembly. Obama is the focus, but he is part of a collective experience in which media entertain and inform a group. The caption notifies the viewer that they are giving their rapt attention to an innovative Superbowl commercial with 3-D visual effects.

In the photo the crowd is both active and passive in their shared practices of looking. Obama clearly takes the lead in the front row, showing the others how to behave. He holds his 3D glasses against his head and braces his elbows against the chair in a pose of anticipation. At the same time, he is the receiver of a message coming from the unseen screen. The photographer is also performing an homage to other iconic photographs of spectators in 3D movie theaters, including Weegee's 1945 "In the Palace Theatre," which is currently in the Metropolitan Museum of Art's collection,[10] and J.R. Eyerman's classic photos shot for *Life* magazine in 1952.[11]

The philosopher of science Bruno Latour has asserted that political representation and visual representation are closely related. In other words, subjects in a system of government learn their assigned roles in the civic

Figure 5.2
President Barack Obama and First Lady Michelle Obama wear 3D glasses while watching a TV commercial during Super Bowl 43, Arizona Cardinals vs. Pittsburgh Steelers, in the family theater of the White House on February 1, 2009. Guests included family, friends, Cabinet members, staff members and bipartisan members of Congress. Official White House Photo by Pete Souza.

order and the rules for expected participation by observing how media perform their representative functions and organize the components of a shared reality. In bringing together the "two different meanings of the word *representation* that have been kept separate in theory," Latour hopes to correct a "bias in much of political philosophy" that ignores the fundamental connection between representative government and artistic and scientific representations.[12]

The Obama selfie-taking image is a particular kind of representation of popular sovereignty and the body politic. Three heads of state from three different forms of representative democracy are engaged in a lighthearted exchange during the somber ceremony of a state funeral. We see these government leaders in a moment of self-representation and media-making together. Depending on one's attitude, this incident might seem to either undermine the trio's executive authority as rulers or humanize them as digital citizens sharing common practices with their constituents.

Obama's team tried to get ahead of the negative publicity about the funeral selfie by giving the story a positive spin about relatability. Obama even recorded a video that lampooned his selfie reputation to promote resources at HealthCare.gov. The video, "Things Everybody Does But Doesn't Talk About," included shots of Obama waving a selfie stick around in the White House library, wearing sunglasses in front of a mirror, and doodling in a sketchpad.[13] Obama also shot a three-person group selfie that featured science educators Bill Nye and Neil deGrasse Tyson.[14] Obama appeared in a selfie with the US women's soccer team. By doing so he implicitly showed support for Title IX, the anti-discrimination statute in higher education that created an important pipeline for female athletes as well.[15] In his final trip abroad as president, images of a town hall at a Peruvian university were filled with clusters of enthusiastic South Americans jockeying to take a selfie with the president.[16] Others in the White House were recruited to promote fitness with the #HealthySelfie hashtag. In these selfies, the diversity of the cabinet was also on display.[17] Each one of these selfies was designed to address at least one aspect of the administration's agenda: national health care, climate science, appreciation of gender equality and racial diversity, and post-Cold War diplomacy.

The Propaganda President

Not everyone who approved of the Johannesburg selfie approved of the president's image management. Santiago Lyon of the Associated Press claimed that "the moment captured the democratization of image making that is a hallmark of our gadget-filled, technologically rich era"[18] However, Lyon praised the selfie in his editorial critiquing Obama's "draconian" restrictions on photographers covering the president. For example, photojournalists were barred when Obama met with the oldest living veteran on the Veterans Day holiday. Lyon complained about the "manifestly undemocratic" policies of the administration's image control, which were enforced in "hypocritical defiance of the principles of openness and transparency" that Obama campaigned upon. These limitations extended to the regular White House press corps and included what had once been standard public relations photo ops. Lyon objected to how the official "visual news releases" from the White House showed "well composed, compelling and even intimate glimpses of presidential life" that were heavily stage managed. By using the term "visual news releases," Lyon was making an unflattering comparison to "video news releases." A video news release, or VNR, is a segment made to look like a news report that is actually created for public relations or advertising purposes. According to Lyon, most White House images were little more than propaganda, even if they seemed to offer an unmediated insider's point of view.

Journalist Margaret Sullivan also warned against this subtle form of censorship. Although the wealth of free content presented a rich and appealing visual narrative of the nation's leader, there were reasons to be suspicious of the White House's largesse. During Pete Souza's tenure as Obama's official photographer, his images showed a multitude of poses and expressions as Obama interacted with many different types of people. But this range might conceal the actual homogeneity of the digital archive and the absence of oppositional perspectives. According to Sullivan, pictures of Obama with a "sour expression" that might invite satiric circulation would no longer be available.[19] Perhaps such image control limited the raw material for racist, sexist, or ageist memes, like the many frowning-Obama-with-beer memes that are still on the internet today. However, restricting journalists to the internal pre-approved, copyright-free photostream of canned images, which were housed first on Flickr and then on Instagram, threatened the livelihoods of photojournalists and the news agencies themselves. After all, news bureaus and image libraries needed to market original content by offering unique moments of spontaneity, demonstrations of emotion, or framings of attention. In response to these restrictions, some news organizations refused to run any images from the official Obama White House image database, even when they seemed essential for illustrating a given story.

Technology in the Frame

State-sanctioned images do much more than merely show the embodiment of power; they also communicate messages in a visual language about how the symbolic order of political sovereignty functions. Such images often show a leader's bodily relationship to a complex assemblage of objects, including devices that sense, record, store, transmit, network, calculate, aggregate, select, and display information. Historically, official portrait paintings have showcased rulers' mastery of other kinds of information technologies, such as maps, charts, books, navigation tools, paintings,

mathematical instruments, timepieces, and cabinets of curiosities. Therefore, it was not surprising to see that the tools of computational media were
often featured in the Obama iconography of digital culture.

The highly curated and constrained photo collection in the official
White House archive also promoted a vision of a shared American technological imagination. From tablet touch-screen computing to 3D motion
capture, the president modeled when and how to be a cyborg in contemporary culture. In the visual record vetted by the White House, Obama
appeared as a fluent technology user—even when he was a novice willing to
try out new platforms and interfaces. He was also shown as someone who
resisted the incursions of technology to maintain independence from its
manipulation and distraction.

Images of human–computer interaction like those on the official White
House website gave the viewer lessons about how to be an ideal user of
new media technologies and how the central political, cultural, and social
space in the country should be occupied, physically and virtually, in the
era of ubiquitous computing. One famous pre-White House photograph of
Obama shows the president-elect pointing directly at the camera as he sits
behind a Pac-Man-stickered Mac laptop surrounded by a number of handheld devices and peripherals.[20] It is an image of the incoming chief executive
as a multitasker. After all, Obama was the first social media president, the
first to regularly carry a mobile wireless device on his person, and the first to
emphasize the integration of computation in a campaign. If the visual rhetoric of candidate Obama accentuated his mastery of multiple screens and
wireless devices, the iconography around communication technology from
his first hundred days in office demonstrated much more separation from
the most commonly used interfaces and platforms in contemporary life.

Ironically, the main message from White House social media seemed to
be that the first digital president should be a detached subject of computer-
mediated messages and no longer an intimately connected producer or
receiver of them. Although his smartphone often appeared in media coverage of the campaign trail, the White House official Flickr photostream rarely
showed President Obama on his famous BlackBerry during his first years
in office. When images did capture him using mobile technology, it was
generally outside of the Oval Office and far from the official spaces of state-
craft. The photostream (figure 5.3) emphasized a visual rhetoric of Obama
checking BlackBerry messages offstage,[21] outdoors,[22] behind his shoes,[23] on

Figure 5.3
Montage of images of Barack Obama with his BlackBerry shot by Pete Souza. Collage
by Mel Horan.

the other side of a barrier,[24] or in the dead of night.[25]A rare shot of him in
public might show him gesturing with the device as an inanimate object[26]
or showing it to others as a curiosity,[27] but digital technologies intended
for everyday use were often relegated to a minor role. Like the cigarettes he
famously hid to conceal his smoking habit, ubiquitous computing devices
could only be indulged covertly.

The digital behavior of others in the White House was also regulated.
Official photographs emphasized that mobile devices should be left at the
door before important meetings (figure 5.4).[28] As Vivek Kundra explained

Figure 5.4
Cell phones are tagged with Post-its during a briefing on Afghanistan and Pakistan in the Cabinet Room of the White House on March 26, 2009. Official White House Photo by Pete Souza.

years later, smartphones were also very difficult for White House staffers to acquire, particularly if they were part of the new digital cohort. Official BlackBerry devices were doled out as a "sign of seniority" based on "the number of years you had been in government" and "the square footage of your office."[29]

The absence of mobile devices in Souza's *The Rise of Barack Obama* is even more striking. Its pages show Obama reading, praying, thinking, swearing in, shaking hands, kissing, gesticulating, speechifying, drinking, bowling and sightseeing, but never texting. The device is just barely visible in his hand as he embraces Ethel Kennedy.[30] When rushing through O'Hare Airport, the object is held behind Obama's head, and the blurred figures in the background indicate that the situation is exceptional.[31] The one example of active engagement with mobile computing in the whole volume is an image of Obama "checking his Blackberry" in a South Carolina conference room, where he is alone and without other claims to his attention.[32] Not only were there no funeral selfies in Souza's carefully curated collection, but the president was presented as a paragon of digital purity, and—whenever possible—smartphones were excluded from the scene.

The Wired President in a Wireless Age

In Souza's presentation of historical record, a traditional phone with a cord tethering the president to his desk was clearly deemed much more presidential. Corded phones were featured in dozens of photographs. Even though his constituents likely no longer used such telephones, President Obama was almost never shown speaking on a wireless device. Instead, we saw him with a wired connection.[33]

The official cover shot for the album of Obama's first hundred days in office shows the president in a leather chair with an old-fashioned corded phone that was clearly designed to remind viewers of Kennedy-esque telephone diplomacy (figure 5.5).[34] Such images alluded to Cold War brinksmanship and represented the lone executive's responsibility to pacify conflict zones abroad. As he holds the traditional phone, Obama looks out the window in deep contemplation. The frame is absent other people or communication devices that might have competed for his attention.

To understand the pre-history of such images, it is helpful to visit the archive of 1960s *Life* photographs shot by Art Rickerby. The Rickerby images

Figure 5.5
President Barack Obama speaks on the phone with Iraqi Prime Minister Nouri al-Maliki in the Oval Office on February 2, 2009. Official White House Photo by Pete Souza.

show Kennedy posed in intense reflection or concentration while using the telephone. They model the sustained attention that was supposedly the hallmark of the pre-digital era. Souza's black-and-white, book-length photo essay about Obama's journey to the presidency, *The Rise of Barack Obama*, also contains a number of such images, including the image facing the volume's introduction, which shows Obama on a traditional telephone in his senate office.[35]

The number of Souza's Obama images that borrow directly from the visual iconography of Kennedy, including those without a phone, is striking. For example, a political photography blog compared an image of Obama running with the new White House puppy Bo with similar photos of the Kennedy family and their pets. The blog argued that the appropriated imagery could convey "any number of meanings, including: vigor; drive, accelerated progress."[36] Not all critics were as enthusiastic about the homages to Kennedy's visual rhetoric. Robert Hariman asserted that these allusions to earlier presidents could quickly be emptied of significance and reduced to kitsch.[37]

Of course, the Kennedy images themselves also borrowed from other visual vocabularies. As David M. Lubin observes in *Shooting Kennedy: JFK and the Culture of Images*, "those pictures borrowed from or played upon the ephemeral popular culture of the period" but also were "derived from enduring works of art and literature produced over a span of centuries."[38] Much as "ancient Greek sculptors established a visual language for depicting male physical beauty," "ancient Roman sculptors taught us what facial expressions to assume and bodily postures to assume when we wish to dedicate ourselves to a noble cause," "seventeenth-century Dutch painters gave us our current notion of what constitutes a cozy, homey environment," and "eighteenth-century French artists provided the prototypes of aristocratic elegance and gravitas," poses and settings in photos of the Kennedy White House drew from an established visual repertoire.

The official rhetoric about the first digital president seemed to be that being online was unpresidential. It was better to be shown with more traditional and private communication technologies, à la Kennedy. Although Obama the candidate was often shown with mobile devices, after the inauguration Obama appeared on a corded telephone at a desk without a computer. Computer screens might surround the president, but he almost never was shown looking at them. Occasionally Obama's attention was directed

Figure 5.6
President Barack Obama talks on the phone with a Member of Congress while
Katie Johnson, the president's personal secretary, works at her desk in the Outer
Oval Office on March 21, 2010. Phil Schiliro, assistant to the president for legislative
affairs, stands nearby. Official White House Photo by Pete Souza.

elsewhere while he spoke on the telephone, as when he appears to be looking over the shoulder at the computer screen of his personal secretary
(figure 5.6), but these moments were rare.[39]

The Keyboard President

On the occasions when Obama had to pose in front of a desktop computer, as he did for the launch of new government websites, the president
appeared uncomfortable. In one image he hunched his body as though
the desk were too small.[40] Official captions informed the public that these
interactions with the computer took place at or near the desk of his personal secretary, Katie Johnson. Sometimes the screen in front of Obama's
gaze was even blank. For example, in a photo in which he "looks over his
prepared remarks in the Outer Oval Office," the viewer can see that Obama
is consumed with a traditional print text on the desk in front of him and

that the neglected computer screen is displaying a screen saver with the official White House logo.[41]

If Obama's hands appear on an actual keyboard, taking part in a form of manual labor usually delegated to female White House employees,[42] a caption informs viewers that Obama was only typing "last-minute edits" rather than engaging in extended composition, which would have required long-term periods of word processing or data entry.[43] In another image, the detachment of a masculine president from the scene of feminized work is dramatized: Obama is shown catching a football pass with Johnson's computer screen in the foreground.[44] Obama's eyes are on the ball in midflight; the information on the monitor is intended for the gaze of woman performing digital labor.

As his second term approached, Obama's image minders became less reluctant to show the president typing on a keyboard. A White House Mac-Book Pro with a presidential seal obscuring the Apple logo became an integral part of key rhetorical scenes.

Obama started a Twitter Town Hall by personally live tweeting, allowing the public to watch him directing his attention to a screen while typing rapidly. Despite careful stage management, the combination of a laptop designed for networked publics and a podium designed for traditional oratory invited satire. In the wake of the federal shutdown in 2013, internet memes promoted the suggestion that the government—like a malfunctioning computer—could be fixed by simply turning it off and turning it on again.

The Mobile President

Images of Obama interacting with mobile technologies became less taboo after "Selfiegate." Some commentators argued that the public had mostly ignored the presence of technology in the scene because they focused exclusively on the characters in the Mandela funeral farce. Through the lens of stereotypes about female competition for male attention, the Danish prime minister was reduced to the role of an attractive bimbo and the First Lady to a jealous shrew.[45]

By Obama's second term it had also become obvious that most public figures were expected to participate in selfie taking with various audiences. The pope agreed to a selfie with teenagers on a pilgrimage to the Vatican.[46]

German Prime Minister Angela Merkel consented to a selfie with a Syrian refugee.[47] Even the famously reserved Vladimir Putin was shown posing for selfies with Sochi schoolchildren on state-sponsored television.[48] Like shaking hands with constituents or kissing babies, taking selfies became part of the established political routine of elected officials.

Rather than show Obama's personal device, these exchanges around mobile technologies and image making for social media usually featured Obama as a user of others' smartphones. For example, in 2015 Souza posted photo of Obama in a Maryland café looking at a group selfie he had just taken with some admirers, and it is clear that the iPhone he is looking at belongs to a young smiling woman in the photo.[49] In Souza's gigantic coffee table book, *Obama: An Intimate Portrait*, an image shot at the newly opened National Museum of African American History and Culture shows Obama using a borrowed smartphone to take a group photo of descendants of an ancestor who had escaped slavery.[50]

Where matters of national security were concerned, however, mobile image-making devices were still expected to remain out of sight during Obama's second term. Famously, an official, behind-the-scenes photo released by the White House documented real-time reactions during the dramatic raid on the compound of terrorist leader Osama bin Laden (figure 5.7).[51] Most of the public's scrutiny focused on the facial expressions of those in attendance. Internet comments frequently mentioned the intense gaze of the hunched Obama or the suspense conveyed by Hillary Clinton's involuntary response.

It might be possible to ask different kinds of questions by focusing on the instruments rather than on the faces in the room. How do the Hewlett-Packard notebooks on the table function as display devices? Why are their screens darkened? Why is Brigadier General Marshall Webb the only one with his hands on a keyboard and his eyes directed to a computer's display? In a moment of national unity experienced "live," why are the computers so extraneous to the drama?

Digital forensics experts have pointed out that this historic document appears to have been altered by image manipulation software, perhaps "to enhance the impression of tension" while also conveying "efficiency and power."[52] In addition to obscuring documents which might reveal classified information, the left side of Obama's face was highlighted, and the colors in Clinton's face were enhanced. In other words, in Souza's image, the faces

Figure 5.7
President Barack Obama and Vice President Joe Biden, along with members of the
national security team, receive an update on the mission against Osama bin Laden in
the Situation Room of the White House on May 1, 2011. Official White House Photo
by Pete Souza.

of Obama and Clinton, like media screens, serve as display interfaces cueing
viewers on how to interpret the scene. In contrast, the laptop screens in the
image convey no information. Forensic analysis using the same software
shows that the screens were also blank in the original shot.

In an ideal world, the laptops in the Situation Room—physical artifacts
integral to a significant event—would now be in the possession of preservationists, much as the clothing of political figures at key events becomes part
of museum collections. Just as archivists must grapple with the vast collection of electronic files that belong in the digital version of Obama's presidential library, his brick-and-mortar library should have planned to store
significant pieces of physical hardware for cultural preservation, including
his historic BlackBerrys and iPhones. Digital archivists would have had
to make decisions about preserving content from these devices, and they
would have had to guard the original digital files against bit rot and other
hazards. Most likely, the machines were wiped in standard government
protocols.

The Flickr President and Instagram Ex-President

Head photographer Souza had previously served as an official White House photographer during the Ronald Reagan years and had covered Obama's rise to power as an Illinois senator while working at the national desk of *The Chicago Tribune*. His daily digital labor intensified once he moved to the White House. One account described how his days began very early with downloading the president's schedule: "Souza sits at his computer, working a mouse on a round pad that boasts the presidential seal, cruising the website for the Executive Office of the President. This daily task is as essential as loading a memory card into his camera."[53]

Souza played a central role in the careful curation of almost two million digital images. He continued to defend Obama's legacy during the Trump administration by recirculating photographs in a variety of formats: from Instagram to coffee table books. After Trump came into office, Souza seemed to delight in "trolling" the 45th president with images of the 44th.[54] For example, Obama's presidential successor caused consternation when he casually allowed classified materials within range of guests' smartphones of at his private club. Shortly after the open terrace of Trump's Mar-a-Lago club was chaotically transformed into an exposed situation room, Souza posted a photo on Instagram of Obama in a Sensitive Compartmented Information Facility erected during a visit to El Salvador. His caption made the comparison between presidents explicit: "When we were on the road, national security discussions and head of state phone calls were conducted in a private, secure location set up on-site. Everyone had to leave their Blackberry outside the area."[55]

In 2019 Souza published *Shade: A Tale of Two Presidents*, a book-length photo essay that documented many of his Instagram juxtapositions. The book's design seemed intended to clearly illustrate contrasts between President Trump and President Obama. On one side of each two-page spread would be a tweet from Trump or a headline about an instance of his unpresidential behavior; on the other side would be a photograph from the Obama presidency. For example, on page sixty-two, a *Washington Post* headline— "Trump Revealed Highly Classified Information to Russian Foreign Minister and Ambassador"—was paired with a photo on page sixty-three of Obama's closed device in its blue and gold case with a caption indicating that it was the "top secret Presidential Daily Brief on a secure, modified iPad."[56]

Only rarely was Obama's digital nonchalance on display in Souza's archive. "Michelle Obama snatches an iPhone away from her husband" faced a page with two different snippets of text: a tweet from Trump alleging improper wiretaps of other world leaders during the Obama administration and a headline about Trump's own sloppiness with "cellphone security measures." Although both Obamas are straight-faced in their phone-snatching vignette, they are clearly playacting. Michelle Obama is wearing a diagonally striped dress that emphasizes the torque of her body. Barack Obama has his feet up on the Resolute Desk in the Oval Office. Near his shoes is a multiline business telephone for office communication that has been sidelined at the edge of the frame.

The scene in which Michelle Obama takes away a smartphone from her husband actually comes from a humorous video shot for the White House Correspondents' Dinner. In the self-deprecating, fictional video, Obama contemplates his impending life in retirement. To occupy himself, now that he is a lame duck president, he fiddles with his wife's phone and expresses pleasure when he discovers that she has the Snapchat app installed on the device. He proceeds to record a video of himself praising his signature achievement, "Obamacare," but he records his message using one of the more ominous Snapchat filters, one that gives him demon eyes, sharp teeth, and a menacing voice that causes consternation and a "breaking news" alert when it is posted.[57]

Although Souza probably gained more internet celebrity during the Trump administration, he had already cultivated a fan base on social media while Obama was in office. Despite being a generation older than most of the platform's users, Souza is the star of a group selfie—complete with selfie stick—in a crowd of Instagrammers visiting the White House for the #WHInstaMeet. The image conveys their affection and adulation.[58] He also experimented with iPhone photography to supplement his more traditional camerawork and generated images specifically for Instagram's preferred square aspect ratio.

Souza starred in *The Way I See It*, a 2020 documentary that placed him in front of the camera rather than behind it. "I never intended to be vocal in any way," Souza said in the film. "I look at myself as an historian, with a camera," documenting "mood, emotion, context," who must "be ready for the fleeting moments both big and small" to compile "the best photographic archive that had ever been done."

In the film, Souza declares that the White House photographer he most admires is Yoichi Okamoto, known for his fly-on-the-wall style of documenting intimate scenes with President Lyndon Baines Johnson during the tumultuous Vietnam War years. Okamoto even shot the president in bed next to his wife. The appearance of complete access in Okamato's work is deceptive, however, because Johnson tightly controlled the presentation of his image and barred Okamoto from witnessing private backroom negotiations. When *Life* magazine ran a sixteen-page photo essay of Johnson with Okamoto's pictures, Johnson selected the images, supervised the layout, and even wrote the captions.[59]

For all of his photographic micromanagement, Johnson didn't seem to understand the most basic principles of the visual language Okamoto had mastered.[60] For example, Johnson preferred images in which he made direct eye contact with the camera. He thought that it established a straightforward rapport with the viewer. Okamoto knew that if Johnson looked at another person in the frame, the image was more rhetorically effective. These kinds of indirect photos showed Johnson making a human connection and allowed the viewer to occupy the imagined position of that intermediary. Notably, Souza was a virtuoso when it came to these kinds of gaze-within-frame pictures. The viewer was invited into the role of White House visitor and validated as the object of Obama's regard.

Although Souza's Flickr stream was safely migrated from an official White House account to one labeled "Obama White House," and Souza's social media images were also made available as compressed files on archival sites, the historians of the future will likely fret about lost content documenting the whole of the administration. Too much of the visual record of political speech in the twenty-first century has been entrusted to social media companies where obsolescent platforms, proprietary algorithms, and rigid user agreements might one day hide materials critical to understanding democratic legacies, technological practices, and internet celebrity. Nothing protects the actual selfie shot in the Maryland café taken by the smiling woman, just as nothing protects Souza's Instagram posts now that he shares them as a private individual.

Flickr was a thriving photo-sharing site at the beginning of the Obama administration. By the end of Obama's time in the White House, it was struggling to stem catastrophic losses to its user base. Dutch media theorist José van Dijck blamed vacillating corporate strategy for Flickr's meltdown, since the company "moved back and forth between various different inter-pretations of online photo sharing and thus between various platform functions: from community site to social network platform, from photo news site to memory service and archival facility."[61] Flickr tried one last monetization gambit before Obama's term ended: the platform attempted to move into the stock photo business by selling pictures uploaded by users with Creative Commons licenses to third parties.[62]

Flickr is still open for business at the time of this writing. For now, 6,668 photos from the Obama White House remain on the site, hosted by an account maintained by the National Archives. Of course, just as Flickr waned in popularity, other Web 2.0 companies that were part of the initial Obama White House social media strategy have experienced decline and obsolescence. In 2016, tens of millions of files that belonged to the users of MySpace were lost in a server migration. In 2018, Digg announced that it would shut down its RSS (Really Simple Syndication) reader. Some White House accounts on Web 2.0 platforms survived but never switched over to the Trump administration for some reason. For example, the White House SlideShare account still showed Obama-era documents during the Trump administration, as did the Socrata site set up to share data like visitor logs or staff salaries in the name of transparency.

Transparent Mediation and Mediated Transparency

Media theorists Jay David Bolter and Richard Grusin have drawn attention to the prominence of "hypermediation" in our society.[63] Hypermediated images emphasize the interfaces of media consumption. Such images may show multiple screens, windows, or devices simultaneously. They promote an aesthetic of intensely mediated multitasking by users who must con-stantly attend to multiple screens or even screens within screens. Hyper-mediation emphasizes the fragmented presence of competing venues for visibility, attention, and representation in today's ubiquitous computing environments. It describes a world in which even a gas pump might be playing a video commercial, and a refrigerator door might be displaying an animated infographic.

Mediated transparency describes a number of White House transparency initiatives that were supposed to demonstrate the administration's com-mitment to making the processes of political deliberation visible, explicit, testable, and straightforward, while also recognizing the limitations of direct democracy by inserting moderators and arbiters or enforcing norms about representational distance. As the chapter on the "rhetoric of transparency" argued, the ideal was to offer citizens a completely "open-source" government. In reality, many of the protocols, procedural logics, and software platforms of the presidency necessarily obscured key pieces of information that were only known to administration insiders with the technical knowledge and political access to decipher meaning using context clues and tacit understanding.

Transparent mediation, in contrast, was illustrated by the fact that Obama's image was often mediated and remediated so that mediating digital technologies become the focus of a scene. For example, the thumbnail images for many of Obama's YouTube weekly addresses displayed lights, camera viewers, computer monitors, and other technological apparatuses prominently.

By emphasizing in state-sanctioned portraits how the president's image appeared in the monitors of official videographers[64] or photographers,[65] the White House both emphasized the existence of an authentic moment not mediated by the technological apparatus foregrounded in the scene and acknowledged the ubiquity of image alteration software and its user interfaces. In these depicted interactions between man and machine, citizens saw a "well composed" digital shot of a public speaker who was also "well composed" as a remediated subject, appearing unconcerned under the glare of media attention and projecting the infamous "Obama cool" to the World Wide Web.[66]

The Body of Evidence

This chapter has argued that even "true" and comprehensive official records, uncontaminated by "fake news," still have significant gaps and blind spots. When it comes to representing representation—depicting a leader of representative government using the tools of artistic and historical representation—the picture is inevitably incomplete. These blank areas can be widened intentionally by digital curation that borders on propagandizing, or unintentionally by careless custodianship of the fragile digital record.

The next chapter will examine how non-human agents might shape—or misshape—the public record of our democratic institutions. As the Obama years progressed, the power to select and organize digital content was increasingly wielded by non-humans through machine learning, computer vision, biometrics, and autonomous sensing.

Souza's vivacious personality put a likable human face to the labor of digital content creation and management. Unlike the work of webmasters or IT managers who performed more mundane tasks behind the scenes, establishing the administration's visual record was seen as historically consequential and artistically creative. In documenting the highest power in representative government, Souza carefully composed and chose what to represent and consequently became a celebrity of visual and digital culture himself. The Obama archive of millions of digital images visually promoted the themes of connection, transparency, access, and participation that were being promulgated in the words of White House speeches and press releases. Souza also framed a particular picture of what digital literacy looks like by presenting a powerful sovereign who had mastered essential tools for calculation, communication, analysis, simulation, and decision-making.

Some of the scenes of human-machine interaction that Souza captured were oddly antiquated, as in the photo of Obama entwined with a corded telephone like an executive from an earlier age. Other scenes were strikingly futuristic; Souza produced many images of Obama posing with robots and other cutting-edge digital technologies. In every photo featuring technological devices, Obama projected confidence and competence. But not all attempts at digital innovation were successful in the Obama White House. And when these failures occurred, neither DC insiders nor Silicon Valley disruptors were eager to accept blame.

6 Identity Politics and Posthuman Technologies

President Barack Obama sat facing a large oil painting of a pensive Abraham Lincoln. The 44th president was separated from the 16th president by an elaborate cage of digital capture and illumination elements. The apparatus was composed of fifty custom-built LED modules, eight high-resolution sports photography devices, and six additional wide-angle cameras, all designed to simulate ten different lighting conditions in the space of a mere second (figure 6.1). The president froze in position as bursts of light danced across his face. He maintained an impassive demeanor as members of the data-gathering team circled him with handheld scanners. Obama was posing for a 3D portrait commissioned by the Smithsonian Institution, which was to be digitally rendered in color and printed as a monochromatic bust.

The enthusiasm of the first Black president for this type of scanning project might be perplexing, given the troubling legacies of scientific racism, phrenology, and physiognomy in the history of human classification and political surveillance. In recent years, Black scholars have emphasized how such software tends to privilege whiteness and how this predisposition perpetuates biased measurement systems resembling those developed through slavery and colonialism.

The prejudices of supposedly neutral systems are most obviously revealed when computer vision misrecognizes Black faces. In 2015, Google was forced to apologize after Black users of its image-recognition photo app discovered that the system labeled them as "gorillas" rather than as human beings.[1] In 2018 Amazon's face recognition system falsely matched twenty-eight members of Congress with mugshots, disproportionately doing so to legislators who were people of color.[2] That same year, media artist Joy Buolamwini demonstrated that many famous Black women—including Michelle Obama—were deemed to be male by computer vision systems.[3]

Figure 6.1
President Barack Obama sits for a 3D portrait being produced by the Smithsonian Institution. Official White House Photo by Pete Souza.

Obama himself was transformed into a white man when a depixelation program was applied to a pixelated image of his face.[4] Such systems were often trained on data sets of white faces, and the Silicon Valley assumptions that set "white" as a default condition were often reinforced in the programming and testing process as well.

Many Black thinkers link these modern biometric technologies to the long history of personal identification methods used to secure captive labor.

Simone Browne's *Dark Matters: On the Surveillance of Blackness* connects the fact that airport scanning machines were likely to have difficulty with Black hair to older mechanisms that policed Black bodies, such as eighteenth-century lantern laws that required Black people to be illuminated at night.[5] Jessica Marie Johnson has observed that the systematic datafication of bodies through "markup" practices continued the "death work of the slave ship register."[6] In *Captivating Technology: Race, Carceral Technoscience, and Liberatory Imagination in Everyday Life*, Ruha Benjamin analyzes the larger sociotechnical apparatus of digital control of Black bodies that includes dashcams in police cars and ankle monitoring devices.[7]

While the Smithsonian Institution was capturing Obama's biometric data, the racial implications seemed to be far from the minds of those present. Tom Kalil of the White House Office of Science and Technology Policy enthused about a "third industrial revolution" finally coming to fruition and with it "the combination of the digital world and the physical world." Adam Metallo of the Smithsonian praised the superiority of "objective 3D scanned data" over "an artistic likeness" because it benefited from the accuracy of "millions upon millions of measurements." The portable light stage transported to the State Dining Room was managed by the Institute for Creative Technologies, an academic research institute known for creating high-tech war games and military training simulations as well as dazzling special effects for action movies. All of these components in the spectacle—biometrics, machine sensing, simulation, and 3D fabrication—were important topics in the technological imagination of the Obama administration. They were also part of a narrative about the role of race in a posthuman future, which promised to be a post-racial future as well.

The Biometric President

Biometric data gathering within the federal government intensified with the Obama White House's aspirations to run the first fully digital administration. For example, the Office of Management and Budget explored schemes for authenticating documents with new kinds of electronic signatures in order to streamline the enormous volume of paperwork generated by agency bureaucracies. Experts explored confirming identity with a biometric supplement to electronic signatures, "such as fingerprints, retinal patterns, and voice recognition."[8]

Visitors to Biometrics.gov could read about "Biometrics in Government Post-9/11," the "Identity Management Task Force," and the "National Biometrics Challenge." The latter envisioned a partnership between government, industry, and academia to promote the interoperability and consistency of recognition programs that would allow computers to categorize individual people while also maintaining privacy protections and safeguards on personal data.

Despite assurances about civil liberties, the images of over 117 million Americans were stored in law enforcement databases by the end of Obama's presidency, making them subject to a "perpetual line-up" every time a crime was committed.[9] Residents of other countries were also compelled to participate in these massive data-gathering efforts. Many US military service members were equipped with handheld biometric recording equipment, including SEEK (Secure Electronic Enrollment Kit), which could transmit data from fingerprints, irises, and faces back to an FBI database.[10]

The Machine Vision President

Once gathered, enormous quantities of data were filtered, correlated, and sorted by machine vision algorithms. These algorithms were designed to police national security, public safety, intellectual property, civic propriety, medical normality, and gender conformity.

The administration celebrated companies that used these technologies for their ingenuity and economic promise. For example, Kairos, a Black-founded facial recognition firm, was chosen for the 2015 White House "Demo Day."[11] Kairos advertised a range of services that included age and gender detection with its "easy to code API."[12] Kairos wasn't the only computer vision company invited to Demo Day. At the Partpic booth, two Black representatives showed Obama how to use his smartphone camera to find a matching replacement part.[13] Of course, the big players in the machine vision industry were not startups like Kairos or Partpic, which were run by Black entrepreneurs. They were established companies like Apple and Amazon with white tech evangelist figureheads. In fact, just a year after she appeared at Demo Day, Partpic cofounder Jewel Burks sold the company to Amazon.

Granted, there was some resistance to adopting machine vision too wholeheartedly, even within the large multinational corporate entities that were profiting from it. For example, the president of Microsoft issued a warning on the company's blog that these issues "go to the heart of fundamental human rights protections like privacy and freedom of expression."[14] Yet, major tech firms continued to incorporate more computer vision capabilities into their platforms.

The perils of surveillance were relatively obvious during the Obama years because foreign governments were already seeking to deploy these technologies to police dissidents, crack down on protestors, and spy on ethnic or religious minorities—often with the help of US technology firms and institutions. For example, in 2018 I visited the Hong Kong offices of SenseTime, which boasted of years of close collaborations with well-known US entities, such as Qualcomm and MIT. I was encouraged to try "fun" activities for "entertainment," like having the computer measure my "attractiveness rating," which included guesses about my age and gender. Practical applications on display included those designed to catch thieves, ticket traffic offenders, and monitor sleepy or inattentive drivers. Using machine learning algorithms and data derived from the profiles of over a billion Chinese citizens, SenseTime promised that misbehavior could be eliminated, along with anonymity. The same company was placed on the Bureau of Industry and Security's 2019 blacklist for contributing to human rights abuses in Uyghur regions of mainland China.

Despite its potential risks, computer vision was very appealing to administration officials as a way to promote safety and efficiency. It was seen as a cheaper, easier, and more reliable alternative to human oversight. In contexts where careful scrutiny by federal officers was no longer practical, such as at the nation's borders, computers could take over from beleaguered human beings. To manage the traffic of products and people under the purview of the Department of Homeland Security, the department recruited senior leadership with "expertise in computer science, data science, information security, user experience, and other technical disciplines."[15]

Information about hostile countries and terrorist organizations might also be hiding in plain sight. Forms of "open-source intelligence" could be gathered from publicly available sites like YouTube without relying on espionage or camouflage. Intelligence agencies could then analyze these troves of data from the safety of their government offices. However, finding specific data about imminent threats required the manpower to sift and sort through massive archives of online material.

At least hypothetically, the drudgery of analyzing open-source intelligence could be automated using computer vision and machine learning. Millions of disorganized clips on YouTube that would take centuries for a human being to watch could be examined much more rapidly by specialized software. Extrapolating from training data that was already labeled, a computer program could tag the content of unfamiliar videos. For example, Google's 2012 "artificial brain" was quickly able to find cat videos on its own.[16]

During the Obama administration, hundreds of computer scientists built tools to make sense of uncategorized "video in the wild." Often, they were looking for material related to national security. For example, content related to "explosion," "fire weapon," "government leader," "meeting," and "prisoner" were all discoverable with the University of Amsterdam's concept detection software. Software to find "flag burning" and "protest" was also developed.[17] Understandably, some state department officials were wary of government contractors selling software they claimed could predict revolutions,[18] but many other policy makers—particularly in intelligence agencies—were eager customers of these technologies.

Obama associated himself and his presidency with machine vision by publicizing digital activities in which "seeing" was performed by computer technologies. For example, in 2013 he visited the DreamWorks animation studios. While actors in tight-fitting black suits covered with green targets pranced and gesticulated in front of the president, director Dean DeBlois explained the basic principles of how motion capture worked to create real-time special effects.[19] Obama even held the virtual camera himself.[20]

In the industrial sector Obama promoted self-driving vehicles, which used machine vision to locate routes and obstacles. As president, he "highlighted the advances in computing, sensors, and machine learning" that "made autonomous vehicles possible," and he doubled federal investments in developing prototypes. In 2015 the White House announced new initiatives for "American Innovation in Autonomous and Connected Vehicles." Obama "proposed doubling federal investment to help bring these technologies to commercial deployment, given that autonomous vehicles, coupled with soon-to-be-ubiquitous vehicle-to-vehicle communication could save thousands of lives annually, give new independence to those like the elderly or the blind who until now have been unable to drive, and help reduce greenhouse gas emissions." The announcement also made an appeal to the self-interest of "the average American who spends 50 minutes a day commuting to and from work," since "autonomous and connected vehicles could free up hundreds of hours a year for other pursuits."[21] Self-driving cars were also tied to initiatives for "smart cities."[22]

Near the end of his presidency, in an interview with *Wired* magazine, Obama described how "machines can make a bunch of quick decisions" much faster and more wisely than mere humans and thereby begin to tackle difficult problems with traffic fatalities, gridlock, and emissions.[23] At the same time, he acknowledged that human values must be embedded in such high-tech machines. He referred obliquely to the famous "trolley problem," a thought experiment in philosophy in which a runaway vehicle could either kill one person on one trajectory or multiple people on another, depending upon the flip of a switch. According to Obama, the behavior of a car might be similarly governed by "a moral decision, not just a pure utilitarian decision."

The Drone President

Self-driving cars weren't the only autonomous vehicles promoted by the Obama administration with the potential to kill. Drone warfare initiatives were also greatly expanded during these years. The decision to keep Secretary of Defense Robert Gates in the cabinet, even though he had been a Republican appointee, was a crucial step in promoting the pro-drone agenda.

In his memoir, *Duty*, Gates recalls seeing the otherworldly Reaper and Predator drones shortly after Obama took office: "They both look like giant bugs, with long spindly legs, a broad wingspan, and a camera pod that looks like a huge, distended eyeball."[24] There is a photograph among his official papers, which happen to be archived at my university, that documents Gates's encounter with the machine. In the hanger, the drone is posed against an American flag. It is shot from below to be almost nose-level with the Secretary of Defense. Gates appears to be studying his new ally intently. Although he describes this uncanny 2008 meeting as a new experience, Gates's memoir also documents quests to develop drone technology at the CIA as early as 1992.

Gates distanced himself from uncritical technophiles. He described himself as "skeptical" of "systems analysis," "computer models," and "game theories." He took pride in caring for the needs of soldiers rather than the high-tech gadgets with which they were armed. In particular, Gates recounted advocating for the drone pilots who operated in the "spartan" conditions of Creech Air Force Base in Nevada, "where the whole enterprise resembled a very sophisticated video arcade—except these men and women were playing for keeps."[25] According to Gates, the pilots complained of long commutes, the absence of places to eat out or work out, and promotion structures that favored fliers with service in traditional manned planes. In his memoir, Gates tells of trying to improve working conditions for drone operators.

Both the Predator and the Reaper were described by commanders as the "Swiss army knife" of the skies. Their equipment inventories included a day-time camera, an infrared sensor, an image-intensified camera, and a laser designator and illuminator.[26] By 2014 officials reported that over 11,000 servicemen were flying or supporting Predator and Reaper missions, a five-fold increase in strength, with more needed in the training pipeline.[27] In addition to Creech, drone operations were headquartered at the Al-Udeid military and air base in Qatar, which was graced with a visit by the First Lady in 2015. Rather than reinvest in risky "knock-and-talk" missions that put soldiers in harm's way, the Obama administration prioritized remote-controlled combat.

With the rise of the "killer robot" that incorporated more artificial intelligence and machine learning, new ethical considerations came into play. To keep human operators in the loop, Gates invested heavily in systems for Intelligence, Surveillance, and Reconnaissance, or ISR. However, achieving real-time responsiveness in the air over hostile territory was an IT nightmare, particularly when the drone was connected to its operator by a data stream that was limited in bandwidth and clouded by glitches. The drone's perspective might give contradictory information about the theater of war, requiring frequent recalculation and recalibration of enemy strategy and strength. The data lag made designing for independent drone decision-making desirable, but the "killer robot" scenario was horrifying to ethicists still clinging to traditional notions of "just war."[28]

The drone remapped the topography of human experience from the air. It transformed political subjects into political objects as it scanned the landscape, separating potential targets from non-targets. Much of the drone's electronic sensorium was designed to identify data at the scale of the human figure, looking for the heat signature that distinguished the living from the inanimate.

Media scholar Lisa Parks observes that "drone-based infrared imagery reinforces already existing power hierarchies by monitoring and targeting certain territories and peoples," even if it ignores "the visible light registers of ethnic/racial difference."[29] According to Parks, human beings become media interfaces for the drone's consumption, like pixels on a digital display. Some have the knowledge or the technology to cloak themselves from the drone's scrutiny, but those living in poverty generally do not.

In addition to being seen by a drone's camera or its infrared sensor, one could also be targeted based on an internet use location or a connection to the so-called internet of things. In his larger book about the perils of datafication, *We Are Data*, John Cheney-Lippold describes human beings as mere "statistical bodies" to the drone. He argues that machines are too easily encouraged to equate patterns of behavior or material in digital dossiers with identity or personhood. For example, he notes that "having a SIM card match the data signature of a suspected terrorist can put someone at the receiving end of a drone strike."[30]

Sociologist Lisa Hajjar has documented how Obama personally participated in authorizing drone attacks. Obama justified both "personality strikes," in which a drone strike targets a particular individual based on their identity, and "signature strikes," in which identity is not known but a "pattern of life" or behavior indicates involvement with terrorist activity.[31] Hajjar describes a growing body of legal knowledge called "lawfare," which combines warfare with legal action. Such lawfare must acknowledge "efforts to challenge a state's military practices and national security policies in court." As a former law professor, Obama could certainly understand the legitimacy of strategies to contest his drone policies, but his pro-drone administration said little publicly about these objections.

Peter Asaro, a prominent critic of "killer robots," has appealed to traditional theories of "just war" to dispute rationales for autonomous armed vehicles in combat.[32] Obama devoted several paragraphs of his Nobel Peace Prize acceptance speech to the topic of "just war," but he made no mention of his administration's widespread adoption of drone technologies as a means for resolving geopolitical conflicts.[33]

Although the lethal violence of the drone would appear to be no laughing matter, Obama actually made a joke of his mastery of deadly force at the White House Correspondents' Dinner in 2010: "The Jonas Brothers are here; they're out there somewhere. Sasha and Malia are huge fans. But boys, don't get any ideas. I have two words for you, 'predator drones.' You will never see it coming. You think I'm joking."[34] Not surprisingly, many in the media took the joke to be in poor taste, given the potentially devastating human costs of high-tech warfare under Obama.

Near the end of Obama's term in office, a Black sniper killed five police officers at an otherwise peaceful protest against police killings of Black civilians. The shooter became the first person killed by a drone on US soil. According to two researchers, "Dallas police attached a bomb to a remotely controlled small aircraft designed to investigate suspicious packages, thus creating an improvised drone."[35] When Obama eulogized the five officers "upholding the constitutional rights of this country," he made no mention of the extrajudicial killing that took place in the aftermath of their deaths.[36]

The Robot Ambassadors

Although mentioning killer robots could be taboo, coverage of peacemaking robots was welcomed. In 2010 Obama was happy to be photographed with the HRP-4C in Yokohama, Japan. This lifelike female robot, nicknamed "Miim," had a silicone head and an armor-like metallic torso.[37] Among other stunts, she could "sing" Japanese pop songs.

One news account described Miim flexing her muscles before the American president,[38] but the actual video of her meeting shows a much more subservient encounter. Obama smiles, but he does not deign to address her. "This exhibition shows Japan's strengths and attraction," she says to him. "Please see, touch, and feel Japan's advanced technology."[39] Despite the invitation, Obama does not touch Miim. He strokes the fur of a robotic seal instead. The way that technology is gendered and raced in the scene with Miim goes without comment.[40]

It is interesting that Obama interacted exclusively with robots who were either Asian, white, or raceless—rather than Black like himself, despite the fact that Black robots played a significant role in the American cultural imagination.[41] In the 1930s, the Westinghouse Electric Corporation exhibited "Rastus Robot," who was billed as a "Mechanical Negro." He could bow, say a few words, and sit obediently with an apple on his head while an arrow was aimed at it. According to Simone Browne, Rastus may have been created "to soothe concerns around robots replacing human workers," because, "unlike Westinghouse's other robots of the time, this robot was a symbol of Black servitude."[42] Browne argues that Rastus was intended to comfort white members of the working class by reminding them of their racial superiority. Like other technology companies praised on the White House website, Westinghouse was frequently lauded as an exemplary corporation. No mention was made of their earlier racist ventures in robotics.[43]

Instead of presenting robots merely as labor-saving devices, the Obama communications team presented them as symbols of human connection and empathy. Robots could also dramatize the reciprocal ties between a political leader and his constituents. For example, in 2015 the president was shown in the White House conversing via a telepresence robot with Alice Wong, a disabled activist and journalist based in San Francisco (figure 6.2). Wong has a neuromuscular disorder and lost her ability to walk as a child. Wong's telepresence robot allowed her, as a person with a disability, to "stand" facing the president. The most advanced telepresence

Figure 6.2
Alice Wong, Disability Visibility Project founder, via telepresence robot on July 20, 2015, the twenty-fifth anniversary of the Americans with Disabilities Act. Official White House Photo by Pete Souza.

robots could actually be controlled by a person's brain signals, so the device could navigate a room. Pete Souza published a photo on his Instagram feed that depicts an intimate, eye-level exchange between Obama and Wong.[44] Another photo shows Wong's robot being ushered out of the room by one of the "social aides" managing the reception line so that the president could meet with the next visitor with a disability.

The following year, another robotic encounter with a visitor with a disability—also captured in official photos—became a talking point in speeches. To dramatize the importance of brain research, Obama told the story of Nathan Copeland, who was paralyzed as a college student by a car accident, and how Copeland had agreed to have four microelectrode arrays implanted into his brain that communicated with a robotic arm.

> Nathan is also the first person in human history who can feel with his prosthetic fingers. Think about this. He hasn't been able to use his arms or legs for over a decade, but now he can once again feel the touch of another person. So we shook hands. He had a strong grip, but he had kind of toned it down. (Laughter.) And then we gave each other a fist bump.[45]

Souza's official photo of the first bump focuses closely on the two hands at the moment of contact. Two of Obama's knuckles touch two of the knuckles of the robotic arm. The background is blurred to emphasize the intimacy of the touch. The composition alludes to iconic images like Michelangelo's *The Creation of Adam.*

Obama was not alone in greeting robot ambassadors warmly. Other world leaders shared the stage with non-human entities during this period of intense innovation in robotics. Pictures of politicians shaking hands with robots became a recognizable public relations genre. In other photo ops with robots, the political leaders of Germany, Canada, Switzerland, France, Austria, Denmark, Turkey, Russia, India, China, South Korea, Japan, Israel, and the Emirates all shook hands with android counterparts of varying shapes and sizes.[46]

Obama's encounters with robots were often part of a narrative about the education of young people in STEM fields. For example, the White House screening of *Underwater Dreams* publicized the story of young, undocumented Mexican immigrants assembling "Stinky," an underwater robot, from Home Depot parts and triumphing over a team of more privileged students from MIT. RoboNaut, "NASA's own fist-bumping robot," also appeared at the event and shook the hand of a young Black girl.[47] In a curated collection of photos on the White House website titled "President Obama and Robots—Our 5 Favorite Moments," three of the five photos show high school students showing off their robots to the president.[48]

Obama's interactions with robots were depicted by conservatives as alarming. During a visit to Japan in April of 2014, Obama played soccer with the famed Honda robot Asimo and also courted controversy by showing deference to the foreign non-human. "US President Bows to Japanese Robot" the *Drudge Report* screamed.[49] The headline in the *New York Post* also emphasized Obama's subservience: "Obama bows to robot in Japan, finds it 'scary.'"[50] Such anti-Obama tech stories became a staple of right-wing news. They were often consumed by those who identified as older and white. Some were people displaced from jobs in manufacturing by the acceleration of the revolution in robotics.

The Simulation President

"It's important to fix a broken system, treat people with respect and have confidence in our ability to assimilate people."

These words were originally spoken by United States president George W. Bush in a television interview with ABC News, but researchers at the University of Washington demonstrated that those same words could be put convincingly, on video, into the mouths of Barack Obama, failed presidential candidate Hillary Clinton, Japanese president Shinzo Abe, reporter Piers Morgan, and actor Ian McKellen, all enunciating the same sentence elements.

In the paper accompanying this startling demonstration, researchers described how their machine learning algorithm could "reconstruct a controllable model of a person from a large photo collection that captures his or her persona" without requiring any actual 3D scanning. They could also mimic "personality and character" using "a novel combination of 3D face reconstruction, tracking, alignment, and multi-texture modeling."[51]

Thanks to these technologies, politicians, movie actors, and other frequently recorded public figures could now be reconstituted as virtual humans from a database of examples. Members of the research team could also generate lifelike replicas of Obama working with audio-only source material so that the former president could seem to be giving an identical speech in two different rooms at the White House wearing two different outfits. In their demo video the Obama twins echo each other, even as they manifest slight differences in their facial performances with identical audio. In describing the Orlando mass shooting both Obamas show gravitas and solemnity, but they emphasize different words and nod in different places. In many ways the "artificial" Obama appears to be more natural than the "natural" Obama. The "real" Obama is addressing reporters standing in a large and impersonal ceremonial space, while the "unreal" Obama was composited from hundreds of instances of footage from Obama's weekly addresses, which were often staged as more intimate fireside chats for You-Tube audiences.

The University of Washington researchers benefited from decades of research in computer animation to generate more realistic faces by imitating the subtlest features of anatomy. They could recreate the smallest motions from complex muscle interactions or the slightest glimmers of light refracted through subcutaneous tissues. Integrating information from dozens of scientific papers on topics such as micro-expressions or subsurface scattering, researchers were able to generate more lifelike and photorealistic composites of recognizable people.

At the 2016 SIGGRAPH conference on emerging technologies in computer graphics, another team of researchers showcased Face2Face, a program that could generate simulated speeches by combining source footage from You-Tube videos and real-time reenactments via commodity webcams. Through real-time facial capture, the grins and grimaces of actors are mirrored in George W. Bush, Vladimir Putin, Donald Trump, and Barack Obama.[52] That same year, at the Adobe MAX conference, Zeyu Jin showed off how Voco, popularly dubbed "the Photoshop of voice," could generate sentences seemingly spoken by actor Jordan Peele that he never actually said.[53] Using twenty to forty minutes of the desired target's speech, the software could output soundalike voice clips, including phonemes that were not present in the example material. Like WaveNet, produced by Google's DeepMind machine learning project, the speech synthesis capabilities of Voco verged on becoming completely indistinguishable from a real human's voice. Peele subsequently created a public service announcement warning of the dangers of fake news using Adobe After Effects and FakeApp.[54] To publicize the potential for highly realistic, computer-generated "deep fakes" circulating on the internet to dupe gullible audiences, the announcement features a simulated Obama saying bizarre, out-of-character things. The video showed how the combined suite of tools developed by academic and commercial researchers could allow bad actors to create convincing videos that showed political figures making policy pronouncements and even declarations of war that they never actually made.

A 1967 essay by computer pioneer Vannevar Bush warned the public about technology's potential for duplicity: "We watch a girl on the screen moving her mouth and someone else is doing the singing. One can put into a man's mouth for all to hear words he never spoke." For Bush the "readily alterable record" destabilizes the organic coherence of the past and makes it "easy to fool people."[55]

Simulation marks a radical shift in existing systems of knowledge. Representation—using a medium to make a likeness of an original—was a common feature of traditional culture. In contrast, simulation—using an authoring platform to make a likeness composited from elements derived from databases of prior representations—typifies digital culture.

"We cannot go back ideologically or materially," Donna Haraway wrote. She listed the move from "representation" to "simulation" as first on her "chart of transitions" tracking shifts from "the comfortable old hierarchical dominations" to the interconnected anarchy of "scary, new networks."[56] Jean Baudrillard similarly predicted an end to the traditional "theater of representation," which was to be replaced with simulation generated by "the black box of the code."[57] According to Baudrillard, the advent of copies without originals could be extremely destabilizing.[58]

Simulated humans might be particularly unsettling. In his 1970 seminal essay on "The Uncanny Valley," roboticist Masahiro Mori asserted that, as technologies of simulation advance, virtual humans elicit disgust because they have come too close to realism without quite achieving it.[59] Mori rationalizes this response as an instinctive withdrawal from nonliving entities like corpses. In a somewhat different vein, cultural historian Hillel Schwarz has claimed that commonly held repulsion to the "knock-offs and replicas" created through simulation indicates that we are unsettled when confronted with "uncomfortable parts of ourselves—emotional, cultural, historical" that we may wish to avoid acknowledging.[60]

In contrast, the Obama administration expressed nothing but optimism about simulation technologies. In its 2012 Progress Report on Modeling & Simulation for the Economy, simulation is applauded as a solution to a wide range of contemporary problems, including obstacles faced by small businesses, manufacturing, clean technologies, space exploration, health care, and education.[61]

To promote these technologies, Obama himself appeared in simulators and spoke of his experiences operating simulators in speeches. A Pete Souza photograph shows Obama preparing to drive a Saturn SL1 automobile simulator following two red sportscars in the virtual lanes ahead.[62] In one of his weekly addresses, Obama marveled about his "chance to fly a space flight simulator where [he] docked a capsule on the International Space Station."[63] These encounters were always staged to be positive experiences that Americans should envy rather than fear.

Yet the connection between military might and simulation technologies was often a not-so-subtle subtext beneath White House rhetoric.[64] In one of the stranger moments of Obama's major 2011 "American Renaissance" speech, he described how federal agencies were "working with private companies to make powerful, often unaffordable modeling and simulation software easier to access." He recounted how "Procter & Gamble teamed up with the researchers at Los Alamos National Labs to adapt software developed for war to figure out what's happening with nuclear particles, and they are using these simulators to dramatically boost the performance of diapers." This anecdote was interrupted with laughter several times. "Yes, diapers. Folks chuckle, but those who've been parents—(laughter)—are always on the lookout for indestructible, military-grade diapers. (Laughter and applause.)"[65]

In this speech, in which simulation was mentioned six times, Obama also asserted the importance of the Defense Advanced Research Projects Agency, which he described as "the folks who brought us stealth technology and, by the way, who brought us the Internet." As with his drone joke at the Correspondents' Dinner, Obama used humor to naturalize the link between computer-mediated communication in everyday life and the exercise of armed force by the state.

The Posthuman President

The term "posthuman" describes many of Obama's performances with technology; the White House promoted enthusiastic engagement with artificial intelligence, computer vision, simulation, and robotics. In her 1996 book *How We Became Posthuman*, N. Katherine Hayles traces the development of

three stories: "how information lost its body," "how the cyborg was created as a technological artifact and cultural icon," and "how a historically
specific construction called the human is giving way to a different construction called the posthuman."[66] For Hayles, the "dream" of science fiction to
transcend the body might actually be a "nightmare."

The Obama administration celebrated all three of these narratives. Big
data was no longer confined to a single container and could be repurposed
and reconfigured easily; robots were the proof that a more just, empathetic,
and advanced society was possible; and technology demanded that humans
rapidly evolve for their own betterment.

The posthuman future presented by the White House was in many ways
also a post-racial one.[67] It celebrated the coming of a color-blind, high-
tech utopia in which Black entrepreneurs, Mexican immigrants, and Asian
activists had equal opportunities for success. This was a future in which
fist-bumping would no longer signify membership in a particular racial
subculture.[68] Instead, the fist bump would become a universal symbol for
affirmation, for the human and the nonhuman alike. It was a vision of
progress that for Obama was informed by the optimistic science fiction
TV shows of his youth, like *Star Trek*, which posit a color-blind world in
which a cast of multiethnic and multispecies characters could solve problems collectively.[69]

In contrast to this post-racial vision of a technological future, media
scholar Beth Coleman has pointed to ways that race itself serves as a kind
of technology that may have the power to liberate as well as to oppress.
According to Coleman, race operates as a "levered mechanism" that "creates movement and diversifies articulation." Rather than being "a trap," it
can function as "a trapdoor."[70] Coleman argues that Obama mastered techniques for operationalizing his Blackness. Perhaps Obama also attempted to
hack the existing racial repertoire with its own code, by playing off assumptions about racial difference.[71]

The Programmer President

In 2014 Obama was celebrated as the first US president "to write a line of
code" and dubbed "Coder in Chief" in White House press releases.[72] This
allowed him to adopt the position of a particular kind of cultural hero: the
hacker. Optimistic visions of hacking already abounded in White House

Figure 6.3
President Barack Obama fist-bumps a middle school student participating in an "Hour of Code" event to honor Computer Science Education Week in the Eisenhower Executive Office Building on December 8, 2014. Official White House Photo by Pete Souza.

rhetoric. Hackers were even presented as potential saviors through "civic hacking"[73] and "hacking for humanity."[74]

At the event where he earned his honorary title, Obama participated in an "hour of code" with New Jersey middle school students learning JavaScript (figure 6.3). Obama wore a baseball cap from Code.org, a self-directed online curriculum funded by Bill Gates, Mark Zuckerberg, and other Silicon Valley titans. The coding exercise used material from the Disney princess movie *Frozen*. To craft the syntax of his instruction to the machine—moveForward(100);—the president needed extra help to select the correct punctuation and capitalization for his program. A Black girl guided him through each step.

During the exchange, the president joked that he was an "old man" and encouraged the young people present to "make [their] own games." He also briefly lectured the students about "zeros and ones" that could be "translated into electrical messages." In saying this, Obama had actually mischaracterized the difference between a programming language and computer processing instructions in binary code. Other adults in the room quickly stepped in to clarify the president's explanation and suggested a "list of instructions" as the best terminology to use. In the background, Vice President Joe Biden worked through the programming task with another Black girl. He was flanked by a white robot on his other side. Later Biden assured them that "girls can do anything," as another Black girl in a hijab listened.[75]

Adrianna Mitchell, the young Black woman patiently instructing the president about composing lines of code, did not fit right-wing stereotypes about Black female technology users like the Obamaphone lady. She was not a freeloader, schemer, or damsel in distress. She was a programmer.

However, digital literacy specialists have questioned the Obama administration's emphasis on coding as a direct and unambiguous path of escape from racism, sexism, and poverty. Digital literacy scholar Annette Vee has examined how the moralism and class snobbery of nineteenth- and twentieth-century literacy campaigns persist in twenty-first-century computer programming education.[76] Media scholar S. Craig Watkins has chronicled the shortcomings of a game design class serving Black and Brown students in a yearlong study of a low-income Texas high school that turned out to be "technology-rich" but "curriculum-poor."[77] Digital humanities scholar Miriam Posner has ridiculed the urge to "exhort everyone to code" without considering why the tech sector lacks diversity.[78] Computer historian Janet Abbate has looked at how what she calls "the pipeline argument" in programs like Girls Who Code "blames women and minorities themselves for not preparing sufficiently" and "reinforces stereotypes about the kinds of people who succeed in tech, equating the masculine pattern of early, obsessive interest in computers with talent and commitment."[79] All of these critics question the misplaced enthusiasm of politicians and educators for privileging computer programming over other kinds of competencies that are also needed for success. According to this line of thinking, treating coding as a meritocratic skill that served as both the ends and the means of social justice displaces the importance of systemic change and sustained investment in communities of practice. In other words, superficial, short-term "hours of code" or "hackathons" aimed at quick results for photo-ops were much less likely to promote democracy.

The Maker President

In 2014, the White House Christmas tree in the Blue Room was festooned with 3D-printed ornaments in the form of white plastic snowflakes, stars, and DC landmarks. In October, a contest had been announced to promote a "unique and interactive holiday experience."[80] Among hundreds of entries, five grand prize winners would be selected to have their ornaments 3D printed and displayed in the White House. The winners' ornaments would also be preserved for posterity in the political history division of the Smithsonian's National Museum of American History. To run the contest the White House partnered with Instructables, a platform specializing in user-created, do-it-yourself projects and currently owned by Autodesk.

Earlier that year, the White House had sponsored its first "Maker Faire." The event's website affirmed that "America has always been a nation of tinkerers, inventors, and entrepreneurs . . . think of Benjamin Franklin, Benjamin Banneker, George Washington Carver, Ida B. Wells, Henry Ford, Grace Hopper, and so many more." According to the White House narrative of progress, this multiracial cast of pioneers of innovation provided the foundation for a radical technological revolution. "Americans have gained access to technologies that support making, such as 3D printers, laser cutters, easy-to-use design software, and desktop machine tools, along with freely available information about how to use, modify, and build upon these technologies." In combination with "growing networks of maker enthusiasts and crowd-funding platforms," these tools were "enabling more Americans to design and build almost anything."[81] Standing next to a black 3D-printed sculpture of the soundwaves from his State of the Union address, Obama declared that "today's DIY is tomorrow's Made in America."[82]

The executive branch under Obama expressed powerful enthusiasm for 3D printing technology as a way to improve entrepreneurship, small business, job training, and STEM education. In his 2013 State of the Union address he told an inspiring story about digital transformation in the so-called Rust Belt of the United States: "Last year, we created our first manufacturing innovation institute in Youngstown, Ohio. A once-shuttered warehouse is now a state-of-the art lab where new workers are mastering the 3D printing that has the potential to revolutionize the way we make almost everything."[83]

This embrace of the do-it-yourself ethos became an important theme during Obama's second term and the phrase "DIY" frequently appeared on official web pages. For example, the White House blog lauded "DIY savings" in manufacturing laboratory equipment for biology education, launched a "DIY Space Race," and profiled a "DIY Neuroscientist." One of the "Champions of Change" celebrated by the White House was Marcin Jakubowski, a Polish immigrant who created "a modular, low-cost, DIY, high-performance platform" that provided open-source blueprints for farm machines to allow anyone to build their own tractor or harvester from scratch.[84] Jakubowski's TED Talk about his "Global Village Construction Set" hailed the achievements of "DIY maker culture" and boasted of using 3D printing technologies for a "civilization starter kit."[85]

Not everyone was so enamored with 3D printing. Media theorist Toby Miller pointed out that heated thermoplastic extrusion machines can produce dangerous aerosol emissions.[86] In addition to the air pollution caused by ultrafine particles, there was the waste created by the nonbiodegradable objects themselves, particularly when makers were encouraged to produce multiple disposable prototypes and tolerate a high probability of defective versions. Given the scope of global supply chains, such small batch producers could also have little impact on the economy.[87]

There was also the fact that the same technology that could produce Christmas ornaments could also produce firearms. 3D printers could allow gun rights advocates anonymous and untraceable access to do-it-yourself manufactured weapons. If they weren't made of metal, they could pass through metal detectors. Such guns could potentially be used to assassinate Obama, one of one of the most hated presidents in US history according to threats monitored by the Secret Service.

In 2012 Defense Distributed disclosed their plan to design a working plastic gun that could be downloaded and reproduced by anyone with a 3D printer, which was realized in 2013. The company also designed a 3D-printable, AR-15-type assault weapon capable of firing hundreds of rounds. During the Obama administration, the United States Department of State demanded removal of the gun's instructions from the Defense Distributed website on the grounds of violation of the Arms Export Control Act. The company's founder Cody Wilson subsequently sued the government on the basis of freedom of speech. In 2018 the Trump administration settled with Wilson, closing the case with an acknowledgment of his right to publish the gun's instructions.

Overall, 3D printing provided little utility for consumers during the Obama administration. Unlike the tangible products of manufacturing, agriculture, or mining, the extractions of the information economy appeared to be much more abstract. They also seemed to reward coastal elites who had received STEM college educations. As a result, messages from Obama to blue-collar workers about retraining for twenty-first-century skills, which were intended to be comforting, were often perceived as tone-deaf platitudes. Obviously, members of the working class did not welcome being displaced by robotics and computerization. Furthermore, the rise of the gig economy facilitated by mobile smartphone applications like Uber or Instacart forced desperate members of the labor force into more precarious, lower-wage, service sector jobs without access to contracts or collective bargaining.

These concerns about the potential disruptions of the new industrial revolution were often minimized in White House messaging that seemed to ignore how new solutions could create new problems. Change was always presented in hopeful terms, a continual process of shifts toward the "more perfect union" Obama constantly referenced. Borrowing from the language of Silicon Valley, the administration embraced "2.0" as a signifier for iteration, versioning, and reform. Declarations were made about a "WhiteHouse 2.0," and the "2.0" label was attached to several other federal projects and initiatives. There was the "Federal Register 2.0," "Rulemaking 2.0," "State of the Union 2.0," the "Advanced Manufacturing Partnership Steering Committee 2.0," and, by 2013, "We the People 2.0."

In Code We Trust?

President Obama had become so closely associated with historic reforms to the US health-care system that key provisions of the Affordable Healthcare Act of 2010 were often referred to as "Obamacare." However, the much-touted online marketplace where Americans without insurance coverage were supposed to be able to shop for cost-conscious plans was a spectacular technological failure once it went "live." Due to heavy demand, the website was down within two hours of launch because it was unable to handle traffic from hundreds of thousands of people. A banner read: "The system is down at the moment. We're working to resolve the issue as soon as possible. Please try again later."

The HealthCare.gov site was obviously unready for heavy internet traffic. It turned out that just "hitting 'apply' on HealthCare.gov" caused "92 separate files, plug-ins and other mammoth swarms of data to stream between the user's computer and the servers powering the government website."[88] A damning McKinsey Report boiled the fiasco down to a grim PowerPoint presentation, which showed that the normal design/build/test stages of software were not sufficiently articulated to optimize prototyping and iteration. Moreover, what should have been an initial phase of determining policy and technical requirements expanded to dominate the entire process.[89] Not surprisingly, anti-Obamacare hacktivists had also attempted to bring down the site through distributed denial-of-service, or DDoS, attacks, although their tools seemed to be too unsophisticated to do much damage.[90] More compromising were flaws in the system's privacy controls over sensitive data, which alarmed computer security experts.

For people able to get through to HealthCare.gov, the user experience was aggravating. Time-consuming online forms seemed to never save data after it was entered, and fears about data privacy and accuracy stoked by HealthCare.gov horror stories undermined confidence. Worse yet, the website looked obviously unfinished. For example, some drop-down menus were incomplete,[91] and important code appeared to be untested.[92] President Obama had promised a very different user experience to the American people. Choosing subsidized health insurance on the website was supposed to be similar to other kinds of online shopping. According to the president in a speech made in October 2013, using HealthCare.gov would be as familiar as shopping for "a plane ticket on Kayak or a TV on Amazon." Despite all the fanfare leading up to the site's debut, only six people were able to complete health insurance applications by the end of the launch day. Yet Obama continued to repeat comparisons to efficient online shopping experiences.

In 2014 I traveled to the Library of Congress to inspect the digital fragments remaining from the botched rollout of the HealthCare.gov website. At the time, the Library of Congress did not seem well equipped for researchers like me, who wanted to study its born-digital collections in person. To examine the remains of that early HealthCare.gov website, I was directed away from the public reading rooms with which I was familiar and led to a lonely workstation only accessible through a maze of back offices. The situation seemed entirely improvised. I was afraid to leave my assigned desk to take breaks because I worried I might not find it again. The room was so remote that employees of the library even forgot I was there. At one point, all the lights went out. I had to find my way out in darkness, feeling for obstacles in my path.

Much as an archeologist might expect elements of an artifact to be missing, I knew that the digital record of HealthCare.gov would be incomplete.[93] The browser reminded me of these gaps in the record repeatedly: "External links, forms, and search boxes may not function within this collection." In browsing the HealthCare.gov pages, I often came across "404" messages that files were unavailable, particularly in the "marketplace" designed for users to shop for insurance. Some parts of the site had been stripped of the aesthetic niceties that the web designers had included to give HealthCare.gov visual coherence and brand authority.

There are two general philosophies for preserving digital media: *migration* and *emulation*. In migration, the approach to preservation is predicated on an assumption of constant tech obsolescence. Migration specialists plan for every platform to eventually be discontinued. Ideally, a lifeboat to the next platform is part of the design process, but programmers and preservationists tend to have very different goals. In migration, data from rich media must be stored as numerical information to allow the files to be reconstituted from their states of suspended animation once a platform becomes defunct. For example, by using the information from a loud and colorful videogame written in computer code, it is possible to adapt the existing formulas of assets and instructions to bring the game back to life on a new platform.

Emulation, on the other hand, focuses on simulating the front-end user experience rather than the resuscitating the back end, where the data had been stored. Many videogames from the classic arcade era are emulated rather than migrated. Nobody has access to the original code anymore, so designers have to guess how to imitate the game's look and feel.

If HealthCare.gov had been properly migrated, the Library of Congress would have had all of the original materials from the sixty-odd companies that worked on the HealthCare.gov site, perhaps sitting in the climate-controlled petabytes of storage that they managed somewhere far away from the reading rooms. If HealthCare.gov had been emulated, I could have re-experienced what it had been like as a user filling in forms and navigating the hyperlinks and menus in those chaotic first days.

Among the plethora of HealthCare.gov memes, the "Obamacare girl" became the face of the failure of the government's efforts to imitate technology companies. Also known as "Glitch Girl" and the "Mona Lisa of health care," "Adriana" had posed for an unpaid stock photo that was used by the Center for Medicare and Medicaid Services for the website.[94] Allegedly she had signed away the rights to her image in exchange for "free family photographs."[95]

Little did she know that her smiling image would be featured upon the landing page of HealthCare.gov (figure 6.4), where it would soon become an object of mockery and derision. Internet jokesters combined Adriana's photograph with commentary about her assumed personality as the mascot of the website's cruelty or naiveté.[96] *The Onion* digitally altered the appearance of Adriana's eyes and eyebrows to illustrate the headline "People in

Figure 6.4
HealthCare.gov landing page prior to launch.

Healthcare.gov Stock Photos Now Visibly Panicking."[97] One meme swapped
out her face to replace it with the agonized figure from Edvard Munch's *The
Scream*. Later Adriana appeared on ABC News to complain about the cyber-
bullying she had been subjected to by online trolls.[98]

Researchers of digital culture know very well that the "epic fail" is often
as beloved as the "epic win," and it is certainly considered more humorous.
In her in-depth ethnographic study of the online collective Anonymous,
Gabriella Coleman describes the "lulz" made possible by the humiliation
of others. According to Coleman, the shared delight at the spectacle of an
embarrassing vulnerability can be explained anthropologically as a man-
ifestation of a culture's need to expose "any information thought to be
personal, secure, or sacred" and expose it to "sharing or defilement in a
multitude of ways."[99] HealthCare.gov attracted legions of such tricksters.
Reddit users picked the site's code apart to show spelling errors in string
names, such as a "feild"/"field" typo.[100]

I had also traveled to Washington, DC to speak with digital archivists
more generally about their preservation work. I wanted to ask about what
was being saved and what was being lost from our growing legacy of material documenting the new digital politics. By that point, midway into
Obama's second term, it was obvious that much of what constituted political discussion in the United States was taking place online. It wasn't in piles
of yellowing newspapers, nor in reels of magnetic tape. It was in ephemeral
mobile feeds that were constantly refreshing, displayed differently for different users, and interspersed with advertisements.

Abigail Grotke was an expert in saving civic discourse for posterity. She
led the digital archiving team at the Library of Congress, which was scoop-
ing up seventeen terabytes a month when we spoke. There were obvious
things of historical significance to preserve: midterm elections, the activities of the legislative branch, and matters of public policy. Librarians and
technicians had already started crawling the web in March 2014 for the
November 2016 election. They were even trying to use sophisticated digital
tools to trace the influence of political action committees, or PACs, which
functioned independently from the established political parties.

Unfortunately, the activities of many other non-state actors had to be
documented as well in order to understand the recent past. For example,
the humiliating memes and labyrinthine conspiracy theories of the alt-
right inevitably had to be a part of the digital cultural record, no matter

how objectionable their online tactics. In choosing which digital news sites merited archiving, it was necessary to cover a broad political spectrum. Grotke was grappling with how to preserve evidence from a range of digital artifacts, from web comics to Reddit posts. At one point, Grotke admitted, "nobody was capturing Instagram."[101]

I was curious about how a historic internet failure like HealthCare.gov might be documented. After all, social media companies were going out of business every month all around the world, taking millions of accounts loaded with user-generated content with them, and noncommercial entities were often even more vulnerable. As Grotke pointed out, "you can't play it all back in the Wayback Machine." The services of the Internet Archive, including the Wayback Machine, were obviously critical for saving a select collection of digital snapshots of publicly accessible websites. However, the full record of dynamic websites was much more fragile. The data might be behind membership logins or have complex file structures that were regularly updated. Such sites also served as staging areas for third-party widgets and middleware. In other words, these web pages were populated with information that was constantly being generated anew and could not easily be reduced to a static specimen.

Lessons Not Learned

Former White House director of new media technologies Tom Cochran described the chain of cascading failures for the HealthCare.gov website as a "classic game of telephone." Although Cochran wasn't employed by the federal government at the time, he had ample experience with the ways that bureaucracies obstructed problem-solving during his stint as a civil servant.

> The engineer on the ground knows there's a problem and says, "Red alert! We have a huge problem here!" He tells that to the project manager. The project manager goes to his or her boss and says, "I think we might have an issue." And then that person goes to their boss and says, "A couple of hiccups here, but I think we're okay." Then that person goes to the head of HHS and says, "We should be fine. Nothing we can't handle." And that person goes to the Chief of Staff and says, "All systems go. Don't worry about it. We'll get there." And then he goes to the president and says, "We're ready to launch." So. Who's at fault there?[102]

Secretary of Health and Human Services Kathleen Sebelius was one of the intermediaries in Cochran's telephone game scenario. She was the highest-ranking official to step down in the aftermath. "You deserve better," she testified before Congress. "I apologize. I'm accountable to you for fixing these problems and I'm committed to earning your confidence back by fixing the site." While she was issuing her *mea culpa* in the House chamber, the HealthCare.gov site was down again. This inspired a split-screen media display on cable television that showed the "system down" message from HealthCare.gov on one side and the cabinet secretary defending the administration against charges of gross negligence on the other.

After the HealthCare.gov site failed spectacularly, Obama walked back his confident assurances about simple and fluid user experiences. He insisted that "we did not wage this long and contentious battle just around a website."[103] Nonetheless, government websites are never "just" websites, because they are always part of the symbolic landscape of a citizen's encounters with the federal government—a model for how interaction between sovereign and subject is staged. Political scientist and technology theorist Jane Fountain has called this paradigm of power expressed through computational media systems "the virtual state."[104] The importance of this symbolic register explains why activists and adversaries often attack government websites with DDoS attacks.

It is worth remembering that HealthCare.gov was not the only highly anticipated government website with a failed launch. It was certainly the most expensive IT disaster under the Obama administration—the budget ballooned from 93.7 million dollars to an ultimate cost of 1.7 billion—but critical lessons could have been learned from earlier snafus. One researcher cited that "over the past 10 years, 94% of large federal information technology projects were unsuccessful, more than 50% were delayed, over budget, or didn't meet expectations and a total of 41.4% were judged to be complete failures."[105] Veterans of .gov websites like Cochran reference similar statistics. As he put it bluntly, "'IT failure' and 'government' are words that often go together."[106] Another IT expert complained about an antiquated bureaucratic procurement process "designed to buy a website like you buy a battleship."[107]

The 2009 launch of Cars.gov, the portal of the "cash for clunkers" program, was similarly mismanaged during the development process. The website was created to provide resources for consumers seeking to benefit from the CARS Act, which encouraged automobile owners to trade in less fuel-efficient vehicles for more fuel-efficient ones and collect a rebate if certain eligibility criteria were met. The site presented the requirements that a vehicle had to meet, information about eligible dealers, and FAQs regarding the

CARS Act. It also had a section for questions. The website was in operation until January 2012. When Cars.gov launched, users complained of periodic system crashes.[108] However, the news on Cars.gov wasn't entirely bad. Cars.gov used a "community cloud" approach, and some experts praised the US federal government for embracing more efficient cloud computing.[109] This improved technology also supported the back end of Forms.gov, Flu.gov, USA.gov, and Apps.gov.

Much as HealthCare.gov became the subject of right-wing conspiracy theories, Cars.gov was viewed with suspicion by prominent conservatives. On Fox News, a popular television show hosted by Glenn Beck pointed out problems with the site's functionality. It also focused on some very strange fine print in the Cars.gov user agreement that seemed to allow the government access to the computers of private citizens. Beck complained about the dangers of "malware and tracking cookies" coming from a government website.[110] The legalese at Cars.gov actually stated that once the terms were accepted, "your computer is considered a federal computer system and is property of the United States government" and asserted that "users have no explicit or implicit expectation of privacy." Ominous warnings included notifications that "all files on this system may be intercepted, monitored, recorded, copied, audited, inspected and disclosed to authorized CARS, DOT and law enforcement personnel, as well as authorized officials of other agencies, both domestic and foreign." After Beck's viewers expressed outrage, government webmasters apologized for accidentally posting language that was intended for "the portion of the Web site accessible by car dealers and not the general public." This frank admission of failure in quality testing during the digital design process further solidified anti-Obama sentiments about technology.

Macon Phillips was changing jobs from the White House to the State Department the week the HealthCare.gov website "went live and broke." But he was philosophical about having been "part of the team" that created the initial HealthCare.gov architecture. He explained how the informational parts of the site had been developed independently over a span of two years, and that the dysfunctional exchange section had been represented with a placeholder during the development process. He argued that there could be "a lot of silver lining" from such a failure that might lead to "reform in how the government used technology."[111]

As late as the 2020 election, memory of the HealthCare.gov failure had yet to recede. As evidence for a narrative about government waste and technocratic vaporware, the story of the over-budget website continued to be used to score political points. For example, in 2019 one of Donald Trump's sons reposted a popular meme with a quotation falsely attributed to comedian Tim Allen: "President Trump's wall costs less than the Obamacare website."[112] Fact checkers pointed out that this assertion about the relative cheapness of an enormous steel barrier along the US-Mexico border was nowhere close to the truth, and Facebook tagged similar posts with this claim as misinformation.[113]

It certainly didn't help that White House hype had set expectations unrealistically high. The president himself had posted a video demo using an idealized version of the site back in July 2010.[114] As Obama clicked through the options on a prototype "dummy" site, he pretended to be a much younger version of himself first settling down as part of a couple in Chicago. In this fantasy of easy digital access to information, he was able to find satisfactory results in less than three minutes.

Plans for the government to enter the field of large-scale but agile software development were probably never realistic, but the administration's optimism read as fresh and hopeful.[115] By pursuing non-commercial alternatives that were developed at taxpayer expense, the administration was also catering to an understandable wish to lower vendor costs and to avoid long-term dependence on corporate algorithms that were riddled with proprietary secrets. Unfortunately, government bureaucracy and civil service pay scales made it difficult for the "virtual state" to perform like Kayak, Amazon, or Google. And the ethical systems of these companies with "silicon values" were also incommensurate with representative democracy.

But what about the women of color who were figureheads of the administration's technological ambitions? Both the "Adrianna" of the Hour of Code and the "Adriana" of HealthCare.gov have since receded into anonymity. Yet the ways that these public faces were coded as gendered and raced were important.

Certainly, computer programmers and DIY makers have become diminished as cultural heroes in recent years. The rise of technologies that use machine learning and computerized sensing have destabilized long-held assumptions about human mastery and personal agency. Although the writing, reading, and sharing of code will continue to be an important form of literacy for many more years, a literacy that still enables some elite forms of access to and participation in an increasingly technologically mediated and embedded world, computer programming knowledge isn't always adequate for decoding the increasingly complex relationships between cause and effect in contemporary life.

Obama-era technocrats championed artificial intelligence as a way to enable faster, fairer, and better decision-making. They also promoted accelerating the robotic revolution that would transfer menial, dangerous, or cumbersome labor to autonomous agents. Shifting away from human brains and brawn as the basis of political sovereignty to a more posthuman philosophy of governance was a risky strategy that was extremely unpopular in areas of the country that were already suffering with the shift to a service and information economy. Even the administration's efforts to elevate human creativity in tech fields were likely to backfire for many who felt excluded from hackathons and maker fairs that required special skills and equipment. Resentful conservatives took pleasure in humiliating failures like HealthCare.gov in which the administration's techno-optimism proved to be ungrounded.

As president, Donald Trump would not be writing computer code or shaking hands with robots. He would reverse the White House's confidence in simulation, artificial intelligence, machine vision, and other advanced computer technologies. As a candidate and as president, Trump asserted an urgent need for a future in which humans remained the ones in control. For example, after an automated system caused two crashes of Boeing jets, he tweeted his skepticism about a machine's capacity to make "[s]plit second decisions" wisely. "Airplanes are becoming far too complex to fly. Pilots are no longer needed, but rather computer scientists from MIT. I see it all the time in many products. Always seeking to go one unnecessary step further, when often old and simpler is far better."[116] In office, Trump was quick to reverse policies that had supported investments in self-driving cars[117] and artificial intelligence in government decision-making.[118]

Despite Trump's nostalgia for a pre-technological past, he proved himself adept at mastering the new lexicons of social media platforms and deploying the language of connection, transparency, participation, and access that promised political change. He also knew how to exploit the dissatisfaction and suspicion about technology brewing in the populace, even if he also benefited from the widespread adoption of social media and mobile computing that had characterized the Obama presidency.

7   Gender and Digital Privacy

Somewhere out there, there is a version of WhiteHouse.gov on which Hillary Clinton is the president of the United States. This official website likely contains a biography of the 2016 Democratic candidate that imagines she had run a triumphant race. It probably also includes the issues and policy positions that characterize her barrier-breaking administration.

This website is not part of an alternate reality. It was actually created as part of the planned presidential transition by Hillary Clinton's digital team, many of whom knew staffers from the Obama administration who had experienced the earlier handoff from George W. Bush. The 2009 White-House.gov launch had not been entirely smooth, and no one wanted to repeat any mistakes.

Tom Cochran, the first director of new media technologies for the Obama administration, noted that the transition was "only the second time" that a fully formed and complex WhiteHouse.gov—one that incorporated blogs and digital video—had moved from one digital team to another, and "it was the first time that it involved social media."[1]

"Clinton's team had a website ready to go," Cochran observed. Yet strangely the victorious Trump campaign didn't seem to understand the challenges of creating a brand-new federal government website for the executive branch within seventy-two days. "They had no idea how to do anything in government," Cochran recalled. And now they were responsible for making "the most attacked website in the world." Obama's digital team was especially confounded when a month went by and no one from Trump's transition team had returned their phone calls. "Now it's December, and they still don't have a website," Cochran remembered. He then articulated the obvious conclusion to be drawn: "They didn't expect to win."

According to Cochran, after dispensing with the idea of doing find-and-replace with the existing presidential website and after jettisoning templates from the real estate industry with which the Trump organization was familiar, the new team for WhiteHouse.gov brought on Ory Rinat, the web guru of the Heritage Foundation, to make sure that the basics would be ready in time. Rinat still moved ahead cautiously. The day before the inauguration Politico published a story that the Trump transition team would be preserving "for now—the basic shell and design built under the leadership of President Barack Obama" of WhiteHouse.gov, "including the fonts, format and blue colors that have come to be associated with many aspects of the outgoing Democratic administration."[2]

What happened to the website of President Hillary Clinton that was produced months before the website of President Donald Trump? The Library of Congress has archived the website from Clinton's career as a senator from 2001 to 2009 as part of its mandate to preserve the institutional memory of the legislative branch.[3] It has also conserved materials from both her 2008 and her 2016 runs for the highest office as part of its collection of political ephemera from presidential candidates.[4] Clinton's WhiteHouse.gov website, which was never launched, is certainly of historical significance, yet the Library of Congress, the organization that should serve as its chief digital custodian, seems not to have a copy of it.

The Administration That Wasn't

Many will insist that Hillary Clinton lost the 2016 US presidential election solely because of her gender. They will argue that implicit bias and toxic misogyny doomed her candidacy and that the physical appearance, voice, and manner of a sixty-nine-year-old professional woman were unacceptable attributes of a political leader, either because they conformed to gender expectations or because they violated them. Even before the election, literary critic Elaine Showalter described the public's mood as "witch-burning ecstasy."[5] According to media scholar Kelly Wilz, gender essentialism among Democrats in the primary weakened her from the start.[6] Communication scholars argued that sexism in both parties was already a major factor in the 2008 election,[7] as was the "pornification" of female candidates.[8] Clinton even seemed to pose a threat to gender norms during her earlier tenure as First Lady.[9]

Others will assert that Clinton lost because of technology and that it was impossible for her to survive a series of scandals stemming from a two-sided attack on her online practices: an extensive FBI investigation of a private computer server located in her home and hacktivist exposure by WikiLeaks that made her emails available in a searchable database. A post-election intelligence report asserted that foreign powers also sought "to undermine public faith in the US democratic process, denigrate Secretary Clinton, and harm her electability and potential presidency"[10] through a concerted cyber-espionage campaign by pro-Russian hackers. Covert electronic messages swirling around the Clinton digital persona seemed to show a practitioner of the dark arts of insider politics. If technology, rather than gender, was the problem, either her secretive wizardry or her sloppy vulnerability disqualified her from office.

My hypothesis is that it was the conflation of gender *and* technology in the popular imagination that contributed to Clinton's stunning defeat, which many pollsters had not predicted.[11] After all, ideas about digital privacy are often strongly gendered. For example, discussions of computer privacy often make analogies to modest clothing or the sanctity of the home. Furthermore, the metaphors for inappropriate digital behavior often invoke sexual misconduct, and these forms of misconduct often have harsher repercussions for women than for men.

The victory of Donald J. Trump—a man who famously refused to write email—may indicate that sympathies could not be aligned with Clinton because she became affiliated with digital media and all its ambiguities. Electronic files can easily reach unintended audiences and be used for unanticipated purposes. They can also be altered to disguise the provenance and character of a piece of digital evidence.

In contrast, Trump—throughout his real estate, hospitality, entertainment, lifestyle marketing, and political careers—had avoided personal computing, with the exception of broadcast channels like Twitter. In sworn depositions Trump declared that he didn't "do the email thing" and preferred to send traditional letters typed by secretaries directly to correspondents.[12] In his view, messages could only be securely transported by human agents using analog means. According to Trump, "if you have something really important, write it out and have it delivered by courier, the old-fashioned way, because I'll tell you what, no computer is safe."[13] At the geopolitical level, he believed this policy should be adopted by nation-states.

"We will never have great national security in the age of computers—too many brilliant nerds can break codes (the old days were better)."[14]

The New Digital Diplomats

As Obama's Secretary of State from 2009 to 2013, Hillary Clinton couldn't avoid using email. She was expected to embrace digital culture and reflect the governing philosophy of the new commander in chief. The technological transformation process in the State Department was comprehensive, much more expansive than just initiating Obama's new digital public diplomacy policy. Like the digital teams based at the White House, digital teams at the State Department were interested in how technology could promote connection, transparency, participation, and access.

Alec Ross, Clinton's senior advisor for innovation, described the scope of his own ambitions broadly: "I was really focused on harnessing the power of technology to address foreign policy challenges, whether that was throttling back the influence of the cartels in Mexico or enabling mobile payments to soldiers in Afghanistan, or using it to reduce sexual violence in Congo."[15]

Mobile phones would be an essential tool for performing the work of international aid and diplomacy in an increasingly networked world. In *The Industries of the Future*, Ross tells the story of being sent to the Mugunga refugee camp. At Mugunga he discovered that 42 percent of the residents had access to a mobile phone despite their "abysmal" living conditions.[16] If even the poorest recipients of foreign aid had cell phones, certainly they were essential tools for State Department staff.

Ross described the deeply dysfunctional information technology culture at the State Department as "horrendous" and "a nightmare." Despite an IT budget of "over a billion dollars a year," employees were stuck with "clunky old desktops."[17] This antiquated model assumed that people would always be sitting in embassies rather than traveling in the field. Clinton herself was described as "the most-traveled Secretary of State in history." She visited 112 countries and traversed 956,733 miles during her tenure.[18]

"With email, you're exchanging information in real time," Ross said. "[Clinton's] in Islamabad, and her staff's in DC, and another group of key people are in Brussels. You've got to communicate in real time."[19]

With the new administration, there was a mandate for change. "What I saw take place at the State Department came from both the top down and the bottom up," Ross observed. "You had these new diplomats, legions of people who had gone to college using these tools. And for them they were second nature." This bottom-up generational shift coincided with "an imperative from the top down out of Secretary Clinton's office to get with the times."

Molly Moran laughed about the State Department being "the last users of the Wang computer."[20] During the Clinton years, Moran served as a design strategist and new media advisor. She described how little in this government agency had changed technologically and culturally since telegraph cables were first laid on the ocean floor during the nineteenth century.[21]

When Hillary Clinton assumed her new position at the State Department, she held a town hall to discuss promoting a deeper culture of listening in the organization. Clinton proposed an internet site where employees could submit ideas and then debate their pros and cons. Anonymous submissions would be accepted to ensure that people could speak freely.

As Moran listened to the town hall, she was particularly impressed to hear Clinton's announcement that the site would be accessible in just two days. "I was like 'Wow! I wonder who is building that?'" Moran recalled. She soon realized that "no one was building it."

"We had to pull people together and basically hackathon the software together and build it in forty-eight hours," Moran remembered. "It wasn't very pretty at first, but it worked. Over time it gained traction. It became very popular."

Clinton's "Sounding Board" presented serious challenges to the State Department's existing "clearance culture" and hierarchical bureaucracy. One of Moran's senior colleagues said, "We may promote democracy, but this organization itself is not a democracy."

The Sounding Board brought a sense of personal connection to the leader of the agency, even if that wasn't its main purpose. It was often called "The Secretary's Sounding Board" by State Department employees.

According to Moran, the site made State Department employees less frustrated with the "non-answers" that were often provided at official town halls. Material from the Sounding Board could also be reviewed in advance so that answers provided at public meetings felt less perfunctory to participants. In one situation, Clinton had to respond to employees' irritation at being forced to use an outdated internet browser. There were "behind-the-scenes" reasons to keep using the old browser having to do with security, rollout, training, and contractual issues. When Clinton announced that State Department employees would finally be getting a more current browser, employees responded euphorically. Moran described the celebration in the town hall as like being "in the studio audience for an Oprah show."

Not everyone was happy with the Sounding Board. Senior officials objected to the thumbs-up/thumbs-down feature of the site because they didn't want to be outvoted by the crowd. Moran encouraged them to view it as a mechanism for useful information gathering, a tool offering "a data point" that wouldn't necessarily force a particular outcome. According to Moran, senior decision-makers were also wary of appearing weak if they seemed to be relying on input from subordinates. Despite fears that the site allowed behavior that might be "indecorous," even the people reluctant to post were reading the Sounding Board every day. Supervisors liked how it functioned as a "safety valve" to prevent leaks or a "safety net" to address issues early. It also allowed State Department employees to practice using social media tools internally before using them externally with public audiences. "It was like training wheels for social media," Moran said.

One of the most vexing aspects of Clinton's announcement about the site was her promise to allow for anonymous submissions. Moran knew IT industry best practices were nearly unanimous in discouraging "anonymous stuff within a workplace." But nobody wanted "the new Secretary of State to look like a liar," so the digital team obliged. As a result, they had to provide constant vigilance as site moderators. They aimed to read and review every post, although keeping up with all the comments was impossible.

Moran's group also established rules for user behavior. There could be no contradiction of foreign policy decisions. The focus could only be on management within the organization: "it's not *what* we do in diplomacy; it's *how* we do it." Personal gripes were also forbidden since the issues discussed had to be of concern to everyone. Despite its success, SoundingBoard.State. gov was shut down in 2018 under the Trump administration, like so many Obama-era digital initiatives.

In addition to her other duties, Moran had to teach email etiquette to State Department employees. For example, diplomatic cables had traditionally been written in all caps, but all-caps emails were often interpreted by younger recipients as "shouting."

As a member of Obama's cabinet, Clinton was expected to be an important voice on digital culture. She gave two major speeches on internet freedom: "Remarks on Internet Freedom" in 2010 and "Internet Rights and Wrongs: Choices & Challenges in a Networked World" in 2011.

Both speeches used the metaphor of the public square, but the first speech was more hopeful than the second. "This freedom is no longer defined solely by whether citizens can go into the town square and criticize their government without fear of retribution," Clinton said in the first speech. "Blogs, emails, social networks, and text messages have opened up new forums for exchanging ideas—and created new targets for censorship."[22]

The second 2011 speech took a less interventionist tone on censorship. Clinton insisted that American policy was opposed to telling "people how to use the internet any more than we ought to tell people how to use any public square, whether it's Tahrir Square or Times Square."[23] While the first speech claimed that internet freedom supported "peace and security," the second speech was more circumspect about potential trade-offs between "liberty" and "security."

According to Ross, "She was never naive about this," never one of the "utopians" when it came to digital technologies. "People get lynched in the public square," he observed darkly.

Shame and Humiliation

In 2008 the network server for clintonemail.com was registered by someone named Eric Hoteham.[24] "Eric Hoteham" was presumably a mangled version of "Eric Hothem," the name of a former Clinton aide. His name also appeared in news reports about other delicate matters that became minor scandals, such as wire transfers to Bill Clinton's brother and discrepancies in the White House's furniture inventories.[25] In 2009 the internet domain clintonemail.com was registered in the name of Justin Cooper, a longtime advisor to the former president. Hillary Clinton's email was set up as hdr22@clintonemail.com.

As she began her service as Secretary of State, private email addresses were allowed as a channel for some government work but discouraged as a general practice. In 2012 Clinton's private email server was revamped with Google as the backup server. A few weeks later congressional investigators asked Clinton if she used personal email in her official capacity as Secretary of State.

The email scandal story didn't really become a story until 2013, when the news-and-gossip site Gawker reported the existence of embarrassing correspondence between Obama foe Sidney Blumenthal and Clinton's personal account at clintonemail.com that had been revealed by a foreign hacker called "Guccifer" who had infiltrated Blumenthal's account.[26] Because Clinton's original email address was revealed in the article, she changed it to hrod17@clintonemail.com.[27] The Clintons also updated the clintonemail.com server so that it would back up to a McAfee-owned company. By the end of the year, the National Archives and Records Administration asserted that personal email accounts could only be used by government officials in "emergency situations." Any emails from personal accounts that were part of federal correspondence were to be recorded and managed in accordance with established record-keeping practices.

As the public clamored for more information, Clinton handed over approximately thirty thousand emails to investigators in 2014, excluding emails deemed to be "personal." By this point President Barack Obama had signed an update to the Federal Records Act prohibiting "the use of private email accounts by government officials unless they copy or forward any such emails into their government account within 20 days."

A flurry of new activity around the Clinton email story occurred in March of 2015. The emails were released in batches to the press and to WikiLeaks in response to their Freedom of Information Act requests. While the State Department was slowly and methodically reviewing the emails for clearance, Clinton held a twenty-minute "press encounter" at the United Nations in which she protested assumptions being made about sinister motives. She insisted that the emails she had held back for personal reasons were truly personal. She also maintained that her use of private email for public duties was purely a matter of convenience. "I trust the American people to make their decisions about political and public matters," she declared, "and I feel like I've taken unprecedented steps for these emails to be in the public domain. I went above and beyond what I was requested to do."

Stories that Hillary Clinton had destroyed digital evidence began to circulate shortly afterward. A senior Republican senator alleged that she had chosen "to wipe her server clean and permanently delete all emails from her personal server" rather than comply with investigators. When it was revealed that Clinton used both an iPad and a BlackBerry for email and that she had ignored questions from Congress back in 2012 about her email, requests for transparency became more insistent. When the State Department said it would need until January 2016 to release all the emails, full-blown conspiracy theories began to take root.

Clinton defended herself by claiming that past secretaries of state had had similar habits of using personal accounts when convenient and deleting irrelevant emails without documenting their removal. It turned out that her assertions about precedent were largely true. During a 2016 State Department review of the emailing practices of the past five secretaries of state, it was revealed that her predecessors Colin Powell and Condoleezza Rice had both received emails containing classified information through personal accounts.

As Clinton was wrapping up her nomination as the Democratic Party candidate in the 2016 election against Republican candidate Donald Trump, FBI Director James Comey made a public announcement that both exonerated Clinton and chastised her. He stated that he would not recommend charges to prosecute her for use of a private email server during her time as Secretary of State. However, he did characterize Clinton and her aides as "extremely careless" in handling classified information.

The same day that Comey seemed to close the case against Clinton, more damaging stories about potential negligence appeared. One story in the *New York Post* titled "Clinton directed her maid to print out classified materials"[28] revealed multiple layers about class, gender, and national security. The maid was an inappropriate intermediary for digital state secrets because of her subordinate position by gender and class, and Clinton also seemed to be exploiting her labor by "directing" her to do work that a secretary of state should be able to do for herself.

The most damaging blow to Hillary Clinton hit just eleven days before the end of the 2016 race. FBI Director Comey announced that the Clinton email investigation was being reopened because emails belonging to Clinton had been found on the laptop of disgraced Congressman Anthony Weiner. Weiner had once been a rising star in the Democratic Party, but in 2011 his habit of sharing lewd messages and pictures of his genitals was revealed. After an initial denial, Weiner expressed contrition, but later he was discovered to be sexting again under a new name. This revelation stymied his attempts to revive his political fortunes. Weiner's wife was Huma Abedin, deputy chief of staff to Clinton in the State Department and a top aide in the Clinton presidential campaign. When another sexting scandal was uncovered in 2016, Abedin and Weiner separated.

Because one of Weiner's sexting scandals involved a minor, the FBI sought possession of Weiner's laptop. Once the laptop was in their possession, they discovered email chains that included material from Clinton's account. Comey said during testimony before the Senate Judiciary Committee that "Huma Abedin appears to have had a regular practice of forwarding emails to him, I think to print out for her, so she could then deliver them to Secretary of State."[29]

After Comey's October 28 announcement, the FBI reinvestigated. The laptop contained 1,355,980 items and approximately 650,000 emails. Technicians were able to narrow material to fewer than 50,000 Clinton-related emails. Among those emails, the FBI identified 6,827 that were either to or from Clinton, and they deemed 3,077 of those emails "potentially work-related." Peter Strzok led the FBI team that scrutinized these messages, poring over them with little time for sleep. They found thirteen email threads containing confidential information, although none were marked as classified. All were duplicates of emails that had already been examined in the initial investigation.[30]

The FBI notified Congress of their exculpatory findings on November 6, just two days before the presidential election. There was little time for the information that should have exonerated Clinton to circulate through the social media ecosystem.

Sexting by Association

After the election, Clinton's name continued to be associated with sexually improper digital communication. One debunked story that circulated on social media read as follows:

> While the NYPD was conducting a forensic analysis of the Weiner/Abedin laptop, it was discovered that the hard drive contained 350,000 of Hillary Clinton's emails and 344,000 Blackberry communications. . . . Here's what you were never told by the HRC-BHO protective media. These were never reviewed by the FBI investigators assigned to help lead agent Peter Strzok. Nor, was any attempt made to analyze the newly discovered files until after the election was over.[31]

In addition to including many misstatements of fact, the story amplifies Clinton's connection to Peter Strzok. Although the language of the fake news item is not obviously salacious, Trump loyalists would immediately associate sexual impropriety with Strzok's name.

In addition to handling the Clinton email investigation at the FBI, Strzok also worked on investigations of Russian interference in the 2016 election. He made headlines because of his extramarital relationship with former FBI lawyer Lisa Page. They exchanged thousands of messages via their FBI-provided mobile phones, many of which contained erotic language. Some of their messages also "expressed political opinions about candidates and issues involved in the 2016 presidential election, including statements of hostility" toward Donald Trump "and statements of support for" for Hillary Clinton."[32]

For years Trump relished reminding his followers about Strzok's sexting scandal. For example, in 2020 he retweeted a message from Charlie Kirk, cofounder of Turning Point USA.

> Fact: Robert Mueller's office deleted 19,000 text messages between Lisa Page and her lover Peter Strzok How is that not obstruction of justice? What were they trying to cover up? We still don't know.

The tweet included the "thinking face" emoji popular among conspiracy theorists, which Trump had already used in retweets multiple times. Like the tale of the 350,000 unexamined Clinton emails, this story about nineteen thousand deleted text messages was debunked by fact-checking sites.[33] Citing large numbers in the thousands made the post sound authoritative and the danger real. It was true that nineteen thousand messages were not initially logged by the FBI because of technical glitches with their data-collection tool when it tried to access Samsung devices. But the messages were eventually recovered.

Although Clinton was never involved in sexting herself, the connections made between her and Weiner and Strzok damaged her reputation. Her name became associated with scandalous and sexualized digital communication in which erotic exchanges were intermingled with what should have been purely professional matters. This hybridity was obviously inappropriate, and—through guilt by association—it became part of Clinton's public persona, along with her own ill-advised digital behavior.

Digital Literacy and Illiteracy

By intermingling personal and professional communication, Clinton violated an expected boundary. As she explained in her UN news conference, "I opted for convenience to use my personal email account, which was allowed by the State Department, because I thought it would be easier to carry just one device for my work and for my personal emails instead of two."[34]

Reporting by Politico showed that Clinton's one-device/two-accounts explanation was much more plausible than it had initially seemed.[35] Politico analyzed nearly 250 pages of interviews and reports available through the Freedom of Information Act. Despite the depictions of Clinton on Fox News as an adept cybercriminal, it appeared from the Politico coverage that she often hesitated to learn new digital skills. Her attachment to her outdated BlackBerry with a trackball made her even more reluctant to try a second device.[36] Politico also revealed that Clinton struggled to use a desktop computer, an account confirmed by my own interviews with State Department insiders.[37] According to the *Daily Mail*, Clinton was a poor typist as well.[38] It is strange to think that one of the oldest of the new media practices—typing—played a role in the downfall of a twenty-first-century, female, would-be commander in chief.[39]

Of course, typing has reinforced gender segregation even in relatively recent memory.[40] Clinton's resistance to learning a skill associated with feminized labor is understandable. After all, J. C. R. Licklider famously wrote that one "can hardly take a military commander or a corporation president away from his work to teach him to type."[41] In Clinton's aspiration to escape the conventional gender roles of secretary or office girl for life as an executive or commander, she hadn't intended to acquire the basic skills of the office worker.

In her memoir Clinton discussed her tendencies to avoid email and characterized herself as a late adopter. With amusement she described how email was often used as a channel for arranging phone calls or faxes, modes of communication that were much more her style.[42]

Naked Transparency and Feminine Privacy

It might sound reasonable to defend a general right to email privacy. When Stanford law professor and transparency advocate Lawrence Lessig read disparaging remarks made by the Clinton campaign about his own bid for the presidency, he refused to condemn his political detractors or exploit the fact that they had been exposed. "We all deserve privacy. The burdens of public service are insane enough without the perpetual threat that every thought shared with a friend becomes Twitter fodder."[43] Lessig had already come out against what he called the "naked transparency" movement, which he saw not as a force for accountability but one for pushing "any faith in our political system over the cliff."[44] He used the metaphor of nudity as a way to explain the profound feeling of vulnerability created by constant technological exposure.

In Clinton's memoir *What Happened*, written in the aftermath of the 2016 election, she lamented the allure of "any gossipy nugget" in her email data dumps. She also put forward a rationale for privacy grounded in notions of legal and medical privacy much like Lessig's argument for clothing the naked citizen.

Law professor Julie Cohen argues that the "privacy of the home" has served "as a sort of cultural shorthand for a broader privacy interest against exposure" to imagine a space that "affords a freedom of movement that is both literal and metaphorical and that has physical, intellectual, and emotional dimensions." In our homes, "we can move from room to room, we can speak our minds and read whatever interests us, we can pursue intimacy in relationships."[45] Of course, the home also can be a highly gendered environment for enacting feminine domesticity and masculine patriarchal control.[46]

Legal scholar Jeannie Suk posits that "privacy is a woman" in much of the discourse of American technology law. For example, in interpreting *Kyllo v. United States*, a case in which the government used a thermal-imaging device to secure a search warrant for a man growing marijuana inside his house, Suk notes how the logic of penetration and domination might be countered by claims to privacy for a female domestic sphere. In a Supreme Court decision, Justice Antonin Scalia speculated that the heat-sensing device might well disclose intimate information—such as "at what hour each night the lady of the house takes her daily sauna and bath." Suk is struck by the premises of Scalia's example, which draw upon very old tropes, including biblical stories about Bathsheba and David or Susanna and the Elders. She observes that Justice Scalia imagines not just any detail of the home; he imagines a woman, specifically a "lady." In this scenario, "privacy is figured as a woman, an object of the male gaze."[47] As this gaze becomes equipped with more sophisticated snooping devices for tracing, probing, scoping, and spying, it is only the trope of female modesty that constrains its purview.

There are long histories of imagining digital privacy as a feminine trait. For example, in the introduction to Claude Shannon's *The Mathematical Theory of Communication* Warren Weaver compared an "engineering communication theory" to "a very proper and discreet girl accepting your telegram."[48] It may be no accident that the "girl," often associated with secrecy, was such an important metaphor in many of the founding documents written by the pioneers of computer science.[49]

In defending her own personal privacy, Clinton often claimed feminine privilege. For example, she described many of the more than thirty thousand deleted emails as not pertinent to the government's inquiry because they were about her "daughter Chelsea's wedding, her mother Dorothy's funeral, her yoga routines and family vacations"[50] rather than worldly professional matters. All of these items depict Clinton assuming traditional female roles as a caretaker of the home and manager of family rituals of birth, marriage, pilgrimage, and death. Even the mention of yoga routines suggests a feminized activity. These explanations were widely ridiculed by her opponent, his surrogates, conservative news organizations, and internet meme generators in the alt-right community.

What does this confluence of privacy, gender, and technology reveal about the investigation of Hillary Clinton? And why was her use of email so damaging in the court of public opinion?

Multitasking Promiscuity

Critics of visual culture watching the television coverage of Clinton's email scandal on Fox News would have observed a particular pattern. Whenever news anchors discussed her use of emails, the accompanying B-roll showed a montage of images of Clinton on her BlackBerry. Some reporters even spoke in front of screens with these images. The images were not flattering. They generally show Clinton as a multitasker who ignores other people or expresses negative emotional states like irritation or boredom. In one of the most commonly used images on Fox News, her eyes are veiled by sunglasses, and she seems completely withdrawn from her environment.[51] In comparison, President Obama was always much savvier about avoiding the appearance of digital distraction and multitasking with others present.[52]

The association of Clinton's computer practices with impurity was also facilitated by implicit and explicit comparisons with her husband and his

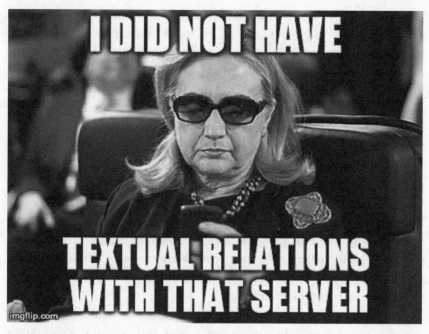

Figure 7.1
"I Did Not Have Textual Relations with that Server" meme, attributed to Charlie-
Physics. Accessed via Imgflip on October 25, 2020, https://i.imgflip.com/qwbeq.jpg.

infidelities. A popular internet meme showed Hillary Clinton's image juxtaposed with typography that read "I did not have textual relations with that
server," which echoed Bill Clinton's famous line to the American people:
"I did not have sexual relations with that woman." The meme (figure 7.1)
suggests that former Secretary Clinton is denying her own digital promiscuity. The fact that the traffic on the Clinton family's servers was intermingled
was also considered suspect for those who continued to propagate conspiracy theories about her husband.[53]

As Wendy Hui Kyong Chun contends in *Freedom and Control*, any puritanical vision of digital privacy ignores the promiscuity of how computers
actually work. For Chun, the dialectic of freedom and control associated
with technology is a false binary that denies the interdependence of
machine-to-machine communication and the fact that information flows
incessantly through public machines.[54]

To conceptualize the barriers between outside and inside, digital scholar
James J. Brown Jr. sees "hospitality" as the heart of digital communication.

The machine must welcome input and allow output with the generosity of a host to a guest. In Brown's analysis, the social contract of such hospitality is construed very generally so as not to require specific invitations. But it also assumes that not all comers should automatically be allowed to pass into the public part of a private dwelling. Brown supposes that the boundary between the home and outside is drawn by "the master of the house," but he grants that such boundary-drawing is a mutual process that involves "the other that arrives" as well.[55]

Transgressive activities like hacking or spreading viruses blur the boundaries of personal computing, according to media theorist Alexander Galloway. For example, the businesslike Transmission Control Protocol "handshake" links sender and receiver in a shared transactional grasp,[56] while the "I Love You" virus in Microsoft Outlook can sow eroticized chaos.[57] According to Galloway, such challenges to the norms of technological communication and conventional gender roles can be read as threatening and a cause for defense of the traditional status quo.[58]

The presence of printers and other peripherals made the existing dynamic around security, transparency, and technological dependence even more problematic for Clinton. Her textual relations with computational media were already fraught. The need to print out documents only made her difficulties with technology worse. As comedian Samantha Bee noted in a humorous routine with Sarah Paulson, "Pls print" was one of Clinton's most common directives.[59]

Masculine Penetration

Like Clinton, Donald J. Trump also asked his staff to print out digital materials for him constantly. According to news accounts, each morning Trump directed his subordinates to produce on paper the top results that came from inputting his name into the search engine for Google News.[60] Clinton and Trump are both senior citizens, so their preference for paper might not be surprising.[61]

Trump's own digital practices also involved a mixture of informational streams. Digital forensics on Donald Trump's Twitter feed during the course of his 2016 candidacy demonstrated that two devices uploaded messages to one account.[62] A Samsung Galaxy produced the angrier tweets that seemed to originate with Trump personally (often outside of business hours), and an Apple iPhone emitted more positive messages that appeared to be written by a more diplomatic PR staffer. Somehow the kind of digital double-face that Trump presented was completely acceptable to his supporters.

Trump made his two-device policy directly relevant to his own enthusiasm for corporate brand shaming after a 2015 attack by a radicalized Muslim married couple in San Bernardino, California. Trump tweeted: "I use both iPhone & Samsung. If Apple doesn't give info to authorities on the terrorists I'll only be using Samsung until they give info." It appears significant that Trump made access to a secure technology something tied to gendered traits in his rhetoric: "Apple won't allow us to get into her cell phone—who do they think they are? No, we have to open it up."[63] In his tweeting Trump addresses a collective "we" with the right to "get into" and "open up" the closed recesses of the proprietary technology that secured the data of the female attacker. Scientist Evelyn Fox Keller observes that learning the hidden secrets of the world is frequently compared to male sexual penetration.[64] In other words, Trump's aggressive approach to digital forensics was a way to assert his masculinity. His inquisitive logic demanded access to both Hillary Clinton's server and to the female attacker's cell phone. This affirmed his dominant position in the gender hierarchy.

As in the case of Suk's *Kyllo v. United States*, Apple's refusal to unlock the shooter's phone connected the concept of privacy back to the rhetoric of maintaining control of space. CEO Tim Cook also used the metaphor of a fortified sanctuary. Heeding Trump's calls to create a single decryption instrument would, for Cook, breech the bastions of personal security. "In the physical world, it would be the equivalent of a master key, capable of opening hundreds of millions of locks—from restaurants and banks to stores and homes. No reasonable person would find that acceptable."[65]

Wendy Hui Kyong Chun agrees that it is risky to desire such "master keys" to complex systems. In *Programmed Visions*, she expresses skepticism that digital forensics is the best way to discover the truth. She reminds us that "our interactions with computers cannot be reduced to the traces we leave behind" because "the exact paths of execution" are ephemeral.[66] In other words, computers are constantly erasing themselves. The electronic signals in their circuits are transitory. All the evidence of Hillary Clinton's emails might never have been shown.

The Double Standard

A few weeks before I interviewed Alec Ross, he had shared a "long, wine-drenched dinner on Lake Como" with Hillary Clinton. Both gender and technology were topics of discussion as they reflected on Clinton's loss in the presidential race. "If it's a woman, it's different." Over the meal, the two agreed that "the fascination with the private lives of individuals" and "the way that people respond" had been deeply gendered in Clinton's case.

During his interview Ross referred to another scandal from the Obama era in which email served as a "political tripwire" that could end a government career. A cyber-stalking investigation that examined the email accounts of top military commanders revealed that a four-star general was having an extramarital affair with his biographer. In addition to his adulterous indiscretion, General David Petraeus was also using a private account rather than his official government email.

Snooping into people's digital private lives "can push people out," Ross said. It can also "push people into more encrypted third-party apps." "People obviously have a lot more email hygiene now than they did then, but I think what that probably produces is a lot more secrecy." He pointed to how Jared Kushner, Trump's son-in-law and advisor, communicated in his official capacity and to the secretive behavior of others in Trump's orbit. "They do so with zero traceability," he complained. After Clinton's travails, "people become much more circumspect."

Evidence that Trump's daughter and son-in-law were using private email and WhatsApp encrypted text messages led to few consequences.[67] Despite White House policy, Kushner received no sanctions. After the story of his digital indiscretions broke in the media, he continued to privately talk and text with Mohammed bin Salman, who was also known to favor WhatsApp, even after the Saudi Arabian prince was linked to the murder of a prominent journalist who was a US resident.[68]

Email in the Public Memory of the Future

On September 12, 2019, Hillary Clinton spent an hour in an art installation at the Venice Biennale. The exhibit was intended to be "somewhere between a library, a theatre stage and an embassy."[69] According to the artist's statement, "the language of digital bureaucracy" would be "transformed" as the audience experienced his artwork. The exhibition consisted of sixty-two thousand printed pages of Hillary Clinton's emails connected to the clintonemail.com domain years earlier. It was difficult to decipher Clinton's expression as she turned the pages. She sat behind an exact replica of the famed Resolute Desk in the White House Oval Office, pondering an artwork about why she wasn't sitting behind the real one. The artist had described the emails—perhaps sarcastically—as "the most important documents of our time."

In Clinton's memoir she imagines a history class taught thirty years in the future, in which young people have to be told about a time in which email was once considered important. In the lesson the students are astonished to learn that there was once a "primitive form of electronic communication that used to be all the rage."[70]

Hillary Clinton was certainly a flawed candidate when it came to digital policy and computational practice. She declared the internet to be "the public space of the twenty-first century" and yet refused to post her own speeches on her own website. She hectored State Department employees about cybersecurity in official videos and yet ducked responsibility for basic data preservation.

However, acknowledging her limitations—if not outright hypocrisy—in matching her practices to her principles does not discount the harm of paternalistic digital purity myths. These myths establish unrealistic standards that disproportionately punish online conduct marked as feminine or behavior associated with women's digital identities. It is striking that Fox News claimed that Clinton's email server was located in a "restroom"[71] and urged her to "look into the mirror."[72] Making such references to a bathroom as a shameful separate sphere and commanding Clinton to occupy a site of reflection and penitence was clearly intended to be harsh chastisement for her perceived digital transgressions. Other news organizations described closets or basements as sites of Clinton's covert server in her New York home but avoided associating her digital incrimination with biological humiliation or filth.

Digital purity is a strange amalgam of the fantasies of digital transparency and those of digital security, and it is easier for women to have such purity tainted. Moreover, male users tend to benefit from unfounded assumptions that they always have better digital skills.[73] From his position of perceived dominance, Trump also exploited a social media ecosystem that targeted, harassed, and silenced women.[74] Furthermore, Trump's acquisition of online literacy was aided by a huge cadre of supportive followers who helped him refine his social media style, amplified his messages, and trolled his critics. Despite the presence of large, feminist-friendly Facebook groups like Pantsuit Nation, Clinton faced a deep disadvantage when it came to the new digital politics. Her staffers watched helplessly as she was pummeled online, unable to make her own messages about connection, transparency, participation, or access stick. As the next chapter will show, decisions by social media companies and new interface features also aided in Trump's rise to power.

8 Trump's Rhetoric of Connection

Peter Costanzo had precisely seven minutes on Donald Trump's calendar to explain social media to a man in his sixties who did not use a computer. Not ten. Not five. Seven.

"I just remember having my laptop in front of him and just showing him Facebook," Costanzo said in an interview for this book.

In 2009 Costanzo had considered himself to be one of only a handful of digitally savvy book publicists working in Manhattan. He had cultivated relationships with a new generation of online retailers and social media companies that had begun to reshape the entire business model of publishing. Using behavioral data, it had suddenly become possible to "fish where the fish are," which was a huge boon to an industry averse to risk. Costanzo was employed by the parent company of Vanguard Press, which was scheduled to publish Trump's latest business advice book, *Think Like a Champion*.[1]

Costanzo pointed to a column written by *New York Times* tech writer David Pogue in early 2009 as Twitter's breakout moment in this new form of marketing. Although Pogue supplied a list of "rules" to help people get started as users of the platform, he insisted that Twitter could still be anything to anyone.[2] Significantly, Pogue included screenshots from Twitter documenting the Obama inauguration and statistics about Obama's 254,484 followers on the platform.

Costanzo was convinced that a social media campaign would be a fantastic way to promote Trump's book. He also believed that this advertising plan would require the participation of the man himself—rather than just the Trump Organization—in order to have the requisite authenticity to be popular online. To make this pitch to Trump, Costanzo had seven minutes.

One of the factors working in Costanzo's favor was the fact that Trump's identity had already been appropriated by an online impostor. The fake Trump was drawing thousands of Trump's potential fans to counterfeit Twitter and Facebook accounts. Although news stories have sometimes described these as "parody" posts,[3] Costanzo said that the pseudo-Trump didn't seem to have any satiric intent. Instead, the pretense probably grew out of admiration rather than of mockery. "He was putting posts up the day after a new *Apprentice* episode would air, and it was not malicious. I don't think to this day anybody knows who it was."

In the meeting with Trump, which actually lasted fifteen or twenty minutes, Costanzo easily got the real estate developer's attention with the examples he had loaded onto his laptop. He showed accounts from other celebrities Trump might know who were using social media to promote their personal brands.

But it was the existence of the fake Trump that was the key to closing the deal. "I was showing him the impostor, what the impostor was doing, and I told him that I had already reached out to Facebook. I alerted them that if he was definitely willing to do this that I could have this remedied. They would switch the two-hundred thousand followers to his new Facebook page automatically. Those fans would have no idea that there was this actual change."

Facebook's willingness to give those two-hundred thousand unearned followers to Trump was an extraordinary windfall for his social media ambitions. It is important to remember that this was a relatively prestigious follower count at the time; scrambles among celebrities to top the million mark were not yet underway. This handover was one of the truly extraordinary pieces of luck from which Trump benefited to stage his internet breakout.

Trump did not have it as easy with Twitter. He had to build a following from scratch. Apparently, Costanzo didn't have the same kind of connections to insiders at Twitter. This was long before the company introduced its verification checkmark program. To solve the brand confusion problem, Costanzo suggested "@realDonaldTrump" as a way to distinguish the famous developer's messages from his bogus alter-ego.

An agreement was reached in which the Trump Organization would approve generic announcement tweets that Costanzo wrote before they went live, but more personal tweets—such as a thank you or birthday wishes—had to be vetted by Trump himself.

Trump/Costanzo's very first tweet in 2009 was written from an odd third-person perspective. It also focused on television spectatorship rather than engagement with online fans. "Be sure to tune in and watch Donald Trump on Late Night with David Letterman as he presents the Top Ten List tonight!" Presumably this impersonal tweet did not require Trump's individual stamp of approval.

Costanzo was a relatively conservative custodian of the Trump account.

"I was very cautious with retweeting because I remembered reading about people getting themselves into a bit of hot water, because at the time Twitter was so new you still didn't really know who the source was and who it wasn't." Mostly Costanzo tweeted announcements about appearances or quotations attributed to Trump. Sometimes there were contests. The winner might be promised a keychain and a signed copy of *Think Like a Champion*. Because the Trump Organization encompassed so many different ventures at the time, including Trump University and a chain of golf courses, Costanzo's tweeting often extended beyond what might strictly be deemed book publicity.

Whatever the message, Costanzo kept it consistent and neutral. Costanzo was seen as so inoffensive and amiable that the Trump Organization kept him listed as the backup administrator for years. He continued to receive Twitter and Facebook notices long after he had moved on from working with Vanguard's authors.

After about six months of "being very happy with the results and happy with me frankly," Trump's entourage asked Costanzo the next logical question: "What do we do next?" Costanzo had an answer ready: "YouTube is another platform that's really growing and getting a lot of attention, particularly with young people. . . . I'd love to sit down and interview Mr. Trump for about twenty minutes, so we can create a two-minute video to promote the book on YouTube. We'll get it on Barnes & Noble's site and Amazon." His proposition was accepted.

The video recording of Trump by Costanzo for YouTube was arranged at Trump Tower with a very small crew. "He came extremely prepared. He really answered the questions in a way that you would want someone who's trying to sell a product to do." As Costanzo described him, Trump was an experienced salesperson. To promote his particular gospel of wealth, he was apparently very good at staying on message. In this case, he focused on the specific appeal of spending money to buy the book in order to make more money.

Costanzo described Trump as "very cordial," "very polite," and "very pleasant" in their interactions. One memory stood out among the pleasantries. Costanzo asked about President Obama: "And he actually had kind words. He said, 'So he seems like a very nice man, nice family man. But I really hope he can fix the economy. Oh, but if he doesn't fix the economy, I'm thinking of running for president.'"[4]

The Formative Period

For most of Barack Obama's first term, Donald Trump expressed very few personal opinions on the internet. His minimal efforts at self-expression were focused on NBC as a broadcast network. He wanted to earn top ratings for starring in *The Apprentice* and saw social media as a means to that end. His reality TV show also served as a vehicle for rebuilding the national reputation Trump had once enjoyed during the 1980s and '90s, a time when shows like *Lifestyles of the Rich and Famous* and magazines like *People* had celebrated Trump and other members of the moneyed classes. During that period Trump-related content also saturated tabloid newspapers, which were highly visible on American supermarket shelves. According to media scholar Geoffrey Baym, the tabloid media of the '80s and '90s served up more than just "sex and scandal" because their gossip-laden pages also "engaged in largely overlooked acts of political storytelling, constructing and politicizing the Trump character."[5]

Trump must have been motivated by money as well as ego. Financial reporting revealed *The Apprentice* to be much more profitable as an income stream than much of his real estate portfolio. With his unstable finances and investments in risky ventures, Trump's personal brand was his most valuable asset.[6]

The Apprentice was a show in which workplaces were depicted as places with extremely little bureaucracy to navigate and very few rules. It was a very different world from the one at the White House, which stressed compliance with government regulations and posted lengthy digital forms for job applicants. In Trump's free-wheeling enterprise, things could be extremely unpredictable. *The Apprentice* allowed Trump to arbitrarily single out contestants to be castigated as they competed for the "ultimate job interview." Dramatic scenes with on-the-job harassment or hostile work environments only boosted the ratings.

Logically, the launch of Trump's successor show *Celebrity Apprentice* in 2008 should have required even greater investments in social media. Contestants who appeared on the show were public figures. Many already had established brands to promote or were being coached to use social media to amplify their fame. Trump's children also regularly appeared in the show, so the family's reputation network would have benefited from further enhancement on the internet. But even with Costanzo's help, it still took a while for Trump to prioritize online influencing. Eventually, he began to channel his aspirations into political ambition by capitalizing on existing antipathies to Obama as a way to build his audience.

The writer Matt Porter has surmised that Trump's personal interest in the Twitter platform remained dormant up until it was roused by Obama's 2011 Twitter Town Hall. As a consequential moment in the history of political disintermediation, this town hall spectacle captured a particular sector of the public imagination at the time. Porter argues that Trump's "first real tweet" was on July 6, 2011.[7] It was a message with capitalized "shouting" focused on solidifying opposition to the Democratic president: "Congress is back. TIME TO CUT, CAP AND BALANCE. There is no revenue problem. The Debt Limit cannot be raised until Obama spending is contained." The next day @realDonaldTrump posted a message that reiterated his "CUT, CAP AND BALANCE" slogan and specifically called out the president with his @BarackObama Twitter username.

Porter makes a compelling case about Trump's motivation. It makes sense in light of how Obama's embrace of social media inspired his competitors to pursue similar strategies. However, I would argue that Trump first exerted control over his Twitter account months earlier when the main activity of his feed suddenly veered away from promoting upcoming media appearances and fan contests. By 2011 Trump had clearly become interested in exploring other ways to defend his reputation digitally. He had figured out that social media could give him a way to respond to journalists doing investigations and to retaliate against celebrities who snubbed him with dismissive comments. One of his strategies was to upload videos to YouTube of his oral rebuttals to his perceived enemies and then tweet the links to the videos. For example, in March of 2011 he confronted an unnamed antagonist to air grievances about news coverage. Embarrassing stories had highlighted Trump's paltry charitable giving and his bizarre hospitality to Libyan despot Mu'ammar Al-Qadhdhāfī. Trump's callout seemed to be

directed at Pulitzer Prize-winning *Washington Post* reporter David Fahrenthold, although, at least in the remaining traces of the exchange, he never
names Fahrenthold directly.

It is difficult to pinpoint the precise references in these online grudge
matches now that almost all of the response videos in the "From the Desk
of Donald Trump" YouTube playlist are marked private. However, by watching the few videos in the series that remained public after the election, critical readers could infer that Trump used a confrontational stance that was
consistent with his role as a gruff and stern TV personality. In one of these
performances, he appears full of bluster to express his deep offense at the
treatment of then-presidential candidate Herman Cain. Trump clearly identified with Cain as a fellow Republican who similarly traded on his political
identity as an outsider, businessmen, and successful capitalist.

A reconstruction of Trump's Fahrenthold response video by Factbase,
which also reconstituted dozens of his other YouTube videos,[8] shows a similarly combative style. In an explanatory caption for its "From the Desk of
Donald Trump" collection, Factbase describes the scope of its project.

> Donald Trump maintained a video log (Vlog) on The Trump Organization's You-
> Tube channel from February, 2011 through 2014. Prior to the election, nearly
> all were deleted or made private. There were 108 of these entries that we could
> locate, spanning 2 hours, 46 minutes and 29,941 words. Of these, six are still
> available on the Trump Organization's YouTube channel. We located the video
> for 99 of the 108 in total, and located transcripts of an additional six.[9]

The recovered videos cover topics ranging from California freeways to
industrial outsourcing to Japan. Trump is usually shot from above in an
expressive close-up.

The reconstructed copy of Trump's anti-Fahrenthold video opens with
him alluding vaguely to a "great amount of comment" about his interactions with Al-Qadhdhāfī rather than referencing any specific reporting.[10]
Near the midway point of the short video Trump alleges that "a lot of the
comment was very positive," because Trump supposedly took advantage of
Al-Qadhdhāfī and then gave the spoils of his business conquest to charity.
Near the one-minute mark, as he begins to wrap up, Trump insists that "I'm
sort of good at that stuff; I'd like to be good at this stuff for this country."

Trump's decision to take up video blogging on YouTube in 2011 was
probably influenced by his earlier experiences with Costanzo. Using it com-
batively was almost certainly connected to changes in his online strategy

that coincided with new staffing on his social media team. In February of that year, he hired twenty-four-year-old Justin McConney as his director of social media. McConney had a fundamentally different attitude about engagement in online spaces from traditional publicists like Costanzo. It was perhaps no coincidence that emoji-marked retweets began to appear in the Trump feed shortly after McConney was hired. Trump's tweets were no longer being filtered out by a professional trained in more conventional media industries.

McConney collaborated much more closely with Trump, and he seems to have encouraged more reality-show-style rivalries as well.[11] In the beginning of Trump's Twitter experimentation phase, the @ sign was more often used as a literal "at" to indicate a time or place. During the pre-McConney period, Trump's account posted only a few tweets mentioning others' Twitter usernames. For example, a few months into operation, @realDonaldTrump pointed out the existence of daughter @IvankaTrump's account and encouraged his followers to follow her as well. These early tweets under Costanzo generally didn't try to bring attention to or get attention from other accounts on Twitter. In contrast, McConney saw the value of signaling two-way engagement with other voices and facilitating the appearance of public dialogue, even if these exchanges were usually staged very theatrically as one-sided blasts.

The strictly benevolent tone Costanzo had crafted in 2009 and 2010 was abandoned during the beginning of McConney's tenure. Tweets began to present Trump as a verbal sparring partner. At first, the "mentions" in his tweets seemed like good-natured joshing: "Hey @SnoopDogg @ItstheSituation @SethMacFarlane: Oh, I'm real scared. #TrumpRoast airs tonight at 10:30/9:30 on @Comedy Central." But as his feuds with the media and liberal politicians escalated, this superficial decorum disappeared. Trump's instigation also became laced with profanity, including words like "bullshit" and "damn." Some of these swear words came from retweeted content, but some came from Trump himself. As McConney tolerated more unfiltered language on Trump's feed, Trump's follower counts grew.

Earlier in the process of his experiments with connectivity, Trump had been reluctant to seem too personally invested in direct forms of composition. He wanted to project the image of a busy corporate leader who delegated menial digital labor to underlings. For example, in 2011 Trump bragged that he chose to "dictate" his tweets to a female "executive assistant." However, it was difficult to preserve the aloofness of the managerial class when Trump embraced "live tweeting" televised events in 2012.

It began relatively innocuously with Trump's announcement that he would be live tweeting *Celebrity Apprentice*. For the episode "Blown Away," Trump posed questions that invited audience participation like, "Aubrey has a lot of self confidence—but will it be warranted?" Often these questions were clearly teasers designed to amplify suspense, such as "How will the client react? They've got both Elle Magazine and Chi to please."

The tone of this early live-tweeting experience seemed to have been established by a publicist rather than by Trump himself. Furthermore, the "Blown Away" episode had already been recorded, and Trump had been a participant. Therefore, describing this stunt as a supposedly unscripted "live" event appeared ludicrous, given its lack of spontaneity. However, Trump seemed to want to create a name for himself as a real-time virtuoso, perhaps to build a reputation for speed and agility in online verbal combat.

Five months later he announced his plan to live tweet the town-hall-style debate between President Obama and Republican challenger Mitt Romney, and after live tweeting the event, Trump was clearly eager to do more. Over the course of the next four years, he formally scheduled to live tweet over a dozen television shows—ranging from political events to awards shows—right up until the inauguration. This included the debate involving his own vice-presidential nominee Mike Pence. Informally, he was live tweeting television much more often, especially broadcasts of his beloved Fox News. Each time he saw a salient nugget of information on his television screen, he leaped into action with commentary on Twitter.

Media scholar Richard Grusin has discussed how Trump's television live tweeting continued into the Oval Office. It became a highly effective way to dominate the news cycle; stations scrambled to cover the president's cascade of outrageous tweets.

> Indeed in many cases Trump's twitter feed is doing little more than live-tweeting his television viewing. But such tweets work to replicate themselves through a cascade of remediations in a kind of algal bloom in the media lagoon.

Grusin was dismayed by the incessant Fox-News-Trump-Twitter churn, in which Trump retweeted Fox broadcasts and then Fox broadcasted his tweets. Once these cycles began, alternative perspectives were choked out. Other social media accounts connected to Trump could amplify this recursiveness, either by circulating Trump's tweet of Fox or Fox's coverage of Trump's tweet.

> His live-tweeting, like all his tweets, is remediated by other social media users through retweets, mentions, favorites and shares, then remediated again by formal and informal media—blogs and other print, televisual, and networked news (and fake news) outlets. The end result of this process is that Trump uses 140-word character Tweets to redevelop media neighborhoods under his name and crowd out other competitors for as many news cycles as he can control.[12]

According to Grusin, Trump optimized the algorithmic processes that were inherent in digital information ecosystems to multiply his messages and pollute the entire news space.

As Newt Gingrich pointed out in *Understanding Trump*, the 2016 Republican candidate "decided to use Facebook and Twitter as his main vehicles for media outreach." He "then trained the media to cover his tweets, and suddenly he was getting millions in earned coverage at no cost."[13] The language about "training" is indicative because it positions Trump as a media master capable of domesticating and instructing others.

But how can we understand Trump's own period of training before the campaign began? How did he develop the digital literacy that allowed him to dominate the existing media ecology and ultimately win the election against seemingly long odds, given his lack of political experience and his limited access to expensive resources for outreach, electioneering, advertising, and analytics? In other words, how do we understand the ways that the host of *The Apprentice* completed his own apprenticeship in learning successful social media practices?

The Callout Candidate

Digital media scholars Jean Burgess and Nancy Baym have told Twitter's coming-of-age story by examining specific stages in the site's development.[14] Their book, *Twitter: A Biography*, focuses on the advent of three specific design affordances: the mention, the hashtag, and the retweet. Burgess and Baym treat the addition of each of these features as life events in the platform's progression toward maturity.

The "@" convention that allowed people to "mention" other usernames and be notified if their own usernames were mentioned was the first—and in many ways the most important—innovation. It made Twitter a medium for conversation. It was essential for creating, maintaining, and enlivening connections among users. In a platform designed initially "to announce rather than to converse," it reflected users' needs to recognize "in order to socialize."[15] When users began retweeting others' messages, two essential tasks could be accomplished: "quoting people accurately" and giving them "credit for their words."[16]

The three milestones of Burgess and Baym's analysis can also be applied to the development of Donald Trump as a Twitter user. However, his progress was more erratic than the gradual story of the platform's development that they describe. Trump's mastery of social media reflected important trends as new design features were incorporated, and he built political influence by exploiting these new modes of connection.

The "mention" was critical to his growing social media confidence under McConney's guidance. Trump employed the "@" symbol to malign both people and corporations. Sometimes he accosted brands for political reasons, invoking "tough on crime" or national security rhetoric. However, his corporate callouts also reflected his promotional deals, personal investments, and pitches as an advertising spokesperson. In addition, just as regular citizens express dissatisfaction with products and services online, Trump initiated callouts based on the idiosyncrasies of his own individual consumer preferences, brand loyalties, and personal experiences. For example, personal pet peeves seemed to be behind his frequent strikes against @TMobile.

By the time Trump had gravitated to the center of the "birther" controversy, he had refined his callout technique to combine appeals to connection with appeals for transparency. "Birthers" like Trump questioned the legitimacy of Barack Obama's presidency by claiming that he was born outside of the United States in Kenya and was thus ineligible to hold the nation's highest office. When Obama produced a birth document that contradicted these claims, Trump tagged @BarackObama to declare it a "fake" and a "fraud."

With 729 references to the @BarackObama handle on his Twitter profile, it appears that hailing Obama became an established routine in Trump's online repertoire. Fourteen times he even called to a nonexistent @Obama, as he was learning how to use the mentions feature correctly. He usually omitted the honorifics of the presidency. Trump only used @POTUS six times—in four anti-Obama retweets and in two tweets that repurposed negative statements Obama had made about Hillary Clinton in the past. In looking at the early tweets directed at Obama, it is also worth pointing out that Obama wasn't Trump's only political Twitter nemesis. Republican leaders like former Speaker of the House John Boehner were also targets for refining his technique.

Trump used hashtags relatively sparingly in comparison to his much freer use of mentions and retweets. For example, in 2011 there were two main hashtags in Trump's feed: "#trumpvlog" for his vlogging activities on YouTube and "#TimeToGetTough" for *Time to Get Tough*, his first book about politics and economic policy. Neither hashtag was really designed to encourage conversation with other Twitter users; they merely promoted his personal brands. Obviously, the #MAGA hashtag for his "Make America Great Again" slogan appeared in his Twitter stream hundreds of times, but he didn't become a regular hashtag user until he began working with more experienced social media handlers during the 2016 campaign.

Elsewhere, I have argued that "a hashtag can assure people that they are connected to other people" because it "affirms that a communication channel is open, that being heard is possible, and that an interdependent web of social ties between equally viable nodes can be made visible for navigational purposes when necessary."[17] In this way, a hashtag "promises that the preconditions for amplifying a collective signal have come into existence."[18] During his formative period as a Twitter user, Trump appeared to be less interested in using hashtags as an open channel for collective communication and more interested in using individual mentions and retweets as a way to engage one-on-one with influencers and elites.

Trump's adoption of the retweet was noticeably perverse. He began his career as a manual retweeter, copying and pasting text into quotation marks rather than using the convenient retweet button provided by the platform. Journalists noticed that Trump's idiosyncratic technique defeated the entire point of the retweet feature, which was intended to promote accuracy and attribution in using the words of others.[19] A *Washington Post* reporter remarked on the fact that "Trump either deletes or forgets to close the quotation marks around the quoted tweet, blurring the line between his commentary and that of someone else."[20] His distinctive style of retweeting got him in trouble when he manually retweeted and then deleted a tweet mocking residents of Iowa in 2015.[21] Trump blamed the retweet on an anonymous intern, which seemed a dubious claim, given that it was a manual retweet like the ones that he had personally authored. Shortly after this incident manual retweets stopped appearing on the @realDonaldTrump account.

Once Trump demonstrated mastery of the retweet button, the Trump account began retweeting even more content that Trump would later disavow. His cavalier approach to retweeting not-so-subtle messages from militias or white supremacists could be justified by denying ill intent. Trump claimed to be innocent even when the usernames he retweeted should have raised red flags. For example, he retweeted content from "@Ilduce2016" and "@WhiteGenocideTM." Trump's denial of responsibility extended to face-to-face interactions. A vulgar "pussy" insult directed at a supposedly weaker Republican opponent was justified as being "like a retweet," merely echoing the sentiments of others.

As president, Trump's retweeting verged into the absurd. From 2016 to 2020 @realDonaldTrump retweeted @realDonaldTrump almost a thousand times, producing a literal echo chamber on his timeline. Near the end of his presidency, he added "So true!" to a retweet of his own tweet that read, "THE SILENT MAJORITY IS STRONGER THAN EVER!!!"[22] (The phrase "silent majority," which was popularized by Richard Nixon, was one of Trump's favorites.) This was at least the fourth time that Trump had added "So true!" to one of his self-retweets that year.

Is a Picture Worth a Hundred and Forty Characters?

To understand Trump's rise to internet prominence, it is useful to examine one additional design feature: the emoji. Emojis are small digital images used to express emotions or ideas that can be added to a social media post or text message. When emojis became standardized after the launch of Unicode 6.0 in 2010, they became a powerful way to enhance text with symbols. Emojis might vary in their appearance, depending on the device, and they also might vary in meaning, depending on the cultural context. But this pictographic language has been useful for many rhetorical purposes.

For example, six months into the Trump presidency, Fox News personality Stuart Varney exuberantly praised the performance of the stock market on television, claiming that four trillion dollars of wealth had been created thanks to optimism about the new Republican administration. That same day, Varney tweeted the TV clip along with the message, "STU'S TAKE:

Figure 8.1
Original Stuart Varney tweet and @realDonaldTrump version with emojis.

'Six months in, it's the hope of growth that's making America $4 trillion richer.'"[23] When @realDonaldTrump tweeted its own, more generously capitalized adaptation of Varney's message the next day, the tweet included an American flag emoji, a moneybag emoji, a positive chart emoji, and a projector emoji (figure 8.1).[24]

This strategy of adding emojis raises some basic questions about the state of presidential rhetoric today. Why did emojis turn out to be significant for the Trump administration, and how did they come to be a normal part of today's political discourse, even for a relatively dry topic like fiscal policy? What do these digital symbols say about economies of writing, particularly when attention might be in short supply? What do they reveal about the investment of emotional labor in social media? And why has traditional media largely ignored the existence of Trump's emoji tweets?

Networks devoted hours of cable news coverage to Trump's rhetorical performances on Twitter, and yet these stations were strangely silent about his use of emojis. News analysts and pundits mocked Trump's misspellings of common words or his overuse of capitalization, but the presence of non-alphabetic characters in his tweets generally went without comment.

For example, during the week leading up to the 2018 midterm election, Donald Trump tweeted the US flag emoji thirteen times. Yet somehow messages like "THANK YOU FLORIDA! Get out and VOTE Republican! #MAGA 🇺🇸" were almost never shown in news stories about his Twitter feed. This gave the public an incomplete picture of his digital practices if they didn't follow Trump on social media themselves.

In November 2019, the *New York Times* devoted a huge headline story in its Sunday edition to "THE TWITTER PRESIDENCY." Using investigative journalism and data visualization, the story asserted that Trump's social media consumption habits had been shaped by narrow circles that made the president subject to "conspiracy-mongers, extremists, and spies."[25] This special coverage—which also made no mention of emojis—argued that the intensity, periodicity, and powerful negative or positive affect in Trump's twitter behaviors had strengthened over time.

By focusing on the subset of cases in which Trump deployed emojis, it might be possible to understand more about how he developed his digital literacy and the ways that his campaign and presidency exploited the design features of social media platforms. After all, many social media users have found that emojis perform important rhetorical work in condensed, discursive spaces like Twitter. As technology scholar Jason Farman has argued, texting is a medium that requires interpretation and the decoding of patterns.[26] Emojis make this interpretive labor simpler and quicker.

Furthermore, the number and frequency of emojis provides a measure of public sentiment. Because there are fewer emojis than words, companies can more easily use the data analytics from emojis to identify potential emotional appeals, exploit private information, map social networks, and target advertising. Emojis also stand out easily when users are scrolling rapidly through long social media streams.

The one time Fox News covered the presence of emojis in tweets by the Trump administration, it focused on a nonsensical tweet from the three-year-old son of White House press secretary Sarah Huckabee Sanders. The child had apparently enjoyed fiddling with the emojis for traffic lights, Easter Island heads, world maps, and Disney castles. His mother used the hashtag #neverleaveyourphoneunlocked to explain the sudden onslaught of emojis in her feed.[27]

Nonetheless, the use of pictures and text together in short-form, online political communication was a serious concern for Trump strategists. And their use of emojis in social media raised important issues about regulating social media, platform governance, and free speech.

From Verbal to Nonverbal Language

Trump was essentially using emojis even before they appeared on his feed because he was already using short verbal versions of these visual symbols. This pattern can be seen during Trump's breakthrough period on Twitter from 2012 to 2014, when he began to gain followers rapidly by sowing doubt about Obama's birthright citizenship. Certainly, there were long-winded messages with conspiracy theories or narcissistic rants that extended to the boundaries of the Twitter text limit, which was 140 characters at the time. In contrast, many of Trump's messages directed to specific followers were remarkably concise.

For example, on a representative day during this period, Trump woke up and tweeted at @karlrove six times, complaining about Rove's attacks on the actor Ashley Judd. Trump wrote nineteen more tweets that morning. Two were inspirational quotations (one from himself and one from Samuel Goldwyn). The remaining tweets could be categorized as extremely brief correspondence with those who had tried to get his attention on Twitter. Trump rewarded these users by writing monosyllabic sentiments like "thanks," "good," "good luck," "good idea," and "it's about time" and mentioning their handles in his tweets so that his bursts of polite acknowledgment were directed appropriately to specific users. About half these messages to fans were generic messages of thanks.[28]

Although these posts got almost no "likes" or "retweets," they were remarkably efficient in building social capital as one-off messages of regard. They also functioned much like emojis. "Good" could be replaced by the okay sign emoji or "good idea" by the thumbs-up emoji. Trump—or one of his staffers—already understood the necessity of performing routine affective labor to attend to the feelings of his followers and to maintain basic cohesion in the group. This required condensed but unambiguous quick responses.

Under McConney's tutelage, emojis began to appear in the @realDonaldTrump feed as Trump cultivated a less stuffy persona. On February 28, 2013, Trump retweeted an admiring comment from @Candynecklace2 that included a face-blowing-a-kiss emoji and a heart emoji. The tweet came from his personal Android phone. On March 2 he used emojis again to another admirer with a female username, and again he used his Android device. After @NicoleWallace04 complained about a lack of responses to her messages with a tearful face and broken heart emoji, Trump retweeted her message—complete with its emojis—and added an assurance of "Not anymore Nicole, thanks." All of these early emoji exchanges were clearly staged as playful heterosexual flirtations.

On April 19, 2013, Trump retweeted an ego-affirming thumbs-up "the man is the man" message from @_ayooPRINCESS and replied with his own "So true!" On May 20, he copied and pasted a blue heart emoji message from @lisaloren11 describing "laughter and tears of joy" derived from watching his reality show, and on May 25 he similarly validated a pink heart emoji message from @FashionistaBtch. On July 31 Trump documented how @anniehepburn described him as a "role model" with the heart emoji, and on August 1 he encouraged a member of the *Real Housewives* reality show to "keep her chin up," as he reiterated elements from @sabrinarose2012's message, which was ornamented with two hearts and a star. In all of these cases the repetition of his fans' emojis showed Trump participating in highly gendered digital exchanges with his female devotees who had displayed their adulation with emotional symbols.

As a commercial salesman exploiting his fame as a public figure, Trump was also learning to retweet testimonial messages with emojis that were intended to enhance the reputation of Trump-branded products. For example, various emojis were present in endorsement retweets about Trump hotels, Trump clothing and accessories, and Trump's own motivational books. Use of the thumbs-up emoji or the okay emoji communicated his approval and signified affirmation of the ostentatious lifestyle that Trump promoted and his male followers desired to emulate. These exchanges did not involve the heart emoji.

Collaborative Literacies

Specialists in composition argue that writing is a collaborative activity, never a product generated by a lone individual genius in isolation. Despite Trump's language in which he casts himself as a great man of history, the story of his developing Twitter literacy reveals jointly constructed sentiments and borrowed textual practices. His claim to be the "Ernest Hemingway of a hundred and forty characters"[29] was true to the extent that his model for twentieth-century prose was perpetually intertextually entangled with others. As a writer, Trump was fundamentally reactive, as perhaps we all are. For him, writing was a defense mechanism.

When Trump tweeted from a mobile device for the first time in 2013, without the assistance of intermediaries, it was a response to words uttered in a television show: "Thanks @SherriEShepherd 4 your nice comments today on The View. U were terrific!" He posted the message, which incorporated youthful text messaging abbreviations, a few hours after airtime. This delay in Trump tweeting about a TV show was not uncommon. What was surprising about this posting, according to McConney, was that it was posted without McConney's assistance or help from anyone else on Trump's staff. "The moment I found out Trump could tweet himself was comparable to the moment in 'Jurassic Park' when Dr. Grant realized that velociraptors could open doors," McConney recalled in an interview. "I was like, 'Oh no.'"[30] After leaving the Trump team, McConney went on to manage the social media presence of the rock band Aerosmith and posted images of their concerts on Instagram.

Although McConney stayed on as social media director of the corporate organization until 2017, Trump began to consult another youthful social media expert in 2013, soon after he'd started tweeting directly from his personal phone. Former golf course caddy Dan Scavino had drawn Trump's attention with his sycophantic posts, and Trump had begun praising Scavino effusively while mentioning his Twitter handle. This all happened just a few months after McConney realized that his dual role as gatekeeper and enabler had become obsolete. Scavino served as director of social media for the Trump campaign and then for the administration. He was profiled by the *New York Times* as "the man behind the president's tweets,"[31] and he was named as an accused alongside the president in lawsuits involving the blocking of critics on Trump's account. Scavino helped energize "Keyboard Warriors" to flood social media channels with pro-Trump content. "Thank you to all of my great Keyboard Warriors," Trump tweeted at one point. "You are better, and far more brilliant, than anyone on Madison Avenue (Ad Agencies)."

Scavino was an enthusiastic emoji user. He even included the American flag emoji in his Twitter handle. To emphasize the fierceness of his patriotism in the final days of the Trump presidency, Scavino added an eagle emoji to the flag emoji. Scavino also telegraphed his loyalty to Trump by using the 100 emoji frequently in his tweets.

Unlike more rigid emoji users who relied on the old 2010 Unicode lexicon of symbols, Scavino often inserted novel emojis into his existing repertoire. For example, in a December 2018 visit to Ramstein Air Base in Germany, Scavino included the selfie emoji when he posted pictures of service people shooting selfies with the president. This tweet was promptly retweeted by @realDonaldTrump.

As collaborative tweet-writing between Trump and White House staff became an established practice, proximity to the president could be measured by influence on his composition process. Some took umbrage when Trump's personal assistant Madeleine Westerhout tried "to weigh in on drafting Mr. Trump's tweets."[32] Some admired how White House communications director Hope Hicks would "supply the choicest put-downs" with "absolute daggers."[33]

Polarizing Affects

Trump researchers observed two distinct Jekyll and Hyde personalities on the @realDonaldTrump feed. During the campaign Trump appeared to write tweets outside of business hours on a personal Android device where he could express himself without interference using a distinct vocabulary of negative words ("badly," "crazy," "weak," etc.).[34] In contrast, his handlers produced "announcement" tweets that integrated links and pictures into positive messages. The announcement tweets incorporated emojis as well, perhaps to project the hyperbolic personality of Trump as a chief executive or to reflect the strong emotions of his political base. Providing some macroanalysis of Trump's patterns of everyday Twitter use, data visualizations showed chronological trends among his tens of thousands of tweets. For example, as election day approached it appeared that he was persuaded to tweet less from his personal device and to engage in less retweeting.[35]

As the 2016 election unfolded, a strong correlation began to appear between mentions of @realDonaldTrump and the use of emojis. Messages on Twitter about the race that included emojis were far more likely to mention Trump than his challengers. According to the *Washington Post*, there were 1.3 million "illustrated tweets" about Trump, compared to 501,000 about Bernie Sanders and 122,000 about Hillary Clinton, which the *Post* attributed to her "comparatively older following."[36] The story was accompanied by an emoji cloud created by Zignal Labs that showed emojis associated with pro-Trump memes like Pepe the Frog, as well as the locomotive emoji that signified the "Trump train," which was tweeted at Trump almost a quarter million times.

Zignal labs monitored emoji reactions during the Democratic National Convention.[37] While Clinton's acceptance speech was being broadcast, her supporters tweeted hearts in various colors, as well as fist bumps, high fives, thumbs-up, and other gestures of positive regard. In contrast, Republican users tweeted money bags, prison chains, and rats. Interestingly both groups were likely to use the 100 emoji among their top twenty-five results, perhaps to indicate the magnitude of their deeply polarized sentiments. This emoji was commonly used as shorthand for "100 percent," meaning "keeping it real" or a similar sentiment affirming top performance, authenticity, or 100 percent agreement.

On election night, emotions were expressed by emojis representing both the body and the face, and different expressions and gestures were correlated to mentions of different candidates. Pro-Trump supporters registered their feelings about the outcome in emojis with clapping hands, thumbs-up, and raised middle fingers.[38] The defeat of Clinton was memorialized with crying and frowning digital icons.

Certainly, these platforms privilege strong emotional expressions over neutral statements, as many social media researchers have pointed out.[39] From the perspective of Web 2.0 companies like Twitter or Facebook, clear affective signals are much more informative for tracking user attraction and repulsion. Emoji analysis allows their advertising clients to better gauge how consumers might be directed to particular pieces of content or objects of attachment. What was good for these social media companies was also good for Donald Trump and vice versa.

A Battle Over Digital Property

Of course, the Trump team's relationship with Twitter could be contentious, even if it was mutually beneficial. Gary Coby, a digital advertising manager for Trump, described his showdown with Twitter head Jack Dorsey. Twitter had issued last-minute prohibitions against pre-approved #CrookedHillary emojis that would automatically insert bags of money when users deployed the anti-Clinton hashtag. The "custom emoji" was part of a five-million-dollar deal with Twitter to promote Trump's campaign.[40] Twitter argued that the emojis were too defamatory. According to them, the image suggested that Clinton had been involved in theft, embezzlement, or illegal appropriation of funds. Coby's account of this incident follows.

> They claimed to fear litigation from HRC. I told them we were trying to show she's gotten wealthy from public office—they did not budge. I asked, why were able to use (still approved) emojis that showed emails being destroyed or phones being destroyed (which could also represent committing a crime)—they could not explain. I asked, if the Clinton Foundation were being investigated for financial crimes, could we use it—they said no. Dan [Greene] apologized and admitted TW's wrongdoing in pulling back an emoji that was previously approved. To me, this was clearly a BS reason that was made up to give them an out.[41]

Even emojis depicting money bags in a state of flight with no representation of a human Clinton were deemed too controversial.

The issues raised in this case are interesting ones about who controls the production of intellectual property in privately owned public spaces like Twitter, what constitutes free speech in highly compressed pictographic language optimized for algorithmic design, and how the line between defamation and political satire can be policed when the evidence is composed of virtual objects.

The #CrookedHillary hashtag was one that Trump has used only a few dozen times, despite the fact that it was a nickname that he relished uttering in speeches, interviews, and non-hashtagged tweets. Moreover, Trump could still use an emoji to demonize Clinton without the permission of

Twitter as a company, as he did when retweeting content from Brian Fraser in June of 2016. After Clinton's name the tweet shows the "smiling face with horns" emoji, a purple demon that appears more diabolically red on Google Android devices.

Trump began to complain about Twitter much more vociferously after the custom emoji contract was allegedly breeched and the promised "discounts, perks, and custom solutions" were supposedly withheld. As coverage of investigations into Russian interference in the 2016 election and revelations about fake news gained visibility, Trump had other reasons to vilify the platform. Before winning the presidency, Trump usually presented Twitter as a pro-Trump venue for connection and transparency that could challenge the entrenched interests of the existing political order. After winning the presidency, he expressed much more ambivalence.

Common and Rare Emojis

During his process of gaining emoji literacy, the American flag became without question Trump's favorite symbol. During his political life Trump used the US flag emoji on @realDonaldTrump over four hundred times. It first appeared in his feed on September 5, 2013, when he retweeted a message from a follower urging him to run for office.

The use of other flag emojis became part of his diplomatic endeavors as president. The emoji flags of Israel, India, Japan, Canada, Australia, Britain, Mexico, Ghana, Kenya, Malawi, Egypt, France, Spain, Portugal, Ireland, South Korea, and China all appeared on the @realDonaldTrump feed alongside the US flag to signal foreign policy overtures or accords. The flags of rivals such as Iran or North Korea did not appear.

Even an emoji that was used relatively rarely could be a useful marker for rhetorical analysis to understand how the Trump political operation managed expressions of online sentiment. For example, on January 22, 2019, @realDonaldTrump celebrated Mariano Rivera's elevation to the Baseball Hall of Fame with the 100 emoji. The 100 emoji can express pride or acceptance as well. It was also a logical addition because Rivera had received 100 percent of the votes from 425 submitted ballots, which was an added achievement.

> Congratulations to Mariano Rivera on unanimously being elected to the National
> Baseball Hall of Fame! Not only a great player but a great person. I am thankful

for Mariano's support of the Opioid Drug Abuse Commission and @FitnessGov. #EnterSandman #HOF2019💯 https://t.co/reU1gKWHSQ.

In addition to using hashtags for the event and Rivera's "Sandman" nickname, the tweet endorsed Fitness.gov, an online initiative promoting physical exercise that originated during the era of George W. Bush. Users were also reminded that the administration cared deeply about prescription drug abuse as a public health issue. With all this rhetorical work to be accomplished in just one tweet, the 100 emoji signified complete commitment, mirroring the total dedication of the athlete the message lauded. Yet this was an emoji that @realDonaldTrump hadn't used in years.

The 100 emoji played an important role in Trump's followers' online adulation. His supporters used it to indicate their admiration of his supposedly "straight talk" and their unwavering dedication as members of his political base. Even during the month-long government shutdown when Trump's poll numbers plummeted, his enthusiasts regularly posted 100s to engage with him on his Twitter account.

Theorizing Emoji

Assertions about affective labor are at the heart of Luke Stark and Kate Crawford's seminal essay about "the conservatism of emoji." With its "highly compressed lexicon," Stark and Crawford argue that "the emoji character set vividly illustrates the constraints on affective labor under informational capital."[42] They claim that "emoji should be understood both as a rearguard action to enable sociality in digital networks and also the means to quantify, measure, signal, and control affective labor, and reinforce existing regimes of inequality and exploitation."[43] In other words, the liberatory and oppressive potentials of the emoji are simultaneously present.

Emojis are less flourishes than markers of architectural style; they signal a particular framework for inhabiting social space. They provide information that is central to interpreting a given message, even if—as researchers have found—emojis tend to create rather than resolve ambiguity, and their decoding is highly dependent on particular cultural contexts. As Kate Miltner has argued, emoji designers claim to be eager to lessen the "cognitive load" of reading by simplifying racial and gender attributes, but she claims that these rationales appear dubious, given that "configuring the user" is part of how standards to simplify representation operate.[44]

Crying Laughing

Certain objects played major roles in the Trump allegorical system. If Hillary Clinton was speaking, money bags, prison chains, and rats were emblems of antipathy. A snowflake served as another object of contempt, representing the supposed oversensitivity of liberal feelings. In contrast, a freight locomotive represented the powerful drive and determination of "the Trump train."

So what are we to make of the use of the crying laughing emoji by Trump and his supporters? The emoji is officially called the "face with tears of joy" emoji and is often used for joking or teasing. It signals ironic distance and disengagement from social norms, even as it shows deep investment in emotional performance. It has consistently been one of the most popular emojis on social media. For Trump supporters, the crying laughing emoji was the antithesis of the corporate happy face.[45] While the happy face was intended to hide conflict, crying laughing celebrated disputes. Like GIFs, image macros, and other memes that circulated among Trump's supporters, the emoji also flouted conventions about what were expected, measured, and appropriate emotional responses. The hyperbole of the crying laughing emoji undermined the assumed gravitas of politics and political institutions as well.

Political aesthetics scholar Jonathan Flatley has argued that America's political state under Trump was characterized by "the emotification of affirmation and the fetishization of contestation." In emoji terms this dichotomy presents a world divided between celebratory acts of solidarity represented by balloons, confetti, flexed muscles, and thankful praying hands and instances of literal demonization in which an electoral rival might be depicted as a purple devil with horns.

New design features for user engagement—such as emojis, user handles, hashtags, and retweets—turned up the emotional temperature in social media in ways that Trump could exploit. He also benefited from direct collaborations with social media companies, although not all of these special agreements worked out to his satisfaction. Facebook handed him 200,000 unearned followers, but Twitter took his custom emoji away. Both incidents showed how alliances with these powerful platforms could reshape the social contract and deform systems of political allegiance.

Trump espoused a rhetoric of connection, even when it relied on antagonistic words, images, and actions. Much as the users of MyBO were urged to reach out and connect to candidate Obama with appeals that made them feel seen as individuals, Trump facilitated connection via Twitter using his own unique style of personalization, which could be either combative or appreciative. Trump's frenetic late-night and early-morning flurries of tweets also modeled the behavior encouraged by social media companies: to be connected anytime, anywhere.

Although Trump went through many social media handlers, Peter Costanzo still recognized residual signs of his contributions years later. The @realDonaldTrump profile photo was still the cover photo for *Think Like a Champion*. "I uploaded that photograph," Costanzo recalled. "That was his favorite photograph."

Costanzo mused about how his advice for Trump to be more personally involved and to appear less filtered was eventually adopted wholeheartedly. This perceived authenticity became the core of Trump's successful presidential run. The disintermediated intensity of Trump's eventual deep investment in social media contrasted sharply with the aloofness of his approach at the beginning of his digital literacy process.

"It certainly wasn't at the level where it is now," Costanzo said. "And it's a different beast now. I mean you can't disconnect his Twitter account from who he is as a person."

9 Trump's Rhetoric of Transparency

On December 4, 2016, a few weeks after Trump succeeded in his improbable bid for the presidency, Edgar Maddison Welch, a 28-year-old man from Salisbury, North Carolina, fired three shots inside the Comet Ping Pong pizzeria in Washington DC with an AR-15-style rifle, striking walls, a desk, and a door before he was taken into custody. No one was physically hurt in the restaurant, but those held hostage while Welch searched for a nonexistent basement were traumatized by the event. Welch surrendered willingly to the authorities after he found no evidence to validate the fake news stories he had read online about child sex slaves being held captive in the basement of the eatery at the behest of powerful leaders of the Democratic Party.

Although this wild pedophilia conspiracy theory should have lost credibility once Welch was arrested and the basement story was debunked, it has persisted in the misinformation ecosystem to this day. People who believed in the so-called Pizzagate conspiracy picketed the Obama White House during its last days, and they demanded an official inquiry from the incoming Trump administration.[1] Over time, a vast mythology about Democratic Party child sex trafficking was expanded with a pantheon of new characters. Years later it helped fuel the outrage that drove extremist Trump supporters to storm the Capitol. A distinctive rhetoric of transparency kept this conspiracy theory alive.

Pizzagate is often cited as the natural result of Trump's logic of radical relativism, the inevitable conclusion of fostering "whataboutism"[2] or "alternative facts"[3] in which everything should be interrogated and anything could be true, especially when distilled to its most toxic and viral form. Implications of sexual impropriety were already linked to Clinton's name in discussions of her email, even if there were only tenuous connections to the sexting scandals of Anthony Weiner and Peter Strzok. Escalating accusations against her to allege direct participation in child sex slavery was in keeping with the general theme of wrongdoing associated with her activities.

Looking closely at the digital documents in Pizzagate's constellation of fictions, I believe there is more to the story than deranged internet conspiracy thinking that can be easily dismissed. When the structures of its densely packed referential claims are untangled, Pizzagate represents not only the fallibility of digital systems for truth telling but also their influence in distorting the information environment of daily life. This analysis examines how conspiracy theories often exploit citizens' understandable desires for transparency when they are forced to negotiate the hidden operations of social media companies and computational culture more generally.

Some important trends help explain the connection between fake news and transparency: the shift from authority to authorization, from authenticity to authentication, and from veracity to verification.[4] Each of these three propensities was manifested in the Pizzagate conspiracy.

From Authority to Authorization

To follow the full trajectory of what led Welch to invade Comet Ping Pong, we can look at how legitimate information flows went off course many months earlier. Pizzagate began with a simple phishing email of the kind that most users receive on a regular basis. It arrived on March 19, 2016, and was addressed to Clinton campaign chief John Podesta. It announced that a suspicious sign-in attempt to his Gmail account had been made from an IP (Internet Protocol) address in the Ukraine. The email advised Podesta to change his email password immediately and conveniently provided a link.

It is important to note that Podesta was not as credulous as other internet users might be. He had written a 2014 report on cyberprivacy for President Obama and was wary of compromising an email account with over 60,000 messages that he had maintained for a decade. However, given the heavy traffic of email to leaders of the Democratic Party, passwords were often shared between trusted insiders.

In response to this ominous warning, one aide forwarded the email to a computer technician to make sure it was a valid message before anyone clicked on the "change password" button. Unfortunately, another IT aide—Charles Delavan—authorized the password change before anyone could investigate. "This is a legitimate email," he wrote in response to the initial alert. "John needs to change his password immediately."[5] In defending his conduct in the months that followed, Delavan claimed that he had identified the email correctly as a phishing attempt, but he said he had accidentally made a typographical error in his message to Podesta, accidentally omitting the word "not."[6] He also pointed out that he had included the official Gmail change password link along with other security advice.

Rather than go to the authentic "change password" page, Podesta's assistant followed the directions in the original phishing email and gave hackers a treasure trove of electronic documents, which were then published on the WikiLeaks website, where they became fodder for crowdsourced conspiracy theories. Readers flocked to the WikiLeaks website looking for juicy tidbits. In the documentary *The Perfect Weapon* Podesta lamented that "if it's secret or if it's stolen, it must be more sexy."

Only when the breach became apparent did DNC staffers realize they had been targeted by electronic interlopers for months. Back in September 2015 Special Agent Adrian Hawkins of the Federal Bureau of Investigation had called the DNC "to pass along some troubling news about its computer network." Hawkins had spent years tracking the activities of "the Dukes," a cyber-espionage team linked to the Russian government. They had played havoc with the unclassified email systems of the White House, the State Department, and the Joint Chiefs of Staff.

> Yared Tamene, the tech-support contractor at the D.N.C. who fielded the call, was no expert in cyberattacks. His first moves were to check Google for "the Dukes" and conduct a cursory search of the D.N.C. computer system logs to look for hints of such a cyberintrusion. By his own account, he did not look too hard even after Special Agent Hawkins called back repeatedly over the next several weeks—in part because he wasn't certain the caller was a real F.B.I. agent and not an impostor. "I had no way of differentiating the call I just received from a prank call," Mr. Tamene wrote in an internal memo.[7]

Recommending a course of action in case of a security breach is a critical responsibility of information technology professionals. Tamene's decision to underreact and dismiss the warning from Hawkins was the inverse response from Delavan's decision to overreact and implement a password change. An authoritative message was taken as illegitimate because it couldn't be authorized, and a message that pretended to have authority it lacked was authorized because the Clinton campaign thought it had completed the necessary procedures of double-checking.

Traditional forms of authority are constituted by the decisions of a designated representative—judge, arbiter, or referee—who either legitimates or delegitimates an exercise of power. Although authorization upholds the integrity of one party granting permission to another, gatekeeping functions are automated through protocols. Many authorization processes are distributed rather than centralized, so the same piece of code manages multiple transactions simultaneously. Without a human agent involved, trust in the entire system can be undermined.

From Authenticity to Authentication

In the next stage of Pizzagate, readers scrutinized the stolen emails on WikiLeaks and looked for patterns. Some assumed that odd word choices might reflect a kind of secret code. Reddit users quickly focused on the most common terms. A user called DumbScribblyUnctious began to catalog possible meanings associated with the odd frequency of the word "pizza" in Podesta's emails. Of course, "pizza" is a relatively common word in the electronic correspondence of organizations that depend on a labor force that is young, volunteer, and likely to work late hours. Yet DumbScribblyUnctious was eager to sow doubt about Podesta's intentions and posted a key for reading the "true" meaning of the emails on November 3: "'hotdog'=boy," "'pizza'=girl," "'cheese'=little girl," "'pasta'=little boy," "'ice cream'=male prostitute," "'walnut'=person of color." He was a regular poster on pro-Trump forums. He also alleged that "Obama spent about $65,000 of the taxpayers money flying in pizza/dogs from Chicago for a private party at the White House."[8]

The terms "authentication" and "authorization" might sound similar, but they are actually based on fundamentally different security concerns. Authentication confirms that users are who they say they are. It establishes a user's identity. Authorization grants users permission to access a resource or perform a function. Generally, there are three factors that can be used for authentication: something you know (such as a password or an answer to a security question), something you have in your possession (such as a personal identification number, or PIN, mailed to your address or access to a particular smartphone that can receive a text), or something you are (such as a biological marker, like a fingerprint or retinal scan). Two-factor authentication is more secure than authentication based on a single factor. These processes of authentication often apply probabilistic logics, based on the unlikelihood that a random try could provide the same result.

Those who believed the Pizzagate conspiracy also relied on probabilistic assumptions when they asserted the likelihood of seemingly unlikely scenarios. For example, they discussed high-frequency words, matching patterns of visual icons, and unusual internet behavior. Often these probabilistic intuitions were confirmed by crowdsourcing procedures that demonstrated a truth arrived at through a seemingly more trustworthy quantitative, rather than qualitative, process. The conspiracy theorists searched for connections between the Clinton campaign and pizza establishments in the Washington area. With strong assumptions about normative heterosexuality, they also scoured those links for possible ties to sexual perversion and religious heresy, with the assumption that pedophilia and child imprisonment would be revealed, much as anti-Semitic persecutors perpetuated the blood libel in centuries past.[9]

Reddit users seized upon the figure of Comet Ping Pong owner James Alefantis. Alefantis had been in a romantic relationship with David Brock, a professional opposition researcher who had worked closely with both of Clinton's presidential campaigns. Alefantis soon began receiving threatening messages on his social media accounts.[10] Eventually the workers who staffed his establishment were also terrorized. Pizzagate's conspiracy theorists posted screen shots of Alefantis's Instagram account and annotated pages that they deemed suspect. A baby posed next to stacks of currency, or a little girl taped to a table by her wrists, were seen as trophy pictures documenting salacious acts of perversion. Although Alefantis made his accounts private, images from his @jimmycomet Instagram had been carefully copied with "highlights preserved on the Steemit blockchain" and also "archived on the Pizzagate Wiki."[11] In addition to items categorized as "strange pictures of children," Pizzagaters pored over homoerotic pictures juxtaposing pizza with male torsos or penises, pizza pies sliced into satanic pentagrams, excavations of basements, and a bearded drag performer in rhinestones and high heels covered with what appeared to be blood. Morbid humor, queer irony, campy statements, and flirtatious puns were all treated as evidence as the Reddit audience scoured the images for clues.

Right-wing internet users also tied these strange images back to another theme they had supposedly uncovered in Podesta's emails: spirit cooking. Among the hacked emails was one from performance artist Marina Abramović, who had invited Podesta and his brother Tony to a dinner themed after one of her multimedia installations, *Spirit Cooking*. Abramović's artwork was a ritualistic interpretation of recipes that used coagulated pig's blood as paint. One conspiracy theorist, True Free Thinker, opined that "being invited to one of Marina Abramovic's Spirit Cooking sessions appears to be the mere top of an iceberg which is melting away to reveal some very troubling aspects about elitism in general."[12] He also tied the Podesta brothers to the disappearance of Madeleine McCann in Portugal and argued that police sketches could be analyzed biometrically to prove their culpability, a claim propagated by Victurus Libertas with similar image-matching as supposed proof.

The hunt for satanic symbols migrated to Voat, which was a website less policed for accuracy than Reddit,[13] although it deployed similar upvoting procedures. Even though the heading for "Satanic/Muslim symbols" in the Comet Ping Pong case was eventually labeled "debunked,"[14] in its heyday followers claimed that they were merely observing rigorous logic, similar to the logic of computational systems that find word patterns or biometric proportions. At one point the Pizzagate group on Voat had over fifteen thousand followers.

According to a *Rolling Stone* exposé, Pizzagate conspiracy theories also blossomed on the website 4chan, where someone calling himself FBIAnon identified himself as a "high-level analyst and strategist" for the Bureau. He announced that "Bill and Hillary love foreign donors so much. They get paid in children as well as money."[15] FBIAnon did not assume that people would accept his representations without question. He encouraged his audience to "dig deep" to expose the investigative work he had done for the agency. Sources in the Pizzagate/Pedogate scandals were often authenticated by access to insider knowledge. They were FBI agents, police officers, technical wizards, and hackers. One poster claimed to have penetrated the back end of the Comet Ping Pong website and showed evidence that images from the Africa Muslim Party were stored in its database.

The structure of 4chan itself also helped the Pizzagate story gain credence, according to digital scholar Marc Tuters and a team of researchers who used computer visualization to analyze threads on 4chan. In examining strategies for "keeping a conversation alive after a thread has been purged," the researchers argued that "general threads were crucial to the process of framing those discussions going forward." In managing an otherwise unwieldy archive of posts, respected users could enhance their reputations further by distilling a more coherent story from disorganized fragments. This process of concentrating the history of prior conversations tended to consolidate multiple threads that may have emerged in the "real-time collective research effort," thereby investing "a single author (as opposed to the anonymous mass)" with "significant authority" to decide "which parts of a prior thread to include or exclude."[16] According to Tuters's group, this comprehensive approach to reframing the whole enterprise of knowledge production tends to favor grand narratives and founding mythologies, such as the role of the "deep state" as a nefarious actor in government.[17]

Enthusiasm for the campaign against Comet Ping Pong went mainstream with adoption of the #Pizzagate hashtag, which was picked up by conservative bloggers like Pam Jones for Liberty.[18] Jones published a more complete version of the email code, which included terms like "pillow," "sauce," and "chicken" as possible search terms for Podesta's email archive.

As a piece of metadata, the #Pizzagate hashtag assisted with authentication procedures on other sites as more users deployed the hashtag for filtering search results for their desired conspiratorial content. #Pizzagate even became used on largely innocuous sites like Pinterest as a place to curate related memes.

From Veracity to Verification

The fact that the conspiracy had essentially no bases in reality was not important to Pizzagate followers. Upvoting verified their suppositions. The use of the hashtag verified them. The migration of content from Reddit, Voat, and 4Chan to social media sites like Facebook and Pinterest verified them. But for Welch, finding verification with redundant information wasn't enough. He needed to investigate in person to find out if it was true, and he needed to bring his rifle to be sure.

According to the police report, Welch had come because "he had read online that that the Comet restaurant was harboring child sex slaves and that he wanted to see for himself if they were there."[19] News stories often emphasized the credulousness of Welch rather than his skepticism, but his desire to verify the story as a firsthand witness rather than accepting it without question is often overlooked. Clearly, he believed it enough to come armed for protection and perhaps to rescue the imprisoned children, but his curiosity and doubt are also important factors. It could be argued that Welch tangled with law enforcement not because he accepted a fake news account but because he wanted to check it out for himself rather than rely on online sources.

Unlike Welch, other users focused on third-party verification as a way to sort fact from fiction. Sites to verify questionable information like Snopes. com were heavily trafficked as a result. Many went to other supposedly neutral sites like Wikipedia for verification purposes as well. However, internet traffic to pro-Pizzagate sites was actually driven by those searching for rigorous fact checking. For example, those in quest of Pizzagate information might go to the *Renegade Tribune*, which purported to fact-check the fact-checking services of the *New York Times*.[20]

Fact-checking services also shaped the career of Alefantis's former boyfriend. In addition to his work for liberal causes, David Brock founded Media Matters for America, which described itself as a watchdog group calling out media bias and inaccuracies in news coverage. Much of the content Media Matters produced was devoted to rebutting the claims of fake news sites. Alex Jones of InfoWars was a frequent subject of its debunking activities.

However, those seeking more information about Brock from Wikipedia might have only been made more suspicious. Brock's Wikipedia page at the time of the Comet Ping Pong shooting used clearly politically slanted terms by describing him as an "operative." At one time the article had been flagged for violating the site's "no point of view" policy, but the label disputing its neutrality "left by 4.158.63.161" was removed in 2004 by a Wikipedia editor who asserted that "the neutrality of this article hasn't been disputed—apparently not even by him!" As justification, editor Ex1le cited existing procedures for verification: "If he wants that label added, let him contest it here."[21]

Media Matters ran over a hundred stories contesting different aspects of the Pizzagate narrative, which remained remarkably durable as it became part of the QAnon conspiracy that Donald Trump refused to disavow. Even after Welch's arrest, former national security advisor Michael Flynn spread the "spirit cooking" tale about Clinton's campaign manager. Almost a year after the Pizzagate shooting, widely read conservative media outlets like PJ Media were still circulating the story, albeit with a link to the fact-checking website Snopes.com.

In the Trump era, everything began to seem like a simulation. Rather than debunk Pizzagate messages after the shooting, deeply invested conspiracy theorists were quick to identify Welch as a "crisis actor." According to them, Welch had participated in an elaborate simulation designed to discredit Pizzagate believers. After the Comet Ping Pong assault, those Googling Welch's name found his IMDB page and his credits as a small-time actor in independent films. They spread suppositions that the capture of a seemingly crazed man was part of a planned performance. Such crisis actors were assumed to be part of staged events intended to justify limiting civil liberties by an authoritarian deep state, particularly by enforcing gun control. In the Pizzagate case, third-party verification with a supposedly neutral third-party reference site—IMDB—confirmed paranoid delusions.

Ultimately, Pizzagate spanned Wikipedia as well as WikiLeaks, IMDB as well as InfoWars, fact-checking sites as well as fake news sites, and photo archiving sites as well as photo doctoring sites. Security technologies like blockchain, designed to establish trust in an untrustworthy world, even played a role. In other words, to understand fake news as the product of a lack of gatekeeping is to misunderstand how gatekeeping systems rose to prominence in the story.

A Brief History of Fake News

Although Welch was a relative newcomer to social media, the fake news stories he consumed had longer legacies. There are many varieties of internet fake news—including those involving content-neutral clickbait—but three types were particularly significant: those structured around satire, those structured around information warfare, and those structured around indeterminacy.

Of course, fake news and moral panics have long histories that predate digital technology. During the sixteenth century, when the technology of printing was still relatively new, adherents of astrology circulated books that created widespread hysteria about natural disasters that would supposedly sweep away European cities in massive floods. Americans similarly panicked during Orson Welles's 1938 radio broadcast adaptation of *The*

War of the Worlds because they feared the twentieth-century version of the apocalypse.[22]

Although the term "fake news" had once been used to describe the dangers of Nazi propaganda, it had become a surprisingly positive term by the time internet browsers and social network sites first came along. During this period, "fake news" was associated with lighthearted political satire in the United States, a formation I have dubbed Fake News 1.0. This content lampooned traditional reporting and often celebrated subversive digital practices.[23] *The Daily Show*, *The Colbert Report*, and other late-night shows on the cable channel Comedy Central featured segments with mock reporters who interviewed real political figures and covered real political stories. Clips were posted online using blogging and video-sharing platforms. This kind of hybrid news consumption—of both real and fake news— also bridged the experiences of watching television and participating in social media.

In a 2014 Pew survey, "nearly a quarter (22%) of 18- to 29-year-old males" said they got "news about politics and government from the parody news show *The Colbert Report* in the previous week." Overall, about ten percent of adults online described it as a source of news, and young males were particularly likely to identify it as a trusted source.[24] A 2007 Pew study indicated that *Colbert Report/Daily Show* viewers scored higher on their news knowledge level, measured by tasks such as identifying the roles of public political figures.[25] Viewers of fake news satire shows even outperformed those who relied on public broadcasting, which was generally considered to be informative and nonpartisan.

The fake news produced by Comedy Central was generally not confused with actual news. However, several stories produced by the satirical Onion News Network were picked up and redistributed as real news by media channels. The *Washington Post* compiled a list of foreign news services from countries as diverse as China, Iran, Singapore, Bangladesh, and Denmark that had used *The Onion* as a source for news stories.[26] US media outlets from the *New York Times* to ESPN have also taken *Onion* items as fact.

Fake News 2.0 was quite unlike Fake News 1.0. Instead of impertinent humor, it assumed a tone that was often dark, menacing, and conspiratorial. Fake News 2.0 was also much more likely to be taken as authentic when circulated among internet audiences. The 9/11 terrorist attacks were the first major topic in this variant. For example, *Loose Change*, a grim, feature-length documentary, promoted a paranoid "false flag" anti-establishment narrative. The film suggested that members of the federal government, rather than jihadists from abroad, had instigated the attacks. The story had initially been pitched as a fictional film by its creator, who had wanted to make a heist movie about using a national security crisis as distraction to steal a stockpile of gold from the World Trade Center.

Loose Change built a large audience through its free distribution on You-Tube, where it received hundreds of thousands of views. It soon attracted financial backing from professional conspiracy theorist Alex Jones of InfoWars. Jones fronted a broadcast organization that specialized in doubting official accounts of news events. Jones and his followers believed that federal authorities were implementing a secret agenda to prohibit the ownership of weapons so as to enforce the dictates of a totalitarian regime. As Jones uncovered supposed conspiracies to drug, assassinate, or incapacitate potential whistle-blowers, he expressed his agitation for transparency in his video performances with shouting and gesticulations.

Fake News 2.0 imagines political life as extremely polarized. Information warfare is staged between diametrically opposed sides. News is a weapon to be used in these deeply antagonistic ideological conflicts. One side champions truth, and the other propagates deception. According to Fake News 2.0, the supposedly liberal mainstream media has obscured dangerous conspiracies with distracting spectacles in order to undermine democracy and deprive citizens of their civil liberties. Fake News 2.0 also tends to be fascinated with the secret and the arcane. Although it deploys the rhetoric of transparency, it actually has little investment in definitively resolving the truth.

Despite their differences, Fake News 1.0 and Fake News 2.0 sometimes simulate each other. For example, during the Trump presidency, the website America's Last Line of Defense was an energetic purveyor of fake news with headlines such as "BREAKING: Dem US Senator KNEW His Serial-Killer Daughter Was Chopping Up Men In His House" or "BREAKING: Muslim School Bus Driver Refused To Let Child Off Bus Till She Converted To Islam." Such clickbait appealed to readers' fears of foreigners, people of color, and women who might displace white, male, native-born Americans. Fact-checking sites devoted many pages to debunking scores of America's Last Line of Defense stories, including one about Obama's older daughter being arrested for participating in a million-dollar shoplifting ring.

The "About Us" page of the original website advertised two very different identities, presenting first its conspiratorial Fake News 2.0 identity and then replacing it with an ironic 1.0 ethos.[27] Above a red, white, and blue star-spangled fist, text read:

> We are a group of educated, God-fearing Christian conservative patriots who are tired of Obama's tyrannical reign and ready to see a strong Republican take the White House. We are sovereign citizens who want our government to keep its nose out of our business. We believe in guns, God and the Constitution and will go to any lengths to take OUR country back from the whiny, politically correct liberal masses.

Below the picture of the fist, the message seemed to be completely contradicted:

> DISCLAIMER: America's Last Line of Defense is a satirical publication that may sometimes appear to be telling the truth. We assure you that's not the case. We present fiction as fact and our sources don't actually exist. Names that represent actual people and places are purely coincidental and all images should be considered altered and do not in any way depict reality.

In the US legal context, this verbiage denied any responsibility for content. The exculpatory language was an attempt to protect America's Last Line of Defense from potential lawsuits. In the United States, humor is protected legally as a form of constitutionally sanctioned cultural expression. In some cases, satire is better protected than journalism, documentary production, and nonfiction storytelling. Declaring this parodic form of political speech openly and explicitly shields the producing party from claims of libel. An assertion of satire can even provide a safe harbor from copyright infringement cases.[28] In this way Fake News 2.0 (online conspiracy clickbait) could claim the legal privileges of Fake News 1.0 (comedy news). Eventually America's Last Line of Defense went out of the fake news business. Its business model changed to peddling gear for self-defense enthusiasts and survivalists. But during its heyday as a fake news site, it regularly drew tens of thousands of viewers and dozens of corrections on Snopes.com.[29]

Donald Trump became the figurehead for Fake News 3.0 by inverting the labels that had once distinguished mainstream sources from questionable ones. He suggested that the *New York Times*, the *Washington Post*, and other respected outlets for journalism were all venues for "fake news." Trump's political career was launched with a Fake News 2.0 audience willing to believe that Obama's birth certificate was a forgery to cover up his Kenyan birth. During his campaign Trump also praised Alex Jones and others who promulgated Fake News 2.0 "false flag" theories of deceptive media coverage. At the same time, Trump courted the hosts of late-night comedy shows specializing in Fake News 1.0 as a way to capitalize on access to free airtime from those eager to view him as a buffoon.[30]

In Trump's Fake News 3.0, the corrections and retractions that are common in legitimate reporting are seen as proof of their vulnerability. The content of such papers of record could be dismissed as unreliable because alt-right news sources like the *Daily Caller* or the *Breitbart News Network* never issued apologies for inaccuracies. Trump seemed to delight in deriding traditional journalism. From inaccurate polling to op-ed pontificating, they were all "lamestream" news. His spokespeople defended the radical relativism of "alternative facts" as a way to challenge conventional notions of credibility. While Fake News 1.0 had in some ways led to greater media literacy, Fake News 3.0 left audiences confused about basic information.

Opening the Gates

Conspiratorial conversations sprawled across different social media platforms, including relatively mainstream sites such as Reddit and Pinterest with clearly defined norms for user behavior and histories of governance. They also spanned sites known for radical libertarianism and boundary crossing, such as Voat, 4chan, and 8chan.

Despite their professed abhorrence of political censorship, many conspiracy groups ended up restricting digital speech, especially the digital speech of women, queer people, and people of color. The "-gate" suffix was often associated with very intense campaigns of suspicion, libel, outing of private information, and online and off-line harassment. When agitated, these online communities of frequently anonymous members exploited regulatory environments extremely effectively. They capitalized on rules for upvoting procedures, domain name registration, IP addresses, and the protocols of crowdfunding and customer service.[31] Using these exploits, they aligned their interests and coordinated their hostile labor.

The collective storytelling efforts of Pizzagate—and other conspiracy theories promulgated by anonymous sources—promoted a certain kind of positive social vision along with their bizarre theories. During his drive from North Carolina to the pizza parlor in Washington, DC, Welch recorded a two-and-a-half-minute video for his daughters with his smartphone positioned on his dashboard.

As the car rumbles over the tree-lined highway in the video, the viewer can see Welch speaking of the lesson he will soon be reinforcing for his "girls" about one's "duty to people who can't protect themselves."[32] He declares his love for them and explains that he "can't let you grow up in a world that's so corrupt by evil without at least standing up for you, for other children just like you."

Welch used his mobile device to create a martyr's farewell. His rhetoric also invoked conventional cinematic images, by positioning himself as the lone sheriff standing up against evildoers. Notably, Welch used one of Trump's favorite words—"corrupt"—to explain his planned assault on a fallen world. Trump tweeted about "corruption" and the "corrupt" over five hundred times.

Russiagate, Spygate, and Obamagate

Trump himself has only engaged with five "-gates" on Twitter directly: "Watergate," "Russiagate," "Spygate," "Obamagate," and "Phonegate."

Trump referred to Watergate over a dozen times on Twitter, usually as a point of comparison for crimes supposedly committed by the Obama administration or the Clinton campaign. Essentially, he argued that the misdeeds of the Nixon administration were dwarfed by those of Democratic leaders. Examples of supposed corruption by Democrats were described as "bigger than Watergate" or "more important than Watergate" on Trump's Twitter feed.

In the era of print journalism, Watergate was perceived to be a high point for the media's role in holding the powerful accountable through investigative reporting. Before the collapse of newspapers, which coincided with the rise of digital news, conservative commentator William Safire identified many other possible "-gate" situations that diluted the achievements of Watergate. The "-gates" coined by Safire during the Carter, Reagan, Bush, and Clinton administrations included "Billygate," "Briefinggate," "Contragate," "Nannygate," "Scalpgate," and "Troopergate."[33] Technological politics scholar Alexandria Lockett observes that, in the digital age, the name "Watergate" has become a signifier of information overflow and leakage that refuses to be gated and managed.[34]

"Spygate" referred to allegations that the Trump campaign was illegally surveilled by the Obama administration in order to stifle political opposition. In some versions of the conspiracy, FBI agents were embedded in Trump's campaign, supposedly enabling them to share secrets of his inner circle with Democratic operatives to gain strategic advantage.

In contrast, "Russiagate"—the investigation into Trump's possible collusion with the Russian government to influence the 2016 election and his obstruction of justice designed to hamper the search for truth—was mentioned only sparingly and only in the context of retweeting. For example, in the final weeks of the 2020 campaign, Trump retweeted "BOMBSHELL: Clinton Allegedly Approved Russiagate Falsehood As Distraction From Email Scandal." In contrast, "Spygate" appeared in Trump's tweets much more frequently and was often capitalized and called out with a hashtag.

On two separate occasions Trump plugged Dan Bongino's *Spygate: The Attempted Sabotage of Donald J. Trump* on Twitter. With much less paranoia than that surrounding wilder theories like Pizzagate, the book told the story of a network of Democratic Party sympathizers. It argued that four entities—the Obama administration, the Clinton campaign, law enforcement, and foreign operatives—had "messy and complicated" shared objectives to thwart the Trump campaign. The book even declared it would offer no Hollywood drama in the form of a "smoke-filled room" or "Doctor Evil."[35] After its publication, Bongino built a reputation as a Trump loyalist and went on to cultivate a media presence as a radio host with over 3.6 million Facebook followers.[36]

Other more conspiratorial versions of the Spygate story emphasized uncovering global plots by much more nefarious powers.[37] For example, the pro-Trump website *Gateway Pundit* presented Pizzagate-style decoding of leaked text messages between FBI employees.

BOMBSHELL- From DECEMBER 2015–The word LURES is redacted by FBI but not OIG; OCONUS LURES; OCONUS= Outside Contiguous US LURES= In this context LURES = SPIES—multiple—Is this an admission that the FBI wanted to run a baited Sting Op using foreign agents against Trump?[38]

In *Gateway Pundit* stories, one tweet alleging an outrage was enough to be cited as definitive evidence. When *Gateway Pundit* founder Jim Hoft received a press credential for the White House in 2017, journalists from traditional news organizations with more rigorous fact-checking were flabbergasted.[39]

Like many other recent "-gate" controversies, Spygate also entailed sifting through massive electronic document releases. In this way supporters could decode insider communications from antagonists, share their decryption activities with supporters, and shame conventional news outlets for inaction. For example, on June 5, 2018, Trump tweeted a message of astonishment at Spygate's early planning and suggested that more detective work needed to be done.

> Wow, Strzok-Page, the incompetent & corrupt FBI lovers, have texts referring to a counter-intelligence operation into the Trump Campaign dating way back to December, 2015. SPYGATE is in full force! Is the Mainstream Media interested yet? Big stuff!

Much as conservative talk radio built on its intimate address to its listeners,[40] Trump used his internet presence to dominate his audience's attention and thus their political bandwidth. By stoking controversy with Spygate, he also encouraged his followers to become participants in the distorted forms of world-building that would be necessary for him to inhabit a Trump-centered reality.[41]

More subtle shifts in language could also be operationalized to amplify a "-gate" conspiracy. Journalists pointed out that "an 'informant' is not the same as a 'spy,' . . . 'Being investigated' is very different than 'being spied upon.'"[42] Yet conservative media outlets such as Fox News spread the Spygate story far and wide.

Some "-gate" conspiracies received no detailed elaboration from the president. When reporters asked Trump for a precise definition of "Obamagate," they received non-answers. Trump spoke vaguely about how "some terrible things happened, and it should never be allowed to happen in our country." It appeared that Trump might have been just rebranding Spygate with a catchier title because the older allegations about a sinister Democratic Party cabal that included the Ukrainians had fizzled.[43] What could be better than using something as memorable as "Obamacare" or "Obamaphone"?

For those who believed that Obama had been using his massive powers over telecommunications networks to spy on or interfere with conservative groups, "Obamagate" was a perfect label with a market-tested pedigree. It also seemed to give credence to an earlier unsupported tweet that had garnered lots of attention by claiming that Trump had been a victim of illegal wiretapping. "How low has President Obama gone to tapp my phones during the very sacred election process," Trump wrote on Twitter without correcting his spelling. "This is Nixon/Watergate. Bad (or sick) guy!"

Obamagate showed how far Trump's recruitment of "keyboard warriors" had come. Trump started with a retweet from @retinaldoctor, a bit player on Twitter with only a few thousand followers. The initial tweet read: "#ObamaGate Wow look what's trending on Twitter. I'll bet these guys aren't laughing today." The original post linked to a picture of Trump's adversary, lead FBI investigator Robert Mueller, laughing with Washington politicians. This image of Mueller as a mocking insider was also a popular photo in online memes.

This first message presented an obvious incitement for Trump's followers to start Googling "Obamagate," and the hashtag was designed to encourage sharing. Later that same day, Trump posted the one-word tweet: "OBAMAGATE!" He posted the same tweet again three days later. He then retweeted it twice, continuing his pattern of retweeting himself. He also compared Obamagate to Watergate five times, asserting that the Nixon scandal was "small time" or "small potatoes" in comparison.

Phonegate

In his pre-presidential life, Trump was less adept at driving online engagement. His efforts to stoke curiosity with a "-gate" narrative about his reality television programming would draw far fewer new followers than would conspiracy theories about Obama. But even in the context of his broadcast career, Trump had presented himself as an agent of transparency.

Although this is largely a book about digital media, reality television also shaped Trump's public personality. Television scholars have argued that "reality"-oriented programming has been a driving force in the entire media ecosystem for many decades and that it is designed to fulfill the audience's desires to see people's private lives and unfiltered emotions and to cut production costs by jettisoning professional writers and performers.[44] Its supposedly unscripted story lines depend on highly formulaic genres, characters, tropes, and catch phrases. Reality television also promotes specific political narratives, particularly those that feature drama about gender, sexuality, race, and class.[45] Often these shows are structured around moments of revelation, in which a secret or an act of wrongdoing is exposed.[46] Thus, transparency serves a major theme in reality television, although it takes a peculiar form that normalizes hypervisibility and the exhibition of private life.[47]

In 2015 Trump retweeted two messages using the #Phonegate hashtag: "Can't wait to see how #Phonegate plays out @realDonaldTrump @MsVivicaFox #CelebApprentice" and "By the way—you will NOT want to miss #Phonegate next week on #CelebApprentice. That's all we're gonna say."

In these tweets Trump doesn't preview how the show will caricature Black women and their cell phone use or supply any hints that might link the Phonegate story to right-wing attitudes about technology and identity politics. However, in watching the actual episode of "Who Stole My Phone?" on *The Celebrity Apprentice*, the racist and sexist subtext quickly emerges. After contestant Vivica A. Fox discovers that her smartphone is missing, the actor suddenly finds herself "at a disadvantage" because she is unable to Google information needed by her team to complete tasks. She is also bereft of her list of "contacts" and "personal information." The loss of the phone requires that Fox perform a weird minstrel act for the camera. At one point, she laments in Black dialect that she feels "like I done lost my child with my phone gone." Fox is subsequently revealed that she posted an uncharacteristic update on Twitter during the phone's absence: "This menopause id killing me I can't think straight, im acting a damn fool half the time 50 just isnt sexy."

Fox immediately blames the other Black woman remaining on the show for the sabotage. Speaking as the accused, Kenya Moore from *The Real Housewives of Atlanta* appeals to Trump to serve as Solomon and to decide which woman is telling the truth. Moore denies the charges and attempts to flatter Trump by praising his urban renewal efforts in "the ghetto." Despite Moore's attempts at deflection, most of the other participants seem to share Fox's consternation at her criminality, deception, and exhibitionism. Moore appears to be guilty of both stealing and identity theft.

As opinion turns against her, Moore asks for her own phone twice during the truth-telling part of the proceedings to show the proof that she believes will support her claims. Finally, Trump's son Donald Trump Jr. holds his own phone aloft with the definitive evidence on the screen. He notes that Fox's previous tweets had been about modest topics, such as "someone having a blessed day." Using his powers of deduction, he also observes that having "grammatical errors" would not be consistent with Fox's brand.

Donald Trump Sr. utters very few words in the episode. He expresses disgust during the pair's confrontation and calls Moore "nasty," a term he famously also used against Hillary Clinton in the 2016 election.

Unlike other memes with the "-gate" suffix, Phonegate never really gained much traction. However, it did play on stereotypes about Black women as irresponsible users of technology, and it furthered earlier racist and sexist narratives about the Obamaphone that linked digital literacy and identity politics.

A Secret in Plain View

ACN, formerly American Communications Network, was founded in 1993 as a direct marketing firm in which members sold telecom equipment and services. Business models like ACN's were often called "pyramid schemes" because revenue was generated largely by recruiting new salespeople rather than by actually selling goods and services. Using what little information was available about Trump's tax returns, financial journalists revealed how multi-level marketing became Trump's second most lucrative source of income, as a "side hustle" to supplement profits from *The Apprentice*.[48] According to this reporting, Trump was paid $8.8 million for promoting ACN. During his presidency, Trump was named in a class action lawsuit alleging that he had misled the plaintiffs by claiming ACN was a "great opportunity" and low risk. Yet the impact of the ACN exposé disappeared quickly in the news cycle. Although Trump faced being deposed in the lawsuit,[49] much more news coverage was devoted to his defense in other legal cases, such as those connected to sexual assault allegations.

Trump's questionable promotion of ACN extended to an episode of *Celebrity Apprentice* that focused entirely on the company. "Failure to Negotiate" was full of screen-within-screen shots featuring ACN teleconferencing. The show's contestants plugged the company's Iris 3000 videophone over and over again during the valuable prime-time hour on NBC, giving away an enormous amount of publicity. *Celebrity Apprentice* made being part of the ACN salesforce look like a rewarding venture full of perks; the climax of the show was a splashy event for ACN salespeople with celebrities and dance numbers.

By 2009, this kind of "voice over internet" communication was something of a dinosaur. Videophones had been the futuristic stars of world's fair pavilions in the 1960s, but a half-century later free or low-cost teleconferencing services like Skype had become the preferred method of video chatting. The Iris 3000 videophone could only communicate with other Iris 3000 videophones, which were built with the company's proprietary technology. In addition to needing connection to broadband internet service, the Iris 3000 required regular monthly payments to the company and a contract with an early termination fee.

Despite consumer dissatisfaction with ACN, the phone is introduced to viewers in the "Failure to Negotiate" episode by the members of the female team who gush over how the "beautiful face" of their team leader fills "the whole big screen." They pitch the usefulness of the phone: "you want to see the person you are speaking to." They enthuse about its "emotional appeal": you can "reconnect with someone you haven't seen in a while." They refer to "a feeling of magic." The team imagines scenarios for using the phone like sharing baby's first steps, announcing a wedding proposal, or connecting with a dad "out of town on business." They assert that ACN products are "the phones of the future." The phones are described as "easy," intuitive for a "non-techie," and "exciting."

Despite their enthusiasm for the product, the female team proved to be unsuccessful at judgment time. They didn't display the technological mastery of the male team. Their presentation was marred by "technical problems" with microphone feedback, and their efforts were hampered by unanticipated digital studio production costs. The male team had appealed to the audience's patriotic sensibilities by using a scenario in which a soldier video chatted with his family. The winning team understood the appeal of hypermasculinity and militarism, which were obvious political subtexts in the episode.

Autocratic politics were also commonly featured in Trump's *Apprentice* shows. The exercise of executive power was almost always shown as much more effective than group deliberation. In the "Failure to Negotiate" episode, the male team leader announces: "It's not a democracy. It's a dictatorship." Members of his team are urged to "take direction from the leader" and not to interfere when "the leader is leading." In contrast, the female team leader is criticized for attempting to govern the group by consensus and is called out for "not making decisions."

Shows like "Who Stole My Phone?" and "Failure to Negotiate" presented models for digital literacy that were clearly raced and gendered. In "Who Stole My Phone?" two Black women squabble over access to a digital device and are taught a lesson about the perils of their public visibility. "Failure to Negotiate" shows men to be logical leaders in technology use, given their ties to military culture. Women are relegated to the domestic sphere and must accept their own incompetence. Like Obama's mediagenic web content, Trump's TV episodes were didactic in promoting a politics of digital consumption. Of course, the spectacle on display was Trump's cutthroat capitalism rather than Obama's community organizing.

The Obscurity of Transparency

By fueling conspiracy theories online about Spygate and Obamagate, Trump modeled his administration's version of digital citizenship and promoted his ideologies about transparency. On Twitter, Trump demanded "transparency" dozens of times, often with capital letters and exclamation marks. He also hired former reality TV stars as White House staffers and used reality TV conventions in news conferences and other public appearances.[50] He fired cabinet members far more regularly than any other president, as if keeping up the rivalry and drama for the viewers tuning in. He even bragged that the ratings for his escapades as president were higher than those for popular reality television show finales. [51]

According to its internal logic, the Trump administration's quests for transparency could never reach a resolution. Exposing one set of secrets from the "deep state" could only lead to new mysteries to be interrogated. This rhetoric of transparency depended on maintaining belief in a continuing state of obscurity so that the truth could never be completely unraveled.[52] Unlike the Obama rhetoric in which transparency offered "sunlight," Trump emphasized the "dark" possibilities of the future, warning on Twitter of "dark days," "dark years," "dark corners," and a "dark and dangerous path" ahead.

The administration's optics around transparency also took advantage of the fact that Trump loved posing for photographs with stacks of documents.[53] The purpose of these staged media events seemed to be to demonstrate disclosure without actually disclosing anything. For example, Trump tweeted out a picture of himself signing his tax return when he was a candidate in 2016, but none of the actual information about his finances was visible.[54] All the viewer could see was that the pile of pages was taller than the top of Trump's head in the photo. After being elected, Trump displayed stacks of folders purportedly filled with documents signing over control of his assets to avoid conflicts of interest, but again reporters were prohibited from seeing the contents of the files.[55] In another press conference the details of the health-care plan that was supposed to supplant Obamacare amounted to a much smaller stack of printouts than the stack of regulations it would replace.[56] Reporters complained that many of these theatrically large paper displays used optical illusions and other questionable tactics,[57] but the visual rhetoric of symbolic display could be easily converted into memes that appealed to Trump's followers.

Trump's Digital Erasure

For over a decade, under both Republican and Democratic administrations, quarterly reports on troop deployments were made available on a website by the Department of Defense (DoD). The site displayed a master spreadsheet that showed how many members of the armed forces were stationed in particular states or countries during a given month. The data was separated into columns for active duty and reserve troops in each of the five branches of military service.[58]

A few months into the Trump administration, the entries for Afghanistan, Iraq, and Syria were suddenly blank. There were no zeros in the spreadsheet cells; the values were simply absent. A small asterisk informed the reader that with "ongoing operations, any questions concerning DoD personnel strength numbers are deferred to OSD Public Affairs/Joint Chiefs of Staff."

By November of 2019, the whole page had vanished. Attempting to access the document would result in an error notification and an encouragement to "contact support." Even troop deployment statistics involving US allies were no longer accessible.[59]

This kind of digital erasure during the Trump administration turned data rescue into an act of explicit political resistance. Saving online information became a way to promote true transparency and to preserve digital memory in the face of denials of fact.

Kin Lane, the Obama-era API evangelist, spent his holidays between Trump's election and inauguration desperately migrating data to save it from erasure.

"There was misinformation on the environment, climate change, LGBTQ rights," Lane recalled. "They seemed to be putting out as much information as they could, but it was not accurate, not real. I spent the whole Christmas downloading huge amounts of data and getting ready to put it out in machine-readable ways."

Lane secured a relatively modest $35,000 Knight Foundation Grant and encouraged other tech-savvy citizens to "Adopt an Agency." Lane explained to participants that "you should choose a data set that you can help clean up using GitHub and Google Sheets to track the work so it can be mirrored and shadowed and synched." In the interest of open access, data rescuers could also "improve the data by making a JSON or CSV file."

Lane wasn't alone as a data rescue leader. Danielle C. Robinson, a self-identified "maintainer," organized a data rescue event in Portland. To foster a welcoming environment, the gathering included a code of conduct that specified "a harassment-free experience for everyone, regardless of age, body size, disability, ethnicity, gender identity and expression, level of experience, nationality, personal appearance, race, religion, or sexual identity and orientation"[60]

While the Obama administration strove to make data openly available in digital formats that were legible in multiple contexts, Trump only offered a spectacle of transparency. Trump's version of transparency offered no sunshine. It was dark, occluded, and arcane. Transparency was limited to cryptic references to conspiracy theories like Pizzagate and Obamagate and to photo opportunities posing with stacks of impenetrable paperwork. Trump's advocacy for transparency was further hollowed out by his actual policies regarding digitizing the public record. This was the same president who undid many of his predecessor's efforts to make government data available to the public on the web. Converting PDFs to open formats was no longer a White House priority, and any websites that were up might be taken down. As the records from Obama-era transparency initiatives began to vanish from the internet, volunteer data rescuers had to try to salvage them.

Despite these profound differences between the two administrations, Trump also capitalized upon familiar language about transparency, the same call for transparency that had aided Obama's political fortunes. For example, he often spoke of "draining the swamp" to make the secrets of Washington visible. To solidify his position in office, Trump would also need to create a vast social media network of alternative news providers who could serve as social media influencers. This influence strategy also depended upon promoting a form of digital, white identity politics that foregrounded gender, race, and class as the main ingredients of online discourse. To incentivize this cohort of influencers, it would be necessary to offer access to his person and welcome them into the White House.

10 Trump's Rhetoric of Access

On October 9, 2016, less than two hours before his second presidential debate with Hillary Clinton, Donald Trump appeared on Facebook Live with four women. Each accused the Clinton family of participating in their sexual victimization.[1] It was one of the most dramatic social media moments of the campaign. Even traditional broadcasters from network news seemed compelled to cover the spectacle unfolding in real time with Trump as the master of ceremonies.

Just two days earlier, an audio file with an incriminating sound bite had exposed Trump speaking in private about objectifying women and making unwanted sexual advances. The vulgar language and casual misogyny in this "grab 'em by the pussy" audio was so offensive that several fellow Republicans called on Trump to withdraw. He was also facing the kind of town-hall-style debate that had traditionally disadvantaged Republican candidates.

Trump did not acknowledge being in a defensive position when he appeared on Facebook Live. He presented himself as a calm and supportive ally who was respectfully allowing the women unmediated access to the public stage. Although the camera shook, the sound was muddy, and reporters' questions were ignored, his imitation of a press conference stole the spotlight from media gatekeepers. Most broadcasters had been reluctant to dredge up these old allegations against the Clintons. They had wanted to keep focused on the fresher story that featured vivid evidence of Trump's own sexual misdeeds.

The first woman on Facebook Live, Paula Jones, was a familiar name to the American public because her lawsuit against Bill Clinton had produced a hoard of damning documents.[2] The second woman to speak, Kathy

Shelton, accused Hillary Clinton of taking pleasure as a young attorney in defending Shelton's accused rapist, including "laughing on tape." The third woman, Juanita Broaddrick, made her accusations succinctly: "Bill Clinton raped me, and Hillary Clinton threatened me." The fourth woman, Kathleen Willey, another alleged victim of Bill Clinton, spoke the longest in praising Trump: "I am here to support Donald Trump. . . . The reason for that is the first day that he announced for president, he said I love this country, and I want America to be great again. And I cried when he said that, because I think this is the greatest country in the world. I think that we can do anything. I think we can accomplish anything. I think we can bring peace to this world. And I think Donald Trump can lead us to that."

Pundits described Trump's Facebook Live event as foolhardy. They assumed that the public would perceive it as "bad politics" and dismiss all his online hoopla as a desperate and undisciplined move. But his attempt at distraction may have actually worked. Although it is difficult to credit any single event with stoking enough voter antipathy, more white women ultimately chose Donald Trump over his white female opponent.

In addition to the rhetoric of transparency, the event also employed an obvious rhetoric of access. Regular women who had been in subservient positions—state employee, job applicant, advice seeker—could mingle with a wealthy celebrity who lived a palatial lifestyle. They could also have access to his worldwide media channels, where he would amplify and extend their fifteen minutes of fame. Ironically, the "hot mic" with the "pussy" comment that had threatened Trump's political future came from a television program called *Access Hollywood*, which promised backstage access to the stars. Thus, Trump's version of access had to be even more compelling than the titillating raw audio too intimate for the show.

That same day—in a different part of cyberspace—Diamond (Lynnette Hardaway) and Silk (Rochelle Richardson), two Black sisters who produced an online talk show and plugged Trump incessantly, used their own Facebook Live channel to announce the results of their latest contest.[3] They called the lucky prizewinner to inform her that she and a friend won the privilege of having lunch with the two internet celebrities. Much as they might for a televised awards ceremony, Diamond and Silk wore coordinating outfits and revealed the name of the winner from a sealed envelope.

Diamond was usually the more talkative host, while Silk offered supportive affirmations, such as "yes," "uh huh," "that's right," "that's exactly right," and "girl." The duo followed the familiar social media celebrity format of frequent calls to action, such as sharing, subscribing, commenting, and liking.[4] In the weeks leading up to the contest results, viewers had been frequently encouraged to "like" Diamond and Silk's page as a way to enter.

These two Facebook Live events were obviously very different in fundamental ways. The Trump stream was structured like a formal news conference, whereas Diamond and Silk's episode presented their banter in a domestic interior. Trump had orchestrated a "breaking news" media event, whereas Diamond and Silk imitated the chatter of a talk show. Trump goaded white women to call out another white woman, while Diamond and Silk celebrated cross-racial political alliances.

However, both streams gave average people access to celebrity, whether a micro-celebrity like Diamond or Silk or a macro-celebrity like Trump.[5] They both featured real-time revelations and relied on elements of surprise to keep their audiences engaged. Diamond and Silk would later reenact elements of Trump's news conference. For example, they interviewed Broaddrick and rehashed the other women's allegations about the Clintons as well.

Facebook and Citizen Journalism

The choice for Diamond and Silk, two African Americans, to use Facebook Live in 2016 was weighted with political significance. Livestreaming on Facebook had become extremely important for Black Lives Matter activists protesting police violence against Black civilians that year. Black Lives Matter is a nonviolent social movement founded by Black queer activists after the shooting of Trayvon Martin was alleged to be in self-defense, Unfortunately, Facebook was not optimized to be a source for citizen journalism—just as it wasn't designed as a broadcast platform for news conferences or opinion shows. Yet it soon became an important venue for average people serving as witnesses to events unfolding around them in real time. High-quality digital cameras on smartphones were widely available, and the ability to livestream content was a significant advance in user-friendliness compared to the earlier video-sharing platforms that required lengthy upload times.

In this new era of ubiquitous access, graphic videos of violent events circulated widely. These digital technologies may have aided human rights advocacy by exposing incidents of state violence or abuses of power, but they may also have undermined social justice causes by revealing the identities of witnesses or victims.[6] When the evidence from cell phone videos was altered through editing or annotation, legitimate truth claims suffered.[7] Such were the dilemmas of relying on social network sites as publishing spaces for citizen journalism.[8]

One of the most searing events of the 2016 election season was the shooting of Philando Castile that July. Castile was killed by a Minnesota police officer while complying with the officer's instructions. His bloody death in an automobile seat was captured on Facebook Live in real time by his companion, Diamond Reynolds, as was her poignant questioning of the officer about his lethal behavior during the traffic stop.[9] Because the clip captured the moment of Castile's death, it drew an enormous audience to the spectacle.[10] Viewers recorded their reactions to seeing the video of the Castile shooting while their emotions were most fresh on Facebook Live. They vented their anger, shock, and outrage with displays of raw feeling.

Alton Sterling had also been shot and killed by law enforcement just one day earlier in Baton Rouge. In a somber stream on Facebook Live, Black police officer Nakia Jones described her experience watching the Sterling video "over and over and over and over again" and becoming "so furious" and "so hurt" as a person who "wears the uniform with the blue" and yet identifies with the mothers who have lost their children to officers imbued with racist prejudices.[11]

That September, the shooting of Keith Lamont Scott in Charlotte was followed by a dramatic Facebook Live stream filmed by his daughter Lyric. In the video she walks around police crime scene tape and registers her shock in the immediate aftermath of his death: "The police just shot my daddy four times for being Black."[12]

On Facebook Live, Diamond and Silk often weighed in on Black Lives Matter stories. One of their earliest videos, posted July 8, 2016, focused on the ambush of Dallas law enforcement officers by Black army reservist Micah Xavier Johnson.[13] Five police officers were killed and nine others were injured in the attack. Johnson's motive was said to be retaliation for the killings of Black civilians by the police. Diamond and Silk begin their stream by registering the immediacy of their emotions: "we're very sad; we're very upset; we're somber." Initially they argue for "complexity" and "sensitivity" with attention to "both sides," but quickly they move to a strong advocacy position for law enforcement. "We love our police officers," Diamond declares. She also rebuts messages from Black Lives Matter by asserting that "all lives matter," including "blue lives." She sees those influenced by Black Lives Matter as people with "weak minds" who do "dumb stuff."

Facebook and Celebrity

Before becoming stars in the Trump alternative-media galaxy, Diamond and Silk posted content much more in line with the progressive Democratic politics often associated with Black women. For example, in 2015 the duo posted a "Black Lives Matter" video that juxtaposed images of slavery with videos of police brutality. They also posted a video sympathetic to Sandra Bland, who was found hanged in her jail cell three days after being arrested during a traffic stop. However, Diamond and Silk had struggled to build an audience with their early channel, "The Viewers' View," which was devoted to media criticism. Even posting emotionally invested Black Lives Matter content couldn't make their videos go viral. "We probably had, what, ten people [watching] our YouTube channel?" Diamond told a *Rolling Stone* reporter. "We were just talking about things that we saw that we didn't like. We thought it was a place to vent."[14] Most of the record of their earlier opinion sharing was eventually scrubbed from the internet.[15]

On a typical episode of Diamond and Silk's newer show, "Chit Chat Live," much of the time was devoted to thanking their "haters" and "agitators," expressing their appreciation for gratuities, and offering subscribers a "shout out" for their attention. Videos were labeled with familiar touchstones for right-wing outrage. For example, one video was entitled "Central Park 5, Crime Bill 1994, Nancy Pelosi, President Trump."[16]

Facebook and Misinformation

As their connections to right-wing causes strengthened, Diamond and Silk began to reference established conspiracy theories connected to Pizzagate and other fake news narratives. For example, in one of their segments Diamond instructs her followers to "go to Wikileaks and Google 'Podesta' and 'spirit cooking.'"[17] As Silk signals her agreement, Diamond suggests that Hillary Clinton's campaign chief was likely "using blood and all kinds of stuff," "working roots," and communicating in a "secret code for some-thing." According to the sisters, Podesta's interest in "bodily fluids" indi-cated that his allies could be "witches" using a "potion" or—at the very least—"sick people" or "freaks" involved with "Satan" or "the devil."[18]

In one of their appearances on Fox News, the sisters also spread a fake news story that Democratic Speaker of the House Nancy Pelosi had garbled speech.[19] Diamond and Silk called the house speaker a "non-functioning alcoholic" who "slurs her words" and was "deteriorating" with advanced age. Just hours earlier, Trump had tweeted a video that seemed so show Pelosi struggling to sound articulate. Mainstream news organizations dem-onstrated with side-by-side videos that the original footage of Pelosi had been slowed down.[20] It was a "cheap fake," a fake video that was easily manufactured rather than a "deep fake," which required more extensive digital production resources, but it was still remarkably effective at under-mining Pelosi's dignity and authority.[21]

Like other right-wing social media celebrities, Diamond and Silk only received minor sanctions for spreading false stories. For example, a head-line in 2018 claimed utterly falsely that "Obama secretly gave citizenship to 2,500 Iranians as part of nuke deal." Facebook users flagged the story as misinformation and links to it were removed,[22] but Diamond and Silk were still free to publish new pro-Trump conspiracy fictions. Even as they spread obviously harmful myths about the coronavirus pandemic, their Facebook account remained active. Trump continued to amplify their brand with an April 2020 tweet that declared his continued "love" for Diamond and Silk, which he said was shared by "millions of people."[23]

Facebook and Censorship

The longevity of Diamond and Silk's status as internet influencers can also be explained by their usefulness to Trump in his high-profile campaign against "Big Tech." Although many software engineers identify as libertar-ian, right-wing media platforms love to denounce the supposedly left-wing sympathies of Silicon Valley elites. Trump's love-hate relationship with social media companies probably dates back to the 2016 campaign when Twitter reneged on a deal for the #CrookedHillary custom emoji. The sting of having his power checked by those who had so amplified it was an irri-tant to Trump that became more enraging over time.

In the last two years of his presidency, Trump became fixated on repealing a key provision in established internet law. Section 230 of the 1996 Communications Decency Act prohibited treating any "provider or user of an interactive computer service" as "the publisher or speaker of any information provided by another information content provider." This part of the legislation carved out an exception for free speech in a law that was initially designed to limit it. The parts of the main law that censored sexual content on the internet were struck down in court challenges, but Section 230 survived. Section 230 provided a "safe harbor" that protected social media companies from expensive litigation, since they couldn't be held liable for the actions of their users.[24] Before Section 230, any kind of content moderation provided by these platforms could be interpreted as accepting responsibility for absolutely everything posted on their sites. Repealing Section 230 would both dissuade platforms from moderating content and place them in legal jeopardy with costly lawsuits.

Trump also had personal reasons to seek revenge on tech moguls. Jeff Bezos owned the *Washington Post*, which was constantly investigating his administration. Bill Gates had close ties to the Clintons through their mutual philanthropic work, which Trump felt unjustly burnished his rivals' charitable reputations. Tim Cook of Apple was a major donor to Hillary Clinton's campaign. Only Mark Zuckerberg of Facebook seemed to escape Trump's ire, perhaps because the platform had been so accommodating for so many years.

To gain political power over tech companies, Trump collaborated closely with Josh Hawley, a tech-savvy photogenic junior senator from Missouri. Hawley was also a former law professor. He introduced several pieces of legislation designed to reign in tech companies. He opened investigations, issued subpoenas, and wrote formal letters of complaint to federal agencies. Hawley often used national sovereignty claims to support greater regulation; these multinational companies were often dependent upon foreign partners, investments, and components. Ties to China were a hot-button political issue in particular. Hawley capitalized on bipartisan anxieties about user privacy, pointing to how digital media companies monetized user surveillance. He rightly pointed to the ways that corporate rhetoric about optimizing user experience often deflected attention from how metadata was harvested and individual decision-making was curtailed. Unfortunately, conservative desires to minimize gatekeeping in digital "public squares" also emboldened those who posted hate speech and misinformation.

Just as the Obama administration created a website to gather details about exposure to online misinformation, the Trump administration launched a site to harvest horror stories about tech bias. Users were asked to fill out an online form that asked for their personal information. The form then prompted them "to describe the alleged bias that occurred, which platform it occurred on, and if they had screenshots of any messages they received from the company."[25] Visitors to the White House website were directed away from the URL controlled by the federal government to a site designed by Typeform, a company based in Barcelona, Spain. Some critics complained that Trump's bias reporting initiative was actually "a data collection tool in disguise" that was designed to customize more effective social media appeals targeted to conservatives.[26]

Eventually this opportunity for participation was suspended. Like a Trump tweet, the announcement used "shouting" via capital letters, scare quotes to indicate sarcasm, and praise of Trump as sole creator of the initiative.

> This typeform isn't accepting new responses SOCIAL MEDIA PLATFORMS should advance FREEDOM OF SPEECH. Yet too many Americans have seen their accounts suspended, banned, or fraudulently reported for unclear "violations" of user policies. On May 15, President Trump asked Americans to share their stories of suspected political bias. The White House received thousands of responses— thank you for lending your voice!

This information-gathering campaign deployed a number of access-themed talking points. It asserted that conservatives had the right for their political content to be freely accessible. It claimed user policies were interfering with people's rights to access the internet itself. It assured disgruntled users that they had the ear of a powerful administration capable of seeking redress. Each one of these elements affirmed an access-oriented principle.

Congressional Hearings

The House had more anti-tech crusaders than the Senate, but they lacked Hawley's star power. House adversaries of social media companies included Tennessee's Marsha Blackburn, who had sparred with Twitter over a "baby body parts" post,[27] and Representatives Jason Smith and Vicky Hartzler, who were self-identified Diamond and Silk fans.

Republican legislators were particularly concerned about allegations of "shadow banning" that supposedly affected right-wing news sources disproportionately. Shadow banning describes how social media companies might make content invisible without the knowledge of the original poster. This material might not be technically removed from a platform, but other users may not see it listed or indexed on their feeds.[28] In their defense, Silicon Valley companies claimed that their visibility algorithms were merely intended to discourage self-promotion, spamming, and trolling.

Tech companies tended to explain these barriers to access as temporary "glitches" or "bugs" that needed to be sorted out by human moderators. However, researchers found reasons to be skeptical, given what they discovered in the actual patterns of decreased visibility across large social network sites. However, this data couldn't be reduced to a simple left-right picture of political bias either. Instead, they found an "epidemic process among interacting users" that might "infect" other users based on connections rather than content.[29]

Before Congress, Diamond and Silk presented themselves as clear-cut victims of shadow banning who were muzzled by tech firms for their conservative beliefs. They were invited to a House Judiciary Hearing on April 26, 2018, to make their case to the American public. Unlike the polished briefs that other witnesses supplied, their written statement contained glaring grammatical errors. It emphasized personal grievances rather than universal rights. Their DIY document included screenshots that demonstrated how their Facebook page had been mislabeled as "very liberal." Other proof included user messages complaining about blocked content, graphs showing periods of plummeting engagement, and view counts that seemed not to correlate with their follower counts.[30]

In Diamond and Silk's oral testimony, they bemoaned their supposed mistreatment by Facebook. Silk reiterated her displeasure with the inaccurate "very liberal" metadata label and expressed her frustration with her inability to change this "default setting." Diamond claimed that they were censored for "six months" as "unsafe to the community," although Facebook itself produced emails that showed the error in "enforcement" only lasted a few days. In a separate session of testimony, Facebook head Mark Zuckerberg was forced to defend the actions that had supposedly led to the duo's travails.

Democratic lawmakers in the House majority grimaced at the women's undignified outbursts, but Republicans were deferential. Representative Steve King, who was known for his strong ties to alt-right communities online,[31] questioned Diamond and Silk with great sympathy and respect.[32] In the hearings King also asked that documents from the conspiracy news source *Gateway Pundit* be entered into evidence.

Certainly, the two women were correct that Facebook's filtering and moderation mechanisms were deliberately hidden. However, the fact that they were hidden didn't mean that there was necessarily a vast left-wing conspiracy at work. Facebook had many reasons not to be transparent about how content was made accessible. For example, Facebook's silence about its gatekeeping might have been influenced by its dependence on paid sponsorships.[33]

Motivation to keep the company's "ghost work" out of view may have also been a factor. "Ghost work" describes exploitative offshore labor practices that keep certain workers invisible.[34] Such precarious employees usually don't work for Facebook directly as content moderators.[35] Instead, they toil in foreign countries where they screen user content in deplorable conditions.[36] They are often underpaid and overworked.

In addition, the daunting task of sorting billions of pieces of information was never planned as part of any business model. Social media companies wanted to avoid controversy by promoting what Tarleton Gillespie has called "the myth of the neutral platform."[37] The tendency of Facebook's algorithm to privilege some kinds of content over others was also known to scuttle material from progressive political causes.[38] After all, the company made its profits from "identity economics" rather than liberal idealism.[39]

Finally, it was possible that social media metrics were designed to be difficult to interpret.[40] Facebook wanted to sell its analytics and marketing services to potential customers, so confusing information could help them sell those services to clients who wanted a clearer view of their visibility data.

The Case for Economic Rights

Although the sisters' testimony was ostensibly about censorship, their real gripe seemed to be demonetization. Many of their most persuasive pieces of evidence involved being deprived of revenue rather than losing the actual ability to post material online. Representative Hank Johnson expressed his skepticism that their appearance was really about "exercising your First Amendment rights." He noted that the sisters made "a ton of money off

Facebook" and accused them of only seeking redress because the company was "messing with your money."

A few days after their high-profile congressional testimony, Diamond and Silk were rewarded with personal access to Trump. In a private meeting, they posed for a "selfie" with the president and his eldest son.[41] Donald Trump Jr. posted the photo on his Instagram feed. Despite a lack of experience running large organizations, Diamond and Silk became fixtures at invitation-only, pro-Trump, African American leadership events. They were welcomed into the White House during Trump's last year in office as spokespeople for economic rights in the digital age. In the transcript of their remarks Diamond describes how they met Trump, a "businessman billionaire," who said to them in their very first encounter, "I hope you monetize this." She continues with a negative comparison to his predecessor in the office. "Obama didn't come and say, 'Hey, I hope you monetize it.'"[42] They consistently emphasized economic rights rather than political or civil rights for Black Americans—both on digital platforms and in society as a whole.

Other alt-right content producers might have benefited from "de-platforming" because it would allow them to operate without interference from regulators or scrutiny from law enforcement, but Diamond and Silk were too dependent on Facebook for their livelihoods. At several points, they attempted to move their digital presence to new start-up platforms, but they remained with the major social media sites that offered the potential for mainstream popularity. By the 2020 election season Facebook was regularly flagging their posts as misinformation or hate speech. They experimented again with two conservative alternatives: ChatDit and Rumble. com. Interestingly, the ChatDit terms and conditions mixed the rhetoric of access to free speech with the rhetoric of access to economic opportunity.

> THIS SOCIAL MEDIA SITE IS A NEUTRAL PLATFORM FOR ALL. DESIGNED WITH YOU IN MIND. IF YOU DON'T LIKE SOMETHING, BLOCK YOURSELF. Build your Business, Keep your Business. Build your Platform as long as you are following the policies. You have freedom of speech, not freedom to hate.

Rumble pitched its monetization even more prominently: "One of the things Rumble does best, is providing audiences that will generate revenue for video creators."

Diamond and Silk benefited from the monetization of pro-Trump content and from being accessible on Facebook. Their desires to emulate

Trump's wealth and celebrity lifestyle and their inclusion in gatherings of the prosperous were more valuable to them than being part of the Black Lives Matter community. Unlike the Obamaphone Lady or Kenya Moore, these two Black women were positioned by Trump as responsible users of technology who were getting out his message and receiving insider access in exchange.

The Social Media Summit

In July of 2019 Diamond and Silk joined other honored guests at the White House for a Social Media Summit, where those who produced pro-Trump digital content were celebrated by the president. The day of the summit began with a triumphal tweet from the president: "The White House will be hosting a very big and very important Social Media Summit today. Would I have become President without Social Media? Yes (probably)!"[43]

The entire event was documented in close to real time with hundreds of selfies shot on the White House complex. Some of Trump's most extensive praise at the summit was directed at Dan Scavino, who was introduced as his "senior advisor for digital strategy." During the summit, Scavino busily amplified posts from participants using the #SocialMediaSummit hashtag (figure 10.1).

During Trump's speech at the gathering, Diamond and Silk were singled out for recognition as "two very special people," "two beautiful women," and "African American, incredible women." Each time Trump mentioned them, he added an additional marker of identity politics. Trump credited First Lady Melania Trump with discovering the media talents of the duo. "My wife said, 'You have to see these women. They're incredible. They're genius. And they like you.'"[44] Then Diamond and Silk were invited up to the stage for a warm embrace.[45]

Just as Diamond and Silk had listed their gripes about inconsistencies in their popularity metrics, Trump groused about his fluctuating follower statistics at the Social Media Summit. "A number of months ago, I was at a certain number—you know, many millions—and then all of a sudden, I was down over a million." He expressed dissatisfaction with how social media companies were "doing adjustments" and denied having "fake people" or needing to "buy people."

IWV ✓
@IWV

🔋 iPhones fully charged (☑️) at the @WhiteHouse #SocialMediaSummit▬

6:02 PM · Jul 11, 2019 · Twitter for iPhone

3.1K Retweets   **13.8K** Likes

Figure 10.1
Tweet using the #SocialMediaSummit hashtag from the Social Media Summit, retweeted by Donald Trump.

In contrast, many data scientists and computer security specialists have asserted that Trump's social media numbers were persistently inflated. For example, one study claimed that sixty-one percent of Trump's followers were "bots, spam, inactive, or propaganda."[46]

The list of Social Media Summit invitees included several influencers involved in the Pizzagate conspiracy theory, including Jim Hoft of *The Gateway Pundit* and Jack Posobiec of One America News Network.[47] Posobiec had a long record of manufacturing scandals to generate profitable clickbait. For example, he publicized the existence of a fictional #RapeMelania hashtag. He blamed the offensive hashtag on left-wing agitators, even though he himself had been the chief creator of it.[48] James O'Keefe, the founder of Project Veritas, was also invited to the summit. O'Keefe specialized in releasing secretly recorded videos of his subjects, which were denounced by mainstream journalists because of the deceptive editing techniques involved. For example, O'Keefe had circulated what seemed to be incriminating footage of a Google executive in an attempt to paint the company as politically biased.

At the Social Media Summit, Trump attempted to resurrect the old Spygate/Obamagate narrative, which alleged that Trump had been under surveillance by deep state operatives. Trump also called for "transparency, more accountability, and more freedom."

Despite the libertarian exuberance of the event, the future of social media imagined by Trump and some of his special guests appeared to be a future of regulation. Social media companies as private enterprises were to be reined in by the law. Trump introduced Josh Hawley who attacked not only "the establishment media, the fake media" but also social media, which was filled with "censorship." He accused "social media giants" of planning to "shut us down" and "shut us up" because they were going to reverse "special deals from government" that had been arranged by Democratic administrations. Although the threat to revoke Section 230 wasn't referenced specifically, it was clear what Hawley meant when he said, "here's the bargain: they have to quit discriminating against conservatives."

Influencer Invitations

The hosting of gatherings like the Social Media Summit started years earlier with the so-called DeploraBall events. During Trump's inauguration, DeploraBall attendees included Hoft, Posobiec, and O'Keefe. One of their events took place at the National Press Club, where media bashing was the order of the day.[49] Other DeploraBall celebrations were organized across the country through distributed networks. Trump's supporters expressed their merriment at managing to "meme our way to the White House and elect Donald Trump."[50] However, some complained that more extreme participants from the alt-right social mediascape were excluded from these parties, such as conspiracy theorist Alex Jones.

Significantly, Trump used an important term in his Social Media Summit speech that had not been part of his presidential vocabulary before: "influencer." In discussing this class of online celebrities associated with self-branding and monetizing internet presence, he was inclined to also describe them as "journalists," thus conflating commercial brand ambassadors with non-commercial citizen journalists. "Never before have so many online journalists and influencers—and that's exactly what you are;

you're journalists and you're influencers—come together in this building to discuss the future of social media." He repeatedly also referenced
their "power."

Although "influencer" was a relatively new word in official White House
parlance, it was a familiar term within the Trump family. Episodes of the
Apprentice, which starred Trump and his children, regularly featured product placement. These product placements couldn't be avoided by viewers
as easily as commercials, and they provided additional revenue that wasn't
as likely to be disclosed. During the course of just one month, over a hundred brands were integrated into episodes of *Celebrity Apprentice*.[51] With the
rise of social media platforms in the beginning of the '00s, corporations
began to invest in amateur content creators who were competing successfully against network television franchises like *The Apprentice*. Traditional
celebrities even began to mimic online influencer practices. Reality television producers adapted to the rising cultural profile of the influencer and
scripted new story lines around product placement that expanded the rep-
ertoires of both their famous and non-famous performers.

The original internet micro-celebrities had traded on familiarity, relatability, and trust. They offered food hacks, cosmetics tutorials, clothing
makeovers, and other lifestyle-based self-improvement. The action was
usually staged in DIY home studios. Because members of this new caste
of internet celebrities presented themselves as part of a viewer's social network, they projected stronger "social proof" to validate consumer choices
and behavioral decisions.[52] Unlike a retail salesperson, an influencer was
selling themselves. The fan was offered a social bond that gave them access
to this special person. By necessity, commercial transactions had to be
underplayed to keep the tone focused on friendly solidarity and bonding.
Social media influencers accelerated the already frenetic pace of neoliberal
capitalism in the early twenty-first century by colonizing more aspects of
the private sphere with market relations. From child-rearing to personal
hygiene, everything and nothing was for sale.

Influencer activities require constant maintenance of an entrepreneurial self. Incessant jockeying for status creates precarity for even the most
successful, as they manage carefully calibrated self-presentation techniques
intended to look effortless and spontaneous. Communications scholar
Alice Marwick chronicled the lives of the first generation of these striving
micro-celebrities. In her book *Status Update* she documents their aspirations

to capitalize on a new culture of self-produced media consumption. The influencers Marwick studied were expected to master "creating a persona, sharing personal information about oneself, constructing intimate connections to create the illusion of friendship or closeness, acknowledging an audience and identifying them as fans, and strategically revealing information to increase or maintain this audience."[53]

Digital anthropologist Crystal Abidin has called these tactical maneuvers "emotioneering." According to Abidin, influencers have to balance the demand for "everydayness" with their audience's expectations for special traits, such as "exclusivity," "exoticism," and "exceptionalism."[54] Projecting access was a key element of this complicated juggling act. Thanks to social media, followers could move from the front row to backstage. They could be invited into private parties and onto secluded islands. They could even enter the bedroom and the bathroom unimpeded.

The Influencer First Daughter

Ivanka Trump, the president's eldest daughter, regularly hired people to run influencer campaigns for her now defunct fashion brand, and she served as an influencer herself. Unlike Marwick's influencers, who had to rely on themselves and their own resources, Trump's daughter had a lot more professional assistance. Her marketing consultants created a flurry of posts intended for reposting on Instagram, Pinterest, Facebook, and Twitter, in addition to email marketing and blog posts.[55]

Because Ivanka was an Oval Office advisor and an unsalaried federal employee, online promotional activities for her private business could be controversial. Only a few days after the 2016 election there was consternation when a "fashion alert" was sent via email to style journalists by Ivanka Trump Fine Jewelry. The alert showed Ivanka on the network news show *Sixty Minutes*. Using an image from an official news event, the alert promoted buying "her favorite bangle from the Metropolis Collection," which cost over eight thousand dollars.[56] Federal ethics rules that prohibit use of public office for private gain barred Ivanka from directly advertising or promoting her products from the White House, but more subtle influencer marketing was much harder to regulate.

After her business shut down because of poor sales in 2018, she continued to use her social media accounts to promote the businesses of others.

When the CEO of Goya Foods outraged Latinx activists by praising Trump, he faced a boycott of his company. Ivanka responded by posting a color photo of herself posing with a can of Goya beans. It appeared on Instagram, Twitter, and Facebook. Her brand promotion of Goya in the image is not subtle: the can has an enormous label with the brand name, and she holds it aloft with one hand and gestures at it, just like a spokesmodel displaying a sponsored product. When Ivanka was castigated for violating rules against giving official endorsements to private companies, Trump Sr. responded by posting his own plugs for Goya on social media.

During her father's term, Ivanka Trump was often chastised for insensitivity to social justice issues. Callouts on her social media accounts drew attention to the mismatch between her picture-perfect lifestyle of privilege and the misery of those excluded from such prosperity because of their race, class, religion, or immigration status. For example, controversy flared because of a glamorous photo she posted during the chaos of the "Muslim ban" on refugees. There was also outrage when she posted an intimate mother-child photo while Mexican parents were being separated from their offspring at the border. Like her father she blocked those who challenged her.

By softening the senior Trump's image on social media among white suburban mothers and white professional women, Ivanka played an important role in clearing his path to victory in 2016. In addition to giving stump speeches praising her father, she used her social media presence to project a lifestyle brand that conveyed both privileged pampering and self-help entrepreneurship.

In their symbiotic father-daughter social media relationship, it was significant that Trump's first Twitter mention was his daughter's handle. Their complementary approaches to promoting the family brand might explain why Ivanka chose tactics that were different from the headlines, alerts, and insults that characterized the communication style of the elder Trump.

When Ivanka Trump published her bestseller *Women Who Work*, several critics pointed to its social-media-ready packaging and its hyper-feminine aesthetic. "The section dividers in the book are pale pink and meant to be Instagrammed," one wrote, "with elaborately lettered quotes from other people labelled #ITWiseWords."[57] "It's perfect for a generation weaned on Pinterest and goop.com," another opined.[58] Another noted, "Its title is adapted from a tagline that was adopted in a marketing meeting that has lived most of its life as a promotional hashtag for the Ivanka Trump brand of clothing, jewelry, and, most recently, feminism."[59]

Women Who Work performs many of the classic influencer moves identified by experts on internet celebrity. For example, female influencers often invite followers to share in their most intimate moments while simultaneously expressing their desires for having a refuge from a prying public. In this way they can disclose private details without seeming exhibitionistic or narcissistic. For example, in her book Ivanka promotes her obligation to be "unabashed and transparent" despite her stated wish to retreat because of her personal "preference for privacy."[60]

Rather than claiming a position of individual uniqueness, Ivanka points to the validation of others who comment, like, and share her content, thus justifying her amplification of similar domestic themes and providing a defense against charges of self-aggrandizement. "I wasn't expecting the overwhelming number of comments I received in response to those family snaps," she claims in *Women Who Work*. "So many people expressed surprise and relief that I was comfortable revealing a more private side of myself." In addition to her humblebragging, she also solicits engagement by emphasizing the relatability of her experiences. She writes, "I often heard things like 'It's so inspiring that you're such a hands-on mom and not intimidated to show that part of you,' and 'So amazing! You're not wearing makeup.'"

She credits her appreciative and empathetic audience with helping her overcome her fears that "being a young female executive with a baby" would undermine her authority in the professional world. Naturally, she does not dwell on the degree to which being a social media influencer was, in fact, her profession. Little of the Trump family's brand value was generated by actual goods and services. According to *Women Who Work*, reader comments on social media "emboldened me to share all aspects of my life—not just my more polished persona—more frequently."

Of course, claiming to be showing spontaneous moments—rather than carefully rehearsed and stage-managed online performances—seemed ludicrous, given the careful composition of the elements in the actual content of her feed. For example, several news outlets covered her no-makeup selfie, which commemorated her thirty-eighth birthday with an exaggerated kissy-face expression that had been edited in a third-party app.[61]

Ivanka generally expressed more subtle disdain for reporters than her father's outright contempt, even if it was still rooted in the same disregard

Figure 10.2
A selfie posted to Instagram on January 4, 2021, of Ivanka Trump with Donald Trump in the background.

for gatekeeping. In *Women Who Work*, she writes that she "didn't want the first photo of my daughter to be sold to the press, so I posted an image myself on one of my social media accounts." In this version of the story, she does an end run around the snooping paparazzi by reporting on herself.

However, many images of Ivanka Trump were taken by photojournalists rather than tabloid scandalmongers. Her Instagram documented official meetings with legislators, foreign dignitaries, and cabinet officials. While many reporters were barred from covering Trump's journeys on Air Force One—after they had been banished by the mercurial president—Ivanka advertised her access to the commander in chief. For example, a selfie of the smiling first daughter showed her father in the background, absorbed in his smartphone with nary a reporter in sight (figure 10.2).

Influencers and Identity Politics

It may seem strange to compare Diamond and Silk's social media presence to Ivanka Trump's, but both cases of pro-Trump digital performance perpetuated the logic of identity politics through an emphasis on access. Certainly, the emotional outbursts and animated call-and-response rants of Diamond and Silk were formally and aesthetically very different from Ivanka Trump's dispassionate heteronormative decorum and executive composure. In many ways Ivanka played the role of the "cool girl" in the White House's disreputable cast of characters, projecting an unruffled demeanor that normalized casual misogyny and sexist power plays.[62] In contrast, the affective labor of Diamond and Silk as Black women was never submerged far beneath the surface.

Ostensibly the spotlight on Diamond and Silk existed to undermine belief in identity politics, a matrix of principles that assumed that self-interest and shared oppressions would inevitably spur organizational movements for a particular group's liberation struggles. As Black women they defied assumptions that they would always align with the Democratic Party and notions of multicultural representation and social welfare policy. By refusing to play their expected role and rejecting their earlier connections to Black Lives Matter, Diamond and Silk reinforced familiar tropes in Republican Party ideology, which always claimed to be color-blind.

From the alt-right Breitbart.com to the mainstream *Wall Street Journal*, conservative pundits regularly assailed "identity politics." According to these sources, identity politics was a force for irrational behavior and divisive tribalism that needed to be eliminated. When Diamond and Silk accused Facebook of "censoring two women of color,"[63] their headline-grabbing complaint was not that this censorship was driven by their race or gender, but rather that their political opinions were being curtailed. According to conservatives, this kind of shared political ideology should be the only legitimate basis of solidarity.

The white identity politics of Ivanka Trump were more subtle but pervasive. It might be difficult to say precisely why a particular picture of cupcakes at a birthday party communicates whiteness so strongly. Of course, the photo looks like it was composed by a professional food stylist, but the exact racial coding might be more difficult to pin down. Nonetheless, I would argue that many of the shots on Ivanka's Instagram could easily be stock photos from the popular parody blog *Stuff White People Like*.[64] The sterility of her spotless home also conveys her eugenic fitness, and the absence of signs of any immigrant heritage is striking.[65] This lack of cultural markers is particularly noteworthy, given that Ivanka is a woman with a Czech mother and a Jewish husband. Her stunt with the can of beans was ridiculed partly because of her obvious estrangement from a product so closely associated with ethnic identity.

Her tone-deaf quotations from Black feminists in *Women Who Work* demonstrated the degree to which Ivanka was incapable of reflecting on her own whiteness.[66] Her use of the words of Toni Morrison about slavery were judged as particularly offensive by many. By embracing empowerment feminism, which addressed individual advancement rather than structural oppression, and popular feminism, which centered white celebrities in social media campaigns, Ivanka consolidated her unimpeachable status as a white woman striving for success.[67] Scholars of whiteness have pointed out how a "sense of uniqueness" and "individual narrative" can actually be essential for the kind of white solidarity that is telegraphed by Ivanka's social media presence.[68]

In her life after the White House, Ivanka is likely to use her fame as an influencer even more obviously for economic advantage. She has sought trademark protections in China for many potential enterprises, including wedding dresses, senior homes, semiconductors, voting machines, and sausage casings.[69] Her stepmother, Melania Trump, might also revive her earlier influencer personality as an above-the-fray, jet-setting, penthouse-living supermodel. Before becoming First Lady, Melania was embroiled in a legal case that sought to protect her reputation against stories that she had worked as an escort before dating Trump. As justification for defending her name, her lawyers cited several pending "multi-million dollar business relationships" in which Melania would hawk clothing, shoes, jewelry, cosmetics, and perfume.[70] The female partners of Trump's sons—Lara Trump and Kimberly Guilfoyle—have also pursued influencer deals. It could be argued that all four of the Trump women were peddling a particular economic and racial ideology, along with the fashion, branded swag, and opportunities for favor that they promoted.

Although it sounds strange, the case of Diamond and Silk raised some substantive questions about what kinds of rights were digital rights. The sisters obviously focused on economic rights, property rights, rights to free speech, and rights to self-defense—which were prominent concerns for social media influencers—rather than the privacy rights, political rights, civil rights, or human rights that affected more precarious citizens. But by drawing attention to power disparities between members of the same social media platforms, they centered advocacy for internet regulation as a major concern.

National Security Access

In the fall of 2019, Donald J. Trump posted what appeared to be a classified photo of a secret Iranian military facility to Twitter. Soon after Trump's tweet was posted, the *New York Times* noticed that there was a reflection on the aerial photograph that indicated that it was a cell phone copy of the original, which was probably from a security briefing to the president.[71] Amateur sky-watchers then used their collective intelligence to determine the likely satellite that had captured the top-secret image.[72]

The photo of the launch pad strewn with wreckage was clearly intended to taunt Iranian leadership, which had struggled to develop a twenty-first-century missile program and had often been thwarted by sanctions and espionage. Years earlier, in their battle for image management, the Iranians had even gone to the trouble of using image editing software to cut and paste a picture of a successful rocket launch on top of a picture of a failed test.[73]

Rather than go through diplomatic channels to transmit a bulletin from the White House to the government of a foreign power, Trump sent the message to the entire world digitally. With a press of his finger, he bypassed intermediaries in the State Department and the news media. In addition to the photo, the tweet contained his personal message of professed ignorance (figure 10.3): "The United States of America was not involved in the catastrophic accident during final launch preparations for the Safir SLV Launch at Semnan Launch Site One in Iran. I wish Iran best wishes and good luck in determining what happened at Site One."

As a picture with a punchline, the tweet reflects what Sara Polak has called the "cartoon logic" of the Trump presidency.[74] The details in the caption don't read as an official denial, and the sentiment of "best wishes and good luck" is obviously ironic. The sooty remains of the explosion show an image of an "epic fail" of the ludicrous kind that the internet adores.

By using social media as a method of direct address, Trump continued the public diplomacy efforts of the Obama administration, which had used YouTube, Facebook, and Twitter to bypass gatekeepers and communicate directly with foreign audiences. The trolling tone, however, was something

Donald J. Trump ✔
@realDonaldTrump

The United States of America was not involved in the catastrophic accident during final launch preparations for the Safir SLV Launch at Semnan Launch Site One in Iran. I wish Iran best wishes and good luck in determining what happened at Site One.

6:44 pm · 30 Aug 2019 · Twitter for iPhone

Figure 10.3
@realDonaldTrump tweet of satellite image.

distinctly Trumpian. His tongue-in-check attitude was intended to perplex his adversaries. Here was a high-stakes move in geopolitics that the US appeared to have initiated. Or had it? Had the Americans approved an attack upon an Iranian military operation? Or was Trump just trying to psych them out? Responding to Trump's tweet would be futile, as it would be with other internet trolls. If challenged, the sender could easily shirk responsibility and mock any foe as unable to take a joke.

The Iranian aerial photo incident was part of a larger pattern of the administration's cavalier attitude about access. Trump often flouted national security clearance rules. For example, at his Florida club, a dinner turned into an impromptu security briefing that was held in full view of other guests. To illuminate top-secret documents, assistants used the flashlights on their cell phones.[75]

While the Obama administration had condemned WikiLeaks for breaching national security and putting "the lives of Americans and our partners at risk,"[76] Trump enthusiastically praised WikiLeaks multiple times.[77] The

previous White House had scolded Russian hackers for seeking "close proximity to sensitive information,"[78] but Trump egged them on in pursuit of
his political enemies.[79]

Just as he did with national security, Trump derided concerns about
influence peddling. In his mind, his identity as a wealthy and powerful man
could only benefit American citizens, whose country he was making great
again. Fans showed their love for him by accessing his clubs, his hotels, and
his person. Why shouldn't he benefit financially from these arrangements?
As a social media influencer, his daughter Ivanka similarly muddied distinc-
tions between her own interests and the interests of her followers.

Whether the Trump family was promoting Jacksonian democracy or
empowerment feminism, the racial politics of white privilege couldn't be
covered over easily with superficial gestures, such as hugging Diamond and
Silk or quoting Toni Morrison. The Trumps refused to grapple with larger
questions about access that acknowledged the existence of structural racism. After all, they had already widened their circles to allow a few Black
women in.

When the administration threw itself into the 2020 campaign, the right-
wing influencers from the Social Media Summit became even more necessary to boost Trump's messages about connection, transparency, and access.
They were also important for promoting his brand of participation, which
was typified by large in-person rallies. As the election season got into full
swing, the rallies abruptly became public health hazards. Although Trump
was reluctant to adapt to the coronavirus pandemic, his opponent was
willing to explore new political strategies. Digital technology proved to be
essential for his success.

11 Together Alone with Biden

At the start of a "virtual event," a disclaimer from Joe Biden's campaign read: "This Illinois virtual town hall had technical issues that delayed its start and led to unclear audio. This is an edited version."[1]

Even in the cleaned-up edition of the video, which presented the salvageable parts of Biden's Zoom session, the Democratic contender appears to struggle with digital technology. For the entire final third of the video, Biden speaks awkwardly into a smartphone that he holds up to his face. As he interacts intently with the mobile device, he sometimes forgets to face the camera and even goes out of the frame. At another point in the original livestream, the virtual background image moved into the foreground, completely obscuring the candidate.[2]

Facebook Live was also supposed to broadcast the Biden town hall, but the attempt was doomed: "That Facebook stream went up late and lasted around four minutes before going dark."[3]

The main event on Zoom had started three hours after it was supposed to, and it went downhill from there. The crackling, echoing, and distorted audio was even worse than the visual footage of Biden's fumbling performance. "Once Biden did start speaking, his staff had to restart his entire speech because there was no audio," one witness recounted. "As he started reading off his prepared remarks again, Biden's audio was suddenly painful to hear and impossible to understand, at least until they replaced whatever mic he was using with a smartphone."[4]

It wasn't Biden's only cringe-worthy performance with a smartphone at a podium. At his very first campaign event in Florida, the Democratic nominee hoped to win over Latinx voters by appearing with Puerto Rican pop singer Luis Fonsi. The former vice president pulled out his phone, held it up to the microphone, and played Fonsi's Spanish-language hit "Despacito" for a few seconds while he danced awkwardly to the tune. It was a made-to-be-memed moment that quickly went viral.

Because being adept at the new digital politics had become so central to presidential campaigning, it seemed impossible for Biden to succeed.

The Zoom Candidate

As the 2020 coronavirus pandemic disrupted public life in the United States and all around the world, the traditional in-person rallies and fundraisers that usually characterized an election season needed to be completely re-imagined to honor requirements for social distancing in which participants would be limited in number, spaced at least six feet apart, and guarded with personal protective equipment such as face masks. Often it seemed simpler, safer, and more culturally virtuous to create digital events that served as surrogate experiences for connecting with a candidate.

These telepresence arrangements brought a new Silicon Valley company into political prominence: Zoom Video Communications. While Google, Apple, Facebook, and Microsoft had all previously developed video chat applications for their customers, in 2020 Zoom managed to capitalize on its existing market share in education and business to become the corporation most associated with new forms of remote learning, teleworking, and online socializing.

As Zoom became the preferred platform of choice, things only got worse for Biden. Another online campaign event, a "virtual rally" in Tampa, Florida, was marred by multiple snafus. Even the pledge of allegiance was bungled. Elected officials, who were unaware that they were on camera, grimaced weirdly or fiddled with crumpled facial tissues.[5] The candidate summed up his sense of all the opportunities that had been lost: "I wish we could have done this together, and it had gone a little more smoothly."[6]

Biden was essentially confined to his home for almost two months during a critical period in the campaign season. He was living much like other Americans who were sheltering in place to reduce infection rates from a highly contagious and potentially fatal disease that could be transmitted by asymptomatic carriers. He may have gained points with some for modeling compliance with government stay-at-home orders. However, his opponent refused to follow basic public health rules at the White House and even called for defiance of them in the name of liberty.

Political commentators worried Biden was "losing the internet" by focusing only on the content produced in his home studio. He was making YouTube videos in the basement of his Delaware residence, which went out to an embarrassingly small viewership. With these online videos, he failed to boost his social media presence or impact coverage on the mainstream news. Meanwhile, Trump was dominating the entire media ecosystem by holding center stage at frequent coronavirus task force briefings and flooding his Twitter stream with new content.[7]

Like other politicians, celebrities, and cultural commentators during the pandemic, Biden was videorecorded in front of what became known as a "credibility bookcase." The *New York Times* described this kind of prominent bookcase as a background that "signals class, education, and money" while also borrowing from the design aesthetics of Instagram and other platforms.[8] Biden's carefully stage-directed white bookcase included a folded American flag, a weathered old football, and other memorabilia that conveyed patriotism, masculinity, and traditional Americana, in addition to bookish expertise.[9] At the Joe Biden online store the campaign suggested that fans could download three different versions of "Joe's Library" as Zoom backgrounds for their own daily teleconferencing activities (figure 11.1). One description under Free Team Joe Swag read, "Make the most of

Figure 11.1
Zoom background from Biden campaign online store.

staying-at-home during coronavirus by taking Zoom calls from Joe's library (now with a soft blue tone)."[10]

Biden's digital director Rob Flaherty had a very different resumé from the Obama upstarts at Blue State Digital. Flaherty had been a senior partner at a global public relations firm, and he claimed a dossier of experiences in crisis management.[11] His online presence was considerably more understated than his counterpart in the Trump campaign, Dan Scavino, who posted animated GIFs and other memes mocking Biden at home.

Blue State Digital still occupied a prominent position as developers of the Biden 2020 website. As they had done for Obama, Blue State designed Biden's site with digital persuasion in mind. The website encouraged visitors to submit their email addresses at the first point of access and then donate a modest amount at the second.

While some pundits urged a radical push into different digital spaces, others argued that Biden's success among so-called low-information voters might pay off.[12] For example, the presence of bingo cards on the website made a clear reference to an analog pastime of senior citizens. His campaign also played on nostalgia for older media by staging events at drive-in movie theaters, which enjoyed a resurgence during the pandemic. Of course, the drive-in could also be seen as a reaction to the new medium of television[13] and as a place associated with second-run or low-budget films rather than glitzy new releases with Hollywood stars.[14]

This is not to say that the Biden campaign didn't make any attempts to reach out to digitally savvy young voters. Biden attended a Democratic virtual event at Club Quarantine on Instagram Live in which over 100,000 participants grooved to the music of influencer D-Nice, who had gained fame for his online dance parties. Before the pandemic, D-Nice was known as an in-person disc jockey, beatboxer, rapper, and producer.[15]

To exploit Biden's obvious weakness, the Trump campaign was relentless in ridiculing Biden's digital literacy. The designers of the DonaldJTrump.com website even built in a surprise easter egg mocking their opponent. The website's error message (figure 11.2) was an image of a befuddled Biden with text reading, "It appears you are as lost as me."[16]

Snapchat Campaigning

Biden's messages weren't getting out on upstart platforms that emphasized micro-video blogging, augmented reality filters, temporary content that

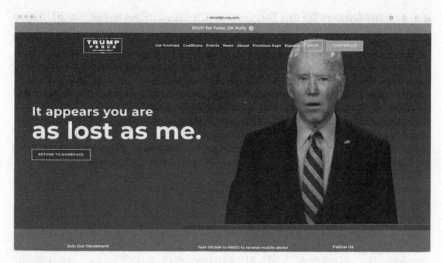

Figure 11.2
Screenshot of error page from DonaldJTrump.com on June 16, 2020.

vanished after a short period of time, or other forms of media meant for quick consumption or changing moods. For many potential voters, social media was becoming even more ambient and ephemeral on a daily basis. Yet there were superficial similarities between the approaches of the two septuagenarian candidates.

On Snapchat, both campaigns utilized built-in facial recognition algorithms to attach humorous accessories to users' heads or faces. Potential voters could advertise their political loyalties in stories to friends, either by wearing a red baseball cap emblazoned with a pro-Trump slogan or by sporting Biden-style aviator glasses.[17] Both campaigns also featured "highlights" on their Snapchat public profiles that were designed to appeal to the same two key constituencies: Black voters and female voters.

The main differences boiled down to the volume of followers and the depth of engagement. Donald Trump boasted of having over 1.5 million followers on Snapchat,[18] a number that tripled during his 2020 reelection campaign, while the Biden operation said little about its own decidedly more modest follower count. Successful Snapchat stories published by the Trump campaign were designed to give users a sense of momentary connection with and access to the candidate. For example, the Trump digital team published a Snapchat story that imagined a "backstage pass" designed to build anticipation for an upcoming rally. They also published one looking back to his famous Trump Tower escalator announcement of his 2016 candidacy. The story places the viewer close to Trump, even brushing past a doorman giving him entry to the building.

The Trump campaign demonstrated knowledge of Snapchat's specific interface features and common visual clichés, such as the crude digital stickers that were often applied to photos and videos for humorous commentary. At one point in the campaign, after a testy exchange with an African American radio host, Biden had declared, "if you have a problem figuring out whether you're for me or Trump, then you ain't Black." In a pro-Trump Snapchat video posted shortly afterward, Biden's words were integrated into a popular "coffin dance" meme showing Africans dancing at a funeral. The "Biden for President" logo was superimposed on the casket.[19]

Some of Trump's advantages on meme-driven mobile media started to erode in the summer of 2020. After many years of deflecting responsibility for content moderation, Silicon Valley companies finally began gatekeeping. This meant that some of the most influential misinformation and hate on their platforms would be barred. Trump found his content under attack by site moderators and platform designers who had belatedly become more willing to intervene as the nation moved through a series of Trump-exacerbated crises. His abilities to monopolize attention by seizing on public fear and anger were tested as disasters escalated, the virus raged through vulnerable populations, unemployment skyrocketed, the streets filled with racial justice protestors, and Americans questioned the safety of in-person voting during a public health crisis.

Snapchat announced that it would no longer promote Trump campaign content under its "Discover" tab, although the material would still be posted and accessible through search.[20] The company cited hate speech that might lead to violence as its main concern. On Trump's account the response to the new policy was an extremely lengthy—by Snapchat's standards—two-paragraph screed.

> Snapchat is trying to rig the 2020 election, illegally using their corporate funding to promote Joe Biden and suppress President Trump. Radical Snapchat CEO Evan Spiegel would rather promote extreme left riot videos and encourage their users to destroy America than share the positive words of unity, justice, and law and order from our President. Snapchat hates that so many of their users watch the President's content and so they are actively engaging in voter suppression. If you're a conservative, they do not want to hear from you, they do not want you

to vote. They view you as a deplorable and they do not want you to exist on their platform.[21]

In addition to capitalizing on Trump's authority as a sitting president, the statement uses the vocabulary of both the left ("voter suppression") and the right ("deplorable").[22] By depriving Trump of algorithmic amplification while still allowing him access to the platform, the issue might have been one of "freedom of reach" rather than "freedom of speech."[23]

Checks and Balances with Twitter

Twitter attempted a highly visible enforcement strategy against Trump after continued violations of their terms of service by the administration and the 2020 campaign. The president's feud with his old perceived nemesis, CEO Jack Dorsey, was reignited by the company's decision to label some of Trump's tweets with additional information that provided corrections from other sources. For example, when Trump claimed on Twitter that there was "NO WAY (ZERO!) that Mail-In Ballots will be anything less than substantially fraudulent," the company added a blue exclamation mark with a link to reporting from the news station CNN that contradicted the president.[24] In response, conservative commentators complained that "social media" was becoming "socialist media."[25] Trump soon signed the "Preventing Online Censorship" executive order that demanded investigations into social media companies by a range of agencies, including the Federal Trade Commission, the Justice Department, and the Office of Management and Budget.[26]

Although defending free speech might seem laudable, some civil libertarians expressed alarm at Trump's legal justifications for regulating digital companies, particularly the citation of the 1980 *PruneYard Shopping Center v. Robins* Supreme Court decision. While other Supreme Court decisions evoked an idealized concept of the "public square" as a way to advocate for free access to digital content on the internet, Trump's executive order rested on comparing social media platforms to shopping malls. Furthermore, because the original case involved pro-Palestinian teenagers who were ousted from private property by a shopping center's security guards for seeking signatures for a petition, the Supreme Court's affirmation of the young people's free speech rights had been seen by many conservatives as liberal overreach into the rightful sphere of private enterprise that endangered the "takings" clause of the Fifth Amendment. As one constitutional scholar noted, Trump's executive order could "gut the First Amendment" as well by redefining public speech, [27] Despite these ideological contradictions, Trump was willing to use his executive authority—and the PruneYard decision—to justify the government effectively exercising eminent domain in cyberspace.

The TikTok Crusade

Republican ire against social media platforms was grounded in other concerns as well. Like Snapchat, TikTok was a youth-oriented mobile app utilized by candidates from both political parties in the 2020 US election. To address potential controversy, TikTok posted a relatively neutral warning below some of the hashtags associated with partisan election content, such as #Trump2020. The TikTok statement affirmed that the platform simultaneously valued "creativity and expression" and "authenticity and integrity." According to its statement of principles, TikTok would not tolerate "bullying, harassment, threats, misleading information, or other violations of our Community Guidelines." Users were also instructed by the site to verify "facts using trusted sources" to protect against fake news.

As TikTok took off in the United States, legislators expressed alarm about widespread use of the foreign-owned data capture service and amplified fears about potential meddling or espionage by the Chinese. Although the company maintained an office in California, it had begun as Shanghai-based Musical.ly, a lip-synching video app that became globally popular among teens and preteens. It was acquired in 2017 by ByteDance Ltd., which was headquartered in Beijing, and became TikTok in 2018. In China the company ran a similar app called Douyin, which had more advanced e-commerce and search features.

In addition to lip-synching, TikTok's fifteen-second video format is commonly used for dance challenges, pratfalls, mini DIY tutorials, and political rants. It is also a forum for first-person "storytimes," hot takes, and micro-documentaries. TikTok has filled a market niche that was vacated when the six-second video hosting service Vine went out of business in 2016, after its parent company Twitter decided to cease its support.[28]

Given the company's Chinese roots, Congress was extremely skeptical about TikTok as a new mobile platform. The interagency Committee on

Foreign Investment in the United States opened a national security investigation based on concerns about the app's censorship practices and its collection of users' personal data.[29] Senator Josh Hawley made anti-TikTok rhetoric a key part of his tech agenda and introduced the National Security and Personal Data Protection Act to prohibit TikTok's parent company and others from transferring the personal data of Americans to China. He also introduced a bill to ban TikTok on government devices.[30] The United States Navy, Army, and Transportation Security Administration banned TikTok from all of their government-issued devices. They also prohibited their personnel from posting on the platform for outreach and recruitment purposes.

Unlike Snapchat, which served as a key platform for the Trump campaign, TikTok was much more difficult to co-opt as a conduit for right-wing memes. Although anti-Biden hashtags like #creepyunclejoe did appear, anti-Trump content was much more likely to go viral, given TikTok's user demographics. Audio from Trump speeches became popular tracks for lip-synching, particularly for aspiring comedians stuck at home during COVID-19. Sarah Cooper's performance mouthing along to a soundtrack from one of Trump's rambling commentaries was picked up by TV networks.[31] In her carefully timed TikTok lip-synching, Cooper's funny faces and use of cramped spaces made already unpresidential diatribes seem even sillier.[32] Gender-bending, "drunk girl" performances of Trump's audio became a TikTok staple, particularly after social-worker-turned-film-student Kylie Scott uploaded "drunk in the club after covid." The video shows Scott lip-synching in a sparkly top to an incoherent speech from Trump about antibiotics and germs. As she channels Trump's voice, Scott waves a cocktail around under colored lights.[33] Even seemingly pro-Trump TikToks would often suddenly switch to anti-Trump "gotcha" messages.

When Trump announced a massive rally to be held in June in an indoor venue with nineteen thousand people, despite the risk of spiking the infection rate in the host city of Tulsa, Oklahoma, a fifty-one-year-old grandmother decided to act. She posted a video on TikTok tagged "Did you know you can make sure there are empty seats at Trump's rally? #BLM," which was shared over a half-million times.[34] In her video she explained how to troll the Republican campaign by reserving rally tickets. By taking tickets out of circulation with no intention of using them, Trump would be deprived of his audience. The campaign fielded requests for over a million tickets. Journalists questioned the real influence of TikTok on the disappointing turnout,[35] but Trump was clearly irritated by the large empty sections in the arena. A few weeks later the president issued an executive order on "Addressing the Threat Posed by TikTok" that declared the need to exercise emergency powers.

> I, DONALD J. TRUMP, President of the United States of America, find that additional steps must be taken to deal with the national emergency with respect to the information and communications technology and services supply chain declared in Executive Order 13873 of May 15, 2019 (Securing the Information and Communications Technology and Services Supply Chain). Specifically, the spread in the United States of mobile applications developed and owned by companies in the People's Republic of China (China) continues to threaten the national security, foreign policy, and economy of the United States. At this time, action must be taken to address the threat posed by one mobile application in particular, TikTok.[36]

A week later he followed up with another executive order aimed at its parent company ByteDance, which ordered TikTok to be divested of its foreign ownership.[37]

The company sued the administration in federal court,[38] alleging that it had been denied due process, but the following month the Department of Commerce moved forward with new rules that would ban the app from being downloaded from the Apple and Android stores.[39] A series of unlikely corporate suitors then came forward to attempt to acquire TikTok, including Microsoft, Walmart, and Oracle.

If TikTok had been anti-Trump before the administration's regulatory moves, its users became much more focused on revenge as the election loomed. Videos showed how to vandalize "TRUMP PENCE" campaign signs, turning them into "I PUMP PENIS" messages, and how to make the president's reelection operation spend money on materials that could be repurposed to promote anti-Trump causes.

Because TikTok was a new content platform that was able to reach a young demographic unlikely to read newspapers or watch network news, journalists and news organizations were experimenting with TikTok at the same time that the Biden campaign was tinkering with different approaches to the platform. This led to an unlikely team effort between a presidential candidate, a media gatekeeping organization, and a mobile app—all in the name of a public health announcement. Producer and writer Dave

Jorgenson of the *Washington Post* collaborated with Biden in a nineteen-second TikTok skit about wearing a face mask while dog walking.[40] In the video, the candidate seems to interrupt his own "Here's the Deal" campaign podcast to chide the bearded urbanite reporter.

"Dave, what the hell!" Biden exclaims. "I told you to wear your mask outside!"

Jorgenson expresses surprise at being addressed personally from his mobile phone: "Mr. Vice President?"

"Yeah, Dave, it's me," Biden replies.

"How are you doing this?" Jorgenson inquires.

Instead of answering him, Biden reminds Jorgenson to wear his mask again, and then Biden expresses exasperation that "he's never going to learn."

The video also incorporates the trope of a cut/costume change, a common TikTok transformation motif that had already appeared in tens of thousands of videos. Because the app was designed to allow recording to stop and start multiple times, Jorgenson could magically change from a maskless dog walker to a masked dog walker in an eyeblink.

A Virtual Convention

With new peaks in the coronavirus pandemic worsening the health crisis, the Democratic National Convention decided to cancel any large, in-person gatherings. For the first time, they would organize an all-digital event instead. The roll call, featuring the delegate announcements from all fifty states, might have been the most ambitious part of their production. Through creative uses of landmarks and local costumes, states showcased particular attributes for tourism or corporate investment. Some states even poked fun at themselves as they vied for internet celebrity. A DNC official made suggestions to the show's director via an earpiece, but it took five separate takes for a satisfactory "live" performance. To make sure that production values were sufficiently professional, the DNC "shipped every state and territory a boxful of equipment . . . including ring lights, a tripod, signs and sign bases, and a phone for filming."[41]

Because party leaders were eager to avoid technical glitches or unintentionally viral moments, much of the convention footage was prerecorded.[42]

However, in keeping with expectations for a prime-time event, many of the speeches from major leaders of the party were live, with the exception of former First Lady Michelle Obama.

Despite the amount of airtime devoted to the party's political celebrities, teleconferencing technology that put domestic interiors on display created a leveling effect with viewers at home. This egalitarianism was enhanced by the presence of citizen-participants who had recorded their own messages. In some shots, apparatuses for digital home production were visible. Other speakers seemed to be watching themselves on mobile phones with selfie lenses. *Wired* magazine declared that "the convention gave America a sense of how everyone—even political heavyweights—might look if they air-dropped into your company's Zoom call."[43]

Viewers also spotted subtle background elements or wardrobe accessories that made stronger statements than the words that were spoken at the convention. For example, Elizabeth Warren spoke from a classroom with blocks spelling out "BLM" in the background. These clues about deeper political sentiments were then shared on social media. In this way, personal staging at home created new forms of political performance that deployed semiotic systems capable of sharpening, particularizing, or challenging official messages.

By the time of the convention, Democratic Party operatives had refined possible ways to use Zoom for registration drives, get-out-the-vote campaigns, and fundraisers. On the last night of the convention, I attended a Zoom fundraiser with Hollywood writers who had created fictional stories about the White House. Donors to the event were able to ask questions of the writers, who had produced both comedies and dramas. The virtual event covered the writers' sources, their political attitudes, and their predictions for the future. Jen Psaki, who would later go on to be Biden's Press Secretary, skillfully moderated.

The Republican National Convention adopted a much more traditional format, but social media still played a starring role—speakers made frequent references to its supposedly detrimental effect on society. For example, 26-year-old Charlie Kirk of the conservative campus organization Turning Point USA blasted "kicking doctors off of social media yet promoting Chinese state-funded propaganda on major tech platforms." He complained that "the American way of life" to "speak your mind without retribution" was under attack now that one could be "kicked off social media by a self-righteous censor in Silicon Valley." White House spokesperson Kellyanne Conway argued that the Republican Party did more for women's empowerment that "strangers on social media." First Lady Melania Trump lamented "how mean and manipulative social media can be." She also emphasized the need to communicate to the young "the downside of technology and their relationships with their peers." Perhaps the most dramatic condemnation of digital culture came from Ann Dorn, a law enforcement widow, who described how her husband's killers "livestreamed his execution and his last moments on earth" while the victim's grandson "was watching the video on Facebook in real time not realizing he was watching his own grandfather."

According to the Republican lineup, social media was creating a new class of perverted pseudo-citizens who were silencing, harassing, and spreading cruelty while true patriots suffered. Of course, there was also some implicit criticism of digital culture at the Democratic National Convention, but it was much more subtle. For example, before observing a moment of silence for Black civilians killed in encounters with the police, the brothers of victim George Floyd called for remembrance of those who might be unmourned "because their murders didn't go viral."

Kamala Harris on Instagram

Biden's choice of Kamala Harris as his running mate was significant not only because of the historic significance of having the first Black and Asian woman as a vice-presidential candidate on a major party ticket, but also because she brought a different style of campaigning to her social media presence. On Harris's Instagram account, she strove for a casual style of relatability and a softer image than the one associated with her career as a prosecutor, attorney general, and senator. She depicted herself in conversations that modeled female friendships, particularly with women of color, using the popular split-screen feature of the platform. She even posted an Instagram Live conversation with TikTok star and Trump lip-syncher Sarah Cooper. In her online videos, Harris often interacted with potential voters in kitchens and highlighted her culinary skills. She also projected a maternal personality in fielding questions and comments from children.

Her awareness of the camera and issues of self-presentation in her video blogging was particularly striking. For example, at the beginning of many of her videos on Instagram, there would be a noticeable pause before she began speaking, during which she smiled while adjusting her pose. This established that she had not edited the footage and had no camera crew to manage the start of the action.[44]

In addition to her aptitude as an internet influencer, Harris also brought strong ties to Silicon Valley. According to the *New York Times*, "tech industry critics worry that a Biden administration with Ms. Harris would mean a return to the cozy relationship that Silicon Valley enjoyed with the White House under President Barack Obama."[45] Her close ties to the Big Tech donors that she once represented as a California officeholder and her personal friendship with Facebook chief operating officer Sheryl Sandberg seemed likely to shape her loyalties.[46] In the US government, vice presidents play a relatively minor role in the executive branch, but "as a former state attorney general Ms. Harris is expected to have a say in Mr. Biden's political appointments at the Justice Department, including officials who oversee antitrust enforcement" and "could also have a significant influence on tech policy in a Biden administration, since Mr. Biden has largely focused on other issues."

Interactivity and Political Appeals

The Biden campaign used its website for some of the same kinds of interactive interfaces that had worked during the Obama era. Just as the Obama "tax calculator" was designed to draw potential supporters, a "tax calculator" on the Biden website was created to publicize the fact that Trump had only paid a paltry $750 a year in taxes during his first two years in office.[47]

The Biden digital team also pursued visibility in online games, just as the Obama campaign had done when it had purchased in-game ads that appeared in nine Xbox videogame titles near the end of the 2008 campaign.[48] The already popular game *Animal Crossing* had become more so during the pandemic, as its multigenerational fan base surged with housebound players. Biden's island in *Animal Crossing* was decorated with patriotic bunting and Biden–Harris lawn signs.[49] Players were directed to visit IWillVote.com and urged to sign up for campaign text messages. Players could also decorate their own properties with Biden swag and dress their avatars up in Biden gear. Fans of the game were impressed by small details that indicated that the developer had familiarity with possible in-game exploits that could be utilized, such as "time traveling" to an earlier version of the game to get multiple train cars for a train set; they also noticed that even relatively innocuous sarcastic comments were removed by moderators.[50]

Despite the Biden campaign's initial stumbles addressing an online public, it gained momentum in real-time responsiveness as the election entered the home stretch. Staffers demonstrated that they could finally improvise quickly enough with digital technology by the time of the televised debates. In these debates, candidates were expected to present their "closing arguments" to the public. During the vice-presidential debates, a fly landed on the snow-white hair of Vice President Pence and was clearly visible to audiences. Although the insect was only viewable for a little over two minutes, this was a century in internet time. Users posted TikTok videos of household members slapping TV screens and green-screen videos of talking flies. Snapchat filters were soon available for superimposing Pence's hair and the fly on users' heads. The Biden campaign also came up with a quick comeback. They set up a FlyWillVote.com website that forwarded to Biden's IWillVote.com. The Biden e-commerce platform also offered a commemorative fly swatter that quickly sold out.

Images of Harris also circulated through the media ecosystem. Stereotypes about gender and race—caricaturing her heritage as a Black and South Asian woman—were also noticeable in these memes. For example, footage of her reactions to interruptions during the vice-presidential debate was quickly turned into familiar kinds of reaction GIFs in which Black women express outrage. As a looping animated video that could be appropriated for almost any rhetorical situation, Harris's image traveled through social media.[51] Clips of Harris dancing at campaign events were also looped and reposted. The dancing Harris meme became the digital property of both the left (signifying celebration and joy) and the right (signifying perfunctory performance and tokenism).

The pandemic revived conflicts around technology that had come up during previous administrations. These struggles were exacerbated by social distancing requirements. For example, journalists reported on new concerns about secure communication now that so many Trump appointees were working from home.[52] Other reporters anticipated that a

Trump-Biden transition might prove to be even rockier than previous transfers of power because "building a government over Zoom" was likely to be
challenging.[53]

Returning to the 2016 Playbook

In the final weeks of the campaign, as Trump's poll numbers stagnated,
his staffers still hoped to generate the kind of free media coverage that
had benefited Trump in the 2016 campaign. Known as "earned media"
in the parlance of public relations, this kind of coverage could be created
through travel and speaking engagements, such as Trump's pre-election
visit to Mexico. It could also be created by having the campaign's surrogates respond to a provocative statement posted by Trump on Twitter. Even
a seemingly damaging event, such as the leaked *Access Hollywood* audio
that contained demeaning and vulgar language, could lead to days of
earned media.

In the 2020 campaign, Trump's campaign manager released a memo
addressed to "Interested Parties," which asserted that "President Trump's
travel" to campaign rallies "earned $40.1 million in calculated broadcast
value" over one seven-day period.[54] He cited data from Cision software as a
measure of Trump's earned-media windfalls.[55] The campaign insisted that
significant digital ad buys were being made as well.

At the same time, conservative news coverage returned to familiar
themes, focusing on emails and portable computing because these stories had been so effective against Hillary Clinton. *The New York Post* and
Fox News amplified stories about incriminating emails that would supposedly not only provide evidence of foreign influence peddling with
Ukraine by son Hunter Biden but also demonstrate Joe Biden's awareness of it.

Soon the publication of a story alleging that a computer repairman had
acquired incriminating emails from the laptop of Hunter Biden, social
media companies began delisting and deplatforming processes.[56] Facebook
announced it would limit the distribution of the story so it could fact-check
claims, and Twitter blocked the article entirely because it included people's personal data and thus violated the company's privacy policies about
hacked material.[57] Within two days, both companies had backtracked to
allow access to the story again.[58] Despite promises to avoid the spread

of deceptive information on their networks, companies were fearful of a potential repeal of Section 230 and a loss of their immunity to lawsuits involving user-generated content.[59]

A second round of anti-Biden allegations focused on China rather than Ukraine. Here, the mouthpiece was Tony Bobulinski, a former business associate of Hunter Biden. Many journalists were skeptical when he "showed three phones spanning 2015 to 2018 as evidence" and "said he would be meeting with the Senate and the FBI to hand over the electronics."[60] Text messages and material from WhatsApp were offered as proof of Hunter Biden's shady dealings.

To elevate these stories about digital proof of the alleged payoffs to the Bidens by foreign governments, the Trump campaign had hoped to get the cooperation of the *Wall Street Journal*. Unfortunately for Trump, the prestigious newspaper consented to only very minimal reporting,[61] although many months after the election they spoke approvingly of the basic journalism. The bulk of the Hunter Biden coverage was relegated to more clearly partisan news sources and online sites.

Clinton's email scandals were also resurrected during the last days of the 2020 campaign. A mere month before the election, secretary of state Mike Pompeo announced that he would be releasing a new tranche of emails from Clinton's time at the State Department, satisfying an explicit request from President Trump. Pompeo emphasized "transparency" explicitly in his statement and boasted of making over 35,000 Clinton emails available on a State Department website. He also took the opportunity to chastise Clinton again for relying on "a system designed to evade State Department rules and regulations."[62]

In the final weeks of the campaign, perhaps the most critical thing for the Trump campaign to achieve was to win back white women, the demographic that had delivered him victory over Hillary Clinton in 2016. Female members of the Trump family were important in this push for female voters by encouraging identification through online image-sharing practices. They also needed to provide different optics on mask wearing, which had become a widely accepted public health measure despite mockery by Trump himself. For example, a selfie by Lara Trump showed four women from the Trump family wearing masks.[63]

With just a few days to go, the Trump campaign website was defaced by hackers. The intruders claimed they had acquired sensitive data. "Multiple devices were compromised that gave full access to Trump and relatives," they asserted, which supposedly provided access to "secret and internal conversations" and "strictly classified information." Their scheme to collect cryptocurrency was somewhat more complex than a conventional ransomware attack. People were encouraged to vote for two possible outcomes: "Yes, share the data" and "No, Do not share the data."[64] It was a disastrous end to Trump's digital campaign.

Although the Biden digital campaign got off to a rocky start, it eventually adapted. It responded effectively to a radically different environment in which most citizens were dependent on digital video teleconferencing technologies for working, learning, and socializing. In the early days of the campaign, Biden events were often "Zoom bombed" by bad actors spewing fascist, racist, sexist, homophobic, or scatological hate. By the end of the campaign, "Zoom bombing" was given a positive spin; Hollywood celebrities surprised Biden volunteers on Zoom calls as a reward for their hard work.[65] The final Biden get-out-the-vote effort was managed with a system of Zoom trainings and check-ins that included sessions with special guests, such as former first daughter Chelsea Clinton. These Zoom cameos provided incentives for the final push of phone calling and door knocking. With all of these elements of digital campaigning in place, Biden won both the popular vote and the Electoral College tally.

As Americans grappled with being housebound during the first phase of the pandemic, they shared a collective experience of physical isolation and digital overconnectivity.[66] During the "Great Pause" people "doomscrolled" on their smartphones.[67] As a result, they were inundated with unending bad news about surging COVID-19 caseloads, police shootings, and fires all over a planet seemingly in its death throes. Biden's "low-information" strategy provided some respite from the overload. While Trump was tweeting an average of thirty-five times a day—a new high in his social media use—the Biden campaign only posted a few items daily. With the gift of time freed up from less commuting or traveling, many citizens aspired to go back to nature or to learn analog skills, such as knitting or baking.[68] Biden's appeals to nostalgia and low-key approach may have hit just the right note for those aspiring to unplug a bit more from contemporary digital life.

Trump lost the election, but he still had his social media following. His messages about connection, transparency, and access still resonated with his audience. He also had a new message about participation, even if it was far too late for his followers to cast a vote.

Before he lost the 2020 race, Trump was a political leader who had driven the news cycle incessantly forward into the future. Now his call to action demanded that time be wound back to just before election day. Together with his followers, he planned to "stop the steal" and prevent Joe Biden from ever taking office.

On January 6, a mere two weeks before the formal transition from the 45th president to the 46th, thousands of pro-Trump supporters violently stormed Capitol Hill. They had been egged on by a speech in which their leader pronounced that "you will never take back our country with weakness" and directed them to "walk down to the Capitol."[1] Many in the crowd listening to Trump's fiery oratory were men who came from militant extremist organizations like the Proud Boys, the Boogaloo Bois, the Oath Keepers, and the 1st Amendment Praetorian, but there were also women with strollers and even a group of nuns in the audience.[2]

Digital communication was a central theme in Trump's incendiary, hour-long diatribe. During his extensive rant, Trump expressed his displeasure with broadcasting outlets that he felt had covered him unfairly. He mentioned "cameras" five times, "media" seventeen times, and "fake news" five times. Also prominent was his disgruntled attitude about social media now that his free access to those platforms had been limited out of concern for propagating falsehoods about the coronavirus pandemic and the 2020 election. "Big Tech" appeared six times as an adversary in his speech. He explicitly called for eliminating Section 230 twice.[3]

At the Capitol, the two houses of the legislative branch were intent on what had traditionally been a pro forma ceremony, the bureaucratic blessing of the accepted election results. Representatives were tasked with accepting the Electoral College votes, which had already been certified, adjudicated, and ritually accepted several times before reaching the final federal tier of the process. However, Josh Hawley and several pro-Trump members of both the Senate and the House had decided to challenge the results, alleging election fraud. But because they had no legal help from the judiciary or process to sway the vote, the lawmakers could not change the outcome.

In the alphabet of states, legislators had made it to the results from Arizona. It was just the beginning of what was expected to be hours of ultimately ineffectual debate. Unbeknownst to the participants, the Capitol police were woefully understaffed. They wouldn't be able to protect the proceedings from the huge swarm of Trump supporters that had gathered outside.

The crowd was extremely agitated. In addition to urging them on with his speech, Trump had been stoking their emotions on Twitter. Late the night before, Trump had retweeted an update from his social media director, Dan Scavino. "🔊WOW! We hear you from the West Wing—THANK YOU♡▬🦅 https://t.co/onytmaJUhp." Scavino linked to a video clip shot from just outside the White House in which music and cheering from another pro-Trump rally is audible.[4] Scavino's footage from the West Wing is moody. In it, dusk has fallen, clouds are gathering, organ-like music swells, and the crowd sings along in eerie unison.[5] Followers reported "goosebumps" and "chills" as reactions. It amplified their feelings and reminded them of the solemnity and sanctity of their mission.

Trump's retweet of Scavino's emoji-filled message obviously played on themes of connection and access. The protestors were being listened to by the president. The sound of the crowd had penetrated the perimeter that surrounded him. Trump had told them that their voices could be heard in the White House. Soon they might be heard in the Capitol as well.

In Trump's speech, the marauders had been instructed to "cheer on our brave senators and congressmen and women." He meant people like Hawley, who were leading their futile last stand. Trump's supporters also knew that they would be looking for enemies. He had told them that "we are probably not going to be cheering so much for some of them."

Although many probably ran amok on a spur-of-the-moment impulse, several aspects of the assault on the Capitol had been carefully planned on social media. Violent tactics had been discussed on far-right sites like Gab and Parler.[6] Gab had a user interface that was similar to Twitter's design, but it tolerated a much higher volume of hate speech.[7] Parler was endorsed by many conservative public figures and benefited from being a platform for right-wing influencers who had been expelled from other sites.[8] Both Gab and Parler defended free speech vigorously in the face of accusations of incitement.

Because the vice president had refused to overturn the election, some of the attackers roamed the halls calling his name and shouting, "Hang Pence!" Others were focused on Democrats who had been demonized on social media for years. At best, the intruders were planning to obstruct the legal exercise of democracy. At worst, they were planning to take elected officials hostage or assassinate them.

Hundreds of millions of people all around the world watched the horrific spectacle of mob rule. News coverage captured rioters scaling walls, breaking windows, vandalizing offices, defiling the sanctuaries of government, and even stealing the podium of the Speaker of the House. Some of the most harrowing scenes showed legislators who had gotten down on the floor to evade possible gunfire as they waited to be evacuated to secure locations. These defensive protocols had been designed for terrorist attacks. Escape hoods were distributed to dazed lawmakers to protect them from potential gas. Photographers shot surreal images of bubble-headed representatives navigating the besieged Capitol as though it were another planet.

Major television stations chose not to air some of the goriest video. One clip, shot on a cell phone, showed a bloodied woman wrapped in a Trump flag dying from a gunshot wound.[9] She had been shot by a Capitol police officer when she attempted to climb through a smashed entryway to access the legislative chamber. The footage of her final moments on the marble floor circulated on Twitter and other social media platforms.[10]

The dead woman, Ashli Babbitt, had been an active Twitter user. She frequently retweeted content from far-right influencers like Jack Posobiec, Juanita Broaddrick, and—of course—Trump himself. In the days leading up to the assault on the Capitol, Babbitt had retweeted a video that emphasized the rhetoric of participation. The video alerted recipients that "THIS COULD BE THE BIGGEST EVENT IN WASHINGTON DC HISTORY" and goaded them to "BE A PART OF HISTORY."[11] It was clearly designed to stir feelings of FOMO ("fear of missing out") to incentivize participation, fueling anxieties about being left out of a once-in-a-lifetime event. It also stimulated intense sentiments of connection by showing footage of large crowds.[12]

The video Babbitt retweeted advertised the March for Trump/Save America rally, also known as the Stop the Steal rally. It had been organized by a group called "Women for America First," who described the event's purpose as a "First Amendment rally" to "demand transparency and protect election integrity."[13] Diamond and Silk were listed as potential speakers on the permit for the protest. The embattled president, who would end up dominating the stage for an entire hour, was not. However, the video that Babbitt shared was clearly a teaser, suggesting that Trump himself might make an appearance. By showing clips of Trump riding by in his limousine, it promised the possibility of access to him.

As people like Babbitt anticipated the climax of all their preparatory activity, they produced a huge volume of social media content, often with posts mere seconds apart. These updates were intended to be both alarmist (an existential danger to your life has erupted) and reassuring (your friends are paying attention, assembling, and keeping you regularly informed). Digital communications scholar Wendy Hui Kyong Chun has distilled this pattern of comfort and anxiety on social media to a recognizable formula: "habit + crisis = update."[14]

Babbitt strengthened her connections to the gathering crowd by participating in the chatter of travelers headed to the rally. Many in her social networks complained of canceled flights and mask requirements. "Nothing will stop us," she tweeted the day before her death, "they can try and try and try but the storm is here and it is descending upon DC in less than 24 hours. . . . dark to light!"[15] Like many Trump supporters, Babbitt's Twitter username was peppered with emojis and hashtags that telegraphed the concentration and intensity of her feelings of attachment: "#Veteran #AMERICA #Libertarian #2A #KAG- I ♡ my dude, my 🐾 & above all, my country-■ #FREEDOM."[16]

Before coming to Washington, DC, Babbitt had often turned her smartphone upon herself, using the selfie lens to document what she believed to be important incidents, as she progressed from radical to revolutionary.[17] For at least two years Babbitt had practiced recording herself as she sought to develop a compelling social media personality. In her role as a would-be citizen journalist, she promised her viewers to deliver the truth "despite what the media tell you."[18] The topics she covered included immigration, drug addiction, and homelessness.

In an early video posted to Twitter Babbitt described herself as not yet "proficient" as a producer of alternative media. Although she didn't see her footage as adequately polished, she defended its authenticity in comparison to mainstream media, which was "lying" to the American public by broadcasting to "echo chambers" and distorting information with "wide-angle lenses."[19] In the video Babbitt is seated in the driver's seat of a moving car, which is a specific format for social media self-production that conveys immediacy, movement, and risk. Often such in-transit videos feature an angry rant.

In Babbitt's last video, streamed live on Facebook, she is also in motion as she walks with Trump's supporters to the Capitol. To describe the moving crowd, she uses both the term "mob" and the term "patriots."

According to news coverage, Babbitt—who had been a fervent Obama supporter—become detached from reality as she descended deeper into the QAnon conspiracy theory.[20] QAnon had succeeded Pizzagate as the pre-eminent online myth about Democratic Party child sex trafficking. Unlike Pizzagate, Trump played a central role in this mythology.[21] QAnon also had a stronger purpose-driven narrative than Pizzagate. According to QAnon lore, historical events would lead up to a clear endpoint with a "great awakening" followed by "the storm." Many QAnon enthusiasts relied upon encrypted online services, such as Telegram, to organize their activities.[22]

The constant selfie taking by the insurrectionists was particularly striking. As in the case of the Social Media Summit, smartphones were raised up high over the heads of many participants. By holding their phones aloft, they could capture both their own self-documenting activities and the context of the crowd surging around them. These selfies appeared in broadcast news, image databases, and FBI wanted posters. Using livestreaming services such as DLive, the infiltration of the building was captured in real time by right-wing influencers. Many of them were counting on monetizing their exclusive experience by offering their followers privileged access to the event.[23]

Like Ashli Babbitt, many who stormed the Capitol typified "horseshoe" politics, in which a passionate political participant might move from the extreme left to the extreme right.[24] They included a former BuzzFeed content creator who had been a supporter of democratic socialist Bernie Sanders[25] and a former labor union official who had attended the Obama inauguration.[26] In other words, the Obama–Trump voter might not always be a centrist merely seeking a change agent. Instead, it is possible for that person to be an extremist, capable of flipping political loyalties to the other end of the spectrum. This kind of citizen was never invested in the civic rituals of representative government.

For hours Trump refused to condemn the rioting of his supporters. He expressed his "love" for them and called them "very special people." A relatively tepid commitment to an "orderly transition" from Trump was not made until the next morning.[27] Trump's lukewarm commitment to normalcy was delivered via Dan Scavino.

Trump's accounts on Twitter, Facebook, and YouTube were seriously sanctioned. On January 8, Trump was permanently suspended from Twitter. The day before his account was terminated, he called for "TRANSPARENCY" twice. Facebook had opted for an indefinite ban rather than termination.[28]

There were also consequences for others in Trump's cast of high-tech rebels.

The Parler social media service was abandoned by other tech companies. When Parler's head defended use of his social network site by those who stormed the Capitol on free speech grounds,[29] Apple and Android removed the app from their stores, and Amazon ceased to provide hosting services for Parler's data. Apparently libertarian philosophies that rejected any real content moderation and refused to alert law enforcement to threats from terrorists were no longer an acceptable part of the Silicon Valley business model. Users also fled Parler after it was hacked, and 30 terabytes of data were made available to the public.[30]

After the breach of the Capitol, Josh Hawley's publisher Simon & Schuster pulled plans to release his book *The Tyranny of Big Tech*.[31] Hawley had alleged that big tech companies, such as "Facebook, Google, Amazon, and Apple" now "represent the gravest threat to American liberty since the monopolies of the Gilded Age," because they "wield enormous market power and political influence, which they deploy to curb competition and turn massive profits."[32] Hawley also criticized "Big Tech" for "collecting more personal and private information from their users than any other company or government in the world" to influence "decisions about their families, politics, and health." It was certainly true that such corporations colluded to "organize, manipulate, and direct the conversations that Americans are having," as Hawley charged. But Trumpism might prove to be part of the problem rather than the solution.

It is significant that Trump never denounced the behavior of his campaign staffers for hiring election consultants Cambridge Analytica, who scraped eighty-seven million Facebook profiles by using a bogus research scheme that encouraged people to feed their information—and the information of their unwitting friends—into a database for experiments in political manipulation. He never mentioned the people who were duped by the ruse of an online personality test. Not one of Trump's fifty-thousand-plus tweets contained the words "Cambridge Analytica." The details of the case pointed to an obvious need for enhanced privacy laws.[33]

Under Trump's presidency, the Federal Communications Commission reversed a rule from late in the Obama administration that had provided some privacy protections for data that could be harvested from citizens' phones.[34] With this new legal latitude, the administration expanded intelligence gathering from mobile devices, with a particular focus on undocumented immigrants and Black Lives Matter activists. In other words, internet privacy was a cause for which Trump never expressed much enthusiasm, unless it involved the privacy of Trump himself. If anything, Trump merely wanted to make an unfair system even less fair by skewing it to the authoritarian right.

After the attack on the Capitol, Trump was stripped of his powerful social media identity, a persona that Peter Costanzo had helped him begin to craft in 2009. Without his established status with social media companies, Trump returned to the early digital style that he had used for bypassing gatekeepers. Those who remembered Trump's "From the Desk of Donald Trump" video channel, which he used from 2011 to 2014, would have recognized the rhetoric of his 2021 venture, "From the Desk of Donald J Trump," a website that provided a steady stream of short missives that were designed to be reposted to Facebook or Twitter by his surrogates. He also aspired to launch his own social media platform, Truth Social.

Trump continued to solicit participation from his followers by asking them to repost his content to the sites that had banned him. He also organized rallies, campaigned for candidates that challenged his perceived enemies, and served as the figurehead for the Donald J. Trump website, which urged people to contribute to his war chest and exhorted them to "get involved." Section 230 remained a major obsession. He tried to marshal support for his lawsuits against "Big Tech," which asserted that the internet was a "public square" from which no one could be excluded.[35]

"Participation" was not a popular term in the right-wing lexicon in 2021. Conservative commentators liked to mock "participation trophies," which they claimed rewarded liberal alternatives to personal achievement and cutthroat competition. "Participation" was also not a word that ever appeared in Trump's tweets. Instead, he preferred the word "action," which he used over 200 times.

Yet the assault on the Capitol demonstrated the power of Trump's participatory appeals. His followers were given their assigned roles as "patriots" and encouraged to act out their cosplay as fans of the Trump entertainment franchise. Much of this activity was defined by digital performance that demonstrated their political allegiance—posting status updates and shooting selfies as they stormed the country's symbol of representative democracy.

Conclusion: The New Digital Politics

Aaron Fisher looked back on his time as a nineteen-year-old intern at the Obama White House with fondness. "I was at Twitter too when I was younger, but it's hard to one-up the White House." He conceded that the place "burns people out." Nonetheless, "you get nostalgic."[1]

Alec Ross, Clinton's former senior advisor for innovation, adopted a more jaded perspective on the Obama years. "I think that my own views on policy were informed by the decade-plus I spent working in nonprofits in community development work. I can see how using these tools is a way of building political power, and not using them means that you are sacrificing some political power."[2] But Ross had often felt like an outsider among the starry-eyed cyberutopians at the State Department. He had held himself apart from "people who thought that you could disintermediate democracy in an efficient way. I sort of rolled my eyes at that stuff, frankly."

"I'm somewhat skeptical of direct democracy," Ross said. "I'm a bigger believer in representative democracy."

When Macon Phillips, Obama's former director of digital strategy, reflected on how these technologies were used in both the Obama and Trump administrations, he saw them as neutral tools, capable of being the instruments of both good and evil: "You can use a phone to call someone and say you're alive. You can use the phone to call someone and harass them. There's just a lot of different ways to use technology."

To emphasize his point, Phillips used an analogy to equipment in an action movie that could be used by either a hero or a villain. "A great online program is just an Iron Man suit."[3]

Tom Cochran, Obama's former director of new media technologies, laughed about how far he had come from his initial self so quickly. After the 2016 election he had already planned to move on from government service. But he felt relief that the restrictions that had made his day-to-day work in the Obama administration such a hassle would be still in place during the Trump administration.

"I went from hating bureaucracy to 'thank god we have bureaucracy'— within 24 hours."[4]

The Biden Tech Agenda

Several days after the 2020 presidential election, a bare-bones web page appeared. It only contained three sentences. A link to a Spanish-language version of Biden's three-sentence announcement was also provided. Unlike the rich environment for digital interaction that heralded the coming of the Obama–Biden administration in 2008 at Change.gov, this website served as a tentative placeholder.

When Change.gov made its debut twelve years earlier, Biden was shown smiling alongside Obama under stadium spotlights. In that earlier digital moment, the two incoming leaders had appeared under a navigation bar of possibilities that invited visitors to explore the site's extensive content and to become regular readers of its news.

Modern technology was noticeably absent in the visual rhetoric of the Biden–Harris transition website. The main photo (figure 13.1) showed a

The American people will determine who will serve as the next President of the United States. Votes are still being counted in several states around the country. The crises facing the country are severe — from a pandemic to an economic recession, climate change to racial injustice — and the transition team will continue preparing at full speed so that the Biden-Harris Administration can hit the ground running on Day One.

Figure 13.1
Transition page at BuildBackBetter.com.

worried president-elect holding a pen. The pen was clearly the technology of potential executive action, but it was frozen in inanimate suspension while Biden waited for his term in office to begin.

Among the executive actions that could have required Biden's pen were pending regulatory measures to reign in Silicon Valley companies. Such corporations might finally face meaningful limitations on their power. Secretive policies, unpredictable practices, hidden algorithms, legal loopholes, and anti-competitive acquisitions had gone unchecked for many years.

Just a few weeks before the 2020 election, Biden's predecessor Donald J. Trump was energetically pursuing his own actions against technology platforms. On October 20, 2020, the Justice Department filed an antitrust suit against Alphabet, the parent company of Google, charging them with a host of violations. On December 9, 2020, the Federal Trade Commission sued Facebook, alleging that the company was illegally maintaining its personal social networking monopoly through a years-long course of anticompetitive conduct. Rescinding Section 230 would require legislative action, but Trump's executive branch continued to make it a focus in their rhetoric against "Big Tech."

Tech journalist Kara Swisher argued that it was "too little too late" on the regulatory front, given how long Silicon Valley companies had expanded their size, scope, and influence without any serious opposition from government regulators. She was also critical of fixating on Section 230 as a "silver bullet" because there was "no such thing as a single entity called Big Tech."[5] According to Swisher, "challenges plaguing the tech industry are so complex that it is impossible to take action against one without understanding the entire ecosystem, which hinges on many monster companies, with many big problems, each of which requires a different remedy."

Communication scholar Siva Vaidhyanathan agreed that the essential problems with search engines and social media companies were both dissimilar and structural, even if they all shared the blame for poisoning political discourse. "The problem with Facebook is Facebook. The problem with Google is Google. And the problem with both is that long-term, global dependence on them warps our ability to comprehend the world (Google more than Facebook) and ability to change the world (Facebook more than Google)."[6]

Journalists described Biden as "another president skeptical of Big Tech."[7] But Biden brought many veterans of the Obama administration with him, some of whom continued to embrace Obama's tech-friendly cyberuto-pian agenda. Technology and telecommunications companies were major donors to the Biden inauguration ceremonies, including Google, Microsoft, and Qualcomm.[8]

Even as the midterm elections approached, much remained uncertain about platform regulation under the Biden administration, which was sometimes jokingly called "Obama's third term." Would they attempt to change the essential power balance between weak users and powerful plat-forms? Or would they advance a technocratic agenda, creating an even greater role in democracy for technical systems? Evidence from Biden's first year in office pointed both ways.

There were some encouraging signs for those who favored more regula-tion. One of Biden's first tech-related announcements called for real strate-gies to curtail online harassment. It was seen as part of his long-standing commitment to crafting legislation prohibiting violence against women.[9]

Then, in July of 2021, Biden signed an ambitious executive order on "Promoting Competition in the American Economy" that was widely seen as targeting Silicon Valley companies. The order used the "Big Tech" label several times, even though "Big Tech" was a pejorative term that had been popularized by right-wing politicians like Trump and Hawley. In the docu-ment, "Big Tech" was chastised for "purchasing would-be competitors," "gathering too much private information," and "unfairly competing with small businesses."[10]

According to Biden, propagating misinformation was also a major concern that merited more gatekeeping. False claims about the coronavi-rus vaccine—including that it contained toxic chemicals, microchips, or embryonic tissue—were disseminated far and wide on Facebook. In frustra-tion, Biden accused Facebook of "killing people" twice in an NBC inter-view. White House officials grew so irritated with Facebook's noncommittal answers in internal meetings that they "demanded to hear from the data scientists at the company instead of lobbyists."[11]

Biden's choice of a Federal Trade Commission chair signaled another loss for the tech lobby. He selected Lina Khan, a law professor who specialized in antitrust cases. Khan had previously published influential articles that were highly critical of internet companies.

At the Federal Communications Commission (FCC), signals for reform were much more mixed. Like the Federal Trade Commission, the FCC had enjoyed a long history of close ties to lobbying groups, many in telecommunications and internet services. One former chair became a lobbyist for Facebook. Another became a legal advisor for a wireless provider. Still another had been a legal advisor for a wireless provider. In one case, the head of the National Cable & Telecommunications Association (NCTA)—a powerful trade organization for the broadband industry—became FCC chair, and in another case the FCC chair became the head of the NCTA. One of *that* person's protégés at the FCC, who had also been the NCTA's chief operating officer, went on to run the Internet Association, a lobbying group for social media services and mobile apps. Although Biden chose Jessica Rosenworcel as the acting chair of the FCC right after the inauguration, months went by with no word on whether he would confirm her permanent appointment to the post. She was finally confirmed by the Senate in December of 2021. Additional tie-breaking appointees for the FTC and FCC remained blocked from confirmation.

In addition to the executive branch of government, the Supreme Court also has the power to alter the regulatory environment for tech companies. Many of the major decisions that established the current status quo dated from the 1990s. For example, the court legitimized click-through licenses in 1996, struck down censorship of adult content on the internet in 1997, and shielded internet service providers from liability for impersonation and harassment in 1998.

During the '00s, the court often reflected the cyberoptimism of the Obama years. In 2010 it praised the internet for promoting financial transparency and offering "significant information about political candidates and issues." It affirmed that the internet served as a "public square" in 2017, providing a core of civic life. Even with its conservative majority solidified, the justices continued to view social media as an important space for freedom of expression. In 2021 a cheerleader's obscene rant on Snapchat was judged to be protected speech for which she could not be disciplined by her school.[12]

Conceivably, the legislative branch of government might also take action. Perhaps their bipartisan anger could overcome the hurdles of political polarization and the bureaucratic structure of committees from the previous century. Would such legislation target harassment, hate groups, and misinformation? Or would it defend free speech and attack the censorship of community standards and content moderation? Left-wing and right-wing politics might generate very different outcomes.

When Frances Haugen, a former Facebook product manager turned whistleblower, testified before Congress about the company's harms in 2021, CEO Mark Zuckerberg described her allegations as "pretty easy to debunk."[13] Soon afterward, Facebook rebranded as "Meta." Zuckerberg promised that the next platform would "be even more immersive—an embodied internet where you're in the experience, not just looking at it."[14] Obviously, the challenges of content moderation and attempting regulation with virtual reality products would become even more daunting.[15]

Engineering Democracy

Of course, there is a legitimate argument that laws are not the most effective way to change internet behavior in ways that support human flourishing. There are other, non-legal measures that can exert regulatory pressure, such as norms, markets, and the architectures of the digital systems themselves.[16]

As a way to combat misinformation, hate speech, harassment, and political extremism, creating new social norms could provide some solutions. Civic customs of mutual respect, open dialogue, and shared public space could compensate for the disadvantages of our over-mediated interactions and allow us to escape the echo chambers and filter bubbles that we currently inhabit. Greater digital literacy could also counter the fantasies of disintermediation that these platforms encourage. Much of the dysfunction in our collective digital culture could be addressed through more comprehensive education programs that expand the definition of traditional civics to include online citizenship.[17] Explicit instruction in media literacy, data literacy, and platform design would be critical areas for pedagogical intervention. Ideally, this instruction would include forms of expertise that extend beyond the domains of STEM. For example, knowledge of history, foreign languages, philosophy, rhetoric, and aesthetics can be useful for distinguishing fake news from real news.[18] However, the current state of our overloaded school systems doesn't make me particularly optimistic that sufficient time could be carved out for these endeavors.

Furthermore, establishing new norms alone cannot be entirely effective when such fundamental inequities of power still exist between users and platforms. We don't just need digital literacy; we need digital rights.[19] In the present moment, social media platforms and search engines often cannot be held accountable for their products and services. As a consequence, our democracy has suffered. These companies may have idealistic origin stories in which their founders only intended to foster connection, transparency, access, and participation. But we clearly don't live in the egalitarian digital nirvana that was planned for us.

Silicon Valley companies tend to prefer their own solutions to the problems they have created, which would allow them to continue to regulate themselves. They generally emphasize markets and architecture rather than laws or norms. According to their spokespeople, laissez-faire economics and an unfettered marketplace will ensure the best products and services for their customers for free or at very low prices.[20] The public is assured that the technical expertise of their engineers, programmers, and designers will continue to optimize the built environments that they have created for us and to remedy any glitches in the system.[21] The rhetoric of the tech lobby asserts that internet companies represent the pinnacle of American achievement, and their progress to even greater success should not be hampered. For example, statements from the Internet Association—a leading trade group—insist that "content moderation by online platforms has been highly effective" and "companies quickly remove bad actors."[22] Using the power of new tools like artificial intelligence, the public is encouraged to believe that even better outcomes could be achieved very soon.[23]

The Fantasy of the Selective Opt-Out

"With this statement, I give notice to Instagram it is strictly forbidden to disclose, copy, distribute, or take any other action against me based on this profile and/or its contents."

Trump's secretary of energy Rick Perry posted this message on social media in 2019. Using a screenshot of text copied and pasted from other sources, Perry warned that "tomorrow starts the new Instagram rule where they can use your photos!" With this impending "deadline" approaching, Perry spoke ominously about "court cases" and "litigation." He cited reporting from a seemingly authoritative Channel 13 News in support of his declaration.

Of course, Perry had been taken in by a hoax. Similar hoaxes about posting opt-out declarations on social media sites had been floating around on the internet since at least 2012.[24] The boilerplate language that Perry shared reflected common anxieties about the changing legalese in user agreements that often gave consumers little power as users of digital services. His desire to have the power to opt out from one aspect of a potentially coercive agreement was shared by many users of social media platforms. As researchers Joan Donovan and Brian Friedberg pointed out, there was more to the Perry Instagram story than simple technological illiteracy. The appeal of the "with this statement" meme demonstrated a profound desire for two-way communication and power sharing with the managers of powerful social media platforms.[25]

Supporting stronger opt-out protocols is one obvious thing that the Biden White House could pursue. Of course, both the Obama and Trump administrations failed to achieve any progress on opt-out provisions during their tenures in office.

Gamifying Government

Hundreds of thousands of people were captivated by a livestream of congressional representatives Alexandria Ocasio-Cortez and Ilhan Omar playing *Among Us*. *Among Us* was a popular, multiplayer murder mystery game with a colorful cartoony aesthetic. The story they played through was set on a spaceship. The game allowed for deceptive role-playing if a player was assigned an "impostor" rather than a "crew" role. It rewarded a player's stealth and powers of speculation. The game also contained many elements of real congressional politics.[26] Players had to complete tasks, do research, be prepared to "discuss" should an "emergency meeting" be called, and vote. The congresswomen's stunt in the final weeks of the 2020 election publicized resources on the IWillVote.com website as well. While multitasking through various screens and channels, Ocasio-Cortez exhorted her followers to make "a voting plan" or get someone else "registered to vote."

The event was a virtuoso digital performance by two members of "The Squad," a group of young, left-leaning, women of color who had beat out more established Democratic Party incumbents at the beginnings of their congressional careers. Ocasio-Cortez's lively facial expressions could be seen below another screen that showed her avatar's game play. In addition to using Twitch, a popular livestreaming service favored by e-sports celebrities, she joined the *Among Us* group's Discord channel to facilitate large group communication. According to the *Guardian*, "Ocasio-Cortez's Twitch channel garnered a staggering audience of 439,000 viewers, all watching her in real time . . . with approximately 5.2 million viewers watching the stream in aggregate."[27] Edited versions of the performance on YouTube racked up hundreds of thousands of views, and meme-making on other platforms made it a fresh topic of online conversation for many days afterward.

This event represented one possible paradigm for reimagining representative government. Ocasio-Cortez's constituents had the opportunity to watch her in action and to generate a flurry of shared social commentary in real time. However, much like Obama's social media Town Halls of the pre-Trump era, it was largely a one-way spectacle for her remote audience. It was a simulation of representative democracy and political gamesmanship rather than the real thing.

Selfie Democracy

In looking back at Trump's successful use of social media as a politician, we can see that he relied on many of the same rhetorical appeals that had worked so well for Obama: connection, transparency, participation, and access. However, these framing concepts in direct digital democracy, which had been promulgated in Silicon Valley as well as in the White House, had become distorted and grotesque under Trump. Connection had become white identity politics. Access had become influence peddling. Transparency had become conspiracy thinking. Participation had become insurrection.

The promise of pervasive, mobile, personalized, and intelligent technologies revealed the nightmare of the digital populism they could unleash. Obama's high-tech simulations became fake news stories fueling anxieties about false flags and crisis actors. Obama's town halls became Trump's rallies. Citizen journalists became influencers. Distributed networks became pyramid schemes. By the time Trump was tweeting out classified photos to the Iranian government, the public diplomacy initiatives of the Obama administration had completely degenerated into trolling.

What Trump's followers got instead of direct democracy was selfie democracy. They attempted to use their smartphones to reinscribe a human presence in an increasingly posthuman world, but they were doomed to fail because they relied on demagoguery.[28] Certainly, many of their social media fears were legitimate. They were responding to a real situation of becoming increasingly disempowered by the prevalence of digital systems that demanded total subservience to mechanisms of surveillance and decision engineering. Abolishing Section 230 or storming the Capitol to keep their leader in charge to fight Big Tech wouldn't save them. Trump had benefited from the extractive social media model that had been established during the Obama administration.

Selfie democracy combines three key elements to make its heady cocktail of political extremism: ubiquitous computing, identity politics, and hostility to representative government. It presents a fantasy of disintermediation that links a political subject directly to his or her sovereign through an experience of digital copresence. A leader can be hailed by a citizen on social media using a more intimate, second-person address than would normally be possible. When that leader shows up in that person's social media feed, sharing similar thoughts and feelings, that citizen might imagine being spoken to personally, even if their actual queries are going unanswered. Obama's charisma and cult of personality encouraged this dangerous line of thinking, just as Trump's strongman theatrics did.

I don't think participants in selfie democracy are necessarily evil or ignorant. The performance of political identity on social media is a fact of life. Gestures of solidarity, signals of mutual aid, and badges of alliance do real rhetorical work online. The larger cultural shift from representation to simulation also feels inevitable. The technologies that predict outcomes and model behavior are here to stay. To pretend that we are really voting for anything when we promote a particular worldview on these platforms with an outcome in representative government is a delusion.

The rise of personal technology is not the only phenomenon that has made citizens less able to experience self-knowledge or shape their own fates. Media consolidation, the failure of campaign finance reform, manipulative redistricting, and threats from foreign governments to international alliances have all played a role. However, the tools through which technology deepens political divisions and manipulates decision-making are more precise and untraceable, allowing oligarchy and authoritarianism more opportunity to thrive.

If we can't selectively opt out to claim agency as sovereign citizens, and if we don't want to sit back and just passively watch the powerful play, we can learn from the lessons of the Obama and Trump administrations through archival evidence and the testimony of participants like Phillips, Cochran, and Ross.

We need to understand the pitfalls of the new digital politics. We need to acknowledge the powerful appeals of nostalgia for a direct democracy that never was. We need to interrogate our deep social and psychological desires for connection, transparency, access, and participation. And we need to understand the role of class, race, and gender in the assumptions that we make about supposedly neutral platforms. This knowledge will help us make difficult decisions—through our elected representatives and established institutions—about the future role of technology in our democracy.

Acknowledgments

A few months after my first book appeared from this press in 2009, I was invited to give a talk at the Berkman Center for Internet & Society at Harvard University, now known as the Berkman Klein Center. That book, *Virtualpolitik*, focused on the use of digital technology during the administration of George W. Bush, although parts of the text were also devoted to the presidency of Bill Clinton and to digital government initiatives in France and the United Kingdom. That book's emphasis was on desktop computing and the risk that digital files could reach unintended audiences and be used for unanticipated purposes. Its premise was that because the government served as both a regulator and a content creator, the situation was much more complicated than standard cyber-optimism or cyber-pessimism.

My recollection was that I had been expected to speak about *Virtualpolitik* at the Berkman Center, but instead I decided to tackle a new topic: digital technology in the administration of Barack Obama. Obama had only been in office for a few months, so the material felt very spontaneous and fresh. Much of my talk was devoted to privacy concerns about the new White House policy on cookies that gathered data from visitors to government websites. I also talked about the limitations that were already apparent in the promised data transparency that Obama was supposed to bring. I am grateful to David Weinberger for blogging about my Berkman visit.

That same year I was invited to participate in a National Endowment for the Humanities Summer Fellowship housed at the Institute for Multimedia Literacy at the University of Southern California, which was sponsored by the pioneering multimedia journal *Vectors*. There I was fortunate to work with organizers Tara McPherson, Virginia Kuhn, Holly Willis, Steve Anderson, Eric Loyer, Craig Dietrich, and Gabriel Peters-Lazaro. Institute participants N. Katherine Hayles, Alexandra Juhasz, Micki McGee, Nicole Starosielski, and Alex Tarr contributed greatly to the developing project that would eventually become this book. As it was initially imagined as a print book, what was to become *Selfie Democracy* was also to have had a multimedia component. The *Vectors* institute video interviews with Wendy Hui Kyong Chun, Henry Jenkins, Christopher Kelty, Dan Cohen, Siva Vaidhyanathan, Geert Lovink, and Chris Soghoian informed many of the ideas represented here.

Because the issues in this book were so urgent and timely, I kept feeling that finishing the manuscript was always just a few weeks away. I felt this way for twelve years during two terms of Obama, a term of Donald J. Trump, and the beginnings of the presidency of Joe Biden. It wasn't until the storming of the Capitol by right-wing extremists inspired by and organized through social media and smartphones that my end point became apparent.

In the intervening time, I published several other books. What was to be my second book became my third and then my fourth. I changed institutions twice, so my list of acknowledgments now grew to include three different universities: William & Mary, UC San Diego, and UC Irvine. Yet those years were active ones, rich in collaboration, especially with two international research groups.

My friend and colleague Nishant Shah introduced me to MECS, the Institute of Advanced Study on Media Cultures of Computer Simulation, which was funded by the German Research Foundation (DFG) at Leuphana University. MECS was directed by Martin Warnke and Claus Pias. I am grateful for the fascinating conversations that took place in Lüneburg, Berlin, and Tuscany thanks to MECS. Other key collaborators in those intensive sessions of scholarly exchange included Neda Atanasoski, Kalindi Vora, Arianna Borrelli, Anne Dippel, Timon Beyes, and Frank Pasema.

The other—equally important—international research group that shaped the writing of this book was Machine Vision in Everyday Life: Playful Interactions with Visual Technologies in Digital Art, Games, Narratives and Social Media. Machine Vision was a five-year, European Research Council-funded project exploring how new algorithmic images were affecting us as a society and as individuals. It was directed by Jill Walker Rettberg. I first got to know Jill through the Selfies Researchers Network, which was organized by Theresa Senft and Alice Marwick. Rettberg and I did a unit for an open-access "Selfie Course" on "Dataveillance, Biometrics and Facial Recognition." Among the Machine Vision cohort, my other close collaborators were Katrin Tiidenberg, Annette Markham, Anna Nacher, and Anne Karhio. Our discussions at the University of Bergen and at Solstrand were incredibly expansive and intellectually ambitious. Tiidenberg also encouraged me to apply for the Fulbright Scholar Program, and as I complete the copyediting for this book, I have joined her at Tallinn University in Estonia as a visiting scholar.

Parts of this book were developed for publication in the *Video Vortex Reader*, *Video Vortex 2*, and *Rhetorical Machines: Writing, Code, and Computational Ethics*. I am grateful to Geert Lovink, John Jones, and Lavinia Hirsu for their intellectual vision for these volumes.

The staff of the William & Mary Washington Center made much of this book possible. I created Washington Center courses on Online Citizenship, Digital Identity, and Global Rhetoric and Social Media, which allowed me to test out ideas for this book with students and guest speakers. Special thanks to Roxane Adler Hickey, Erin Battle, Elisabeth Merrifield, and Rhys Tucker for all of their work facilitating, as well as to my fabulous teaching assistants Ravynn Stringfield and Jonathan Newby. In Washington, DC, I was able to interview many of the important voices represented in this book, including Macon Phillips, Alec Ross, and Tom Cochran. I interviewed Peter Costanzo in New York. Other interviews with Kin Lane, Aaron Fisher, and Molly Moran were conducted remotely. Material from Jane Cook was gathered via email questions. (I interviewed Abbie Grotke and Kris Anderson long beforehand, for an unpublished op-ed about the Obama inauguration for the *Washington Post*.)

Before retiring from the University of California and coming to William & Mary, I benefited greatly from the research being done at UC institutes and centers. I presented drafts of several parts of this book at Calit2, the California Institute for Telecommunications and Information Technology. Lev Manovich and Benjamin Bratton were particularly significant Calit2 members and friends. The UC Humanities Research Institute also provided critical research infrastructure and opportunities to present works in progress. Special thanks are due to David Theo Goldberg and Mimi Ito for their leadership on digital learning initiatives and to Mariko Oda, Claudia Caro Sullivan, and Mimi Ko Cruz for administrative support. The Institute for Money, Technology, and Financial Inclusion also stimulated me to think about "digital media" much more interdisciplinarily and globally, and director Bill Maurer and manager Jenny Fan made this exploration and expansion possible. I also presented material from this book at what was to become the Institute for Virtual Environments and Computer Games. Before it was an institute, it was a center, and before it was a center it was just a welcoming group of faculty in the Informatics Department at UC Irvine. In particular, Paul Dourish and Bonnie Nardi organized talks that resulted in essential feedback and often changed the direction of my thinking for the manuscript.

The Equality Lab at William & Mary, which I co-founded with Brett Wilson and subsequently directed, could be considered my current base of operations. During the Trump years, when I was particularly busy making sense of social media streams, the lab provided the infrastructure to analyze the enormous corpora of posts from Twitter and other platforms. Donors Gale and Steve Kohlhagen and Duane A. and Virginia S. Dittman directly sustained my work in the lab, as did Joseph Plumeri. Many thanks to Latasha Simms, Jeanne Smith, Jean Brown, and Monika Van Tassel for dealing with the lab's never-ending stream of paperwork with such good humor.

Undergraduate researchers at the Equality Lab—especially Gus Espinosa and Jasmine Geonzon—helped me organize, transcribe, and interpret the voluminous data set of interviews, archival screenshots, and spreadsheets of social media posts that provided the evidence for my central claims. Special thanks go to donor Maggie Glauber for supporting these undergraduate fellowships. Graduate research assistants in the Equality Lab—Khanh Vo, Jessica Cowing, Laura Beltran-Rubio, Sara Woodbury, and Shaun Richards—made time available for writing. These lab leaders organized symposia, lectures, and workshops. Vice provost Dennis Manos, graduate dean Virginia Torczon, and American Studies program director Leisa Meyer made these assistanceships possible. My fellow faculty in Data Science were also incredibly helpful, especially Matthias Leu and Jaime Settle.

These dozen years of work were also supported and sustained by the rich feminist network of scholars, learners, activists, archivists, artists, and friends working on feminism and technology in FemTechNet, which was first activated by Alexandra Juhasz and Anne Balsamo. Because there have been hundreds of people involved in this network, there might be too many FemTechNet names to fit in an acknowledgments section, but I want to thank my fellow co-facilitators Lisa Nakamura and Sharon Irish individually, as well as our successors Anne Cong-Nguyen, T. L. Cowing, Paula Gardner, Veronica Paredes, and Jasmine Rault.

Scholars of Black digital feminism were particularly important for challenging the worldview that I brought to the central questions of theorizing race and gender that have been so critical for what it means to have an American digital presidency. After all, you can't talk about figures like Barack Obama, Hillary Clinton, Donald Trump, or Joe Biden without considering the intersections of race and gender. Intellectual and personal relationships with Jessica Marie Johnson, Beth Coleman, and Moya Bailey were particularly transformative.

Jennifer Cool was a sounding board for the entire twelve-year period of research and writing, as I talked through ideas and benefited from her knowledge about informal histories of digital culture that tended not to be documented. There were also a number of meals during conferences in which I shared my current thinking with trusted friends. I am grateful to Nick Mirzoeff and Joan Donovan in particular for providing feedback during this process of revision and reflection. The group at Microsoft Research who extended their hospitality—including lending me a beautiful office with a view of the Charles River—also merit recognition, especially Nancy Baym, Mary Gray, and Tarleton Gillespie.

Obviously, all of the terrific people at the MIT Press shaped this volume. From the very beginning, when I was just starting to work on *Selfie Democracy* for that Berkman lunch talk, I talked with great excitement to Doug Sery and Gita Manaktala about this book. As an author, I am very fortunate to consider them friends as well as editors. Their enthusiasm and patience with the "new idea" that I pitched during my 2009 visit to Cambridge, Massachusetts, speaks to the depth of their friendship over the years.

When it comes to publishing networks, thanks are due also to Ian Bogost and Chris Schaberg. If it weren't for Ian and Chris, I wouldn't have met MIT Press's Noah Springer at the Object Lessons National Endowment for the Humanities Workshop in 2017. Ian and Chris also provided critical feedback for the book as I refined its framing for more general audiences. Since 2020 Noah has brought the project over the finish line and shepherded it though the feedback process with the anonymous peer reviewers to whom I am also extremely grateful. Special thanks go to "reviewer one," who annotated the entire manuscript. Of course, everyone in the production process at the MIT Press also contributed significantly, especially copy editor Liz DeWolf, assistant editor Liz Agresta, acquisitions assistant Lillian Dunaj, indexer Kendra Millis, and the many excellent design and production professionals at the press.

Throughout it all, my husband Mel Horan was always there. He tolerated me blaring Fox News throughout the house, and he shared in the idiosyncratic delights of my For You page on TikTok. This book is dedicated to him. I look forward to many years of following digital politics together.

Notes

Introduction

1. For example, Israeli prime minister Benjamin Netanyahu had copied Obama's campaign website design, including its distinctive blue color scheme and video-friendly layout. See Ethan Bronner and Noam Cohen, "Israeli Candidate Borrows a (Web) Page From Obama," *New York Times*, November 14, 2008, Middle East, https://www.nytimes.com/2008/11/15/world/middleeast/15bibi.html.

2. Brad Stone, "The High Security Risk Attached to Obama's Belt," *New York Times*, January 11, 2009, Technology, https://www.nytimes.com/2009/01/12/technology/internet/12blackberry.html.

3. Curtis Marez, "Obama's BlackBerry, or This Is Not a Technology of Destruction," *Journal of Visual Culture* 8, no. 2 (August 2009): 219–23, https://doi.org/10.1177/147 04129090080020404.

4. Sharon Begley, "Will the Blackberry Sink the Presidency?," *Newsweek*, February 16, 2009, https://www.ics.uci.edu/community/news/articles/view_article?id=125.

5. John Harauz and Lori M. Kaufman, "A New Era of Presidential Security: The President and His BlackBerry," *IEEE Security Privacy* 7, no. 2 (March 2009): 67–70, https://doi.org/10.1109/MSP.2009.29.

6. *The Tonight Show Starring Jimmy Fallon*, "President Obama Explains His Old-School Blackberry," uploaded June 10, 2016, YouTube video, 3:28, https://youtu.be/aMcKi1TS2Zs.

7. André Brock, *Distributed Blackness: African American Cybercultures* (New York: New York University Press, 2020).

8. Of course, users with disabilities may engage with their devices very differently, as might those who access them without reliable networks or electricity.

9. Donald J. Trump (@realDonaldTrump), "Great—Now Supreme Court Justices Are Talking about a Constitutional Right to a Cell Phone Http://T.Co/6oXWvjnB

Obama, Just Stop Already.," Twitter, October 17, 2021, https://twitter.com/realdon
aldtrump/status/258673336391966722.

10. Melanie Arter, "Justice Stevens: 'Maybe You Have Some Kind of Constitutional
Right to a Cell Phone . . .'," *CNSNews*, October 16, 2012, https://www.cnsnews.com
/news/article/justice-stevens-maybe-you-have-some-kind-constitutional-right-cell
-phone.

11. In this section about the risks and rewards of mobile communication, I use
the term "cell phone" as well as "smartphone," but the distinction between smartphones and "dumber," less expensive phones, or "flip phones," is an important one.
I have tried to reflect the terms used in the original sources appropriately.

12. Terence P. Jeffrey, "Justice Breyer: Can Congress Make Americans Buy Computers, Cell Phones, Burials? 'Yes, of Course'," *CNSNews*, March 28, 2012, https://
www.cnsnews.com/news/article/justice-breyer-can-congress-make-americans-buy
-computers-cell-phones-burials-yes-course.

13. "Original Obamaphone Lady: Obama Voter Says Vote for Obama Because He
Gives a Free Phone," uploaded September 26, 2012, by RealFreedom1776, YouTube
video, 0:44, https://youtu.be/tpAOwJvTOio.

14. Brendan Sasso, "'Obama Phone' Viral Video Puts Spotlight on FCC's Phone-
Access Program," *The Hill*, October 1, 2012, https://thehill.com/policy/technology
/259579-obama-phone-video-puts-spotlight-on-fcc-program.

15. Digital anthropologist Crystal Abidin has described this kind of internet celebrity as an "eyewitness viral star" and has observed that they are often "black persons of low socioeconomic status, whose pity-comedic-likeability dimensions are
premised on an intended middle-class audience's sense of distance from and exoticism toward the everyday lives of the poor and people of color." See Crystal Abidin,
Internet Celebrity: Understanding Fame Online (Bingley: Emerald Publishing, 2018), 40.

16. Lee Fang, "Group Running Racist 'Obama Phone' Ad Has Close Ties to Congressional Republicans," *The Nation*, October 16, 2012, https://www.thenation
.com/article/group-running-racist-obama-phone-ad-has-close-ties-congressional
-republicans/.

17. See Charlton D. McIlwain and Stephen M. Caliendo, "Mitt Romney's Racist
Appeals: How Race Was Played in the 2012 Presidential Election," *American Behavioral Scientist* 58, no. 9 (August 2014): 1157–68 and Anna Everett, "Have We Become
Postracial Yet?: Race and Media Technologies in the Age of President Obama," in
Race after the Internet, ed. Lisa Nakamura and Peter Chow-White (New York: Routledge, 2012), 146–167. In discussing the Obamaphone ad, McIlwain and Caliendo
trace the trope of "the lazy Black" back to Reconstruction and its use by white
supremacists not only as a negative stereotype to keep the formerly enslaved out
of power, but also as evidence of an implied binary logic of who works and who

benefits. According to Everett, a film and media scholar, the racist vitriol so closely tied to the Obama brand demonstrates the persistence of "America's racial scripts" that refuse to be rewritten by "pervasive computing and ubiquitous digital media technologies." The use of "Obama as prefix" ("Obamacare," etc.), she argues, became enough to discredit many "progressive gains on the postracial front."

18. Comm. on the Budget, Concurrent Resolution on the Budget—Fiscal Year 2018, H. R. Rep. No. 115–240 (2017), https://www.congress.gov/congressional-report/115th -congress/house-report/240/1.

19. See Nate Cohn, "The Obama-Trump Voters Are Real. Here's What They Think.," *New York Times*, December 22, 2017, The Upshot, https://www.nytimes.com /2017/08/15/upshot/the-obama-trump-voters-are-real-heres-what-they-think.html and Dana Milbank, "There's No Such Thing as a Trump Democrat," *Washington Post*, August 4, 2017, https://www.washingtonpost.com/opinions/theres-no-such-thing -as-a-trump-democrat/2017/08/04/0d5d06bc-7920-11e7-8f39-eeb7d3a2d304_story .html.

20. Mark Weiser, "Some Computer Science Issues in Ubiquitous Computing." *Communications of the ACM* 36, no. 7 (July 1993): 75–84, https://doi.org/10.1145 /159544.159617.

21. The chapters covering these rhetorics are labeled with each president's name, but phrases like "Obama's rhetoric of connection" should be understood as strategies developed by large teams of campaign operatives, White House staffers, programmers, designers, and data analysts rather than by the president alone.

Chapter 1

1. Macon Phillips (former director of digital strategy for President Obama), in discussion with the author, April 2019.

2. For more on the *Dean for America* game, see Ian Bogost, "Playing Politics: Videogames for Politics, Activism, and Advocacy," *First Monday*, September 4, 2006, https://doi.org/10.5210/fm.v0i0.1617.

3. Phillips, April 2019.

4. Phillips, April 2019.

5. Tom Cochran (former director of new media technologies for President Obama), in discussion with the author, September 2019.

6. David Karpf, *Analytic Activism: Digital Listening and the New Political Strategy* (New York: Oxford University Press, 2016), 1.

7. Karpf, *Analytic Activism: Digital Listening and the New Political Strategy*, 147.

8. Sarah Lai Stirland, "Obama's Secret Weapons: Internet, Databases and Psychology," *Wired*, October 29, 2008, https://www.wired.com/2008/10/obamas-secret-w/.

9. Noam Cohen, "Is Obama a Mac and Clinton a PC?," *New York Times*, February 4, 2008, https://www.nytimes.com/2008/02/04/technology/04link.html.

10. "MyBO Tour," BarackObamadotcom, uploaded September 11, 2008, YouTube video, 6:26, https://youtu.be/uRY72OHE0DE.

11. David Talbot, "How Obama Really Did It," *MIT Technology Review*, August 19, 2008, https://www.technologyreview.com/2008/08/19/219185/how-obama-really-did-it-2/.

12. "Vote Different," uploaded March 5, 2007, by ParkRidge47, YouTube video, 1:14, https://youtu.be/6h3G-lMZxjo.

13. will.i.am, "Yes We Can Song by will.i.am," uploaded February 2, 2008, YouTube video, 4:30, https://youtu.be/2fZHou18Cdk.

14. Lawrence Lessig, *Remix: Making Art and Commerce Thrive in the Hybrid Economy* (New York: Penguin Books, 2009), 56.

15. John McCain, "Celeb," uploaded July 30, 2008, YouTube video, 0:31, https://youtu.be/oHXYsw_ZDXg.

16. Kate Kenski, Bruce W. Hardy, and Kathleen Hall Jamieson, *The Obama Victory: How Media, Money, and Message Shaped the 2008 Election* (Oxford; New York: Oxford University Press, 2010).

17. Funny or Die, "Paris Hilton Responds to McCain Ad," uploaded May 20, 2013, YouTube video, 1:55, https://youtu.be/ySc12uzoxqU.

18. For more on Chad Hurley's computer science and graphic design training at Indiana University of Pennsylvania, see "The YouTube Guy—IUP," https://www.iup.edu/admissions/undergraduate/academics/findyoursuccess/more-stories/the-youtube-guy/.

19. Sean Cubitt, "Codecs and Capability," in *Video Vortex Reader Responses to YouTube*, ed. Geert Lovink and Sabine Niederer (Amsterdam: Institute of Network Cultures, 2009), 45–52.

20. Geert Lovink, "The Art of Watching Databases," in *Video Vortex Reader Responses to Youtube*, ed. Geert Lovink and Sabine Niederer (Amsterdam: Institute of Network Cultures, 2009), 9–12.

21. Alexandra Juhasz, "Learning the Five Lessons of YouTube: After Trying to Teach There, I Don't Believe the Hype," *Cinema Journal* 48, no. 2 (2009): 145–50, http://www.jstor.org/stable/20484456.

22. Jean Burgess and Joshua Green, *YouTube: Online Video and Participatory Culture* (Cambridge: Polity, 2018).

23. Catherine Rampell, "Presidential Tax Calculators," *Economix*, October 14, 2008, https://economix.blogs.nytimes.com/2008/10/14/obama-and-mccain-tax-calculators/.

24. James J. Brown, *Ethical Programs: Hospitality and the Rhetorics of Software* (Ann Arbor, Michigan: University of Michigan Press, 2015), 71.

25. Rahaf Harfoush, *Yes We Did: An Inside Look at How Social Media Built the Obama Brand* (Berkeley: New Riders, 2009), 79.

26. Deborah Lupton, *The Quantified Self* (Malden: Polity, 2016).

27. Gina Neff, *Self-Tracking*, (Cambridge, MA: MIT Press, 2016).

28. Jacqueline Wernimont, *Numbered Lives: Life and Death in Quantum Media* (Cambridge, MA: MIT Press, 2019).

29. W. Lance Bennett, "The Personalization of Politics: Political Identity, Social Media, and Changing Patterns of Participation," *The ANNALS of the American Academy of Political and Social Science* 644, no. 1 (November 2012): 20–39.

30. With the rise of online crowdfunding, it could be argued that this emphasis on the distinct stories of specific individuals who are most likely to be deemed "worthy" by society has only been exacerbated by social media platforms. See Lauren S. Berliner and Nora J. Kenworthy, "Producing a Worthy Illness: Personal Crowdfunding amidst Financial Crisis," *Social Science & Medicine* 187 (August 2017): 233–242.

31. Experts have recognized a range of effects resulting from the politics of personalization. For a relatively benign interpretation that focuses on the shift from "collective action" to "connective action," see W. Lance Bennett and Alexandra Segerberg, *The Logic of Connective Action: Digital Media and the Personalization of Contentious Politics* (New York: Cambridge University Press, 2014). For a darker analysis of personalization, see Inderpal Grewal, *Saving the Security State Exceptional Citizens in Twenty-First-Century America* (Durham, NC: Duke University Press, 2017) on the dangers of "exceptional citizens" who consider themselves empowered to defend the state only if they are above the law.

32. Micah L. Sifry, "Obama's Lost Army," *New Republic*, February 9, 2017, https://newrepublic.com/article/140245/obamas-lost-army-inside-fall-grassroots-machine.

33. Christopher Edley Jr., "RESENDING: Fwd: Movement 2.0 incorporation and fundraising," WikiLeaks Podesta Emails, Email ID: 57558, dated August 21, 2008, https://wikileaks.org/podesta-emails/emailid/57558.

34. Kate Albright-Hanna, "How the Cool Kids Killed Obama's Grassroots Movement," *Civicist*, February 21, 2017, https://civichall.org/civicist/cool-kids-killed-obamas-grassroots-movement/.

Chapter 2

1. Elise Viebeck, "Memo to Obama Aides: Don't Prank Trump or Clinton on Your Way Out," *Washington Post*, September 29, 2016, https://www.washingtonpost .com/news/powerpost/wp/2016/09/29/memo-to-obama-aides-dont-prank-trump-or -clinton-on-your-way-out/.

2. Viebeck, "Memo to Obama Aides."

3. However, a "clean slate" was anticipated; see Richard Wiggins, "The Unnoticed Presidential Transition," *First Monday*, January 8, 2001, https://firstmonday.org/ojs /index.php/fm/article/download/829/738?inline=1.

4. "President William J. Clinton: Eight Years of Peace, Progress and Prosperity," WhiteHouse.gov, January 18, 2001, accessed via Wayback Machine, https://web .archive.org/web/20010118201800/http://www.whitehouse.gov/.

5. Jane Cook, email to author, May 2020.

6. "Welcome to the White House," WhiteHouse.gov, January 20, 2009, https:// georgewbush-whitehouse.archives.gov/.

7. "An American Moment: Your Story," Change.gov, February 12, 2009, http://web .archive.org/web/20090212000015/http://change.gov/page/s/yourstory.

8. "Office of the President-Elect," Change.gov, available online from 2008 to 2013, accessed via Library of Congress Web Archive, https://www.loc.gov/item /lcwa00092811/.

9. Elizabeth Losh, "From the Crowd to the Cloud: Watching the Inauguration on the Internet," *Virtualpolitik* (blog), January 17, 2009, http://virtualpolitik.blogspot .com/2009/01/from-crowd-to-cloud-watching.html.

10. Kate Day, "Barack Obama's Inauguration on Twitter," *Telegraph*, January 20, 2009, https://www.telegraph.co.uk/news/worldnews/barackobama/4296690/Barack -Obamas-inauguration-on-Twitter.html.

11. Pete Cashmore, "Mindblowing Numbers from the Obama Inauguration," *Mashable*, January 20, 2009, https://mashable.com/2009/01/20/cnn-facebook-inauguration -numbers/.

12. Amy Zimmerman, "Jan. 20, 2009: Mr. President, You're Live," *Wired*, January 20, 2012, https://www.wired.com/2012/01/jan-20-2009-obamas-inauguration-crashes -websites/.

13. "Search Findings from the U.S. Presidential Inauguration," *Official Google Blog*, January 20, 2009, https://googleblog.blogspot.com/2009/01/search-findings-from-us -presidential.html.

14. Max Weber, Guenther Roth, and Claus Wittich, *Economy and Society an Outline of Interpretive Sociology* (Berkeley: University of California Press, 1978), 957.

15. Manuel Castells, *The Internet Galaxy: Reflections on the Internet, Business, and Society* (Oxford: Oxford University Press, 2004), 37.

16. Castells, *The Internet Galaxy: Reflections on the Internet, Business, and Society*, 17.

17. Tom Cochran (former director of new media technologies for President Obama), in discussion with the author, September 2019.

18. Erik Berggren and Rob Bershteyn, "Organizational Transparency Drives Company Performance," *Journal of Management Development* 26, no. 5 (January 2007): 411–417, https://doi.org/10.1108/02621710710748248.

19. Rachel Gillett, "Mark Zuckerberg Works at Same Desk As Everyone Else," *Insider*, September 15, 2015, https://www.businessinsider.com/mark-zuckerberg-virtual-tour -frank-gehry-designed-building-2015-9.

20. Daphne Keller and Paddy Leerssen, "Facts and Where to Find Them: Empirical Research on Internet Platforms and Content Moderation," in *Social Media and Democracy: The State of the Field, Prospects for Reform*, ed. Nathaniel Persily and Joshua A. Tucker (Cambridge: Cambridge University Press, 2020), 220–251.

21. Many digital archivists and data managers see JSON as superior to other open formats discussed later in this chapter, such as XML or CSV. For why JSON is supposed to be better than CSV, see "4 Reasons You Should Use JSON Instead of CSV," *Datafiniti* (blog), March 16, 2014, https://blog.datafiniti.co/4-reasons-you-should -use-json-instead-of-csv-2cac362f1943, and for why it is better than XML, see Alyssa Walker, "JSON vs XML: What's the Difference?," *Guru99* (blog), updated November 1, 2021, https://www.guru99.com/json-vs-xml-difference.html.

22. In teaching workshops in rudimentary programming skills, I emphasize the fact that behind every dazzling data visualization there is a humble spreadsheet.

23. For more about theories about smart cities—and the limitations of the ideologies driving the designers of smart cities—see Anthony M Townsend, *Smart Cities: Big Data, Civic Hackers, and the Quest for a New Utopia* (New York; London: W.W. Norton & Company, 2014) and Ben Green, *The Smart Enough City: Putting Technology in Its Place to Reclaim Our Urban Future* (Cambridge, MA: MIT Press, 2019). For an important critique of the smart cities movement, see Shannon Mattern, *A City Is Not a Computer: Other Urban Intelligences* (Princeton, NJ: Princeton University Press, 2021).

24. Tom Cochran, September 2019.

25. "Barack Obama 'Public Will Have 5 Days to Look at Every Bill That Lands on My Desk'," *uploaded February 14, 2009, by Speakmymind02, YouTube video, 1:57*, https://youtu.be/o5t8GdxFYBU.

26. Mary Katharine Ham, "Darkness Falls on Obama's Sunshine Promises," *Washington Examiner*, April 27, 2009, https://www.washingtonexaminer.com/weekly-standard/darkness-falls-on-obamas-sunshine-promises.

27. Macon Phillips, "Update on Sunlight Before Signing," *WhiteHouse.gov Blog*, February 6, 2009, https://obamawhitehouse.archives.gov/blog/2009/02/06/update-sunlight-signing.

28. Macon Phillips, "Change has come to WhiteHouse.gov.," *WhiteHouse.gov Blog*, January 20, 2009, https://obamawhitehouse.archives.gov/blog/2009/01/20/change-has-come-whitehousegov.

29. Jesse Lee, "Transparency and Open Government," *WhiteHouse.gov Blog*, May 21, 2009, https://obamawhitehouse.archives.gov/blog/2009/05/21/transparency-and-open-government.

30. Unlike the positive and hopeful tone of the Obama White House website, the rhetoric of Trump's site warned of a nation under threat. As if to signal its negative orientation, the picture of the White House in the top right corner of Obama's site was replaced by a black version under Trump. With the launch of the Trump site the president's political platform was no longer buried under anodyne labels like "agenda" or "issues." The top navigation read "ECONOMY," "NATIONAL SECURITY," "BUDGET," "IMMIGRATION," "HEALTHCARE"—the issues Trump campaigned on. The Clinton and Bush White House pages had a prominent "FOR KIDS" area, which both the Obama and Trump versions of the site deemphasized.

31. Benjamin H. Bratton, *The Stack—On Software and Sovereignty* (Cambridge, MA: MIT Press, 2016), 49.

32. Safiya Umoja Noble, *Algorithms of Oppression: How Search Engines Reinforce Racism* (New York: New York University Press, 2018).

33. The Obama White House, "Information Technology & Transparency: Vivek Kundra Takes Your Questions," uploaded July 1, 2009, YouTube video, 29:33, https://youtu.be/9HZ-BESVVck.

34. Kin Lane, "Why I Exited My Presidential Innovation Fellowship," *Kin Lane* (blog), accessed August 25, 2019, http://kinlane.com/2013/11/15/why-i-exited-my-presidential-innovation-fellowship/.

35. Kin Lane (known as "the API Evangelist"), in discussion with author, March 2019. The choice to interview Kin Lane was somewhat anomalous in the methodology for choosing interview subjects for this book. In general, interview subjects had appeared in media coverage of technology issues related to the Bush, Obama, or Clinton administrations, and I reached out to them through publicly available contact information. In some cases, I used snowball sampling if a source mentioned a relevant participant who had not received coverage in news reports. Specialized

blogs, such as *Tech President*, also provided information about specific individuals involved with political tech teams. Archivists and faculty members interviewed for this book were selected based on their expertise in particular subject areas. In some cases, however, I was given names of potential interviewees from colleagues and friends who knew about this book project and my search for insider perspectives. Lane was suggested by writer Audrey Watters.

36. Lane, March 2019.

37. Macon Phillips (former director of digital strategy for President Obama), in discussion with the author, April 2019.

38. Mark Fenster, "Seeing the State: Transparency as Metaphor," *Administrative Law Review* 62, no. 3 (Summer 2010): 617–72, http://www.jstor.org/stable/25758547.

39. Evgeny Morozov, *To Save Everything, Click Here: Smart Machines, Dumb Humans, and the Myth of Technological Perfectionism* (New York: Perseus Books, 2013), xi.

40. Morozov, 95.

41. Cass R. Sunstein, "Output Transparency vs. Input Transparency," Social Science Research Network, May 25, 2017, https://papers.ssrn.com/abstract=2826009.

42. "Occupational Safety and Health Administration," United States Department of Labor, February 12, 2016, https://web.archive.org/web/20160212061226/https://www.osha.gov/. This feature was removed by the subsequent Trump administration.

43. For more on Black desires for opacity, see Shaka Mcglotten, "Black Data," in *No Tea, No Shade*, ed. E. Patrick Johnson (Durham, NC: Duke University Press, 2016), 262–286.

44. Wendy Hui Kyong Chun (media theorist), in discussion with the author, August 2010.

45. See James C. Scott, *Seeing like a State: How Certain Schemes to Improve the Human Condition Have Failed* (New Haven, CT: Yale University Press, 1999) for a comprehensive discussion of this issue.

46. Talks at Google, "Innovation Agenda *Barack Obama | Talks at Google*," uploaded November 14, 2007, YouTube video, https://youtu.be/m4yVlPqeZwo.

47. Michael Grunwald, *The New New Deal: The Hidden Story of Change in the Obama Era* (New York: Simon and Schuster, 2012), 320.

48. Barack Obama, *The Audacity of Hope: Thoughts on Reclaiming the American Dream* (New York: Broadway Books, 2007), 139.

49. The White House Office of the Press Secretary, "Remarks by the President Presenting New Management Agenda," WhiteHouse.gov, July 8, 2013, https://obam

awhitehouse.archives.gov/the-press-office/2013/07/08/remarks-president-presenting
-new-management-agenda.

50. Richard D. White, "Executive Reorganization, Theodore Roosevelt and the Keep Commission," *Administrative Theory & Praxis* 24, no. 3 (2002): 507–18, http://www .jstor.org/stable/25611596.

51. Cary Coglianese, "The Transparency President? The Obama Administration and Open Government," *Governance* 22, no. 4 (2009): 529–44, https://doi.org/10.1111 /j.1468-0491.2009.01451.x.

52. Jane E. Fountain, "Bureaucratic Reform and E-Government in the United States: An Institutional Perspective," in *Routledge Handbook of Internet Politics*, ed. Andrew Chadwick and Philip N. Howard (London: Routledge, 2010), https://doi .org/10.4324/9780203962541-15.

53. "1/12/01: Results of Electronic Government Initiatives," accessed November 2, 2019, http://govinfo.library.unt.edu/npr/initiati/it/egovresults.html.

54. David Dayen, "The Android Administration: Google's Remarkably Close Relationship With the Obama White House, in Two Charts," *The Intercept*, April 22, 2016, https://theintercept.com/2016/04/22/googles-remarkably-close-relationship-with -the-obama-white-house-in-two-charts/.

55. "Google's White House Meetings," Tech Transparency Project, April 26, 2016, https://www.techtransparencyproject.org/articles/googles-white-house-meetings.

56. Dayen, *The Intercept*.

57. Colleen Curtis, "Google Science Fair Winners Visit the White House," *White-House.gov Blog*, October 7, 2011, https://obamawhitehouse.archives.gov/blog/2011 /10/07/google-science-fair-winners-visit-white-house.

58. Connor Schmidt, "Students Speak: I Won the Google Science Fair," *White-House.gov Blog*, November 21, 2013, https://obamawhitehouse.archives.gov/blog /2013/11/21/students-speak-i-won-google-science-fair.

59. "2016 State of the Union," WhiteHouse.gov, accessed September 22, 2019, https://obamawhitehouse.archives.gov/node/351116.

60. "Resources on Syrian Refugees," WhiteHouse.gov, accessed September 22, 2019, https://obamawhitehouse.archives.gov/node/349501.

61. Eric Schmidt and Jared Cohen, *The New Digital Age: Reshaping the Future of People, Nations and Business* (London: John Murray, 2014). It is noteworthy that the copyright of the book is granted to Google rather than Schmidt himself.

62. "Obama for America Persuades Voters on YouTube," Think with Google, May 2013, https://www.thinkwithgoogle.com/marketing-resources/obama-case-study/.

63. Adam J. White, "Google.Gov," *New Atlantis*, Spring 2018, https://www.thene watlantis.com/publications/googlegov.

64. Vaidhyanathan has asserted that this process actually predates Obama. He traces it back to the Bush administration, when privatization was pushed by small government advocates to further a "public failure" narrative. In the Obama philosophy, crises were to be avoided by having the government imitate corporations rather than outsource tasks to them. See Siva Vaidhyanathan, *The Googlization of Everything (And Why We Should Worry)* (Berkeley; Los Angeles: University of California Press, 2012).

65. Such rhetoric was also used by Bill Clinton, who advocated "running government like a business." See Richard C. Box, "Running Government Like a Business: Implications for Public Administration Theory and Practice," *The American Review of Public Administration* 29, no. 1 (March 1999): 19–43 for analysis of this business-friendly discourse.

66. Shoshana Zuboff, *The Age of Surveillance Capitalism: The Fight for a Human Future at the New Frontier of Power* (New York: Public Affairs, 2019), 1–2.

67. Jacob J. Lew, "Privacy Policies and Data Collection on Federal Web Sites," memorandum, June 22, 2000, https://georgewbush-whitehouse.archives.gov/omb /memoranda/m00-13.html.

68. Roger W. Baker, "Cookies Letter, 07-28-00 (Text Only)," letter, July 28, 2000, https://georgewbush-whitehouse.archives.gov/omb/inforeg/text/cookies_letter72800 .html.

69. Marc Lacey, "Drug Office Ends Tracking Of Web Users," *New York Times*, June 22, 2000, US, https://www.nytimes.com/2000/06/22/us/drug-office-ends-tracking-of -web-users.html.

70. Arshad Mohammed and Sara Kehaulani Goo, "Government Increasingly Turning to Data Mining," *Washington Post*, June 15, 2006, http://www.washingtonpost .com/wp-dyn/content/article/2006/06/14/AR2006061402063.html.

71. Jane Cook, email to author, May 2020.

72. Many in the academy who might have normally been critical of corporate influence could also be seen as somewhat naïve about the reach of tech companies inside the White House. As an example of the Zeitgeist, see Yochai Benkler, *The Wealth of Networks: How Social Production Transforms Markets and Freedom* (New Haven, CT; London: Yale University Press, 2007).

73. Rahaf Harfoush, *Yes We Did! An Inside Look at How Social Media Built the Obama Brand* (Berkeley, CA: New Riders, 2009), 156.

74. Christopher Soghoain (tech blogger), in discussion with the author, August 2009.

75. Christopher Soghoian, "Chris Soghoian's Comments on Federal Cookie Policies," letter, Scribd, July 30, 2009, https://www.scribd.com/document/17861000/Chris-Soghoian-s-comments-on-federal-cookie-policies.

76. Phillips, April 2019.

77. Vivek Kundra and Michael Fitzpatrick, "Federal Websites: Cookie Policy," *White-House.gov Blog*, July 24, 2009, https://obamawhitehouse.archives.gov/blog/2009/07/24/federal-websites-cookie-policy.

78. Lane, March 2019.

79. Danny Weitzner, "Putting Twitter's 'Do Not Track' Feature in Context," *White-House.gov Blog*, May 19, 2012, https://obamawhitehouse.archives.gov/blog/2012/05/19/putting-twitter-s-do-not-track-feature-context.

80. Tom Cochran (former director of new media technologies for President Obama), in discussion with the author, September 2019.

81. Jillian C. York, *Silicon Values: The Future of Free Speech Under Surveillance Capitalism* (Brooklyn: Verso, 2021).

Chapter 3

1. Aaron Fisher (former Obama intern), in discussion with the author, November 2014. Fisher was suggested as a source by family friend Alice Phillips. See note 35 in Chapter 2 for more information about the methodology of selecting informants.

2. Macon Phillips, "Change has come to WhiteHouse.gov.," *WhiteHouse.gov Blog*, January 20, 2009, https://obamawhitehouse.archives.gov/blog/2009/01/20/change-has-come-whitehousegov.

3. When Twitter went down, the "fail whale" appeared to viewers, which showed a weighty cetacean dragging down the airborne avian mascots of the site.

4. Elizabeth Losh, "Virtualpolitik: The 3AM Phone Call and the 11PM Tweet," *Virtualpolitik* (blog), February 22, 2009, http://virtualpolitik.blogspot.com/2009/02/3am-phone-call-and-11pm-tweet.html.

5. Mike Melanson, "Memo to Gov Agencies: You May Now Tweet, Blog and Facebook," *ReadWrite* (blog), April 8, 2010, https://readwrite.com/2010/04/08/memo_to_gov_agencies_you_may_now_tweet_blog_and_fa/.

6. "Social Media, Web-Based Interactive Technologies, and the Paperwork Reduction Act," Digital.gov, 24:51—0400 400AD, /resources/social-media-web-based-interactive-technologies-and-the-paperwork-reduction-act/.

7. The Verge, "Why Healthcare.gov Came out Broken," uploaded December 3, 2013, YouTube video, 11:46, https://youtu.be/k3M8O83n254.

8. "Part.Public.Part.Lab: in the nature of participation," Part.Lab, accessed October 23, 2020, https://recursivepublic.net/.

9. Christopher M. Kelty, "Too Much Democracy in All the Wrong Places: Toward a Grammar of Participation," *Current Anthropology* 58, no. S15 (December 2016): S77–90, https://doi.org/10.1086/688705.

10. Amitai Etzioni, "Minerva: An Electronic Town Hall," *Policy Sciences* 3.4 (1972): 457–474.

11. Charles Krauthammer, "Ross Perot and the Call-In Presidency," *Time,* July 13, 1992.

12. Silicon Beach is often overlooked in histories of the internet, but entertainment industries were important areas of innovation. The global workflows of media production required robust technical infrastructures, much like how the distributed supply chains of the aviation and defense industries of the Cold War era in Southern California necessitated investment in sophisticated technologies.

13. For more on the Public Electronic Network, see Howard Rheingold, *The Virtual Community: Homesteading on the Electronic Frontier* (Cambridge, MA: MIT Press, 2000) and Elizabeth Losh, *Virtualpolitik: An Electronic History of Government Media-Making in a Time of War, Scandal, Disaster, Miscommunication, and Mistakes* (Cambridge, MA: MIT Press, 2009).

14. Kevin McKeown, "Social Norms and Implications of Santa Monica's PEN (Public Electronic Network)," Kevin McKeown, accessed September 29, 2019, http://www .mckeown.net/PENaddress.html.

15. Jackie Mansky, "The History of the Town Hall Debate," *Smithsonian Magazine*, October 6, 2016, https://www.smithsonianmag.com/history/history-town-hall-debate -180960705/. Despite having triumphed over Bush in this highly structured event on network television, Clinton stumbled in less formal town hall settings. For example, he would come to regret answering a bawdy "boxers or briefs" question during a town-hall-style appearance on the cable music video channel MTV in 1994.

16. A. J. McCarthy, "Dear Pizza Hut, You're Not Helping . . ." *Slate*, October 9, 2012, https://slate.com/news-and-politics/2012/10/pizza-hut-on-presidential-debate-pizza -toppings-an-important-discussion.html.

17. "Part I: CNN/YouTube Democratic Presidential Debate Transcript," CNN, accessed October 3, 2019, https://www.cnn.com/2007/POLITICS/07/23/debate .transcript/.

18. BarackObamadotcom, "Barack Obama After the CNN YouTube Debate," uploaded July 23, 2007, YouTube video, 0:23, https://youtu.be/8ZEOOJ7F9FM.

19. BarackObamadotcom, *"Barack Obama After the CNN YouTube Debate."*

20. Katharine Q. Seelye, "CNN/YouTube Debate Ratings," *The Caucus* (blog), July 24, 2007, https://thecaucus.blogs.nytimes.com/2007/07/24/cnnyoutube-debate-ratings/.

21. LaChrystal Ricke, "A New Opportunity for Democratic Engagement: The CNN-YouTube Presidential Candidate Debates," *Journal of Information Technology & Politics* 7, no. 2–3 (May 18, 2010): 202–15, https://doi.org/10.1080/19331681003772768.

22. Jennifer Stromer-Galley and Lauren Bryant, "Agenda Control in the 2008 CNN/YouTube Debates," *Communication Quarterly* 59, no. 5 (November 1, 2011): 529–46, https://doi.org/10.1080/01463373.2011.614212.

23. NBC News, "NBC News-YouTube Democratic Debate (Full)," uploaded January 17, 2016, YouTube video, 1:53:43, https://youtu.be/ti2Nokoq1J4.

24. The Obama White House, "Online Town Hall," uploaded March 26, 2009, YouTube video, 1:13:48, https://youtu.be/YPPT9pWhivM.

25. The Obama White House, *"Online Town Hall."*

26. Jonathan Beecher Field, *Town Hall Meetings and the Death of Deliberation* (Minneapolis: Univ of Minnesota Press, 2019), 14.

27. Field, *Town Hall Meetings and the Death of Deliberation*, 3.

28. Kristen D. Landreville, Caitlin White, and Sam Allen, "Tweets, Polls, and Quotes: Gatekeeping and Bias in On-Screen Visuals During the Final 2012 Presidential Debate," *Communication Studies* 66, no. 2 (March 15, 2015): 146–64, https://doi.org/10.1080/10510974.2014.930919.

29. CitizenTube, "What Will YOU Ask the Presidential Candidates?," uploaded June 13, 2007, YouTube video, 2:18, https://youtu.be/LSzsRnssUC8.

30. Steve Grove, "Introducing Citizentube," *YouTube Official Blog*, April 5, 2007, https://youtube.googleblog.com/2007/04/introducing-citizentube.html.

31. CitizenTube, "The YouTube Interview with President Obama," uploaded February 1, 2010, YouTube video, 35:46, https://youtu.be/0pqzNJYzh7I.

32. Richard Gao, "Google Removes Its Own CitizenTube YouTube Channel for Some Reason, Reinstates It, but Leaves It Full of Spam," *Android Police* (blog), November 19, 2017, https://www.androidpolice.com/2017/11/18/google-removes-citizentube-youtube-channel-reason-reinstates-leaves-full-spam/.

33. Walt Mossberg and Kara Swisher, "Liveblogging the Facebook Our-ToS-Is-Your-ToS Press Conference," *BoomTown* (blog), December 31, 2013, http://kara.allthingsd.com/20090226/liveblogging-the-facebook-our-tos-is-your-tos-press-conference/.

34. Facebook, "Governing the Facebook Service in an Open and Transparent Way," updated February 26, 2009, https://www.facebook.com/notes/facebook-app/governing-the-facebook-service-in-an-open-and-transparent-way/56566967130/.

35. David Sarno, "Facebook Governance Vote Is a Homework Assignment No One Did," *LA Times Blogs—Technology*, April 23, 2009, https://latimesblogs.latimes.com /technology/2009/04/facebook-governance-vote-is-a-homework-assignment-no-one -did.html.

36. Kalev Leetaru, "Facebook Was A Democracy 2009–2012 But We Didn't Vote So It Turned Into A Dictatorship," Forbes, April 13, 2019, https://www.forbes.com /sites/kalevleetaru/2019/04/13/facebook-was-a-democracy-2009-2012-but-we-didnt -vote-so-it-turned-into-a-dictatorship/.

37. Beth Simone Noveck, *Wiki Government: How Technology Can Make Government Better, Democracy Stronger, and Citizens More Powerful* (Washington, DC: Brookings Institution Press, 2010), 143.

38. James E. Katz, Michael Barris, and Anshul Jain, "Social Media Modalities: Examples and Patterns from the Obama White House," in *The Social Media President: Barack Obama and the Politics of Digital Engagement*, ed. James E. Katz, Michael Barris, and Anshul Jain (New York: Palgrave Macmillan, 2013), 85–108, https:// doi.org/10.1057/9781137378354_8.

39. Micah L. Sifry, "Pot Tops We the People," *TechPresident* (blog), September 26, 2011, http://techpresident.com/blog-entry/pot-tops-we-people-issue-list-how-long.

40. James E. Katz, Michael Barris, and Anshul Jain, "Social Media Modalities: Examples and Patterns from the Obama White House."

41. Norman B. Smith, "Shall Make No Law Abridging . . . : An Analysis of the Neglected, but Nearly Absolute, Right of Petition," *University of Cincinnati Law Review* 54 (1986): 1153, https://heinonline.org/HOL/Page?handle=hein.journals/ucinlr54& id=1165&div=&collection=.

42. Mac Marshall and Alice Oleson, "In the Pink: MADD and Public Health Policy in the 1990s," *Journal of Public Health Policy* 15, no. 1 (1994): 54–70, https://doi.org /10.2307/3342607.

43. Macon Phillips (former director of digital strategy for President Obama), in discussion with the author, April 2019.

44. Tom Cochran, "Farewell to Obama, Our First Digital President," *Vox*, December 1, 2016, https://www.vox.com/2016/12/1/13765002/president-obama-digital-trump -administration-open-source.

45. Fisher, November 2014.

46. Tom Cochran, "Farewell to Obama, Our First Digital President."

47. Eli Rosenberg, "The White House Has Finally Restored a Petitions Site That Is Critical of President Trump," *Washington Post*, January 31, 2018, https://www .washingtonpost.com/news/the-fix/wp/2018/01/31/the-white-house-promised-to -restore-a-petitions-site-that-was-critical-of-trump-it-hasnt/.

48. "★INDICT & ARREST Moon Jae-in for SMUGGLING the ChinaVirus into the US & ENDANGERING the National Security of US & ROK!," accessed October 24, 2020, https://petitions.trumpwhitehouse.archives.gov/petition/indict-arrest-moon-jae -smuggling-chinavirus-us-endangering-national-security-us-rok.

49. Daren C. Brabham, *Crowdsourcing* (Cambridge, MA; London: MIT Press, 2013).

50. Macon Phillips, "Facts Are Stubborn Things," *WhiteHouse.gov Blog*, August 4, 2009, https://obamawhitehouse.archives.gov/blog/2009/08/04/facts-are-stubborn -things.

51. "Sen. Cornyn Sends Letter to President Obama About 'Fishy' Activities Program," John Cornyn United States Senator for Texas, August 5, 2009, https://www .cornyn.senate.gov/content/sen-cornyn-sends-letter-president-obama-about-fishy -activities-program.

52. James E. Katz, Michael Barris, and Anshul Jain, "The Supreme Court Vacancies and the Healthcare Debate," in *The Social Media President: Barack Obama and the Politics of Digital Engagement*, ed. James E. Katz, Michael Barris, and Anshul Jain (New York: Palgrave Macmillan, 2013), 73–84, https://doi.org/10.1057/9781137378354_7.

53. "Sen. Cornyn: White House Must Come Clean on Cancelled 'Fishy' Data Collection Program," John Cornyn United States Senator for Texas.

54. Kyle Mantyla, "Star Parker Sues the White House," Right Wing Watch, August 31, 2009, https://www.rightwingwatch.org/post/star-parker-sues-the-white-house/.

55. Phillips, April 2019.

56. Christopher Kelty (professor), in discussion with the author, August 2009.

57. Kelty, August 2009.

58. Baratunde Thurston, How to Citizen with Baratunde, accessed December 23, 2020, https://www.baratunde.com/howtocitizen.

59. Henry Jenkins, *Confronting the Challenges of Participatory Culture: Media Education for the 21st Century* (Cambridge, MA: MIT Press, 2009).

Chapter 4

1. D. M. Ryfe, "Franklin Roosevelt and the Fireside Chats," *Journal of Communication* 49, no. 4 (1999): 80–103, https://doi.org/10.1111/j.1460-2466.1999.tb02818.x.

2. Macon Phillips (former director of digital strategy for President Obama), in discussion with the author, April 2019.

3. Phillips, April 2019.

4. Lev Manovich, Jeremy Douglass, and Tara Zepel were important collaborators on this project and provided output data from the Software Studies Lab at UC San Diego. This data is also discussed in Manovich's work, *Cultural Analytics* (Cambridge, MA: MIT Press, 2020).

5. Henry Jenkins, "DIY Media 2010: Video Blogging (Part One)," *Henry Jenkins* (blog), January 30, 2011, http://henryjenkins.org/blog/2011/01/diy_media_2010 _video_blogging_1.html.

6. Evan Ratliff and Jez Burrows, "The Wired Presidency: Can Obama Really Reboot the White House?," *Wired*, January 19, 2009, https://www.wired.com/2009/01/ff -obama/.

7. The Obama White House, "President Obama Speaks to the Muslim World from Cairo, Egypt," uploaded June 4, 2009, YouTube video, 54:56, https://youtu.be/Nax ZPiiKyMw.

8. Associated Press, "White House Uses Web during Speech to Muslims," June 5, 2009, https://www.google.com/hostednews/ap/article/ALeqM5gtoEQ22V-CRmdi _vMVIWesHmSqxwD98K25M83.

9. Nadja-Christina Schneider, *Social Dynamics 2.0: Researching Change in Times of Media Convergence: Case Studies from the Middle East and Asia* (Frank & Timme, 2011), 43.

10. Tarek El-Ariss, *Leaks, Hacks, and Scandals: Arab Culture in the Digital Age* (Princeton, NJ: Princeton University Press, 2018), 192.

11. Sam Gregory and Elizabeth Losh, "Remixing Human Rights: Rethinking Civic Expression, Representation and Personal Security in Online Video," *First Monday* 17, no. 8 (July 2012), https://doi.org/10.5210/fm.v17i8.4104.

12. Amelia Arsenault, "Public Diplomacy 2.0," in *Toward a New Public Diplomacy: Redirecting U.S. Foreign Policy*, ed. Philip Seib, Palgrave Macmillan Series in Global Public Diplomacy (New York: Palgrave Macmillan, 2009), 135–153, https://doi.org /10.1057/9780230100855_7.

13. Jeremy Berkowitz, "Raising the Iron Curtain on Twitter: Why the United States Must Revise the Smith-Mundt Act to Improve Public Diplomacy Comment," *Comm-Law Conspectus: Journal of Communications Law and Policy*, no. 18 (2009): 269–310, https://heinonline.org/HOL/P?h=hein.journals/cconsp18&i=278.

14. Anne-Marie Slaughter, *The Chessboard and the Web: Strategies of Connection in a Networked World* (New Haven, CT: Yale University Press, 2018), 16.

15. For more on this topic, see P. W Singer and Emerson T Brooking, *Likewar: The Weaponization of Social Media* (New York: Houghton Mifflin, 2019).

16. Ethan Zuckerman, "Cute Cats to the Rescue? Participatory Media and Political Expression," in *Youth, New Media and Political Participation*, ed. Danielle Allen and Jennifer Light, April 2013, under review, https://dspace.mit.edu/handle/1721.1/78899.

17. Evan Ratliff and Jez Burrows, *Wired*.

18. "Behind the Scenes: The Google Art Project at the White House," The White House, accessed September 15, 2019, https://obamawhitehouse.archives.gov/node/137515.

19. Lauren Berlant, "The Theory of Infantile Citizenship," *Public Culture* 5, no. 3 (September 1993): 395.

20. At the conclusion of Berlant's reflection on infantile citizenship she discusses people who come to Washington, DC to protest rather than to pay homage. Although she observes that demonstrators—like other pilgrims to DC—are constrained by rituals of celebrity and heroism, she hypothesizes that a "legitimate mass political voice uniquely performed outside of the voting booth" could be understood in relation to the small-town and metropolitan spectacle of the "parade." See Lauren Berlant, "The Theory of Infantile Citizenship," *Public Culture* 5, no. 3 (September 1993): 409.

21. In contrast, even a player of the military recruiting game *America's Army*, which is known for promoting nationalistic indoctrination, can commit acts of civil disobedience in the interactive simulation. See Joseph DeLappe, "Dead-in-Iraq," accessed September 22, 2019, http://www.delappe.net/project/dead-in-iraq/.

22. John Cheney-Lippold, *We Are Data: Algorithms and the Making of Our Digital Selves* (New York: NYU Press, 2017).

23. Antoinette Rouvroy, Thomas Berns, and Elizabeth Libbrecht, "Algorithmic Governmentality and Prospects of Emancipation," *Réseaux* 177, no. 1 (October 2013): 163–96, https://www.cairn-int.info/article-E_RES_177_0163--algorithmic-govern mentality-and-prospect.htm.

24. Antoinette Rouvroy, Thomas Berns, and Elizabeth Libbrecht, *Réseaux*. It is important to note that Rouvroy is careful to distinguish her objections from those of civil libertarians who are focused on risks to personal expression and privacy alone; she rejects what she calls "possessive individualism."

25. Felix & Paul Studios, "The People's House—Inside the White House with Barack and Michelle Obama," uploaded May 17, 2017, YouTube video, 22:23, https://youtu.be/bqW2qm02jwI.

26. Such angle-less rooms were also well designed for VR experiences like YouTube 360.

27. See also Charles Musser, *Politicking and Emergent Media: US Presidential Elections of the 1890s* (Berkeley: University of California Press, 2016).

28. Amy Sullivan, "Obama's Summer Reading," *Time*, August 24, 2009, http://swampland.time.com/2009/08/24/obamas-summer-reading/.

29. Thomas Joseph Rickert, *Ambient Rhetoric: The Attunements of Rhetorical Being* (Pittsburgh: University of Pittsburgh Press, 2013), 9.

30. Kori Schulman, "The White House Just Joined Spotify: Listen to the President's Summer Playlist," *WhiteHouse.gov Blog*, August 14, 2015, https://obamawhitehouse.archives.gov/blog/2015/08/14/white-house-just-joined-spotify-listen-presidents-summer-playlist.

31. Gardiner Harris, "President Obama's Emotional Spotify Playlist Is a Hit," *New York Times*, August 14, 2016, US, https://www.nytimes.com/2016/08/15/us/politics/president-obama-spotify-playlist.html.

32. Mark Alfano, J. Adam Carter, and Marc Cheong, "Technological Seduction and Self-Radicalization," *Journal of the American Philosophical Association* 4, no. 3 (ed 2018): 298–322, https://doi.org/10.1017/apa.2018.27.

Chapter 5

1. Helene Cooper, "Obamas Give Queen Elizabeth an iPod," *New York Times*, April 1, 2009, Europe, https://www.nytimes.com/2009/04/02/world/europe/02ipod.html.

2. Jim Holt, "Royal Narcissist! . . . Obama Uploaded HIS SPEECHES To Queen's IPod," *Gateway Pundit* (blog), April 2, 2009, https://www.thegatewaypundit.com/2009/04/holy-narcissist-obama-uploaded-his/.

3. Jim Holt, "AFP Photographer 'Sad' to Make Obama Look Bad in 'Selfie' Shot at Mandela Funeral," *Gateway Pundit* (blog), December 11, 2013, https://www.thegatewaypundit.com/2013/12/afp-photographer-sad-to-make-obama-look-bad-in-selfie-shot-at-mandela-funeral/.

4. "Obama Creates International Incident with 'Selfie' at Mandela Service," Fox News, March 25, 2015, https://www.foxnews.com/politics/obama-creates-international-incident-with-selfie-at-mandela-service.

5. Kate M. Miltner and Nancy K. Baym, "Selfies| The Selfie of the Year of the Selfie: Reflections on a Media Scandal," *International Journal of Communication* 9 (May 2015): 15, https://ijoc.org/index.php/ijoc/article/view/3244.

6. Nicholas Mirzoeff, *How to See the World: An Introduction to Images, from Self-Portraits to Selfies, Maps to Movies, and More* (New York: Basic Books, 2016), 29.

7. Mirzoeff, *How to See the World*, 31.

8. See also Marita Sturken and Lisa Cartwright, *Practices of Looking* (Oxford: Oxford University Press, 2003).

9. Pete Souza, *P020109PS-0339*, 2009, photo, Obama White House Archived, available from: Flickr, https://www.flickr.com/photos/obamawhitehouse/3484819402/.

10. Weegee, *At the Palace Theater*, 1983, photo, Weegee/International Center of Photography, accessed October 21, 2020, https://www.metmuseum.org/art/collection/search/263651.

11. Ben Cosgrove, "LIFE at the Moves: When 3-D Was New," *Life*, September 26, 2013, https://www.life.com/arts-entertainment/3-d-movies-revisiting-a-classic-life-photo-of-a-rapt-film-audience/.

12. Bruno Latour, *Making Things Public: Atmospheres of Democracy* (Karlsruhe: ZKM, 2005).

13. Andrew Gauthier, Ella Mielniczenko, Andrew Ilnyckyj, Adam Bianchi, Maycie Timpone, and Cody D'Ambrosio, "Things Everybody Does But Doesn't Talk About, Featuring President Obama," BuzzFeed, February 12, 2015, https://www.buzzfeed.com/andrewgauthier/the-president-uses-a-selfie-stick.

14. Bill Nye, Instagram post, February 28, 2014, https://www.instagram.com/p/k-jmdbkePN/.

15. Pete Souza, *P102715LJ-0329*, 2015, photo, Obama White House Archived, available from: Flickr, https://www.flickr.com/photos/obamawhitehouse/23941892740/.

16. The Obama White House, "In Photos: A Look Back at President Obama's Last Overseas Trip," *Medium* (blog), November 21, 2016, https://medium.com/@ObamaWhiteHouse/in-photos-a-look-back-at-president-obamas-last-overseas-trip-2955f91b3501.

17. Valerie Jarrett and Sylvia Burwell, "Invest In Your 'Healthy Self' (and Post a #HealthySelfie While You're At It)," *WhiteHouse.gov Blog*, June 11, 2015, https://obamawhitehouse.archives.gov/blog/2015/06/11/invest-your-healthy-self-and-post-healthyselfie-while-you-re-it.

18. Santiago Lyon, "Obama's Orwellian Image Control," *New York Times*, December 11, 2013, Opinion, http://www.nytimes.com/2013/12/12/opinion/obamas-orwellian-image-control.html

19. Margaret Sullivan, "When White House Photos Are 'Visual Press Releases,'" *Public Editor's Journal* (blog), December 6, 2013, http://publiceditor.blogs.nytimes.com/2013/12/06/when-white-house-photos-are-visual-press-releases/.

20. Stijn Vogels, *Barack Has a Mac*. November 13, 2008. http://www.flickr.com/photos/stijnvogels/3027740917/.

21. Pete Souza, *P032310PS-0604*, 2010, photo, Obama White House Archived, Flickr, https://www.flickr.com/photos/obamawhitehouse/4458525548/.

22. Pete Souza, *P031810PS-0013*, 2010, photo, Obama White House Archived, Flickr, https://www.flickr.com/photos/obamawhitehouse/4456732652/.

23. Pete Souza, *P032110PS-1110*, 2010, photo, Obama White House Archived, Flickr, https://www.flickr.com/photos/obamawhitehouse/4455979689/.

24. Pete Souza, *P021209PS-0407*, 2009, photo, Obama White House Archived, Flickr, https://www.flickr.com/photos/obamawhitehouse/3484824308/.

25. Pete Souza, *P121310PS-1173*, 2010, photo, Obama White House Archived, Flickr, https://www.flickr.com/photos/obamawhitehouse/5267470022/.

26. Pete Souza, *P033009PS-0087*, 2009, photo, Obama White House Archived, Flickr, https://www.flickr.com/photos/obamawhitehouse/3484850774/.

27. Pete Souza, *P062510PS-0443*, 2010, photo, Obama White House Archived, Flickr, https://www.flickr.com/photos/obamawhitehouse/4753023841/.

28. Pete Souza, *P032609PS-0451*, 2009, photo, Obama White House Archived, Flickr, https://www.flickr.com/photos/obamawhitehouse/3484849578/. Security was obviously a factor in excluding these devices. Nonetheless, this image—which highlights individual ownership and personal responsibility—also reflects ideas about digital moderation and limiting screen time.

29. "Vivek Kundra Keynote at the Cloud Computing Forum & Workshop," 2010, YouTube video, https://youtu.be/USfYrYKfYgI.

30. Pete Souza, *The Rise of Barack Obama / Photographs and Text by Pete Souza* (Chicago: Triumph Books, 2008), 70.

31. Souza, *The Rise of Barack Obama*, 78.

32. Souza, *The Rise of Barack Obama*, 130.

33. Obviously, security was a factor in the White House's communication choices as well. But the echoing of Kennedy imagery is significant.

34. Pete Souza, *P020209PS-0181*, 2009, photo, Obama White House Archived, available from: Flickr, https://www.flickr.com/photos/obamawhitehouse/3484005995/.

35. Souza, *The Rise of Barack Obama*, 4.

36. Michael Shaw, "'Bo-Bama,'" *BagNews* (blog), April 13, 2009, http://www.bagnews notes.com/2009/04/bo-bama/.

37. Robert Hariman, "Two Senses Of A Usable Past," *Reading the Pictures* (blog), January 20, 2009, *https://www.readingthepictures.org/2009/01/two-senses-of-a-usable-past/*.

38. David Lubin, *Shooting Kennedy: JFK and the Culture of Images* (Berkeley: University of California Press, 2003), xi.

39. Pete Souza, *P032110PS-0673*, 2010, photo, Obama White House Archived, Flickr, https://www.flickr.com/photos/obamawhitehouse/4455975307/.

40. Pete Souza, *P070209PS-0559*, 2009, photo, Obama White House Archived, Flickr, https://www.flickr.com/photos/obamawhitehouse/3818144278/.

41. Pete Souza, *P062310PS-0245*, 2010, photo, Obama White House Archived, Flickr, https://www.flickr.com/photos/obamawhitehouse/4753683646/.

42. For more about gender and office labor, see Alice Gambrell, "Stolen Time Archive," *Vectors: Journal of Culture and Technology in a Dynamic Vernacular* no. 1 (2005), http://vectors.usc.edu/projects/index.php?project=10.

43. Pete Souza, *P100810PS-0062*, 2010, photo, Obama White House Archived, Flickr, https://www.flickr.com/photos/obamawhitehouse/5098342319/.

44. Pete Souza, *P030409PS-0208*, 2009, photo, Obama White House Archived, Flickr, https://www.flickr.com/photos/obamawhitehouse/3484831226/.

45. Carolyn Edgar, "The Sexism of 'Selfie-Gate': America's Dangerous Suspicion of Women Working with Men," *Salon*, December 12, 2013, https://www.salon.com /2013/12/12/the_sexism_of_selfie_gate_americas_dangerous_suspicion_of_women _working_with_men/.

46. Harriet Alexander, "Pope Francis and the First 'Papal Selfie,'" *Telegraph*, August 31, 2013, http://www.telegraph.co.uk/news/worldnews/the-pope/10277934/Pope -Francis-and-the-first-Papal-selfie.html.

47. Melissa Eddy, "How a Refugee's Selfie with Merkel Led to a Facebook Lawsuit," *New York Times*, February 6, 2017, Business Day, https://www.nytimes.com /2017/02/06/business/syria-refugee-anas-modamani-germany-facebook.html.

48. Ruptly, "Russia: Ever Seen Putin Take a SELFIE?," uploaded October 11, 2014, YouTube video, 0:55, https://youtu.be/MJRIjmNDlnk.

49. Pete Souza, *P011515PS-0406*. 2015, photo, Obama White House Archived, available from: Flickr, https://www.flickr.com/photos/obamawhitehouse/20283628 443/.

50. Pete Souza, *Obama: An Intimate Portrait* (New York: Little, Brown and Company, 2017), 320.

51. Pete Souza, *P050111PS-0210*, 2011, photo, Obama White House Archived, Flickr, https://www.flickr.com/photos/obamawhitehouse/5680724572/.

52. "Bin Laden Raid: 'Situation Room' Photo Airbrushed by White House," France 24 Observers, accessed January 10, 2018, http://observers.france24.com/en/20110516 -bin-laden-raid-situation-room-photo-airbrushed-white-house-usa-propaganda.

53. John B, Bredar and Pete Souza. *The President's Photographer: Fifty Years inside the Oval Office* (Washington, DC: National Geographic, 2010), 21.

54. Sam Wolfson, "Photographic Memory: Pete Souza Trolls Trump with Just the Right Obama Photos," *Guardian*, August 15, 2018, US news, http://www.theguardian.com/us-news/2018/aug/15/pete-souza-obama-photographer-trump-trolling.

55. Pete Souza (@petesouza), "When we were on the road, national security discussions and head of state phone calls were conducted in a private . . . ," Instagram post, February 13, 2017, https://www.instagram.com/p/BQd5lB7hNK1/.

56. Pete Souza, *Shade: A Tale of Two Presidents* (New York: Little, Brown, and Company, 2019), 63.

57. Maya Rhodan, "President Obama Spoof Video Shows How He'll Spend His Retirement," *Time*, May 2, 2016, https://time.com/4314589/president-obama-video-retirement.

58. The Obama White House (@obamawhitehouse), "To round out the #WHInsta-Meet, these Instagrammers took a group photo . . . ," Instagram post, March 21, 2015, https://instagram.com/p/0gzztTwitR/.

59. "Special Issue: The Presidency," *Life*, July 5, 1968, http://www.theguardian.com/world/2008/jul/15/barackobama.usa.

60. See Erina Duganne, "The Photographic Legacy of Lyndon Baines Johnson," *Photography and Culture* 6, no. 3 (November 2013): 303–23, https://doi.org/10.2752/175145213X13735390913241.

61. José van Dijck, *The Culture of Connectivity* (New York: Oxford University Press, 2013), 91.

62. Dan Gillmor, "How Yahoo Could Make up for Its Decision to Sell Flickr Users' Photos," *Slate*, December 4, 2014, https://slate.com/technology/2014/12/how-yahoo-could-make-up-for-its-decision-to-sell-flickr-users-photos.html.

63. Jay David Bolter and Richard Grusin, *Remediation: Understanding New Media* (Cambridge, MA: MIT Press, 2000).

64. Pete Souza, *P033009PS-0221*, 2009, photo, Obama White House Archived, available from: Flickr, http://www.flickr.com/photos/obamawhitehouse/3484850660/

65. Pete Souza, *P102009PS-0789*, 2009, photo, Obama White House Archived, available from: Flickr, http://www.flickr.com/photos/obamawhitehouse/4050328699/

66. William Jelani Cobb, "The Genius of Cool: The 25 Coolest Brothers of All Time," *Ebony*, August 2008.

Chapter 6

1. Steve Lohr, "Facial Recognition Is Accurate, If You're a White Guy," *New York Times*, February 9, 2018, Technology, https://www.nytimes.com/2018/02/09/technology/facial-recognition-race-artificial-intelligence.html.

2. Jacob Snow, "Amazon's Face Recognition Falsely Matched 28 Members of Congress With Mugshots," *American Civil Liberties Union Blog*, July 26, 2018, https://www.aclu.org/blog/privacy-technology/surveillance-technologies/amazons-face-recognition-falsely-matched-28.

3. Joy Buolamwini, "AI, Ain't I A Woman?," uploaded June 28, 2018, YouTube video, 3:32, https://youtu.be/QxuyfWoVV98.

4. Isobel Asher Hamilton, "An AI Tool Which Reconstructed a Pixelated Picture of Barack Obama to Look like a White Man Perfectly Illustrates Racial Bias in Algorithms," *Business Insider*, June 22, 2020, https://www.businessinsider.com/depixelator-turned-obama-white-illustrates-racial-bias-in-ai-2020-6.

5. Simone Browne, *Dark Matters: On the Surveillance of Blackness* (Durham, NC: Duke University Press, 2015).

6. Jessica Marie Johnson, "Markup Bodies Black [Life] Studies and Slavery [Death] Studies at the Digital Crossroads," *Social Text* 36, no. 4 (137) (December 2018): 57–79, https://doi.org/10.1215/01642472-7145658.

7. Ruha Benjamin, *Captivating Technology: Race, Carceral Technoscience, and Liberatory Imagination in Everyday Life* (Durham, NC: Duke University Press, 2019).

8. "Implementation of the Government Paperwork Elimination Act," WhiteHouse: gov, accessed January 15, 2020, https://obamawhitehouse.archives.gov/node/15075.

9. Clare Garvie, Alvaro Bedoya, Jonathan Frankle, "The Perpetual Line-Up: Unregulated Police Face Recognition in America," Georgetown Law Center on Privacy & Technology, October 18, 2016, https://www.perpetuallineup.org/.

10. "US Military Deploys Facial Recognition Technology in Bin Laden Operation," *Biometric Technology Today* 2011, no. 5 (May 2011): 1, https://doi.org/10.1016/S0969-4765(11)70081-9.

11. The White House Office of the Press Secretary, "Fact Sheet: President Obama Announces New Commitments from Investors, Companies, Universities, and Cities to Advance Inclusive Entrepreneurship at First-Ever White House Demo Day," WhiteHouse.gov, August 4, 2015, https://obamawhitehouse.archives.gov/the-press-office/2015/08/04/fact-sheet-president-obama-announces-new-commitments-investors-companies.

12. "Face Recognition Features," Kairos, accessed January 15, 2020, https://www.kairos.com/features. Kairos became well known for refusing to sell its products and services to law enforcement and for criticizing its competitors for relying on biased training data and harvesting images without user consent.

13. "White House Demo Day Exhibits, Part 1," C-SPAN, August 4, 2015, https://www.c-span.org/video/?327463-101/white-house-demo-day-exhibits-part-1.

14. Brad Smith, "Facial Recognition Technology: The Need for Public Regulation and Corporate Responsibility," *Microsoft on the Issues* (blog), July 13, 2018, https://blogs .microsoft.com/on-the-issues/2018/07/13/facial-recognition-technology-the-need -for-public-regulation-and-corporate-responsibility/.

15. Jeh C. Johnson, "DHS Record of Progress and Vision for the Future," memorandum, U.S. Department of Homeland Security, January 5, 2017, https://www.dhs.gov /sites/default/files/publications/17_0105_exit-memo.pdf.

16. Liat Clark, "Google's Artificial Brain Learns to Find Cat Videos," *Wired*, June 26, 2012, https://www.wired.com/2012/06/google-x-neural-network/.

17. Examples are drawn from presentations at the DMASM conference held at UC San Diego.

18. Alec Ross (Clinton's former senior advisor for innovation), in discussion with the author, October 2019.

19. Amid Amidi, "Watch Dean DeBlois Explain Motion Capture to President Obama," *Cartoon Brew* (blog), November 27, 2013, https://www.cartoonbrew.com /cartoon-culture/watch-dean-deblois-explain-motion-capture-to-president-obama -91551.html.

20. Pete Souza , *P112613PS-0222*, 2013, photo, Obama White House Archived, available from: Flickr, https://www.flickr.com/photos/obamawhitehouse/11665238693/.

21. Jeffrey Zients and John P. Holdren, "American Innovation in Autonomous and Connected Vehicles," *WhiteHouse.gov Blog*, December 7, 2015, https://obamawhite house.archives.gov/blog/2015/12/07/american-innovation-autonomous-and -connected-vehicles.

22. White House Office of the Press Secretary, "FACT SHEET: The White House Releases New Strategy for American Innovation, Announces Areas of Opportunity from Self-Driving Cars to Smart Cities," WhiteHouse.gov, October 21, 2015, https:// obamawhitehouse.archives.gov/the-press-office/2015/10/21/fact-sheet-white-house -releases-new-strategy-american-innovation.

23. WIRED, "President Barack Obama on How We'll Embrace Self-Driving Cars," uploaded October 12, 2016, YouTube video, 8:37, https://youtu.be/P31Fl8bRqUY.

24. Robert M. Gates, *Duty: Memoirs of a Secretary at War* (New York: Knopf, 2014), 131.

25. Robert M. Gates, *Duty: Memoirs of a Secretary at War* (New York: Knopf, 2014), 131.

26. Valerie Insinna, "In the Fight against ISIS, Predators and Reapers Prove Close-Air Support Bona-Fides," *Defense News* (blog), August 8, 2017, https://www.defense

news.com/smr/unmanned-unleashed/2017/03/28/in-the-fight-against-isis-predators
-and-reapers-prove-close-air-support-bona-fides/.

27. White House Office of the Press Secretary, "Remarks by National Security Advisor Susan E. Rice at the U.S. Air Force Academy, Colorado Springs," WhiteHouse.gov, April 14, 2016, https://obamawhitehouse.archives.gov/the-press-office/2016/04/14/remarks-national-security-advisor-susan-e-rice-us-air-force-academy.

28. Peter Asaro, "How Just Could a Robot War Be?," in *Current Issues in Computing and Philosophy*, ed. A. Briggle, P. A. E. Brey, and K. Waelbers (IOS Press, 2008).

29. Lisa Parks, "Media, Hot & Cold| Drones, Infrared Imagery, and Body Heat," *International Journal of Communication* 8 (October 30, 2014): 2519.

30. John Cheney-Lippold, *We Are Data Algorithms and the Making of Our Digital Selves* (New York: New York University Press, 2019).

31. Lisa Hajjar, "Lawfare and Armed Conflicts," in *Life in the Age of Drone Warfare*, ed. Lisa Parks and Caren Kaplan (Durham, NC: Duke University Press, 2017), 58–88, https://doi.org/10.1215/9780822372813.

32. Peter Asaro, "How Just Could a Robot War Be?," *Frontiers in Artificial Intelligence and Applications* 175 (2008): 50–64.

33. White House Office of the Press Secretary, "Remarks by the President at the Acceptance of the Nobel Peace Prize," WhiteHouse.gov, December 10, 2009, https://obamawhitehouse.archives.gov/the-press-office/remarks-president-acceptance-nobel-peace-prize.

34. Max Fisher, "Obama Finds Predator Drones Hilarious," *Atlantic*, May 3, 2010, https://www.theatlantic.com/international/archive/2010/05/obama-finds-predator-drones-hilarious/340949/.

35. Neda Atanasoski and Kalindi Vora, *Surrogate Humanity: Race, Robots, and the Politics of Technological Futures* (Durham, NC: Duke University Press, 2019), 149.

36. White House Office of the Press Secretary, "Remarks by the President at Memorial Service for Fallen Dallas Police Officers," WhiteHouse.gov, July 12, 2016, https://obamawhitehouse.archives.gov/the-press-office/2016/07/12/remarks-president-memorial-service-fallen-dallas-police-officers.

37. For more on the pre-history of the fembot, see Anne Balsamo, *Technologies of the Gendered Body: Reading Cyborg Women* (Durham, NC: Duke University Press, 1996)

38. Tim Hornyak, "Japan's HRP Robot Flexes Muscles at Obama," CNET, November 15, 2010, https://www.cnet.com/news/japans-hrp-robot-flexes-muscles-at-obama/.

39. CBS, "Obama Test Drives Japanese Technology," uploaded November 15, 2010, YouTube video, 2:06, https://youtu.be/CfCTBOTHsVU.

40. In some of her appearances without Obama present, Miim was much more clearly positioned as a sexual object. For example, she was dressed as a bride for one event and adopted a cosplay role—sporting green hair and go-go boots—for another. Feminist scholars have argued that such robots designed for masculine pleasure belittle the value of affective labor and the importance of domestic work. According to one research team, "sex with robots may not be biologically reproductive sex, but it is socially reproductive," because human-robot coupling perpetuates "social norms." See Neda Atanasoski and Kalindi Vora, "Why the Sex Robot Becomes the Killer Robot—Reproduction, Care, and the Limits of Refusal," *Spheres*, March 12, 2020, https://spheres-journal.org/contribution/why-the-sex-robot-becomes-the-killer -robot-reproduction-care-and-the-limits-of-refusal/. According to Jennifer Rhee this "robotic imaginary" also sanctions dehumanizing the most marginalized citizens. See *The Robotic Imaginary: The Human and the Price of Dehumanized Labor* (Minneapolis: University of Minnesota Press, 2018).

41. For more on racism and sexism in Westinghouse robots, see the dissertation of Khanh Vo, "'All the Work, Without the Workers': Robotic Labor in the American Imaginary" (PhD diss., William & Mary, 2021).

42. AI Now Institute, "Thinking A.I. through Rastus Robot, the Westinghouse Mechanical Slave | Simone Browne | AI Now," *uploaded July 25,* 2017, YouTube video, 5:14, https://youtu.be/HvC6kvrwsN4.

43. For more about the role of slavery and oppressive labor conditions in the history of robotics, see Dustin A. Abnet, *The American Robot: A Cultural History* (Chicago: University of Chicago Press, 2020).

44. Pete Souza (@petesouza44), "President Obama Greets Alice Wong, Disability Visibility Project Founder, via Robot before a White House Reception to Mark the 25th . . . ," Instagram post, July 20, 2015, https://www.instagram.com/p/5YQBu TNNO7/.

45. White House Office of the Press Secretary, "Remarks by the President in Opening Remarks and Panel Discussion at White House Frontiers Conference," WhiteHouse.gov, October 13, 2016, https://obamawhitehouse.archives.gov/the-pres s-office/2016/10/13/remarks-president-opening-remarks-and-panel-discussion-white -house.

46. Matt Novak, "Politicians Shaking Hands with Robots, Ranked," *Gizmodo*, March 10, 2015, https://gizmodo.com/politicians-shaking-hands-with-robots-ranked-1690 408820.

47. Richard Voyles and Rafael Lopez, "A Team of DREAMers and a Robot Named 'Stinky,'" *WhiteHouse.gov Blog*, April 14, 2015, https://obamawhitehouse.archives .gov/blog/2015/04/14/team-dreamers-and-robot-named-stinky.

48. Courtney Corbisiero, "President Obama and Robots—Our 5 Favorite Moments," *WhiteHouse.gov Blog*, August 8, 2013, https://obamawhitehouse.archives.gov/blog /2013/08/08/president-obama-and-robots-our-5-favorite-moments.

49. Catherine Taibi, "Drudge Report: 'U.S. President Bows To Japanese Robot'," *Huff-Post*, updated December 6, 2017, https://www.huffpost.com/entry/drudge-obama -robot-japanese-japan-report-headline_n_5205835.

50. Associated Press, "Obama Bows to Robot in Japan, Finds It 'Scary,'" *New York Post*, April 24, 2014, https://nypost.com/2014/04/24/obama-bows-to-japanese-robot -thinks-its-a-little-scary/.

51. Supasorn Suwajanakorn, Steven M. Seitz, and Ira Kemelmacher-Shlizerman, "What Makes Tom Hanks Look Like Tom Hanks," in *2015 IEEE International Conference on Computer Vision (ICCV)* (Dec 2015), 3952–60, https://doi.org/10.1109 /ICCV.2015.450.

52. Matthias Niessner, "Face2Face: Real-Time Face Capture and Reenactment of RGB Videos (CVPR 2016 Oral)," uploaded March 17, 2016, YouTube video, 6:35, https://youtu.be/ohmajJTcpNk?t=289.

53. Adobe Creative Cloud, "#VoCo. Adobe Audio Manipulator Sneak Peak with Jordan Peele | Adobe Creative Cloud," uploaded November 4, 2016, YouTube video, 7:20, https://youtu.be/I3l4XLZ59iw.

54. David Mack, "This PSA about Fake News from Barack Obama Is Not What It Appears," *BuzzFeed News*, April 17, 2018, https://www.buzzfeednews.com/article /davidmack/obama-fake-news-jordan-peele-psa-video-buzzfeed.

55. Vannevar Bush, "Memex Revisited," in *From Memex to Hypertext: Vannevar Bush and the Mind's Machine* (USA: Academic Press Professional, Inc., 1991), 197–216.

56. Donna J. Haraway and Cary Wolfe, *Manifestly Haraway* (Minneapolis: University of Minnesota Press, 2016), 28.

57. Jean Baudrillard, *Selected Writings*, trans. Mark Poster (Stanford, CA: Stanford University Press, 2001), 140.

58. Jean Baudrillard, *Simulacra and Simulation*, trans. Sheila Faria Glaser (Ann Arbor: University of Michigan Press, 2014).

59. Masahiro Mori, "The Uncanny Valley," *Energy* 7, no. 4 (1970): 33–35.

60. Hillel Schwartz, *The Culture of the Copy: Striking Likenesses, Unreasonable Facsimiles* (New York: Zone Books, 1996), 19.

61. Sridhar Kota, "A Progress Report on Modeling & Simulation for the Economy," *WhiteHouse.gov Blog*, February 15, 2012, https://obamawhitehouse.archives.gov /blog/2012/02/15/progress-report-modeling-simulation-economy.

62. David Hudson, "The President Speaks on the Importance of Our Nation's Infrastructure," *WhiteHouse.gov Blog*, July 15, 2014, https://obamawhitehouse.archives.gov/blog/2014/07/15/president-speaks-importance-our-nations-infrastructure.

63. The White House Office of the Press Secretary, "WEEKLY ADDRESS: Ensuring America Leads the World Into the Next Frontier," WhiteHouse.gov, October 15, 2016, https://obamawhitehouse.archives.gov/the-press-office/2016/10/15/weekly-address-ensuring-america-leads-world-next-frontier.

64. The explicit connection between mathematical simulation and the exercise of military dominance dates back to at least nineteenth-century Prussia, according to Pat Harrigan, Matthew G Kirschenbaum, and James F Dunnigan, *Zones of Control: Perspectives on Wargaming* (Cambridge, MA: MIT Press, 2016).

65. "A Renaissance in American Manufacturing," WhiteHouse.gov, accessed August 30, 2021, https://obamawhitehouse.archives.gov/the-press-office/2011/06/24/remarks-president-carnegie-mellon-universitys-national-robotics-engineer.

66. Katherine Hayles, *How We Became Posthuman: Virtual Bodies in Cybernetics, Literature, and Informatics* (Chicago: University of Chicago Press, 1999).

67. For more on this topic, see Anna Everett, "Have We Become Postracial Yet?: Race and Media Technologies in the Age of President Obama," in *Race after the Internet*, ed. Lisa Nakamura and Peter Chow-White (New York: Routledge, 2012), 146–167.

68. For more about how the fist bump was read as code for Black radicalism, the controversy over the *New Yorker* cover depicting Barack and Michelle Obama is illustrative. See Suzanne Goldenberg, "US Election: 'Terrorist Fist Bump' Cartoon Misfires," *Guardian*, July 14, 2008, http://www.theguardian.com/world/2008/jul/15/barackobama.usa.

69. During his tenure as president, Obama often praised the show. See WIRED, "President Barack Obama on the True Meaning of Star Trek | WIRED," uploaded October 12, 2016, YouTube video, 4:16, https://youtu.be/WR2lWEtVe2Q. He also welcomed cast member Nichelle Nichols at the White House and sent official messages of condolences at the death of star Leonard Nimoy.

70. Beth Coleman, "Race as Technology," *Camera Obscura* 24, no.1 70 (January 1, 2009): 177–207, https://doi.org/10.1215/02705346-2008-018.

71. In contrast, Black film critic David Ehrenstein described Obama's deployment of racial classification as a trope of magic rather than technology. According to Ehrenstein, candidate Obama was also running for "an equally important unelected office, in the province of the popular imagination—the 'Magic Negro,'" a "figure of postmodern folk culture" most commonly conjured up in cinematic depictions where a Black helper character with "no past . . . simply appears one day to help the white protagonist." David Ehrenstein, "Obama the 'Magic Negro,'" *Los Angeles Times*, March

19, 2007, https://www.latimes.com/la-oe-ehrenstein19mar19-story.html. This formulation also became a racist meme in the song "Barack the Magic Negro," set to the tune of "Puff, the Magic Dragon." The song was frequently played on right-wing radio and defended by conservatives as parody.

72. Ezra Mechaber, "President Obama Is the First President to Write a Line of Code," *WhiteHouse.gov Blog*, December 10, 2014, https://obamawhitehouse.archives.gov /blog/2014/12/10/president-obama-first-president-write-line-code.

73. Peter Welsch, "Civic Hacking at the White House: We the People, by the People," WhiteHouse.gov Blog, June 5, 2013, https://obamawhitehouse.archives .gov/blog/2013/06/05/civic-hacking-white-house-we-people-people.

74. Aneesh Chopra, "Hacking for Humanity," WhiteHouse.gov Blog, June 3, 2010, https://obamawhitehouse.archives.gov/blog/2010/06/03/hacking-humanity.

75. Code.org, "President Obama Does the Hour of Code," uploaded December 11, 2014, YouTube video, 1:28, https://youtu.be/AI_dayIQWV4.

76. Annette Vee, *Coding Literacy: How Computer Programming Is Changing Writing* (Cambridge, MA: MIT Press, 2017).

77. S. Craig Watkins, Alexander Cho, Andres Lombana-Bermudez, Vivian Shaw, Jacqueline Ryan Vickery, Lauren Weinzimmer, *The Digital Edge: How Black and Latino Youth Navigate Digital Inequality* (New York: NYU Press, 2018).

78. Miriam Posner, "Some Things to Think about before You Exhort Everyone to Code," *Miriam Posner's Blog*, February 29, 2012, https://miriamposner.com/blog /some-things-to-think-about-before-you-exhort-everyone-to-code/.

79. Janet Abbate, "Coding Is Not Empowerment," in *Your Computer Is on Fire*, ed. Thomas S. Mullaney et al. (Cambridge, MA: MIT Press, 2020), 256.

80. Stephanie Santoso and Ryan Xue, "Announcing the Winners of the First-Ever White House 3D Printed Ornament Challenge," *WhiteHouse.gov Blog*, December 3, 2014, https://obamawhitehouse.archives.gov/blog/2014/12/03/announcing-winners -first-ever-white-house-3d-printed-ornament-challenge.

81. "Nation of Makers," WhiteHouse.gov, accessed December 27, 2020, https:// obamawhitehouse.archives.gov/nation-of-makers.

82. The Obama White House, "The White House Hosts Its First-Ever Maker Faire," uploaded June 18, 2014, YouTube video, 15:13, https://youtu.be/7wHorfRvvcE.

83. Today the entity Obama described, America Makes, characterizes itself as "the flagship Institute for Manufacturing USA, the National Network for Manufacturing Innovation," and it is "managed and operated by the National Center for Defense Manufacturing and Machining," which is a 501(c)(3) not-for-profit, organization.

84. Marcin Jakubowski, "The Open Source Industrial Revolution," *WhiteHouse.gov Blog*, June 6, 2013, https://obamawhitehouse.archives.gov/blog/2013/06/06/open -source-industrial-revolution.

85. Marcin Jakubowski, "Open-Sourced Blueprints for Civilization," February 2011, TED video, 3:54, https://www.ted.com/talks/marcin_jakubowski_open_sourced _blueprints_for_civilization.

86. Toby Miller, "The Art of Waste: Contemporary Culture and Unsustainable Energy Use," in *Signal Traffic: Critical Studies of Media Infrastructures*, ed. Lisa Parks and Nicole Starosielski (University of Illinois Press, 2015), 137–156, https://www .jstor.org/stable/10.5406/j.ctt155jmd9.

87. In another essay, Richard Maxwell joined Miller in ridiculing the ideology of the DIY movement. "We've heard this nonsense before: readers become writers, listeners transform into speakers, viewers are stars, fans are academics, cultural-studies students are designers, zinewriters are screenwriters, bloggers are copywriters, bus riders are journalists, and vice versa," they write. "Relatively cheap digital technologies supposedly allow us all to mutate into prosumers (producer-consumers) without the say-so of media gatekeepers." Miller and Maxwell insisted that corporations "continue to rule content distribution," making the "high-tech prosumer an easily exploited agent." Richard Maxwell and Toby Miller, "The Waste of Art and the Art of Waste," *Psychology Today*, October 6, 2013, http://www.psychologytoday.com /blog/greening-the-media/201310/the-waste-art-and-the-art-waste.

88. Sharon Begley, "Analysis: IT experts question architecture of Obamacare website," http://www.reuters.com/article/2013/10/05/us-usa-healthcare-technology -analysis-idUSBRE99407T20131005

89. "McKinsey Report on Problems with HealthCare.Gov," *Washington Post*, accessed September 14, 2019, https://www.washingtonpost.com/apps/g/page /politics/mckinsey-report-on-problems-with-healthcaregov/601/.

90. Joe Johns and Stacey Samuel, "Official: Hackers Tried Repeatedly to Attack Obamacare Website," CNN, updated November 18, 2013, https://www.cnn.com /2013/11/13/politics/hackers-attack-obamacare-site/index.html.

91. ABC123, "The Failed Launch of www.HealthCare.gov," *Harvard Business School Technology and Operations Management: MBA Student Perspectives* (blog), modified November 18, 2016, https://digital.hbs.edu/platform-rctom/submission /the-failed-launch-of-www-healthcare-gov/.

92. Christopher Weaver, Shira Ovide, and Louise Radnofsky, "Software, Design Defects Cripple Health-Care Website," *Wall Street Journal*, October 6, 2013, https:// www.wsj.com/articles/SB10001424052702304441404579119740283413018.

93. The field of media archeology has grappled with the challenges of preserving computer hardware and software for many years. Important scholarship that reflects on the contingency of these artifacts has been produced by Jussi Parikka, Erkki Huhtamo, Lori Emerson, Matthew Kirschenbaum, Eric Kluitenberg, Siegfried Zielinski, Oliver Grau, and many others.

94. Joe Coscarelli, "Everything We Now Know About Adriana, the Obamacare Woman," *Intelligencer*, November 13, 2013, http://nymag.com/intelligencer/2013/11/adriana-obamacare-woman-speaks.html.

95. Juli Weiner, "Meet Adriana, the Smiling HealthCare.Gov Lady," *Vanity Fair*, November 13, 2013, https://www.vanityfair.com/news/2013/11/adriana-healthcare-web-site-interview.

96. "Healthcare.gov: Images," Know Your Meme, accessed September 14, 2019, https://knowyourmeme.com/memes/sites/healthcaregov/photos.

97. "People in Healthcare.Gov Stock Photos Now Visibly Panicking," *The Onion*, October 22, 2013, https://www.theonion.com/people-in-healthcare-gov-stock-photos-now-visibly-panic-1819591430.

98. ABC News, "Exclusive Obamacare Girl Interview: Mystery Face of Obamacare Speaks out on 'Bullying,'" uploaded November 13, 2013, YouTube video, 2:38, https://youtu.be/yid9IhoFqfM.

99. E. Gabriella Coleman, *Hacker, Hoaxer, Whistleblower, Spy: The Many Faces of Anonymous* (London: Verso, 2015), 32–33.

100. u/tweedpatch, "I guess a couple of are trying to sign up for healthcare . . . (a minor bug on the new healthcare website)," reddit post, r/webdev, October 1, 2013, https://www.reddit.com/r/webdev/comments/1nifc5/i_guess_a_couple_of_are_trying_to_sign_up_for/.

101. Abigail Grotke (digital archivist at Library of Congress), in discussion with the author, September 2014.

102. Tom Cochran (former director of new media technologies for President Obama), in discussion with the author, September 2019.

103. The White House Office of the Press Secretary, "Remarks by the President on the Affordable Care Act," WhiteHouse.gov, October 21, 2013, https://obamawhitehouse.archives.gov/the-press-office/2013/10/21/remarks-president-affordable-care-act.

104. Jane E. Fountain, *Building the Virtual State: Information Technology and Institutional Change* (Brookings Institution Press, 2004).

105. Clay Johnson and Harper Reed, "Why the Government Never Gets Tech Right," *New York Times*, October 25, 2013, Opinion, https://www.nytimes.com/2013/10/25/opinion/getting-to-the-bottom-of-healthcaregovs-flop.html.

106. ABC123, "The Failed Launch Of www.HealthCare.gov."

107. The Verge, "Why Healthcare.gov Came out Broken," uploaded December 3, 2013, YouTube video, 11:46, https://youtu.be/k3M8O83n254.

108. The Denver Channel, accessed August 2, 2009, http://www.thedenverchannel.com/news/20162629/detail.html.

109. Prashant Gupta, A. Seetharaman, and John Rudolph Raj, "The Usage and Adoption of Cloud Computing by Small and Medium Businesses," *International Journal of Information Management* 33, no. 5 (October 2013): 861–74, https://doi.org/10.1016/j.ijinfomgt.2013.07.001.

110. "Glenn Beck: Cars.Gov Allows Government to Takeover Your Computer," uploaded July 31, 2009 by markedmannerf, YouTube video, 5:08, https://youtu.be/bWs12ccbOiE.

111. Macon Phillips (former director of digital strategy for President Obama), in discussion with the author, April 2019.

112. Glenn Kessler, "Eric Trump's Four-Pinocchio Claim That the Obamacare Website Cost More than Trump's Border Barrier,"*Washington Post*, September 16, 2019, https://www.washingtonpost.com/politics/2019/09/16/eric-trumps-four-pinocchio-claim-that-obamacare-website-cost-more-than-trumps-border-barrier/.

113. Julianna Rennie, "Will Trump's Border Wall Cost Less than Obamacare Website?," Politifact, March 29, 2019, https://www.politifact.com/factchecks/2019/mar/29/facebook-posts/will-trumps-border-wall-cost-less-obamacare-websit/.

114. The Obama White House, "President Obama Explains Healthcare.gov," uploaded July 28, 2010, YouTube video, 3:20, https://youtu.be/DCQSGnZ0lTg.

115. An anonymous peer reviewer of this book pointed out that this optimism persists in the so-called agile government movement. See https://napawash.org/the-agile-government-center/overview for more.

116. Donald J. Trump (@realDonaldTrump), "Airplanes are becoming far too complex to fly . . . ," Twitter, March 12, 2019, https://twitter.com/realDonaldTrump/status/1105468569800839169.

117. Ryan Beene, "Trump Administration Revises Obama Self-Driving Vehicle Policy," *Insurance Journal*, September 12, 2017, https://www.insurancejournal.com/news/national/2017/09/12/463929.htm.

118. David Shepardson, "Trump Signs Order on Principles for U.S. Government AI Use," *Reuters*, December 3, 2020, Technology News, https://www.reuters.com/article/us-trump-ai-idUSKBN28D357. Trump also increased AI funding in a number of areas, however, in his "Artificial Intelligence for the American People" directive. See https://trumpwhitehouse.archives.gov/ai/.

Chapter 7

1. Tom Cochran (former director of new media technologies for President Obama), in discussion with the author, September 2019.

2. Darren Samuelsohn, "Trump Needs Time to Make Whitehouse.Gov Great Again," *POLITICO*, January 19, 2017, https://www.politico.com/story/2017/01/trump-white -house-website-delay-233860.

3. "Member of Congress Official Web Site—Hillary Rodham Clinton," Clinton. Senate.gov, available online from 2001 to 2009, accessed via Library of Congress Web Archive, https://www.loc.gov/item/lcwa0c001041/.

4. "Official Campaign Web Site—Hillary Rodham Clinton," accessed via Library of Congress Web Archive on November 7, 2019, https://www.loc.gov/item/lcwa N0001413/.

5. Elaine Showalter, "Pilloried Clinton," *The Times Literary Supplement*, October 26, 2016, http://www.the-tls.co.uk/articles/public/hillary-clinton-vs-misogyny/.

6. Kelly Wilz, "Bernie Bros and Woman Cards: Rhetorics of Sexism, Misogyny, and Constructed Masculinity in the 2016 Election," *Women's Studies in Communication* 39, no. 4 (October 2016): 357–360.

7. Diana B. Carlin and Kelly L. Winfrey, "Have You Come a Long Way, Baby? Hillary Clinton, Sarah Palin, and Sexism in 2008 Campaign Coverage," *Communication Studies* 60, no. 4 (August 2009): 326–343.

8. Karrin Vasby Anderson and Kristina Horn Sheeler, "Texts (and Tweets) from Hillary: Meta-Meming and Postfeminist Political Culture," *PSQ Presidential Studies Quarterly* 44, no. 2 (2014): 224–243.

9. Charlotte Templin, "Hillary Clinton as Threat to Gender Norms: Cartoon Images of the First Lady," *Journal of Communication Inquiry* 23, no. 1 (January 1999): 20–36.

10. "Background to 'Assessing Russian Activities and Intentions in Recent US Elections': The Analytic Process and Cyber Incident Attribution," Office of the Director of National Intelligence, January 6, 2017, https://www.dni.gov/files/documents /ICA_2017_01.pdf.

11. Obviously, I am not the first one to suggest that gender and technology are closely allied, given the work done by previous feminist scholars of science and technology studies. For example, Anne Balsamo's *Technologies of the Gendered Body* contradicted the truisms of the nature/culture divide and argued that gendered bodies were always "product" and "process." In *Technofeminism* Judy Wajcman declared that "technology is both a source and a consequence of gender relations." And feminist film theorists have long argued that cinema is one of many "technologies of gender." See Anne Marie Balsamo, *Technologies of the Gendered Body: Reading Cyborg*

Women (Durham, NC: Duke University Press, 1996); Judy Wajcman, *TechnoFeminism* (Cambridge, UK; Malden, MA: Polity Press, 2006); and Teresa De Lauretis, *Technologies of Gender: Essays on Theory, Film, and Fiction* (Bloomington: Indiana University Press, 2001).

12. Michael Barbaro and Steve Eder, "Under Oath, Donald Trump Shows His Raw Side," *New York Times*, July 28, 2015, https://www.nytimes.com/2015/07/29/us/politics/depositions-show-donald-trump-as-quick-to-exaggerate-and-insult.html.

13. Maggie Haberman, "Trump Promises a Revelation on Hacking," *New York Times*, December 31, 2016, https://www.nytimes.com/2016/12/31/us/politics/donald-trump-russia-hacking.html.

14. Donald J. Trump (@realDonaldTrump), "We will never have great national security in the age of computers—too many brilliant nerds can break codes (the old days were better)," Twitter, accessed December 28, 2020.

15. Alec Ross (Clinton's former senior advisor for innovation), in discussion with the author, October 2019.

16. Alec Ross, *The Industries of the Future* (New York: Simon & Schuster, 2017), 84.

17. Alec Ross, October 2019.

18. Kavitha Davidson, "Hillary Clinton: Countries Visited by the Most-Traveled Secretary of State in History," *HuffPost*, February 2, 2013, https://www.huffpost.com/entry/hillary-clinton-countries-travels_n_2602541.

19. Alec Ross, October 2019.

20. Molly Moran, "Social Media and Global Rhetoric," presentation, August 6, 2020.

21. For more on telegraph diplomacy, see David Paull Nickles, *Under the Wire: How the Telegraph Changed Diplomacy* (Cambridge, MA: Harvard University Press, 2003).

22. "Remarks on Internet Freedom," U.S. Department of State, accessed October 25, 2020, https://2009-2017.state.gov/secretary/20092013clinton/rm/2010/01/135519.htm.

23. Hillary Clinton, "Internet Rights and Wrongs: Choices & Challenges in a Networked World," remarks, February 15, 2011, https://2009-2017.state.gov/secretary/20092013clinton/rm/2011/02/156619.htm.

24. Casey Hicks, "Timeline of Hillary Clinton's Email Scandal," CNN, November 7, 2016, https://www.cnn.com/2016/10/28/politics/hillary-clinton-email-timeline/index.html. Subsequent pieces of information without citations about the chronology of events also come from this summary.

25. "The Mystery Man behind Hillary's Email Controversy—POLITICO," accessed October 26, 2020, https://www.politico.com/story/2015/03/hillary-clinton-email-eric-hothem-115764.

26. John Cook, "Hacked Emails Show Hillary Clinton Was Receiving Advice at a Private Email Account from Banned, Obama-Hating Former Staffer, *Gawker* (blog), March 20, 2013, https://www.gawker.com/5991563/hacked-emails-show-hillary -clinton-was-receiving-advice-at-a-private-email-account-from-banned-obama -hating-former-staffer. Eventually Guccifer's real name was revealed to be Marcel Lazăr Lehel. In addition to attempting to hack Clinton, he accessed information from her predecessor Colin Powell and from former president George W. Bush, in addition to celebrities and government officials in his home country of Romania. See Catalin Cimpanu, "Hacker Guccifer, Who Exposed Clinton Private Email Server, Ready for US Prison Sentence," *ZDNet* (blog), October 24, 2018, https://www.zdnet .com/article/hacker-guccifer-who-exposed-clinton-private-email-server-ready-for-us -prison-sentence/.

27. Eugene Kiely, "Clinton's 'Secret' Email Accounts," *FactCheck.Org* (blog), May 22, 2015, https://www.factcheck.org/2015/05/clintons-secret-email-accounts/.

28. Paul Sperry, "Clinton Directed Her Maid to Print out Classified Materials," *New York Post*, November 6, 2016, http://nypost.com/2016/11/06/clinton-directed -her-maid-to-print-out-classified-materials/.

29. Alana Abramson, "Comey: Classified Hillary Clinton Emails Were Forwarded to Anthony Weiner," *Time*, May 3, 2017, https://time.com/4765460/james-comey -anthony-weiner-hillary-clinton-emails-huma-abedin/.

30. Statistics in this section are from James B. Stewart, "How One Agent Forced the FBI to Reopen Hillary Clinton Investigation," *Insider*, October 8, 2019, https://www .insider.com/lone-fbi-agent-reopened-hillary-clinton-investigation-2019-10.

31. Angelo Fichera, "Clinton's Emails, Weiner's Laptop and a Falsehood," *FactCheck. Org* (blog), August 24, 2018, https://www.factcheck.org/2018/08/clintons-emails -weiners-laptop-and-a-falsehood/.

32. Office of the Inspector General U.S. Department of Justice, "A Review of Various Actions by the Federal Bureau of Investigation and Department of Justice in Advance of the 2016 Election," June 2018, https://www.justice.gov/file/1071991/download.

33. John Kruzel, "No Evidence FBI Officials' Texts Deliberately Erased, as Donald Trump Said," Politifact, December 19, 2018, https://www.politifact.com/factchecks /2018/dec/19/donald-trump/no-evidence-fbi-officials-texts-deliberately-erase/.

34. Michelle Ye Hee Lee, "Revisiting Clinton's Claim She Used Personal Email out of 'Convenience,'" *Washington Post*, July 5, 2016, https://www.washingtonpost .com/news/fact-checker/wp/2016/07/05/revisiting-clintons-claim-she-used-personal -email-out-of-convenience-and-it-was-allowed-by-state-department/.

35. Garrett M. Graff, "What the FBI Files Reveal About Hillary Clinton's Email Server," *POLITICO Magazine*, September 30, 2016, http://politi.co/2cFumCq.

36. As intertwined community property, the email server arrangements also necessitated data-sharing services that messily distributed access to computational resources between Hillary Clinton's spouse, ex-president Bill Clinton, and the candidate herself. The family drama of inappropriate access extended to Clinton's aide Huma Abedin, who was married to disgraced Congressmen Anthony Weiner. Thus, by this transitive property, Clinton found herself linked by FBI director Comey to illicit sexual text messages shared with a 15-year-old girl in North Carolina.

37. In the dramatization of the *Politico* story for the radio, one can actually hear the astonishment of reporters over Clinton's lack of familiarity with basic office equipment: "I can get not knowing how to play an Xbox or virtual reality machine or something like that, but, I mean, a desktop computer—I mean this is literally the oldest piece of personal technology available to us today." See Sean Cole, "Act One: Server Be Served," This American Life, November 4, 2016, https://www.thisamericanlife .org/radio-archives/episode/601/master-of-her-domain-name.

38. David Martosko, "Email-Gate Update: Dick Morris Says Hillary 'Doesn't Know How to Type,'" *Daily Mail*, March 24, 2015, http://www.dailymail.co.uk/news/article -3009471/Former-longtime-Clinton-insider-says-Hillary-doesn-t-know-type-email -scandal-swirls-returns-White-House-Obama-visit.html.

39. See Friedrich A Kittler, Geoffrey Winthrop-Young, and Michael Wutz, *Gramophone, Film, Typewriter* (Stanford, CA: Stanford University Press, 1999).

40. I have memories of my own experiences in all-girl typing classes and of my mother advising me to master secretarial skills to ensure steady employment.

41. J. C. R. Licklider and Robert W. Taylor, "The Computer as a Communication Device," *Science and Technology* 76 (1968): 21–31.

42. Hillary Rodham Clinton, *What Happened* (Simon and Schuster, 2017), 293–294.

43. Lawrence Lessig, "On the Wikileak-ed Emails between Tanden and Podesta Re: Me," *Lessig Blog*, October 18, 2016, http://lessig.tumblr.com/post/151983995587/on -the-wikileak-ed-emails-between-tanden-and.

44. Lawrence Lessig, "Against Transparency," *New Republic*, October 9, 2009, https:// newrepublic.com/article/70097/against-transparency.

45. Julie Cohen, *Configuring the Networked Self* (New Haven, CT: Yale University Press, 2012), 142–143.

46. Jessica Sewell, "Dream House: Gendered Fantasies of Home," lecture at William & Mary, October 23, 2020.

47. Jeannie Suk, "Is Privacy a Woman?," *The Georgetown Law Journal* 97, no. 2 (2008): 488.

48. Claude Elwood Shannon and Warren Weaver, *The Mathematical Theory of Communication* (Urbana: University of Illinois Press, 1999), 27.

49. More examples are discussed in Elizabeth Losh, *Virtualpolitik: An Electronic History of Government Media-Making in a Time of War, Scandal, Disaster, Miscommunication, and Mistakes* (Cambridge, MA: MIT Press, 2009).

50. Anne Gearan and Philip Rucker, "Clinton: It 'Might Have Been Smarter' to Use a State Dept. E-Mail Account," *Washington Post*, March 10, 2015, https://www .washingtonpost.com/politics/hillary-clinton-to-answer-questions-about-use-of-private -e-mail-server/2015/03/10/4c000d00-c735-11e4-a199-6cb5e63819d2_story.html.

51. The same images of Clinton in sunglasses using her mobile phone was shared as a meme in many pro-Clinton circles, including the popular Tumblr blog "Texts from Hillary," accessed April 29, 2018, http://textsfromhillaryclinton.tumblr.com/.

52. It is interesting that Clinton was denied access to the kind of secure BlackBerry that Obama used or one like her predecessor Condoleezza Rice had possessed. The workaround of a "private line" was also previously utilized by former secretary Colin Powell. See Sean Gallagher, "NSA Refused Clinton a Secure BlackBerry like Obama, so She Used Her Own," *Ars Technica* (blog), March 17, 2016, http://arstechnica.com /information-technology/2016/03/nsa-refused-clinton-a-secure-blackberry-like -obama-so-she-used-her-own/ and "Ignorance and Indifference: Delving Deep into the Clinton E-Mail Saga," *Ars Technica* (blog), July 15, 2016, http://arstechnica.com /information-technology/2016/07/indifference-and-ignorance-delving-deep-into -the-clinton-e-mail-saga/.

53. Sean Gallagher, "All the Clintons' Servers: Hillary First Used a Power Mac Tower for e-Mail," *Ars Technica* (blog), September 2, 2016, http://arstechnica.com/informa tion-technology/2016/09/fbi-clintons-first-e-mail-server-was-a-power-mac-tower/.

54. Wendy Hui Kyong Chun, *Control and Freedom: Power and Paranoia in the Age of Fiber Optics* (Cambridge, MA: MIT Press, 2006).

55. James J. Brown, *Ethical Programs: Hospitality and the Rhetorics of Software* (Ann Arbor: University of Michigan Press, 2015), 28.

56. Alexander R. Galloway, *Protocol: How Control Exists after Decentralization* (Cambridge, MA: MIT Press, 2004), 42–43.

57. Galloway, *Protocol*, 187–189.

58. Galloway also argues optimistically that new forms of cyberfeminism correspond to digital platforms that encourage multiple couplings: "The universality of protocol can give feminism something that it never had at its disposal, the obliteration of the masculine from beginning to end. . . . In other words, as protocol rises, patriarchy declines."

59. *Full Frontal with Samantha Bee*, "The Fascinating Emails of a Sixty-Something | Full Frontal with Samantha Bee | TBS," uploaded November 7, 2016, YouTube video, 4:58, https://youtu.be/xhM0Htv39aE.

60. Damon Beres, "Trump Campaign Wastes a Lot of Paper Printing Articles about Trump," *Huffington Post*, June 20, 2016, Tech, http://www.huffingtonpost.com /entry/trump-googles-himself_us_57681ab0e4b015db1bca04da.

61. However, I tend to be skeptical of generational myths in which there are always young "digital natives" and old "digital immigrants." See also Siva Vaidhyanathan, "Generational Myth," *The Chronicle of Higher Education*, September 19, 2008, http:// chronicle.com/article/Generational-Myth/32491.

62. David Robinson, "Text Analysis of Trump's Tweets Confirms He Writes Only the (Angrier) Android Half," *Variance Explained* (blog), August 9, 2016, http:// varianceexplained.org/r/trump-tweets/.

63. "TRUMP: WHO DOES APPLE THINK THEY ARE?! | In the Greenroom—Fox & Friends," Fox News, February 18, 2016, http://www.foxnews.com/on-air/fox-and -friends/blog/2016/02/18/trump-who-does-apple-think-they-are.

64. Evelyn Fox Keller, *Reflections on Gender and Science* (New Haven, CT: Yale University Press, 1985).

65. Timothy Cook, "A Message to Our Customers," Apple, February 16, 2016, http:// www.apple.com/customer-letter/.

66. Wendy Hui Kyong Chun, *Programmed Visions: Software and Memory* (Cambridge, MA: MIT Press, 2011), 133.

67. Rebecca Ballhaus, "House Democrats Probe White House Officials' Email Use," *Wall Street Journal*, March 21, 2019, Politics, https://www.wsj.com/articles/house -democrats-probe-white-house-officials-email-use-11553188033.

68. David D. Kirkpatrick, Ben Hubbard, Mark Landler, and Mark Mazzetti, "The Wooing of Jared Kushner: How the Saudis Got a Friend in the White House," *New York Times*, December 8, 2018, World, https://www.nytimes.com/2018/12/08/world /middleeast/saudi-mbs-jared-kushner.html.

69. Kenneth Goldsmith, "HILLARY: The Hillary Clinton Emails," artist's statement, accessed September 13, 2019, via Dropbox, https://www.dropbox.com/sh/sigqyq 4wu9ki87f/AAB8dP0_GK-qAFLZ_3cpbDxSa?dl=0.

70. Hillary Rodham Clinton, *What Happened* (Simon and Schuster, 2017), 289.

71. "WATCH: Video Appears to Show Clinton Lecturing State Dept on Cyber Security," FOX News Insider, October 22, 2016, http://insider.foxnews.com/2016/10/22 /hillary-clinton-appears-lecture-state-department-colleagues-cyber-security-email -server.

72. "Clinton Lectured State Dept. Staff on Cybersecurity in 2010 Video," Fox News, October 22, 2016, http://www.foxnews.com/politics/2016/10/22/clinton-lectured -state-dept-staff-on-cybersecurity-in-2010-video.html.

73. See Eszter Hargittai and Steven Shafer, "Differences in Actual and Perceived Online Skills: The Role of Gender," *Social Science Quarterly* 87, no. 2 (2006): 432–448, https://doi.org/10.1111/j.1540-6237.2006.00389.x.

74. Marjan Nadim and Audun Fladmoe, "Silencing Women? Gender and Online Harassment," *Social Science Computer Review* 39, no. 2 (April 2021): 245–58, https:// doi.org/10.1177/0894439319865518.

Chapter 8

1. According to Costanzo, Roger Cooper, the maverick publisher of Vanguard, was experimenting with a new business model that did not pay authors an advance. Instead, Cooper promised to invest in the book projects he signed with a large budget for 'marketing, which made releasing a book with Vanguard an attractive proposition for the always publicity-hungry Trump, who was attracted to high risk-high reward ventures.

2. David Pogue, "Twitter Is What You Make It," *New York Times*, February 11, 2009, Personal Tech, https://www.nytimes.com/2009/02/12/technology/personaltech /12pogue.html.

3. Jacob Weisbert, "Creating the Monster That is @RealDonaldTrump: Meet the Man Who Got Donald Trump Started on Twitter.," *Slate*, August 17, 2016, https:// slate.com/news-and-politics/2016/08/meet-the-man-who-got-donald-trump-started -on-twitter.html.

4. Peter Costanzo, in discussion with the author, October 2019.

5. Geoffrey Baym, "'Think of Him as The President': Tabloid Trump and the Political Imaginary, 1980–1999," *Journal of Communication* 69, no. 4 (August 2019): 396–417, https://doi.org/10.1093/joc/jqz022. Trump also sought publicity by buying newspaper advertising during this period, most famously for his 1989 full-page ad calling for capital punishment that ran in four New York area newspapers, including the *New York Times*, the *Daily News*, the *New York Post*, and *New York Newsday*. In the ad, Trump called for death to be meted out to avenge the attack on the so-called Central Park jogger, even though the suspects were minors and ultimately exonerated when the real assailant was found years later.

6. David Leonhardt, "18 Revelations From a Trove of Trump Tax Records," *New York Times*, September 27, 2020, US, https://www.nytimes.com/2020/09/27/us/trump -taxes-takeaways.html.

7. Matt Porter, "Trump's First Real Tweet Was on July 6, 2011," *Outline*, July 6, 2011, https://theoutline.com/post/2445/trump-s-first-real-tweet-was-on-july-6-2011.

8. According to their website, Factbase used information from the Internet Archive, YouTube, the Trump Organization, and Democracy in Action to rebuild its "From the Desk" archive.

9. "Search Trump's Deleted Vlogs," Factbase, accessed November 3, 2019, https://factba.se/trump-vlog-search.

10. Factbase Videos, "Donald Trump Vlog—Deleted: From the Desk of Donald Trump—Gaddafi, Land Lease—March 22, 2011," uploaded March 11, 2018, YouTube video, 1:20, https://youtu.be/vZyl1bvVvlE.

11. I reached out to McConney on Instagram for an interview, but I received no response.

12. Richard A. Grusin, "Donald Trump's Evil Mediation," *Theory & Event* 20, no. 1 (March 2017): 92–93, https://muse.jhu.edu/article/650865.

13. Newt Gingrich and Eric Trump, *Understanding Trump* (New York: Center Street, 2018), 46.

14. Those curious about the common last name of the two Bayms cited in this chapter might wonder about their relationship. Nancy Baym and Geoffrey Baym are siblings who conduct research independently of one another.

15. Jean Burgess and Nancy K Baym, *Twitter: A Biography* (New York: NYU Press, 2020), 39.

16. Burgess and Baym, *Twitter: A Biography*, 83.

17. Elizabeth M Losh, *Hashtag* (New York: Bloomsbury, 2020), 62–63.

18. Losh, *Hashtag*, 63.

19. The button's designer eventually distanced himself from his creation on the grounds that easy retweeting spread online vitriol through the information ecosystem. See Alex Kantrowitz, "Man Who Built The Retweet: 'We Handed A Loaded Weapon To 4-Year-Olds,'" *BuzzFeed News*, July 23, 2019, https://www.buzzfeednews.com/article/alexkantrowitz/how-the-retweet-ruined-the-internet.

20. Abby Ohlheiser, "Is a Retweet an Endorsement from President-Elect Trump?," *Washington Post*, November 30, 2016, https://www.washingtonpost.com/news/the-intersect/wp/2016/11/30/is-a-retweet-an-endorsement-from-president-elect-trump/.

21. Eliza Collins, "Trump Blames Intern for Tweet Mocking Iowans," *Politico*, October 22, 2015, https://www.politico.com/story/2015/10/trump-retweet-blunder-215072.

22. Oliver O'Connell, "Trump Ridiculed for Retweeting Himself—Then Agreeing with Himself," *The Independent*, June 16, 2020, https://www.independent.co.uk /news/world/americas/us-election/donald-trump-twitter-so-true-retweets-a9569426 .html.

23. Varney & Co (@Varneyco), "STU'S TAKE: 'Six Months in, It's the Hope of Growth That's Making America $4 Trillion Richer.'," Twitter, July 20, 2017, https:// twitter.com/Varneyco/status/888111111320461316.

24. Donald J. Trump (@realDonaldTrump), "'Six months in—it is the hope of GROWTH that is making America FOUR TRILLION DOLLARSRICHER.' -Stuart @ VarneyCo," Twitter, July 21, 2017, https://twitter.com/realDonaldTrump/status /888420461075476480.

25. Michael D. Shear, Maggie Haberman, Nicholas Confessore, Karen Yourish, Larry Buchanan, and Keith Collins, "How Trump Reshaped the Presidency in Over 11,000 Tweets," *New York Times*, November 2, 2019, US, https://www.nytimes.com /interactive/2019/11/02/us/politics/trump-twitter-presidency.html.

26. Jason Farman, *Delayed Response: The Art of Waiting from the Ancient to the Instant World* (New Haven, CT: Yale University Press, 2018), 23.

27. "More 'Covfefe'?: Trump Spox Lights Up Internet with Strange Emoji'ed Tweet," Fox News Insider, June 10, 2017, https://insider.foxnews.com/2017/06/10 /donald-trump-covfefe-sarah-huckabee-sanders-sends-emoji-tweet-kid.

28. The day was February 8, 2013.

29. Michael Barbaro, "Pithy, Mean and Powerful: How Donald Trump Mastered Twitter for 2016," *New York Times*, October 5, 2015, Politics, https://www.nytimes .com/2015/10/06/us/politics/donald-trump-twitter-use-campaign-2016.html.

30. Ben Schreckinger, "'Oh, No': The Day Trump Learned to Tweet," *Politico*, December 20, 2018, https://politi.co/2Bu2EGX.

31. Robert Draper, "The Man Behind the President's Tweets," *New York Times*, April 16, 2018, Magazine, https://www.nytimes.com/2018/04/16/magazine/dan-scavino -the-secretary-of-offense.html.

32. Katie Rogers, Annie Karni, and Maggie Haberman, "Trump's Personal Assistant, Madeleine Westerhout, Shared Intimate Details of First Family," *New York Times*, August 30, 2019, US, https://www.nytimes.com/2019/08/30/us/politics/madeleine -westerhout-trump-family.html.

33. Draper, "The Man Behind the President's Tweets."

34. David Robinson, "Text Analysis of Trump's Tweets Confirms He Writes Only the (Angrier) Android Half," *Variance Explained* (blog), August 9, 2016, http:// varianceexplained.org/r/trump-tweets/.

35. Jay Lewis, "Trump's Campaign Twitter Usage in 6 Charts," Tableau, January 15, 2017, https://public.tableau.com/views/TrumpTwitter/TrumpTwitter.

36. James Hohmann, "Donald Trump Supporters Love to Use Emojis," *Washington Post*, April 14, 2016, https://www.washingtonpost.com/news/powerpost/wp/2016/04/14/donald-trump-supporters-love-to-use-emojis/.

37. Tom Howells, "From the Primaries to Election Night: How the 2016 Campaign Played Out," *Zignal Labs* (blog), November 11, 2016, https://zignallabs.com/from-primaries-to-election-night-how-the-2016-campaign-played-out/.

38. Hamdan Azhar, "The Top Emojis of Election Day 2016," *Prismoji* (blog), November 25, 2016, https://medium.com/prismoji/https-medium-com-prismoji-the-top-emojis-of-election-day-2016-110def7429b9.

39. See Siva Vaidhyanathan, *Antisocial Media: How Facebook Disconnects Us and Undermines Democracy* (Oxford: Oxford University Press, 2018) and Zeynep Tufekci, "YouTube, the Great Radicalizer," *New York Times*, March 10, 2018, https://www.nytimes.com/2018/03/10/opinion/sunday/youtube-politics-radical.html.

40. Nancy Scola, "Source: Twitter Cut out of Trump Tech Meeting over Failed Emoji Deal," *Politico*, December 14, 2016, https://www.politico.com/story/2016/12/donald-trump-twitter-emoji-crooked-hillary-232647.

41. Gary Coby, "A Call with Jack," *Gary Coby* (blog), November 18, 2016, https://medium.com/@garycoby/twitter-restricts-trump-eb7e48ccf5ff. "Dan" refers to Twitter's Vice President of U.S. Sales, Dan Greene.

42. Luke Stark and Kate Crawford, "The Conservatism of Emoji: Work, Affect, and Communication," *Social Media + Society* 1, no. 2 (2015): 2.

43. Stark and Crawford, "The Conservatism of Emoji," 8.

44. Kate M. Miltner, "'One Part Politics, One Part Technology, One Part History': The Construction of the Emoji Set in Unicode 7.0," *New Media + Society* 23, no. 3 (2020): 515–534, https://doi.org/10.1177/1461444819899623.

45. For more on the corporate origin story of the happy face, see Stark and Crawford, "The Conservatism of Emoji."

Chapter 9

1. Michael E. Miller, "Protesters Outside White House Demand 'Pizzagate' Investigation," *Washington Post*, March 25, 2017, Local, https://www.washingtonpost.com/news/local/wp/2017/03/25/protesters-outside-white-house-demand-pizzagate-investigation/.

2. Doyle McManus, "Trump's Weaponized Whataboutism," *Los Angeles Times*, December 6, 2017, http://www.latimes.com/opinion/op-ed/la-oe-mcmanus-what aboutism-20171206-story.html.

3. Matthew d'Ancona, "Ten Alternative Facts for the Post Truth World," *Guardian*, May 12, 2017, https://www.theguardian.com/books/2017/may/12/post-truth -worst-of-best-donald-trump-sean-spicer-kellyanne-conway.

4. This trio of themes was developed in conversation with Nishant Shah as part of a research group on simulation based at Leuphana university. Many of the ideas also reflect Wendy Hui Kyong Chun's presentations about fake news. For more about why important phenomena in digital culture are dismissed as "fake," see Alexandra Juhasz, Ganaele Langlois, and Nishant Shah, *Really Fake* (Minneapolis: University of Minnesota Press, 2021).

5. Eric Lipton, David E. Sanger, and Scott Shane, "The Perfect Weapon: How Russian Cyberpower Invaded the U.S.," *New York Times*, December 13, 2016, Politics, https:// www.nytimes.com/2016/12/13/us/politics/russia-hack-election-dnc.html.

6. Will Oremus, "I Talked to the IT Guy Whose 'Typo' Helped Russia (Maybe) Hack the Election," *Slate*, December 14, 2016, https://slate.com/technology/2016/12 /an-interview-with-charles-delavan-the-it-guy-whose-typo-led-to-the-podesta-email -hack.html.

7. Lipton, Sanger, and Shane, "The Perfect Weapon."

8. u/DumbScribblyUnctious, "Obama spent about $65,000 of the taxpayers money flying in pizza/dogs from Chicago for a private party at the White House.," reddit post, Pedo Allegations MEGATHREAD #1, r/HillaryForPrison, accessed January 13, 2018, https://www.reddit.com/r/HillaryForPrison/comments/5b23bx/pedo_allegations _megathread_1/.

9. Alan Dundes, *The Blood Libel Legend: A Casebook in Anti-Semitic Folklore* (Madison: University of Wisconsin Press, 1991).

10. Cecilia Kang, "Fake News Onslaught Targets Pizzeria as Nest of Child-Trafficking," *New York Times*, November 21, 2016, Technology, https://www.nytimes .com/2016/11/21/technology/fact-check-this-pizzeria-is-not-a-child-trafficking-site .html.

11. rebelskumin, "James Alefantis' Once-Public Instagram, Jimmycomet, Now Preserved on Steemit Blockchain!," forum post, Steemit, April 27, 2017, https://steemit .com/pizzagate/@rebelskum/james-alefantis-once-public-instagram-jimmycomet -now-preserved-on-steemit-blockchain.

12. "Madonna's Pedophilia Joke On Jimmy Fallon Show," TrueFreethinker, accessed January 13, 2018, via Internet Archive, https://archive.org/embed/Madonnas PedophiliaJokeOnJimmyFallonShow.

13. Becca Lewis and Alice E. Marwick, "Media Manipulation and Disinformation Online," report, Data & Society, May 15, 2017, https://datasociety.net/library/media -manipulation-and-disinfo-online/.

14. "Satanic / Muslim Symbol in the Comet Ping Pong Street Sign—DEBUNKED | Pizzagate," Voat, accessed January 13, 2018, /v/pizzagate/1472692.

15. Amanda Robb, "Pizzagate: Anatomy of a Fake News Scandal," *Rolling Stone*, November 16, 2017, https://www.rollingstone.com/feature/anatomy-of-a-fake-news -scandal-125877/.

16. Marc Tuters, Emilija Jokubauskaitė, and Daniel Bach, "Post-Truth Protest: How 4chan Cooked Up the Pizzagate Bullshit," *M/C Journal* 21, no. 3 (August 2018), https://doi.org/10.5204/mcj.1422.

17. Platform administrators can also play a role in legitimating conspiracy theories, as the 2021 HBO documentary series *Q: Into the Storm* demonstrates. It follows the story of Jim Watkins and Ron Watkins, who ran the imageboard 8chan, and alleges that they shaped the QAnon movement.

18. Ace of Swords, "#PIZZAGATE, CLINTON, & PODESTA: WHAT IS IT, AND IS IT CREDIBLE?" Pam Jones, November 28, 2016, http://pamjonesforliberty.com/2016 /11/27/pizzagate-clinton-podesta-what-is-it-and-is-it-credible/.

19. "Criminal Complaint in Comet Ping Pong Shooting." *New York Times*, December 5, 2016, US, https://www.nytimes.com/interactive/2016/12/05/us/document -Edgar-Welch-Criminal-Complaint-Comet-Ping-Pong.html.

20. Torchy Blane, "The *New York Times* 'Fact Checks' Pizzagate," *Renegade Tribune*, November 22, 2016, http://www.renegadetribune.com/new-york-times-fact-checks -pizzagate/.

21. "Talk:David Brock," *Wikipedia*, December 9, 2017, https://en.wikipedia.org/w /index.php?title=Talk:David_Brock&oldid=814612613. The Wikipedia entry has since been considerably improved with more background material and sources.

22. For a comprehensive account of the "War of the Worlds" broadcast and its aftermath, see A. Brad Schwartz, *Broadcast Hysteria: Orson Welles's War of the Worlds and the Art of Fake News* (New York: Hill and Wang, 2016).

23. See Megan Boler, *Digital Media and Democracy: Tactics in Hard Times* (Cambridge, MA: MIT Press, 2008) for more on "fake news" and what Boler calls "ironic citizenship."

24. Jeffrey Gottfried and Monica Anderson, "For Some, the Satiric 'Colbert Report' Is a Trusted Source of Political News," *Pew Research Center* (blog), December 12, 2014, http://www.pewresearch.org/fact-tank/2014/12/12/for-some-the-satiric-colbert -report-is-a-trusted-source-of-political-news/.

25. "Public Knowledge of Current Affairs Little Changed by News and Information Revolutions," *Pew Research Center for the People and the Press* (blog), April 15, 2007, http://www.people-press.org/2007/04/15/public-knowledge-of-current-affairs-little -changed-by-news-and-information-revolutions/.

26. Adam Taylor, "7 Times the Onion Was Lost in Translation," *Washington Post,* June 2, 2015, World Views, https://www.washingtonpost.com/news/worldviews/wp /2015/06/02/7-times-the-onion-was-lost-in-translation/.

27. "ABOUT US," *Americas Last Line of Defense* (blog), February 8, 2016, http:// thelastlineofdefense.org/about-us/.

28. Siva Vaidhyanathan, *Intellectual Property: A Very Short Introduction* (Oxford: Oxford University Press, 2017).

29. Joshua Gillin, "If You're Fooled by Fake News, This Man Probably Wrote It," Politifact, May 31, 2017, http://www.politifact.com/punditfact/article/2017/may /31/If-youre-fooled-by-fake-news-this-man-probably-wro/.

30. In 2004, Trump appeared on *The Daily Show* with Jon Stewart, and in 2015 he appeared on the *Late Show*, which Stephen Colbert left *The Colbert Report* to host.

31. For the tactics of GamerGate, see Elizabeth Losh, "Hiding Inside the Magic Circle: Gamergate and the End of Safe Space," *Boundary 2* (blog), August 15, 2016, https://www.boundary2.org/2016/08/elizabeth-losh-hiding-inside-the-magic-circle -gamergate-and-the-end-of-safe-space/.

32. "Watch: 'Pizzagate' Gunman Recorded This Video on His Drive to D.C.," *Washington Post,* June 22, 2017, https://www.washingtonpost.com/video/national/watch -pizzagate-gunman-recorded-this-video-on-his-drive-to-dc/2017/06/22/795d76a8 -5783-11e7-840b-512026319da7_video.html.

33. Noam Cohen, "The Smoking Lexicon," *New York Magazine*, February 5, 1996.

34. Alexandria Lockett, "Overflow: The Leaky Politics of Living in the Data Deluge," *Portfolio: The Work and Philosophy of Alexandra Lockett, Ph.D.* (blog), November 8, 2018, http://www.alexandrialockett.com/overflow-the-leaky-politics-of-living-in-the -data-deluge/.

35. Dan Bongino, D. C. McAllister, and Matt Palumbo, *Spygate: The Attempted Sabotage of Donald J. Trump* (Franklin, TN: Post Hill Press, 2018).

36. Davey Alba, "Riled Up: Misinformation Stokes Calls for Violence on Election Day," *New York Times*, October 13, 2020, Technology, https://www.nytimes.com /2020/10/13/technology/viral-misinformation-violence-election.html.

37. On the Gateway Pundit site, digital paranoia flourished. Readers were warned of DDoS attacks. An ever-present sidebar also reminded them that Facebook was interfering with content delivery.

38. Jim Hoft, "Breaking: Senate Releases Unredacted Strzok-Page Texts Showing FBI Initiated MULTIPLE SPIES in Trump Campaign in December 2015," *Gateway Pundit*, June 4, 2018, https://www.thegatewaypundit.com/2018/06/breaking-senate -releases-unredacted-strzok-page-texts-showing-fbi-initiated-multiple-spies-in-trump -campaign-in-december-2015/.

39. Jim Rutenberg, "'Alternative Facts' and the Costs of Trump-Branded Reality," *New York Times*, January 22, 2017, Business, https://www.nytimes.com/2017/01/22 /business/media/alternative-facts-trump-brand.html.

40. Brian Rosenwald, *Talk Radio's America: How an Industry Took Over a Political Party That Took over the United States* (Cambridge, MA: Harvard University Press, 2019).

41. This phenomenon of world-building has also been described by Ethan Zuckerman in his work on the QAnon mythology. See Ethan Zuckerman, "QAnon and the Emergence of the Unreal," *Journal of Design and Science*, no. 6 (July 2019), https://. doi.org/10.21428/7808da6b.6b8a82b9.

42. Jay Willis, "How Right-Wing Media Creates a Conspiracy Theory Out of Thin Air," *GQ*, May 23, 2018, https://www.gq.com/story/spygate-conspiracy-theory-explained.

43. Kevin Roose, "How 'Spygate' Attacks Fizzled," *New York Times*, October 20, 2020, Technology, https://www.nytimes.com/2020/10/20/technology/how-spygate -attacks-fizzled.html.

44. See for example, the range of scholars in television and cultural studies presented in the edited collection by Susan Murray and Laurie Ouellette, *Reality TV: Remaking Television Culture* (New York: NYU Press, 2004).

45. See the essays about identity and politics in Su Holmes and Deborah Jermyn, *Understanding Reality Television* (New York: Routledge, 2011).

46. Anita Biressi and Heather Nunn, *Reality TV: Realism and Revelation* (New York: Columbia University Press, 2005).

47. Vincent Kaufmann, "Transparency and Subjectivity: Remembering Jennifer Ringley," in *Transparency, Society and Subjectivity: Critical Perspectives*, ed. Emmanuel Alloa and Dieter Thomä (Cham, Switzerland: Springer International Publishing, 2018), 307–322.

48. Lisette Voytko, "Trump's Biggest Side Hustle Outside Of 'Apprentice'? Multi-Level Marketing Schemes," *Forbes*, September 29, 2020, https://www.forbes.com /sites/lisettevoytko/2020/09/29/trumps-biggest-side-hustle-outside-of-apprentice -multi-level-marketing-schemes/.

49. David Yaffe-Bellany, "The Legal Threats Trump Will Face If He Loses the Election," *Bloomberg*, October 23, 2020, https://www.bloomberg.com/features/2020 -trump-faces-lawsuits-and-legal-threats/.

50. Stefan L. Brandt, "Donald Trump, the Reality Show: Populism as Performance and Spectacle," *Zeitschrift Für Literaturwissenschaft Und Linguistik* 50, no. 2 (June 2020): 303–21, https://doi.org/10.1007/s41244-020-00170-3.

51. Jan Wolfe, "Trump Brags about High TV Viewership of Coronavirus Briefings," *Reuters*, March 29, 2020, Coronavirus, https://www.reuters.com/article/us-health-coronavirus-trump-tv-idUSKBN21G0TR.

52. Timon Beyes and Claus Pias have written usefully about this fundamental attraction to intransparency and fascination with the arcane. See "Transparenz und Geheimnis" in *Zeitschrift Für Kulturwissenschaften* (2014), 2 | H-Soz-Kult. Kommunikation Und Fachinformation Für Die Geschichtswissenschaften, http://www.hsozkult.de/journal/id/zeitschriftenausgaben-9136.

53. Andrew Beaujon, "Donald Trump Keeps Using Stacks of Papers to Settle Arguments | Washingtonian (DC)," *Washingtonian* (blog), March 7, 2017, https://www.washingtonian.com/2017/03/07/donald-trump-stacks-of-papers/.

54. Jedd Rosche, "Donald Trump Tweets Photo of Tax Returns," CNN, October 15, 2015, https://www.cnn.com/2015/10/15/politics/donald-trump-tweets-tax-return/index.html.

55. Brooke Seipel, "Trump Barred Reporters from Examining Stacks of Folders at Press Conference," *The Hill*, January 11, 2017, https://thehill.com/blogs/blog-briefing-room/news/313907-trump-didnt-allow-reporters-to-see-documents-detailing-split.

56. Inae Oh, "Republicans' Only Selling Point for Their Obamacare Replacement Bill Is How Short It Is," *Mother Jones* (blog), March 7, 2017, https://www.motherjones.com/politics/2017/03/sean-spicer-size-gop-obamacare-repeal-bill/.

57. Philip Bump, "That Giant Stack of Paper Trump Stood next to? A Little Too Giant.," *Washington Post*, December 14, 2017, https://www.washingtonpost.com/news/politics/wp/2017/12/14/that-giant-stack-of-paper-trump-stood-next-to-a-little-too-giant/.

58. "DoD Personnel, Workforce Reports & Publications," accessed February 16, 2019, https://www.dmdc.osd.mil/appj/dwp/dwp_reports.jsp.

59. Of course, this was not the first time that government information had been removed from the internet. These kinds of deletions had happened many times before. In the early days of federal websites, back in May of 1996, the Clinton administration removed a full-text archive of speeches for fear of it being mined by Republican operatives. See Niels Brugger, *The Archived Web: Doing History in the Digital Age* (Cambridge, MA: MIT Press, 2018), 2.

60. Danielle Robinson, "Daniellecrobinson/Data-Rescue-PDX," GitHub repository, updated March 4, 2017, https://github.com/daniellecrobinson/Data-Rescue-PDX.

Chapter 10

1. Donald J. Trump, "Join me in St. Louis, Missouri—as I conclude my debate prep.," *streamed live* on October 9, 2016, Facebook Live video, https://www.facebook.com /DonaldTrump/videos/10157857037430725/.

2. "Washingtonpost.com: Jones v. Clinton Legal Documents," accessed August 30, 2019, https://www.washingtonpost.com/wp-srv/politics/special/pjones/legal.htm. At one point in 1998, Jones had become so famous that she was featured on the cover of *Time* magazine. Because of Jones's lawsuit, President Clinton himself was deposed, and the affidavit of former White House intern Monica Lewinsky—with whom Clinton had had an extramarital affair—was entered into evidence.

3. Diamond and Silk, "Diamond and Silk pick the lucky winner that will hang out with them," *streamed live* on October 9, 2016, Facebook Live video, https://www .facebook.com/DiamondandSilk/videos/718308281651621/.

4. Lindsay Ellis, "YouTube: Manufacturing Authenticity (For Fun and Profit!)," uploaded September 11, 2018, YouTube video, 36:01, https://youtu.be/8FJEtCvb2Kw.

5. Alice Marwick, "Microcelebrity, Self-Branding, and the Internet," in *The Blackwell Encyclopedia of Sociology* (Wiley & Sons, 2017), 1–3, https://doi.org/10.1002 /9781405165518.wbeos1000.

6. Sam Gregory, "Cameras Everywhere: Ubiquitous Video Documentation of Human Rights, New Forms of Video Advocacy, and Considerations of Safety, Security, Dignity and Consent," *Journal of Human Rights Practice* 2, no. 2 (July 2010): 191–207, https://doi.org/10.1093/jhuman/huq002.

7. Sam Gregory and Elizabeth Losh, "Remixing Human Rights: Rethinking Civic Expression, Representation and Personal Security in Online Video," *First Monday*, July 18, 2012, https://doi.org/10.5210/fm.v17i8.4104.

8. For a list of useful guidelines, see "Filming Protests and Police Abuse," *WITNESS* (blog), accessed January 16, 2021, https://www.witness.org/portfolio_page /filming-protests-and-police-abuse/.

9. For more about the digital literacy of Diamond Reynolds, see Elizabeth Losh, "Beyond the Techno-Missionary Narrative Digital Literacy and Necropolitics," in *Handbook of Writing, Literacies, and Education in Digital Cultures*, ed. Kathy A. Mills et al. (New York: Routledge, 2017).

10. Susan Sontag has called this desire to consume images of mortal violence the draw of the "mystery" and "indecency" of "co-spectatorship" at another's death. See Susan Sontag, *Regarding the Pain of Others* (New York: Farrar, Straus and Giroux, 2003), 60. Alexandra Juhasz has written about this desire as deeply problematic when it involves consumption of spectacles of Black death that are triggering and

traumatic to community members when they are disseminated. See Alexandra Juhasz, "How Do I (Not) Look? Live Feed Video and Viral Black Death," *JSTOR Daily* (blog), July 20, 2016, http://daily.jstor.org/how-do-i-not-look/.

11. "Nakia Jones Reacts as a Mother and an Officer," uploaded on October 4, 2018, by Joe Madison—"The Black Eagle," Facebook Live video, https://www.facebook .com/watch/?v=177428416481850.

12. Gianluca Mezzofiore, "5 Facebook Live Streams That Defined the News in 2016," Mashable, December 23, 2016, https://mashable.com/2016/12/23/facebook -live-news-charlotte-black-lives-matter/.

13. Diamond and Silk, "Diamond and Silk live. Discussing the police shootings in Dallas.," *streamed live* on July 8, 2016, Facebook Live video, https://www.facebook .com/DiamondandSilk/videos/668436829972100/.

14. Tessa Stuart, "Meet the Black Women Defending Trump's Record on Race," *Rolling Stone*, September 28, 2016, https://www.rollingstone.com/politics/politics-features /meet-the-black-women-defending-trumps-record-on-race-2-186845/.

15. Emily Stewart, "Diamond and Silk, Fox & Friends' Favorite Black Trump Supporters, Explained," *Vox*, May 1, 2018, https://www.vox.com/policy-and-politics /2018/5/1/17300120/diamond-and-silk-youtube-trump-state-of-the-union.

16. *Diamond and Silk, "Diamond and Silk on Live discussing: Central Park 5*, Crime Bill 1994," *streamed live* on May 28, 2019, Facebook Live video, https://www.facebook .com/DiamondandSilk/videos/diamond-and-silk-on-live-discussing-central-park-5 -crime-bill-1994-nancy-pelosi-/937336113275589/.

17. *Diamond and Silk, "Juicy Gossip: Podesta and his spirit cooking. Lil Wayne vs BLM," streamed live November 4, 2016, Facebook Live video*, https://www.facebook.com /DiamondandSilk/videos/734885999993849/.

18. As noted in the previous chapter, Podesta's "spirit cooking" emails actually referenced a feminist performance project by famed Serbian artist Marina Abramović.

19. Olivia Messer, "'Fox & Friends' Admit Diamond & Silk Mocked Doctored Video of 'Crazy Nancy,'" *The Daily Beast*, May 24, 2019, Politics, https://www.thedaily. beast.com/fox-and-friends-admit-diamond-and-silk-mocked-doctored-video-of -crazy-nancy-pelosi.

20. Sarah Mervosh, "Distorted Videos of Nancy Pelosi Spread on Facebook and Twitter, Helped by Trump," *New York Times*, May 24, 2019, https://www.nytimes .com/2019/05/24/us/politics/pelosi-doctored-video.html.

21. Britt Paris and Joan Donovan, "Deepfakes and Cheap Fakes," report, Data & Society, September 18, 2019, https://datasociety.net/library/deepfakes-and-cheap-fakes/.

22. Amy Sherman, "No Evidence That Obama Secretly Granted Citizenship to 2,500 Iranians as Part of Nuclear Agreement," Politifact, May 5, 2018, https://www.politi

fact.com/factchecks/2018/jul/05/diamond-and-silk/no-evidence-obama-secretly
-granted-citizenship-250/.

23. William Cummings, "'I Love Diamond & Silk': Trump Stands by Controversial
Supporters Who Promoted Coronavirus Conspiracies," *USA TODAY*, April 28, 2020,
https://www.usatoday.com/story/news/politics/2020/04/28/trump-defends
-diamond-and-silk-despite-coronavirus-conspiracies/3039249001/.

24. For a fuller account of Section 230 and its relationship to older legal cases involving bookstores and public access stations, see Jeff Kosseff, *The Twenty-Six Words That
Created the Internet* (Ithaca, NY: Cornell University Press, 2019).

25. Oliver Darcy, "White House Creates Tool for People to Report Alleged Social
Media Bias," CNN, May 15, 2019, https://www.cnn.com/2019/05/15/tech/white
-house-social-media-bias-tool/index.html.

26. Casey Newton, "Trump's Social Media Bias Reporting Project Is a Data Collection Tool in Disguise," *The Verge* (blog), May 16, 2019, https://www.theverge
.com/interface/2019/5/16/18627096/trump-social-media-bias-reporting-scam-christ
church-call.

27. Molly Roberts, "Marsha Blackburn's 'Baby Body Parts' Ad Is Worse than 'Inflam-
matory,'" *Washington Post* (blog), October 10, 2017, https://www.washingtonpost
.com/blogs/post-partisan/wp/2017/10/10/who-cares-whether-marsha-blackburns
-baby-body-parts-ad-is-inflammatory/.

28. For more on user perceptions of shadow banning, see Brooke Erin Duffy,
Annika Pinch, Shruti Sannon, and Megan Sawey, "The Nested Precarities of Creative Labor on Social Media," *Social Media + Society* 7, no. 2 (April 2021), https://
doi.org/10.1177/20563051211021368.

29. Erwan Le Merrer, Benoît Morgan, and Gilles Trédan, "Setting the Record Straighter
on Shadow Banning," in *IEEE INFOCOM 2021—IEEE Conference on Computer Communications*, 2021, 1–10, https://doi.org/10.1109/INFOCOM42981.2021.9488792.

30. "Filtering Practices of Social Media Platforms," House Committee on the
Judiciary, April 26, 2018, https://judiciary.house.gov/legislation/hearings/filtering
-practices-social-media-platforms.

31. Alexandra Minna Stern, *Proud Boys and the White Ethnostate: How the Alt-Right Is
Warping the American Imagination* (Boston: Beacon Press, 2020).

32. To show his deep alliance with the sisters, the following year King introduced
a bill named after them and credited them as coauthors of the legislation. See Joe
Perticone, "Steve King Introduces 'Diamond and Silk Act' in Bizarre Press Conference," *Business Insider* (blog), June 12, 2019, https://www.businessinsider.com/steve
-king-introduces-diamond-and-silk-act-press-conference-2019-6.

33. Disclosing such sponsorship arrangements had less effect on the persuasive
power of regular people than it did for celebrities. See Sophie C. Boerman, Lotte

M. Willemsen, and Eva P. Van Der Aa, "'This Post Is Sponsored': Effects of Spon-sorship Disclosure on Persuasion Knowledge and Electronic Word of Mouth in the Context of Facebook," *Journal of Interactive Marketing* 38 (May 2017): 82–92, https://doi.org/10.1016/j.intmar.2016.12.002.

34. Mary L. Gray and Siddharth Suri, *Ghost Work: How to Stop Silicon Valley from Building a New Global Underclass* (Boston: Mariner Books, 2019).

35. For information about Facebook's contract with Accenture for content modera-tion, see Adam Satariano and Mike Isaac, "The Silent Partner Cleaning Up Facebook for $500 Million a Year," *New York Times*, August 31, 2021, Technology, https://www.nytimes.com/2021/08/31/technology/facebook-accenture-content-modera tion.html.

36. See also the disturbing 2017 documentary *The Cleaners* by Hans Block and Moritz Riesewieck, which follows the lives of content moderators in the Philippines.

37. Tarleton Gillespie, *Custodians of the Internet: Platforms, Content Moderation, and the Hidden Decisions That Shape Social Media* (New Haven, CT: Yale University Press, 2021).

38. Zeynep Tufekci, "What Happens to #Ferguson Affects Ferguson: Net Neutrality, Algorithmic Filtering and Ferguson," *The Message* (blog), August 14, 2014, https://medium.com/message/ferguson-is-also-a-net-neutrality-issue-6d2f3db51eb0.

39. Elisha Lim, "The Protestant Ethic and the Spirit of Facebook: Updating Iden-tity Economics," *Social Media + Society* 6, no. 2 (April 2020), https://doi.org/10.1177/2056305120910144.

40. For a discussion of the deceptiveness of popularity metrics, see Eunsong Kim, "The Politics of Trending," *Model View Culture* (blog), March 19, 2015, https://mod elviewculture.com/pieces/the-politics-of-trending. Kim discusses Twitter's trending algorithm, but her concerns can be applied to other social media companies.

41. Hannah Parry, "Donald Trump and Don Jr Pose with Republican Social Media Stars Diamond and Silk after the Women Were Accused of Lying under Oath about Being Paid by the President's Campaign Team," *Daily Mail*, May 4, 2018, https://www.dailymail.co.uk/news/article-5693497/Donald-Trump-Don-Jr-pose-Republican -social-media-stars-Diamond-Silk.html.

42. "Remarks by President Trump in Meeting with African American Leaders," The White House, accessed November 5, 2020, https://www.whitehouse.gov /briefings-statements/remarks-president-trump-meeting-african-american-leaders/.

43. Donald J. Trump (@realDonaldTrump), "The White House will be hosting a very big and very important Social Media Summit today. Would I have become President without Social Media? Yes (probably)!," Twitter, July 11, 2019, https://twitter.com /realDonaldTrump/status/1149266929565261824.

44. "Remarks by President Trump at the Presidential Social Media Summit," WhiteHouse.gov, accessed August 31, 2019, https://www.whitehouse.gov/briefings -statements/remarks-president-trump-presidential-social-media-summit/.

45. "President Trump Remarks at Social Media Summit," C-SPAN, July 11, 2019, https:// www.c-span.org/video/?462567-1/president-trump-remarks-social-media-summit.

46. Rand Fishkin, "We Analyzed Every Twitter Account Following Donald Trump: 61% Are Bots, Spam, Inactive, or Propaganda," *SparkToro* (blog), October 9, 2018, https://sparktoro.com/blog/we-analyzed-every-twitter-account-following-donald -trump-61-are-bots-spam-inactive-or-propaganda/.

47. Marie C. Baca, "Who Was Who at Trump's Social Media Summit," *Washington Post*, July 11, 2019, https://www.washingtonpost.com/technology/2019/07/11 /who-was-who-trumps-social-media-summit/.

48. P. W. Singer and Emerson T. Brooking, *Likewar: The Weaponization of Social Media* (New York: Houghton Mifflin, 2019), 209–210.

49. John Woodrow Cox, "'DeploraBall' Will Celebrate Victory of Media-Bashing Trump at National Press Club," *Washington Post*, December 22, 2016, Local, https:// www.washingtonpost.com/local/deploraball-will-celebrate-election-of-media -bashing-trump-at-national-press-club/2016/12/22/53958d64-c86f-11e6-8bee -54e800ef2a63_story.html.

50. "DeploraBall 2017," accessed October 20, 2020, http://deploraball.com/.

51. "Celebrity Apprentice Has Most Product Placements in Prime Time," *Product Placement & Advertising News* (blog), May 31, 2011, https://productplacement.biz /201105313381/branded-entertainment/celebrity-apprentice-has-more-product-place ments-in-prime-time.html.

52. Kian Bakhtiari, "Influencer Fatigue Sets Stage For A New Generation Of Cre- ators," *Forbes*, April 6, 2020, https://www.forbes.com/sites/kianbakhtiari/2020/04/06 /influencer-fatigue-sets-the-stage-for-a-new-generation-of-creators/.

53. Alice E. Marwick, *Status Update: Celebrity, Publicity, and Branding in the Social Media Age* (New Haven, CT: Yale University Press, 2013), 117.

54. Crystal Abidin, *Internet Celebrity: Understanding Fame Online* (Bingley, UK: Emer- ald Publishing, 2018).

55. "Ivanka Trump Influencer Program," Vanessa Street Design, accessed January 17, 2021, http://vstreetdesign.com/work/ivanka-trump-influencer-program/.

56. Aliyah Frumin, "Ivanka Trump's Company Scrambles over '60 Minutes' Bracelet Criticisms," NBC News, November 15, 2016, https://www.nbcnews.com /news/us-news/ivanka-trump-s-company-scrambles-over-60-minutes-bracelet -criticism-n684171.

57. Jia Tolentino, "Ivanka Trump Wrote a Painfully Oblivious Book for Basically No One," *New Yorker*, May 4, 2017, https://www.newyorker.com/books/page-turner /ivanka-trump-wrote-a-painfully-oblivious-book-for-basically-no-one.

58. Jennifer Senior, "Having Trouble Having It All? Ivanka Alone Can Fix It," *New York Times*, May 2, 2017, Books, https://www.nytimes.com/2017/05/02/books/review -ivanka-trump-women-who-work.html.

59. Megan Garber, "When Ivanka Trump Quoted Toni Morrison," *Atlantic*, May 5, 2017, https://www.theatlantic.com/entertainment/archive/2017/05/the-borrowed -words-of-ivanka-trump/525621/.

60. Ivanka Trump, "An Exclusive Excerpt from Ivanka Trump's New Book, Women Who Work," *Fortune*, May 1, 2017, https://fortune.com/2017/05/01/ivanka-trump -book-women-who-work/.

61. Charlie Lankston, "Ivanka Trump Pouts at the Camera in Makeup-Free Birth-day Selfie," *Daily Mail*, October 30, 2019, https://www.dailymail.co.uk/femail /article-7630619/Ivanka-Trump-pouts-camera-makeup-free-birthday-selfie.html.

62. Julie DiCaro, "The Dangers Of The 'Cool Girl' Ideal," *HuffPost*, updated January 12, 2017, https://www.huffpost.com/entry/the-dangers-of-the-cool-girl-ideal_b _5873d393e4b0a5e600a78d4e.

63. Eugene Scott, "Trump Fans Diamond and Silk Claim Facebook Is Censoring 'Women of Color.' They Aren't Likely to Gain Much Support.," *Washington Post*, April 12, 2018, https://www.washingtonpost.com/news/the-fix/wp/2018/04/12/trump -fans-diamond-and-silk-claims-facebook-is-censoring-women-of-color-they-arent-likely -to-gain-much-support/.

64. Stuff White People Like, accessed January 19, 2021, https://stuffwhitepeoplelike .com/.

65. For more about how whiteness was constituted by distance from supposedly degenerate immigrant families, see Nell Irvin Painter, *The History of White People* (New York: Norton, 2011).

66. Priscilla Frank, "Ivanka Trump's Book Uses Toni Morrison Quote To Equate Busyness With Slavery," *HuffPost*, May 5, 2017, https://www.huffpost.com/entry /ivanka-trump-book-toni-morrison_n_590c8536e4b0d5d9049bcc01.

67. Sarah Banet-Weiser, *Empowered: Popular Feminism and Popular Misogyny* (Durham, NC; London: Duke University Press, 2018).

68. Robin DiAngelo, *White Fragility: Why It's so Hard for White People to Talk about Racism* (London: Penguin, 2019).

69. Gerry Shih and Jonathan O'Connell, "China Greenlights Large Batch of Ivanka Trump Trademark Applications," *Washington Post*, November 6, 2018, https://www

.washingtonpost.com/world/asia_pacific/china-greenlights-large-batch-of-ivanka
-trump-trademark-applications/2018/11/06/c085e88c-e1c8-11e8-a1c9-6afe99dddd92
_story.html.

70. Nick Penzenstadler, "Melania Trump Plans to Cash-in on Trademarks, Files
New Lawsuit," *USA TODAY*, February 7, 2017, https://www.usatoday.com/story/news
/politics/onpolitics/2017/02/07/melania-trump-plans-cash--trademarks-files-new
-suit/97595954/.

71. David E. Sanger and William J. Broad, "In a Tweet Taunting Iran, Trump
Releases an Image Thought to Be Classified," *New York Times*, August 30, 2019,
World, https://www.nytimes.com/2019/08/30/world/middleeast/trump-iran-missile
-explosion-satellite-image.html.

72. Geoff Brumfiel, "Amateurs Identify U.S. Spy Satellite Behind President Trump's
Tweet," NPR, September 2, 2019, https://www.npr.org/2019/09/02/756673481
/amateurs-identify-u-s-spy-satellite-behind-president-trumps-tweet.

73. Mike Nizza and Patrick J. Lyons, "In an Iranian Image, a Missile Too Many,"
The Lede (blog), July 10, 2008, https://thelede.blogs.nytimes.com/2008/07/10/in
-an-iranian-image-a-missile-too-many/.

74. Sara Polak, "Posting the Presidency: Cartoon Politics in a Social Media Landscape," *Media and Arts Law Review* 22 (2018): 403–419.

75. Russell Brandom, "Donald Trump Used a Phone Flashlight to Read His Briefing
on a North Korean Missile Test," *The Verge* (blog), February 13, 2017, https://www
.theverge.com/2017/2/13/14597700/donald-trump-phone-flashlight-north-korea
-hacking-security.

76. The White House Office of the Press Secretary, "Statement of National Security
Advisor General James Jones on Wikileaks," WhiteHouse.gov, July 25, 2010, https://
obamawhitehouse.archives.gov/the-press-office/statement-national-security-advisor
-general-james-jones-wikileaks.

77. Louis Jacobson, "Trump's Flip-Flop on Leaks and the Release of Secret Information," Politifact, February 16, 2017, https://www.politifact.com/factchecks/2017/feb
/16/donald-trump/trumps-flip-flop-leaks-and-release-secret-informat/.

78. The White House Office of the Press Secretary, "Press Briefing by Press Secretary Josh Earnest, 4/8/2015," WhiteHouse.gov, April 8, 2015, https://obamawhite
house.archives.gov/the-press-office/2015/04/08/press-briefing-press-secretary-josh
-earnest-482015.

79. Aaron Rupar, "Trump Says 'Russia, If You're Listening' Was a Joke. There's Tape
to Prove Otherwise.," *Vox*, September 29, 2020, https://www.vox.com/2020/9
/29/21493319/trump-russia-if-youre-listening-comments-rewrite-history.

Chapter 11

1. Joe Biden, "Illinois Virtual Town Hall | Joe Biden for President," uploaded March 14, 2020, YouTube video, 18:09, https://youtu.be/QxhsV_6dWVs.

2. Katie Glueck and Thomas Kaplan, "'Am I on Camera?' Joe Biden's Foray into Virtual Campaigning," *New York Times*, March 13, 2020, US, https://www.nytimes.com/2020/03/13/us/politics/joe-biden-digital-campaign.html.

3. Makena Kelly, "Joe Biden's First Virtual Town Hall Was an Absolute Technical Nightmare," *The Verge* (blog), March 14, 2020, https://www.theverge.com/2020/3/14/21179466/joe-biden-virtual-town-hall-audio-bernie-sanders-illinois-dick-durbin-nightmare.

4. Makena Kelly, "Joe Biden's First Virtual Town Hall Was an Absolute Technical Nightmare," *The Verge* (blog), March 14, 2020, https://www.theverge.com/2020/3/14/21179466/joe-biden-virtual-town-hall-audio-bernie-sanders-illinois-dick-durbin-nightmare.

5. Don't Walk, Run! Productions, "Joe Biden's "Virtual Rally" Was a Real Disaster!," uploaded May 11, 2020, YouTube video, 6:11, https://youtu.be/pdUbOekBJ7s.

6. Sean Sullivan, "Biden 'Virtual Rallies' Have Mixed Results," *Washington Post*, July 5, 2020, https://www.washingtonpost.com/politics/biden-virtual-tampa-rally-runs-into-glitches-awkwardness-and-blank-screens/2020/05/07/03bb7b36-906d-11ea-9e23-6914ee410a5f_story.html.

7. Kevin Roose, "Biden Is Losing the Internet. Does That Matter?," *New York Times*, April 16, 2020, Technology, https://www.nytimes.com/2020/04/16/technology/joe-biden-internet.html.

8. Amanda Hess and Shane O'Neill, "Why We're Obsessed with Celebrities' Bookcases," *New York Times*, May 12, 2020, https://www.nytimes.com/video/arts/100000007120740/celebrity-bookshelves-coronavirus.html.

9. See also Jessica Pressman, "The Aesthetic of Bookishness in Twenty-First-Century Literature," *Michigan Quarterly Review* XLVIII, no. 4 (Fall 2009), http://hdl.handle.net/2027/spo.act2080.0048.402.

10. "Free Team Joe Swag," accessed June 7, 2020, https://store.joebiden.com/make-your-own.

11. "Rob Flaherty," Institute for Public Relations, accessed June 1, 2020, https://instituteforpr.org/ipr-bio/rob-flaherty/.

12. Pete Hamby, "Why the Uncle Joe-Can't-Internet Criticism Is Mostly Malarkey," *Vanity Fair*, May 18, 2020, https://www.vanityfair.com/news/2020/05/why-the-uncle-joe-cant-internet-criticism-is-mostly-malarkey.

13. B. Schlanger and W. A. Hoffberg, "Effects of Television on the Motion Picture Theater," *Journal of the Society of Motion Picture and Television Engineers* 56, no. 1 (January 1951): 39–43, https://doi.org/10.5594/J05091.

14. Charles Taylor, *Opening Wednesday at a Theater or Drive-In Near You: The Shadow Cinema of the American '70s* (New York: Bloomsbury Publishing Inc, 2017).

15. Shirley Ju, "How DJ D-Nice's Club Quarantine Became an Isolation Sensation," *Variety*, March 29, 2020, https://variety.com/2020/music/news/dj-d-nice-club -quarantine-rihanna-michelle-obama-interview-1203541666/.

16. Erica Davies, "Trump's 2020 Website Using a Confused Joe Biden Saying 'You Are as Lost as Me' as 404 Error Page," *US Sun*, May 13, 2020, https://www.the-sun .com/news/824944/donald-trump-campaign-website-joe-biden-404-error/. In summer the Biden 404 page showed the candidate in aviator sunglasses holding an ice cream cone with this assurance: "LOOKS LIKE THAT PAGE ISN'T HERE. KEEP COOL—I'LL GET US BACK ON THE RAILS." By fall the text had been changed to "WE COULDN'T MASK THIS ERROR, BUT YOU SHOULD MASK YOURSELF," which also showed Biden in his signature aviator sunglasses, but it used a more somber photograph of a masked Biden saluting.

17. Scott Nover, "You Can Now Wear Joe Biden's Aviators on Snapchat," *Adweek*, May 19, 2020, https://www.adweek.com/digital/you-can-now-wear-joe-bidens-aviators-on -snapchat/.

18. Rachel Lerman, "Snap Says It Is No Longer Promoting Trump's Account, Adding to Social Media Backlash against President," *Washington Post*, June 3, 2020, https:// www.washingtonpost.com/technology/2020/06/03/snapchat-stops-promoting -trump/.

19. Headass, "Trump's Coffin Dance Snapchat Ad," uploaded May 23, 2020, YouTube video, 0:38, https://youtu.be/Qc_QPtsb0BQ.

20. Lerman, *Washington Post*.

21. Trump Campaign, "Trump Campaign Statement on Snapchat," Donald-JTrump.com, accessed June 3, 2020, https://www.donaldjtrump.com/media/trump -campaign-statement-on-snapchat.

22. The term comes from Hillary Clinton's characterization of Trump's followers as a "basket of deplorables," which was appropriated by her opposition as a name of honor. For more about the term and its emotional valences, see James Gibson, Christopher Claassen, and Joan Barceló, "Deplorables: Emotions, Political Sophistication, and Political Intolerance," *American Politics Research* 48, no. 2 (March 2020): 252–62, https://doi.org/10.1177/1532673X18820864.

23. Casey Newton, "What Other Social Networks Can Learn from Snapchat's Rebuke of Trump," *The Verge* (blog), June 4, 2020, https://www.theverge.com/interface /2020/6/4/21279339/snapchat-trump-discover-reach-speech-evan-spiegel-snap.

24. Kate Conger and Davey Alba, "Twitter Refutes Inaccuracies in Trump's Tweets About Mail-In Voting," *New York Times*, May 26, 2020, https://www.nytimes.com /2020/05/26/technology/twitter-trump-mail-in-ballots.html.

25. David Krayden, "We Can't Let Social Media Become the Socialist Media.," Human Events, June 6, 2020, https://humanevents.com/2020/06/06/we-cant-let-social-media -become-the-socialist-media/.

26. "Executive Order on Preventing Online Censorship," WhiteHouse.gov, accessed June 17, 2020, https://www.whitehouse.gov/presidential-actions/executive -order-preventing-online-censorship/.

27. Garrett Epps, "The Obscure Supreme Court Decision the Trump Administration Could Use to Gut the First Amendment," *Atlantic*, June 17, 2020, https://www .theatlantic.com/ideas/archive/2020/06/supreme-court-decision-could-gut-first -amendment/612973/.

28. Although Vine was short-lived, the scholarly community of internet researchers was very interested in how Vine promulgated participatory culture through adopting shared production constraints and a particular aesthetic of looping. Some of this work is comparative in nature and focused on how Vine differed from services offered by YouTube, Instagram, and other more durable platforms. For example, see sections on Vine in Jean Burgess and Joshua Green, *YouTube: Online Video and Participatory Culture* (Cambridge, UK; Medford, MA: Polity, 2018) or Stefanie Duguay, "Lesbian, Gay, Bisexual, Trans, and Queer Visibility Through Selfies: Comparing Platform Mediators Across Ruby Rose's Instagram and Vine Presence," *Social Media + Society* 2, no. 2 (April 2016), https://doi.org/10.1177/2056305116641975.

29. This committee had also been concerned about potential Chinese ownership of the gay dating mobile application Grindr and its potential for blackmail. See Robert D. Williams, "Reflections on TikTok and Data Privacy as National Security," *Lawfare* (blog), November 15, 2019, https://www.lawfareblog.com/reflections-tiktok-and -data-privacy-national-security for a discussion about balancing forms of free expression.

30. "TikTok, National Security Threats the Focus of Hawley's 'Dangerous Partners: Big Tech and Beijing' Hearing," Josh Hawley, U.S. Senator for Missouri, March 4, 2020, https://www.hawley.senate.gov/tiktok-national-security-threats-focus-hawleys -dangerous-partners-big-tech-and-beijing-hearing.

31. Siobhan Neela-Stock, "Sarah Cooper Debuts Her New Trump vs. the Bathroom TikTok for Jimmy Fallon," Mashable, June 13, 2020, https://mashable.com/article /sarah-cooper-debuts-bathroom-tik-tok-fallon/. See also James Poniewozik, "Trump Said, 'I Have the Best Words.' Now They're Hers," *New York Times*, May 27, 2020, https://www.nytimes.com/2020/05/27/arts/television/trump-sarah-cooper.html.

32. Jill Walker Rettberg has argued that exaggerated hand gestures are also important for TikTok and its precursors to serve as video emoji. See Jill Walker Rettberg, "Hand Signs for Lip-Syncing: The Emergence of a Gestural Language on Musical.Ly as a Video-Based Equivalent to Emoji," *Social Media + Society* 3, no. 4 (October 2017), https://doi.org/10.1177/2056305117735751.

33. Monica Hesse, "Women on TikTok Have Cracked the Code on How to Satirize Trump," *Washington Post*, May 22, 2020, https://www.washingtonpost.com/life style/style/women-on-tiktok-have-cracked-the-code-on-how-to-satirize-trump/2020 /05/19/d002086e-9602-11ea-82b4-c8db161ff6e5_story.html.

34. Donie O'Sullivan, "TikTok Users Are Trying to Troll Trump's Campaign by Reserving Tickets for Tulsa Rally They'll Never Use," CNN, June 16, 2020, https:// www.cnn.com/2020/06/16/politics/tiktok-trump-tulsa-rally-trnd/index.html.

35. Taylor Lorenz, Kellen Browning, and Sheera Frenkel, "TikTok Teens and K-Pop Stans Say They Sank Trump Rally," *New York Times*, September 14, 2020, Style, https://www.nytimes.com/2020/06/21/style/tiktok-trump-rally-tulsa.html.

36. "Executive Order on Addressing the Threat Posed by TikTok," WhiteHouse. gov, accessed September 22, 2020, https://www.whitehouse.gov/presidential-actions /executive-order-addressing-threat-posed-tiktok/.

37. "Order Regarding the Acquisition of Musical.Ly by ByteDance Ltd," White-House.gov, accessed September 22, 2020, https://www.whitehouse.gov/presidential -actions/order-regarding-acquisition-musical-ly-bytedance-ltd/.

38. Mike Isaac and Ana Swanson, "TikTok Sues U.S. Government Over Trump Ban," *New York Times*, August 26, 2020, Technology, https://www.nytimes.com/2020 /08/24/technology/tiktok-sues-us-government-over-trump-ban.html.

39. "Commerce Department Prohibits WeChat and TikTok Transactions to Protect the National Security of the United States," U.S. Department of Commerce, accessed September 22, 2020, https://www.commerce.gov/news/press-releases/2020/09/com merce-department-prohibits-wechat-and-tiktok-transactions-protect.

40. Kaelan Deese, "Joe Biden Does 'Face Mask Awareness' TikTok Video with WaPo," *TheHill*, May 28, 2020, https://thehill.com/blogs/in-the-know/in-the-know/499925 -joe-biden-does-face-mask-awareness-tiktok-with-wapo.

41. Julia Silverman, "How Oregon's Contribution to That Viral DNC Roll Call Video Came Together," *Portland Monthly*, August 19, 2020, https://www.pdx monthly.com/news-and-city-life/2020/08/how-oregons-contribution-to-that-viral -dnc-roll-call-video-came-together.

42. Taylor Hatmaker, "At the First-Ever Virtual DNC, Democrats Play It Safe," *TechCrunch* (blog), August 18, 2020, https://social.techcrunch.com/2020/08/18/dnc -first-virtual-convention/.

43. Angela Watercutter, "The DNC Is the Best Zoom Meeting of 2020—So Far," *Wired*, August 21, 2020, https://www.wired.com/story/dnc-long-zoom-meeting/.

44. For more on "calibrated amateurism," see Crystal Abidin, *Internet Celebrity: Understanding Fame Online* (Bingley, UK: Emerald Publishing, 2018).

45. Daisuke Wakabayashi, Stephanie Saul, and Kenneth P. Vogel, "How Kamala Harris Forged Close Ties With Big Tech," *New York Times*, August 21, 2020, Technology, https://www.nytimes.com/2020/08/20/technology/kamala-harris-ties-to-big-tech.html.

46. Theodore Schleifer, "Kamala Harris Is the Choice Joe Biden Needed to Win over Silicon Valley," *Vox*, August 11, 2020, https://www.vox.com/recode/2020/8/11/21364027/kamala-harris-joe-biden-vice-president-silicon-valley-donors-tech.

47. "Trump Tax Calculator," Biden Harris Democrats, https://joebiden.com/trump taxes/.

48. Devlin Barrett, "Ads for Obama Campaign: 'It's in the Game,'" NBC News, October 14, 2008, http://www.nbcnews.com/id/27184857/ns/technology_and_science-games/t/ads-obama-campaign-its-game/.

49. Abram Brown, "Joe Biden Now Has His Own Island On 'Animal Crossing,'" *Forbes*, October 16, 2020, https://www.forbes.com/sites/abrambrown/2020/10/16/joe-biden-now-has-his-own-island-on-animal-crossing/.

50. Gene Park, "Joe Biden's 'Animal Crossing' Island Was Definitely Made by a Pro Gamer," *Washington Post*, October 16, 2020, https://www.washingtonpost.com/video-games/2020/10/16/biden-animal-crossing-island/.

51. For more on issues involving "digital blackface," see Lauren Michele Jackson, "We Need to Talk About Digital Blackface in Reaction GIFs," *Teen Vogue*, August 2, 2017, https://www.teenvogue.com/story/digital-blackface-reaction-gifs and Joseph Lawless, "Of Mammies, Minstrels, and Machines: Movement-Image Automaticity and the Impossible Conditions of Black Humanity," *Dissertations, Theses, and Masters Projects*, October 21, 2018, http://dx.doi.org/10.21220/s2-9k63-9m82.

52. David Uberti and Kim S. Nash, "White House Faces Remote-Work, Security Challenges as Trump Treated for Covid-19," *Wall Street Journal*, October 3, 2020, C Suite, https://www.wsj.com/articles/white-house-faces-remote-work-security-challenges-as-trump-treated-for-covid-19-11601683250.

53. Alice Miranda Ollstein and Megan Cassella, "A New Challenge for Transition Planners: Building a Government over Zoom," *Politico*, October 5, 2020, https://www.politico.com/news/2020/10/05/a-new-challenge-for-transition-planners-building-a-government-over-zoom-425528.

54. Mike Allen, "Trump Campaign Manager Says Travel, Grassroots Campaigning Worth $48 Million a Week," *Axios* (blog), September 22, 2020, https://www.axios

.com/trump-campaign-bill-stepien-travel-rallies-impact-74c238d6-4a40-4870-9d1d-c1dd1c176a4a.html.

55. Cision's website promised clients access to media analytics tools able to quantify "prominence," "impact," and "share of voice" by monitoring "all media channels," including Instagram, Facebook, YouTube, and Twitter "in as few as three clicks." See "Earned Media Analytics," accessed October 18, 2020, https://www.cision.com/us/products/analytics/earned-media-analytics/.

56. Jacqui Heinrich, Tara Prindiville, and Thomas Barrabi, "Hunter Biden Email Story: Computer Repair Store Owner Describes Handing over Laptop to FBI," Fox News, October 14, 2020, https://www.foxnews.com/politics/hunter-biden-emails-computer-repair-store-owner-john-paul-mac-isaac; The *Wall Street Journal* Editorial Board, "Hunter Biden's Laptop Is Finally News Fit to Print," *Wall Street Journal*, March 18, 2022, https://www.wsj.com/articles/all-the-news-thats-finally-fit-to-print-hunter-biden-laptop-new-york-post-new-york-times-joe-biden-11647637814.

57. Katie Glueck, Michael S. Schmidt, and Mike Isaac, "Allegation on Biden Prompts Pushback From Social Media Companies," *New York Times*, October 17, 2020, US, https://www.nytimes.com/2020/10/14/us/politics/hunter-biden-ukraine-facebook-twitter.html.

58. Kate Conger and Mike Isaac, "In Reversal, Twitter Is No Longer Blocking New York Post Article," *New York Times*, October 16, 2020, Technology, https://www.nytimes.com/2020/10/16/technology/twitter-new-york-post.html.

59. Kevin Roose, "Facebook and Twitter Dodge a 2016 Repeat, and Ignite a 2020 Firestorm," *New York Times*, October 15, 2020, Technology, https://www.nytimes.com/2020/10/15/technology/facebook-twitter-nypost-hunter-biden.html.

60. Ebony Bowden and Steven Nelson, "Hunter's Ex-Partner Tony Bobulinski: Joe Biden's a Liar and Here's Proof," *New York Post*, October 22, 2020, https://nypost.com/2020/10/22/hunter-ex-partner-tony-bobulinski-calls-joe-biden-a-liar/.

61. Ben Smith, "Trump Had One Last Story to Sell. The Wall Street Journal Wouldn't Buy It.," *New York Times*, October 25, 2020, Business, https://www.nytimes.com/2020/10/25/business/media/hunter-biden-wall-street-journal-trump.html.

62. Reuters, "State Department Reviewing Clinton Emails, Pompeo Says," *New York Times*, video, October 14, 2020, https://www.nytimes.com/video/us/politics/100000007395271/pompeo-clinton-emails.html.

63. "Melania Trump Delights Social Media by Posing for Selfie with Ivanka and Tiffany," *Daily Mail*, September 30, 2020, https://www.dailymail.co.uk/femail/article-8789695/Melania-Trump-delights-social-media-posing-selfie-Ivanka-Tiffany.html. Similar images were first circulated by the first lady months earlier; see Kate Bennett, "Melania Trump Encourages Face Mask Use with Photo of Herself," CNN,

April 9, 2020, https://www.cnn.com/2020/04/09/politics/melania-trump-face-mask-coronavirus/index.html.

64. Nicole Perlroth, "Trump Campaign Website Is Defaced by Hackers," *New York Times*, October 27, 2020, Technology, https://www.nytimes.com/2020/10/27/technology/trump-campaign-website-defaced-hackers.html.

65. Ted Johnson, "How Joe Biden's Campaign Has Mobilized Hollywood With Weekly Zoom Sessions," *Deadline* (blog), October 20, 2020, https://deadline.com/2020/10/joe-biden-zoom-bombs-hollywood-supporters-campaign-1234600877/.

66. The title of this chapter pays homage to two books about telecommunication: Sherry Turkle, *Alone Together: Why We Expect More from Technology and Less from Each Other* (New York: Basic Books, 2017) and Judith S. Olson and Gary M. Olson, *Working Together Apart: Collaboration over the Internet* (San Rafael, CA: Morgan & Claypool, 2014). The Turkle book argues that in regular, in-person social life, people are alienated by technologies of distraction that isolate them from experiencing life in the moment because they are constantly involved with events elsewhere. I have inverted Turkle's title, because during Covid these technologies were a lifeline of connection. The Olsons' book emphasizes the power of collective action online if appropriate situations of trust are established. But the term "apart" lacks the pathos of "alone."

67. For a useful ethnographic account of this period, see Annette N. Markham, "Pattern Recognition: Using Rocks, Wind, Water, Anxiety, and Doom Scrolling in a Slow Apocalypse (to Learn More About Methods for Changing the World)," *Qualitative Inquiry*, October 3, 2020, https://doi.org/10.1177/1077800420960191.

68. Of course, technology played a major role in acquiring knowledge about the outdoors or homespun pursuits.

Chapter 12

1. Maggie Haberman, "Trump Told Crowd 'You Will Never Take Back Our Country With Weakness,'" *New York Times*, January 7, 2021, US, https://www.nytimes.com/2021/01/06/us/politics/trump-speech-capitol.html.

2. For an anthropological account of the Save America rally and its carnival-like features, see Joyce Dalsheim and Gregory Starrett, "Everything Possible and Nothing True: Notes on the Capitol Insurrection," *Anthropology Today* 37, no. 2 (2021): 26–30, https://doi.org/10.1111/1467-8322.12645.

3. Associated Press, "Transcript of Trump's Speech at Rally Before US Capitol Riot," US News & World Report, January 13, 2021, https://www.usnews.com/news/politics/articles/2021-01-13/transcript-of-trumps-speech-at-rally-before-us-capitol-riot.

4. The "Rally to Revival" had a roster of conspiracy theorists such as Alex Jones and Jack Posobiac. Many speakers listed their occupation as "influencer." See, "Public

Gathering Permit 21–0274 Rally To Revival Freedom Plaza Permit—Redacted," uploaded to Scribd by Washingtonian Magazine, January 4, 2021, https://www .scribd.com/document/489865993/21-0274-Rally-to-Revival-Freedom-Plaza-Permit -Redacted. Footage documenting the event shows a relatively modest crowd. See Bloomberg Quicktake: Now, "LIVE: Pro-Trump Protesters Hold 'Rally for Revival' at Washington, D.C. Freedom Plaza," streamed live on January 5, 2021, YouTube video, 4:21:43, https://youtu.be/tRUTm-ZIcow.

5. Dan Scavino Jr. ▰◱ (@DanScavino), "◖◗WOW! We Hear You from the West Wing—THANK YOU♡ ▰◱," Twitter, January 5, 2021, https://twitter.com/Dan Scavino/status/1346584866964598785.

6. Sheera Frenkel, "The Storming of Capitol Hill Was Organized on Social Media.," *New York Times*, January 6, 2021, https://www.nytimes.com/2021/01/06/us/politics /protesters-storm-capitol-hill-building.html.

7. Gabriel Fair and Ryan Wesslen, "Shouting into the Void: A Database of the Alternative Social Media Platform Gab," *Proceedings of the International AAAI Conference on Web and Social Media* 13 (2019): 608–610.

8. Max Aliapoulios et al., "An Early Look at the Parler Online Social Network," ArXiv:2101.03820 [Physics], February 18, 2021, http://arxiv.org/abs/2101.03820.

9. @The_Real_Fly, "POLICE ALLEGEDLY SHOT UNARMED WOMAN," Twitter, January 6, 2021, https://twitter.com/The_Real_Fly/status/1346915933584027652.

10. For the perspective of the videographer, who has been described as a Black activist and citizen journalist, see Tim Dickinson, "'I Don't Think She Deserved to Die': Black Activist Who Filmed Ashli Babbitt Shooting Speaks Out," *Rolling Stone*, January 15, 2021, https://www.rollingstone.com/culture/culture-features/ashli-babbitt-shooting -video-jayden-x-maga-riot-interview-1112949/.

11. Kylie Jane Kremer (@KylieJaneKramer), "BE A PART OF HISTORY!. . . ," Twitter, January 2, 2021, https://twitter.com/KylieJaneKramer/status/1345539000312991750.

12. The data shows that these social media dynamics can be complicated, however. See James A. Roberts and Meredith E. David, "The Social Media Party: Fear of Missing Out (FoMO), Social Media Intensity, Connection, and Well-Being," *International Journal of Human–Computer Interaction* 36, no. 4 (February 2020): 386–92, https:// doi.org/10.1080/10447318.2019.1646517.

13. "Here's What We Know About the Pro-Trump Rallies That Have Permits," *Washingtonian*, January 5, 2021, https://www.washingtonian.com/2021/01/05/heres -what-we-know-about-the-pro-trump-rallies-that-have-permits/.

14. Wendy Hui Kyong Chun, *Updating to Remain the Same: Habitual New Media* (Cambridge, MA: MIT Press, 2017).

15. Ashli Babbitt (@CommonAshSense), "#Veteran #AMERICA #Libertarian #2A #KAG- I 💙 my dude, my 🐺 & above all, my country-🇺🇸 #FREEDOM.," Twitter bio, accessed January 7, 2021, https://twitter.com/Ashli_Babbitt/status/1346531200819 716098.

16. To see how emoji came to dominate Babbitt's social media posts, see Shannon Stapleton, "The Journey of Ashli Babbitt," *Bellingcat*, January 8, 2021, https://www .bellingcat.com/news/2021/01/08/the-journey-of-ashli-babbitt/.

17. Peter Jamison, Hannah Natason, John Woodrow Cox, and Alex Horton, "'The Storm Is Here': Ashli Babbitt's Journey from Capital 'Guardian' to Invader," *Washington Post*, January 9, 2021, https://www.washingtonpost.com/dc-md-va/2021/01/09 /ashli-babbitt-capitol-shooting-trump-qanon/.

18. "Ashli Babbitt, Enthusiastic Video Marching to Capitol Right Before Fatal Shooting," TMZ, January 7, 2021, https://www.tmz.com/2021/01/07/ashli-babbitt -final-video-marching-us-capitol-before-fatally-shot/.

19. Ashli Babbitt (@CommonAshSense) on Twitter, accessed January 20, 2021, https://twitter.com/Ashli_Babbitt/status/1067115172458725377.

20. Jamison, Natason, Cox, and Horton, "'The Storm Is Here'," *Washington Post*.

21. For evidence of the overlap with The_Donald subreddit, see Alvin Chang, "We Analyzed Every QAnon Post on Reddit. Here's Who QAnon Supporters Actually Are," *Vox*, August 8, 2018, https://www.vox.com/2018/8/8/17657800/qanon-reddit -conspiracy-data.

22. Jamie Gangel and Donie O'Sullivan, "Talk of Overturning the 2020 Election on New Social Media Platforms Used by QAnon Followers Sparks Fears of Further Violence," CNN, June 2, 2021, https://www.cnn.com/2021/06/02/politics/telegram -qanon-trump-supporters/index.html.

23. Kellen Browning and Taylor Lorenz, "Pro-Trump Mob Livestreamed Its Rampage, and Made Money Doing It," *New York Times*, January 8, 2021, Technology, https://www.nytimes.com/2021/01/08/technology/dlive-capitol-mob.html.

24. For an argument about horseshoe politics and white identity politics in Europe, see Heinz Handler, "European Identity and Identitarians in Europe," Social Science Research Network, January 31, 2019, https://doi.org/10.2139/ssrn.3338349.

25. Ben Smith, "We Worked Together on the Internet. Last Week, He Stormed the Capitol.," *New York Times*, January 11, 2021, Business, https://www.nytimes.com /2021/01/10/business/media/capitol-anthime-gionet-buzzfeed-vine.html.

26. Connor Sheets, "The Radicalization of Kevin Greeson," *ProPublica*, January 15, 2021, https://www.propublica.org/article/the-radicalization-of-kevin-greeson.

27. Dan Scavino Jr. ▆≶ (@DanScavino), "Statement by President Donald J. Trump on the Electoral Certification . . . ," Twitter, January 7, 2021, https://twitter.com/DanScavino/status/1347103015493361664.

28. In May 2021, Facebook's Oversight Board—an independent panel of journalists, activists, lawyers, and experienced policy makers—upheld Facebook's post-insurrection decision. They also argued that the company should either set an expiration date or commit to a permanent ban. See Mike Isaac, "Facebook Oversight Board Upholds Social Network's Ban of Trump," *New York Times*, May 5, 2021, https://www.nytimes.com/2021/05/05/technology/facebook-trump-ban-upheld.html.

29. "If You Were on Parler, You Saw the Mob Coming," *New York Times*, January 7, 2021, https://www.nytimes.com/2021/01/07/opinion/sway-kara-swisher-john-matze.html.

30. "Parler Data Breach: Archived Posts from Capitol Riots Could Reveal Platform's Role in the Insurrection," *USA TODAY*, accessed January 4, 2022, https://www.usatoday.com/story/tech/news/2021/01/11/parler-hack-platform-archived-hackers-capitol-riots/6629772002/.

31. Elizabeth A. Harris and Alexandra Alter, "Simon & Schuster Cancels Plans for Senator Hawley's Book," *New York Times*, January 7, 2021, Books, https://www.nytimes.com/2021/01/07/books/simon-schuster-josh-hawley-book.html.

32. Josh Hawley, The Tyranny of Big Tech (Washington, DC: Regnery Publishing, 2021).

33. Jim Isaak and Mina J. Hanna, "User Data Privacy: Facebook, Cambridge Analytica, and Privacy Protection," *Computer* 51, no. 8 (August 2018): 56–59, https://doi.org/10.1109/MC.2018.3191268.

34. George W. Croner, "The Intelligence Community and Open-Source Information in the Digital Age—Foreign Policy Research Institute," Foreign Policy Research Institute, February 17, 2021, https://www.fpri.org/article/2021/02/the-intelligence-community-and-open-source-information-in-the-digital-age/.

35. Donald J. Trump, "Donald J. Trump: Why I'm Suing Big Tech," *Wall Street Journal*, July 8, 2021, Opinion, https://www.wsj.com/articles/donald-j-trump-why-im-suing-big-tech-11625761897.

Conclusion

1. Aaron Fisher (former Obama intern), in discussion with the author, November 2014.

2. Alec Ross (Clinton's former senior advisor for innovation), in discussion with the author, October 2019.

3. Macon Phillips (former director of digital strategy for President Obama), in discussion with the author, April 2019.

4. Tom Cochran (former director of new media technologies for President Obama), in discussion with the author, September 2019.

5. Kara Swisher, "The Justice Dept.'s Lawsuit Against Google: Too Little, Too Late," *New York Times*, October 20, 2020, Opinion, https://www.nytimes.com/2020/10/20/opinion/google-justice-lawsuit.html.

6. Siva Vaidhyanathan 🤘🖐 (@sivavaid), "The problem with Facebook is Facebook . . . ," Twitter, accessed September 8, 2019, https://twitter.com/sivavaid/status/1170727418157555713.

7. Sarah E. Needleman and Deepa Seetharaman, "Silicon Valley Gets Another President Skeptical of Big Tech," *Wall Street Journal*, November 9, 2020, https://www.wsj.com/articles/silicon-valley-gets-another-president-skeptical-of-big-tech-11604938267.

8. Eric Lipton and Kenneth P. Vogel, "Major Technology Companies Join List of Biden Inaugural Donors," *New York Times*, January 10, 2021, US, https://www.nytimes.com/2021/01/09/us/politics/technology-companies-biden-inaugural-donors.html.

9. Samantha Cole, "What Does Biden's Ambitious Plan to Tackle Online Harassment Actually Say?," *Vice*, November 12, 2021, https://www.vice.com/en/article/epdnjp/biden-plan-to-end-violence-against-women-online-harassment-what-does-it-say.

10. The White House Briefing Room, "FACT SHEET: Executive Order on Promoting Competition in the American Economy," WhiteHouse.gov, July 9, 2021, https://www.whitehouse.gov/briefing-room/statements-releases/2021/07/09/fact-sheet-executive-order-on-promoting-competition-in-the-american-economy/.

11. Zolan Kanno-Youngs and Cecilia Kang, "Inside the White House-Facebook Rift Over Vaccine Misinformation," *New York Times*, August 10, 2021, Technology, https://www.nytimes.com/2021/08/10/technology/facebook-vaccine-misinformation.html.

12. It is interesting that the Biden administration took the school's side in the case. Alex Swoyer, "Biden Administration Sides against Cheerleader in First Amendment Case," *Washington Times*, March 4, 2021, Politics, https://www.washingtontimes.com/news/2021/mar/4/biden-administration-sides-with-cheerleader-in-fir/.

13. Mike Isaac, Ryan Mac, and Sheera Frenkel, "After Whistle-Blower Goes Public, Facebook Tries Calming Employees," *New York Times*, October 10, 2021, https://www.nytimes.com/2021/10/10/technology/facebook-whistleblower-employees.html.

14. Skarredghost, "Mark Zuckerberg Explains the Metaverse at Facebook Connect 2021," November 1, 2021, YouTube video, 3:32, https://youtu.be/5TJ5ENxCUQs.

15. For some examples of relevant legal case studies, see Dan L. Burk, "Authorization and Governance in Virtual Worlds," *First Monday*, 2010, https://doi.org/10.5210 /fm.v15i5.2967.

16. See Lawrence Lessig, *Code: And Other Laws of Cyberspace* (New York: Basic Books, 1999).

17. See, for example, the work of Erica Hodgin, Carrie James, and Sangita Shresthova at the Digital Civics Toolkit (https://www.digitalcivicstoolkit.org/) or of Joseph Kahne and Hodgin at the Civic Engagement Research Group (https://www .civicsurvey.org/). In the European Union, Athina Karatzogianni, Katrin Tiidenberg, and Dimitris Parsanoglou are publishing useful research on political participation in connection with the Digital Generation project (https://www.digigen.eu).

18. For an argument about the importance of the arts and humanities, see also Kavita Philip, "How to Stop Worrying about Clean Signals and Start Loving the Noise," in *Your Computer Is on Fire*, ed. Thomas S. Mullaney et al. (Cambridge, MA: MIT Press, 2020), 363–376.

19. For example, in 2021 activists and artists at Ars Electronica called for a "new digital deal" that would expand the EU's already more powerful system of checks and balances on social media companies. See "Thema," A New Digital Deal, accessed January 4, 2022, https://ars.electronica.art/newdigitaldeal/de/theme/.

20. Taxation is another intervention into the market that is often unpopular with internet companies. Some tech critics advocate taxing the data that search and social media companies collect and store as a disincentive for harvesting so much private information. See Renu Zaretsky, "Big Tech Has Our Data. Should We Tax Them on It?," Tax Policy Center, March 3, 2021, https://www.taxpolicycenter.org /taxvox/big-tech-has-our-data-should-we-tax-them-it.

21. Some tech critics have also called for more DIY approaches to designing for democracy, which would center Black or queer communities rather than Silicon Valley elites. See, for example, the Design Justice Network (https://designjustice .org/).

22. "Statements Archives," Internet Association, accessed August 16, 2021, https:// internetassociation.org/news/category/statements/.

23. A new generation of cyber-optimists in the academy and the nonprofit sector also believes that intelligent machines could counteract the flaws of a "representational system of government." See George Zarkadakis, *Cyber Republic: Reinventing Democracy in the Age of Intelligent Machines* (Cambridge, MA: MIT Press, 2021). See criticisms of AI from Black scholars and social justice advocates from Black in AI at

https://blackinai.github.io for a counterargument to this faith in the egalitarianism supposedly derived from the intelligence of machines.

24. Alex Kasprak, "Did Rick Perry Fall For A Years-Old Social Media Privacy Hoax?," Snopes, accessed August 21, 2019, https://www.snopes.com/fact-check/rick-perry -instagram-hoax/.

25. Joan Donovan and Brian Friedberg, "Opinion: With This Statement, I Give Notice That Instagram Owns Your Soul," *BuzzFeed News*, August 23, 2019, https://www .buzzfeednews.com/article/joandonovan/i-give-notice-that-instagram-owns-you.

26. For more on the relationship between politics, persuasion, and gaming, see Ian Bogost, *Persuasive Games: The Expressive Power of Videogames* (Cambridge, MA: MIT Press, 2007).

27. Joshua Rivera, "AOC Played Among Us and Achieved What Most Politicians Fail at: Acting Normal," *Guardian*, October 22, 2020, http://www.theguardian.com /games/2020/oct/22/alexandria-ocasio-cortez-ilhan-omar-among-us-twitch-stream -aoc.

28. For another approach to "posthuman democracy," see Zizi Papacharissi, *After Democracy: Imagining Our Political Future* (New Haven: Yale University Press, 2021). Papacharissi interviews people from all around the world to ask them about democracy, citizenship, and the role of technology in the future.

Index